Grievance Formation, Rights and Remedies

In the last century, the treatment of victims of involuntary sterilisation and castration in Nordic countries has varied drastically from state to state, across time and victim groups. Considering why this is the case, Daniela Alaattinoğlu investigates how laws and practices of involuntary, surgical sterilisation and castration have been established, abolished and remedied in three Nordic states: Sweden, Norway and Finland. Employing a vast range of primary and secondary sources, Alaattinoğlu traces the national and international developments of the last 100 years. Developing the concept of grievance formation, the book explores why some states have claimed public responsibility while others have not, and why some victim groups have mobilised while others have remained silent. Through this pioneering analysis, Alaattinoğlu illuminates issues of human and constitutional rights, the evolution of the welfare state and state responsibility in both national and global contexts.

Daniela Alaattinoğlu is an Assistant Professor of Law at the University of Turku. She has previously held an Icelandic Research Fund postdoctoral fellowship at the University of Iceland and visiting fellowships at the Åbo Akademi Institute for Human Rights, the Max Planck Institute for Social Anthropology and the University of Melbourne. She is the co-editor of *Contesting Femicide: Feminism and the Power of Law Revisited* (2019).

Law in Context

Since 1970, the Law in Context series has been at the forefront of a movement to broaden the study of law. The series is a vehicle for the publication of innovative monographs and texts that treat law and legal phenomena critically in their cultural, social, political, technological, environmental and economic contexts. A contextual approach involves treating legal subjects broadly, using materials from other humanities and social sciences, and from any other discipline that helps to explain the operation in practice of the particular legal field or legal phenomena under investigation. It is intended that this orientation is at once more stimulating and more revealing than the bare exposition of legal rules. The series includes original research monographs, coursebooks and textbooks that foreground contextual approaches and methods. The series includes and welcomes books on the study of law in all its contexts, including domestic legal systems, European and international law, transnational and global legal processes, and comparative law.

Books in the Series

Acosta: *The National versus the Foreigner in South America: 200 Years of Migration and Citizenship Law*
Alaattinoğlu: *Grievance Formation, Rights and Remedies*
Ali: *Modern Challenges to Islamic Law*
Alyagon Darr: *Plausible Crime Stories: The Legal History of Sexual Offences in Mandate Palestine*
Anderson, Schum & Twining: *Analysis of Evidence, 2nd Edition*
Ashworth: *Sentencing and Criminal Justice, 6th Edition*
Barton & Douglas: *Law and Parenthood*
Baxi, McCrudden & Paliwala: *Law's Ethical, Global and Theoretical Contexts: Essays in Honour of William Twining*
Beecher-Monas: *Evaluating Scientific Evidence: An Interdisciplinary Framework for Intellectual Due Process*
Bell: *French Legal Cultures*

Siems: *Comparative Law, 3rd Edition*
Stapleton: *Product Liability*
Stewart: *Gender, Law and Justice in a Global Market*
Tamanaha: *Law as a Means to an End: Threat to the Rule of Law*
Tuori: *Properties of Law: Modern Law and After*
Turpin & Tomkins: *British Government and the Constitution: Text and Materials, 7th Edition*
Twining: *General Jurisprudence: Understanding Law from a Global Perspective*
Twining: *Globalisation and Legal Theory*
Twining: *Human Rights, Southern Voices: Francis Deng, Abdullahi An-Na'im, Yash Ghai and Upendra Baxi*
Twining: *Jurist in Context: A Memoir*
Twining: *Karl Llewellyn and the Realist Movement, 2nd Edition*
Twining: *Rethinking Evidence: Exploratory Essays, 2nd Edition*
Twining & Miers: *How to Do Things with Rules, 5th Edition*
Wan: *Film and Constitutional Controversy: Visualising Hong Kong Identity in the Age of 'One Country, Two Systems'*
Ward: *A Critical Introduction to European Law, 3rd Edition*
Ward: *Law, Text, Terror*
Ward: *Shakespeare and Legal Imagination*
Wells & Quick: *Lacey, Wells and Quick: Reconstructing Criminal Law: Text and Materials, 4th Edition*
Young: *Turpin and Tomkins' British Government and the Constitution: Text and Materials , 8th Edition*
Zander: *Cases and Materials on the English Legal System, 10th Edition*
Zander: *The Law-Making Process, 6th Edition*

International Journal of Law in Context: A Global Forum for Interdisciplinary Legal Studies

The *International Journal of Law in Context* is the companion journal to the Law in Context book series and provides a forum for interdisciplinary legal studies and offers intellectual space for ground-breaking critical research. It publishes contextual work about law and its relationship with other disciplines including but not limited to science, literature, humanities, philosophy, sociology, psychology, ethics, history and geography. More information about the journal and how to submit an article can be found at http://journals.cambridge.org/ijc

Grievance Formation, Rights and Remedies

Involuntary Sterilisation and Castration in the Nordics, 1930s–2020s

DANIELA ALAATTINOĞLU
University of Turku

CAMBRIDGE
UNIVERSITY PRESS

CAMBRIDGE
UNIVERSITY PRESS

Shaftesbury Road, Cambridge CB2 8EA, United Kingdom

One Liberty Plaza, 20th Floor, New York, NY 10006, USA

477 Williamstown Road, Port Melbourne, VIC 3207, Australia

314–321, 3rd Floor, Plot 3, Splendor Forum, Jasola District Centre, New Delhi – 110025, India

103 Penang Road, #05-06/07, Visioncrest Commercial, Singapore 238467

Cambridge University Press is part of Cambridge University Press & Assessment, a department of the University of Cambridge.

We share the University's mission to contribute to society through the pursuit of education, learning and research at the highest international levels of excellence.

www.cambridge.org
Information on this title: www.cambridge.org/9781009171687

DOI: 10.1017/9781009171663

First published 2023

A catalogue record for this publication is available from the British Library.

A Cataloging-in-Publication data record for this book is available from the Library of Congress

ISBN 978-1-009-17168-7 Hardback

To be in the margin is to be part of the whole but outside the main body.[1]

Bell Hooks

[1] Hooks 1984: 8.

Contents

Tables

Foreword

Nordic feminist legal scholars have long questioned the Nordic countries' commitments to gender equality, particularly their self-acclaimed status as protectors of women's human rights – often by contrasting lived experiences with law and policy 'in the books'.[2] This monograph, which builds on Dr Alaattinoğlu's doctoral thesis, for which I was an external examiner, follows and develops this critical tradition of investigating the law beyond the books.

Bringing together the experiences of three marginalised groups who have been subject to involuntary sterilisation and castration – socially disadvantaged women, sexual offenders and transpersons – the book juxtaposes legal promises and realities in three Nordic countries – Sweden, Norway and Finland. It provides a compelling picture of how groups marginalised by contemporary societies and deemed unworthy of reproduction, or whose sexual orientations or gender identities have been considered dangerous or deviant, have been the targets of practices of forced and otherwise involuntary sterilisation and castration (1930s–2020s). As such, it uncovers a 'skeleton in the closet' of the welfare states in question.

The work provides an original analysis of the inconsistent way in which these practices have been framed and remedied within international law and how these weaknesses are reflected at the level of national law in the Nordics. The comparisons between the three countries, the different victim groups and the different historical contexts focus on factors and forces that have influenced the regulation of rights and responsibilities in the three countries. These comparisons provide a fresh perspective on tensions between the state prerogative to define the common good through regulation of reproduction and sexuality on the one hand and the human rights narrative emphasising the freedom, autonomy, integrity and equality of all individuals regardless of social status, race, ethnicity, health, sex, sexual orientation and gender identity on the other hand. While on paper acceding to human rights instruments, Dr Alaattinoğlu's detailed study of each country uncovers gaps and inconsistencies.

[2] This criticism has particularly come from scholars within the 'women's law' and 'gender and law' disciplines in the Nordic countries.

Most importantly, the analysis shows how the emerging human rights conceptions of harm, rights and remedies have a different effect on legal recognition of harm claims made in the three countries investigated. Drawing on an impressively wide range of sources – including case law, legislation, *travaux préparatoires*, interviews and secondary literature – Dr Alaattinoğlu points to legal, historical, political and cultural factors that shed further light on the different ways in which the rights claims of sterilisation and castration victims are promoted, adopted or resisted in the Nordics.

All in all, this is a timely, independent and highly original monograph that makes an important and much-needed theoretical and methodological contribution to the fields of socio-legal studies and law in context. By innovatively combining frame analysis, grievance formation and rights development and comparative methodology, Dr Alaattinoğlu develops new knowledge and original analytical tools to investigate how rights are promoted, used, adopted, challenged and resisted in different contexts and settings. Far from confining herself to describing evolving practices and legal standards, the author embraces the socio-legal context and the emergence of social, political and cultural notions and utilisations of rights in the twentieth and twenty-first centuries. This contextual insight is crucial to understand why some victims in some cases have been remedied by states, and why some groups have resorted to legal mobilisation while others have not. It sets the scene for an empirically informed discussion as to why states consider some oppressive practices dark chapters of their history books, while other, comparable practices go unchallenged.

Anne Hellum
Dr Juris, Professor at the Department of Public and International Law
University of Oslo

Acknowledgements

This work would not have been possible without the support of multiple people and institutions. The first words of gratitude are dedicated to my doctoral supervisor Ruth Rubio-Marín, who encouraged me to take on this challenging topic and to develop my skills as a socio-legal academic. She continues to inspire me through her rigorous, engaged and engaging scholarship. The members of the thesis jury, Laura Downs, Anne Hellum and Dinah Shelton, thank you for your thoughtful comments. Thank you, Adrienne Stone, for selecting me as a Kathleen Fitzpatrick Visiting Fellow at the Laureate Programme in comparative constitutional law at Melbourne Law School (2018). The stay provided me with excellent chances to discuss this work in a vibrant academic environment. Special thanks also to Marie-Claire Foblets and the Max Planck Institute for Social Anthropology for hosting me as a guest in January 2019.

I am deeply grateful to the knowledgeable and kind people who have spent their time reading and commenting the text and supported the project. I would especially like to thank Stefano Osella, Kristina Čufar, Nicola Hargreaves, the late Sally Engle Merry, Reva Siegel, Adrian Howe, Hilary Charlesworth, Dianne Otto, Aeyal Gross, Shazia Choudhry, Jemima Repo, Raimo Lahti, Markku Mattila, Veronica Pimenoff, Per Haave, Anniken Sørlie, Malin Arvidsson, Karin Åhman, Mårten Schultz, Mattias Tydén, Jens Rydström, Maija Runcis, Paulina de los Reyes, Nehal Bhuta and the late Reza Banakar.

I am indebted to my interviewees, who have made me understand the topic of this monograph so much better, with all its underlying complexities.

I would also like to thank Johanna Niemi and the anonymous reviewers at Cambridge University Press for their encouragement and helpful comments when reworking the text into a book. Thanks also to Miluska Kooij for your excellent editing and to Marianne Nield and Finola O'Sullivan at Cambridge University Press for your support for this project.

The institutional support, for which I am very grateful, has come primarily from the European University Institute, the Academy of Finland, the Finnish Section of the Nordic Federation of Public Administration (NAF) and the Olga and Kaarle Oskari Laitinen Foundation. Thank you also to the University of Turku and the University of Iceland for allowing this project to come to fruition.

Finally, to my friends and family, my partner and child, I am forever thankful for your love and support.

Abbreviations

ACHPR	The African Commission on Human and Peoples' Rights
ACHR	The American Convention on Human Rights
CAT	The Convention against Torture and Other Cruel, Inhuman or Degrading Treatment or Punishment
CAT Committee	The Committee against Torture
CEDAW	The Convention on the Elimination of All Forms of Discrimination against Women
CEDAW Committee	The Committee on the Elimination of All Forms of Discrimination against Women
CERD	The Convention on the Elimination of All Forms of Racial Discrimination
CERD Committee	The Committee on the Elimination of Racial Discrimination
CESCR Committee	The Committee on Economic, Social and Cultural Rights
CJEU	The Court of Justice of the European Union
CoE	The Council of Europe
CPT	The European Committee for the Prevention of Torture and Inhuman or Degrading Treatment or Punishment
CRC	The Convention on the Rights of the Child
CRC Committee	The Committee on the Rights of the Child
CRPD	The Convention on the Rights of Persons with Disabilities
CRPD Committee	The Committee on the Rights of Persons with Disabilities
ECHR	The European Convention for the Protection of Human Rights and Fundamental Freedoms
ECmHR	The European Commission of Human Rights
ECOSOC	The United Nations Economic and Social Council
ECSR	The European Committee of Social Rights
ECtHR	The European Court of Human Rights

EEA	The European Economic Area
EFTA	The European Free Trade Association
EU	The European Union
FPES	Full Personality Expression Sweden
FRI	The Norwegian Association for Gender and Sexuality Diversity (previously LLH) (*Foreningen for kjønns- og seksualitetsmangfold*)
FTPN	The Norwegian Association for Trans People (*Forbundet for transpersoner i Norge*)
HBRS	The Norwegian Patient Organisation for People Experiencing Gender Dysphoria, Gender Incongruence and Gender Identity Challenges (*Harry Benjamin Resurssenter*)
IACHR	The Inter-American Commission on Human Rights
IACtHR	The Inter-American Court of Human Rights
ICC	The International Criminal Court
ICCPR	The International Covenant on Civil and Political Rights
ICESCR	The International Covenant on Economic, Social and Cultural Rights
ICTR	The International Criminal Tribunal for Rwanda
ICTY	The International Criminal Tribunal for the Former Yugoslavia
ILGA	The International Lesbian, Gay, Bisexual, Trans and Intersex Association
JK	The Swedish Chancellor of Justice (*Justitiekanslern*)
JO	The Swedish Parliamentary Ombudsmen (*Riksdagens ombudsmän*)
KHO	The Finnish Supreme Administrative Court (*Korkein hallinto-oikeus*)
KKO	The Finnish Supreme Court (*Korkein oikeus*)
LGBT(IQ)	Lesbian, Gay, Bisexual, Trans (Intersex and Queer/ Questioning)
N/A	Not applicable
NGO	Non-governmental organisation
OHCHR	The United Nations Office of the High Commissioner for Human Rights
PACE	The Parliamentary Assembly of the Council of Europe
PCIJ	The Permanent Court of International Justice
PKI	The Norwegian Patient Organisation for Gender Incongruence (*Pasientorganisasjonen for Kjønnsinkongruens*)

RFSU	The Swedish Association for Sexuality Education (*Riksförbundet för sexuell upplysning*)
RFSL	The Swedish Federation for Lesbian, Gay, Bisexual, Transgender, Queer and Intersex Rights
TGEU	Transgender Europe
UN	The United Nations
UNGA	The United Nations General Assembly
WPATH	The World Professional Association for Transgender Health

Prologue: Eugenics and the Control of Reproduction and Sexuality

In the context of social control, sterilisations and castrations, early twentieth-century scientists and authorities alike became increasingly interested in the science of the human body.[1] New techniques and medical advancements, such as the use of anaesthesia to decrease pain, chemical agents to minimise germs and eventually, antibiotics, created an increasing scientific fascination with the body. According to the new sciences such as eugenics, sexology and psychiatry, the human body could be measured, categorised and altered in previously undiscovered ways, leading to new forms of standardisation and normalisation.[2] The new sciences were not only concerned with the body of individuals but also with that of the population as 'the species body' or the human race.[3] Thinking of the population as a biological mass allows for the conceptualisation of some elements as desirable, to be encouraged, while viewing the undesirable, abnormal, sick and deviant elements of the population as in need of regulation or even elimination.

Involuntary sterilisation and castration are means of controlling and discouraging the reproduction and sexuality of people considered undesirable or dangerous. Sterilisation aims to permanently destroy the reproductive abilities of a person, for example, through tubal ligation or vasoligation, that is, vasectomy. Castration – or gonadectomy, that is, the removal of the gonads – intends to eradicate the sexual drive of a person, or alternatively, can be part of genital gender-affirming surgery. With these dissimilar aims, the two surgical interventions often target different groups.[4] Nevertheless, a certain continuity can be identified for the two interventions, even though they affect different functions. Both

[1] This is expressed in Honkasalo's account of biopower as operating 'at the level of life, intervening and regulating every vital aspect of a population, including sexuality, health, nutrition, hygiene, reproduction, immigration and death'. Honkasalo J 2016: 273.

[2] See Gould 1996. As such, these practices are part of what Foucault refers to as the '*anatomo-politics of the human body*', the evolution of the power over life viewing 'the body as a machine', integrating it 'into systems of efficient and economic controls'. Foucault 1990: 139.

[3] Foucault 1990: 139; Hanson 2008: 106.

[4] Sterilisation is a surgical intervention; castration can be either surgical or chemical (hormonal), or both. However, the present book primarily focuses on surgical interventions due to space concerns. By doing so, it for example excludes so-called 'chemical castration' of sex offenders, a frequently present topic in contemporary debates.

interventions have targeted individuals considered dangerous to society's well-being, that is, as a threat to public interests.

Surgical sterilisation and castration came into wider use with the advent of medical advancements in parts of the global North at the beginning of the twentieth century. The state-enforced interventions were inflicted on the population to regulate its reproduction and sexuality in a manner which was perceived as modern.[5] The techniques which developed at pace with the welfare state appeared to be a simple solution to poverty, criminality and social misery. Yet, these interventions were not always in line with, and sometimes directly contrary to, the wishes of the individuals involved. Such involuntary interventions often targeted society's marginalised and were generally not conceptualised as violations of rights and not made a topic of discussion by the international community for a long time.

This also holds true for the Nordic countries investigated in this book. Contextually analysing the differences in the establishment, abolition and remedy of involuntary sterilisation and castration practices in Sweden, Norway and Finland, the present work is particularly interested in the reasons behind the limited and inconsistent acceptance of public responsibility for the practices. Moreover, it analyses the socio-legal processes which have led to some victims receiving recognition and redress, while others fail to access remedies.

The three Nordic universal welfare states under examination share many traits when it comes to geographic location, political system, cultural context, demographic structure, economic growth and commitment to international legal instruments.[6] Importantly, all three countries established and enforced similar practices of sterilisation and castration (both voluntary and involuntary) over the last century, not only through legislation but also through administrative regulation and practices. The interventions have targeted similar groups, their administration was centralised and the total number of people who were sterilised or castrated (involuntarily or voluntarily) is comparable in the three countries.[7] The manner in which the states have subsequently come to abolish and conceptualise involuntary interventions, be they directly allowed through legislation or indirectly through implementation with impunity, has

[5] The practices in focus have taken place in many different contexts, but always concern a (public) authority imposing on an individual. This focus excludes some practices of involuntary sterilisation and castration, such as illegal sterilisation carried out on the initiative of individual surgeons without the consent of the patient, or a person forcing their partner to undergo sterilisation. These situations which invoke other questions of liability than the ones posed in this book, remain outside its scope.

[6] The case selection is based on the 'most similar case' model. Hirschl 2014: 245–253.

[7] The administration and amount motivate the exclusion of two other Nordic countries, Denmark and Iceland, from the comparison. In Denmark, sterilisation was implemented in a less centralised manner with an approximate 11,000 registered sterilisations during the period 1929–1967, significantly fewer than in Sweden, Norway and Finland in the corresponding time period. In Iceland, the number of sterilisations on the basis of the 1938 Sterilisation Act is unknown. See Hansen 2005; Shaw 2014.

however differed greatly. Providing a contextual account, the book seeks to understand the 'complex interrelationships among political, legal, historical, social, and cultural elements' in respect of the topic of involuntary sterilisation and castration in the countries of comparison.[8] The issue is underexplored in many ways. The fragmentary nature of the sources also explains that the study is in part fragmented in its analysis.

The Nordic countries often serve as international benchmarks for progressiveness and champions of human rights, a narrative which the present work complicates by taking a closer look at what has been referred to as their 'skeleton in the closet'.[9] This is a trailblazing, comprehensive study that analyses how involuntary sterilisation and castration have been problematised in international law and explores the related emerging remedial standards. It is also a pioneering comparative analysis of the establishment, abolition and remedy of involuntary sterilisation and castration in the countries in question from the perspective of rights and state responsibility.[10] It encompasses comparisons across different geographies, historical contexts and victim groups. The work originally builds on the reality constructed in legal sources, such as case law, legislation and *travaux préparatoires*, the last of which is traditionally given much weight in Nordic legal scholarship.[11] In order to understand the wider sociocultural conceptualisation of the topic, the study complements and contextualises the doctrinal analysis by engaging in comparison, and by using interview material and secondary literature, such as historical research on state practice and policy. The book allows the reader to comprehend how a socio-legal culture of rights has emerged, how the national legal systems are changing, why some victims have mobilised and others have not, as well as why some states respond to claims of rights violations and public responsibility, while others do not. Moreover, this is the first legal study that focuses on the concept of grievance formation in relation to rights, a concept which has great analytical potential for future socio-legal research.

The work advances three main arguments. The first is that the international human rights law framework has provided a master frame, albeit a weak one, for the legal and remedial conceptualisation of involuntary sterilisation and castration in the Nordic nations investigated. Secondly, the book argues that in addition to their role as legal instruments, the notion of rights as sociocultural entitlements has been crucial for victims to forge a sense of individual and group identity, and for them to receive public and institutional recognition as victims of rights violations. Finally, the diverging recognition and remedial responses by states for different victims of involuntary sterilisation and castration can be understood in the context of grievance formation.

[8] Scheppele 2004: 390. [9] See, for example, Lennerhed 1997.

[10] Previous accounts have mainly been country-specific and primarily from a historical point of view. See, for example, Broberg & Roll-Hansen (eds), 2005; Runcis 1998; Tydén 2002; Mattila 1999; Haave 2000a; Weindling 1999.

[11] Husa 2010: 107.

Castration and Sterilisation of the 'Dangerous' and 'Feebleminded'

At the outset, it is important to point out that particularly sterilisation is often traced back to eugenics. Even though sterilisation has been carried out outside the context of eugenics as well, and eugenics movements are about much more than sterilisation, the present work also takes eugenics as its point of departure. At the end of the nineteenth and the beginning of the twentieth centuries, Darwin's evolution theory and its various applications to social life became popular in scientific circles and wider political and public debates. Coined by Darwin's half-cousin Francis Galton in 1883, the term 'eugenics' was understood as the teachings about human breeding for the improvement of the population's hereditary material.[12] Eugenics movements, which were convinced that science could solve social problems,[13] gained worldwide support. Resisting the temptation to simply dismiss eugenics as 'bad science',[14] I rather see it as an expression of science developed from a wish to measure, systematise and classify the world and 'improve the quality of human lives'.[15] Importantly, research tools developed by eugenicists, such as different instruments to categorise and measure populations, still partly underpin modern genetics,[16] statistics, psychological testing, anthropology and other applied sciences.[17] By using explanations and hierarchies that seemed particularly reasonable in the zeitgeist, eugenics nevertheless provided political arguments for existing oppressions as well. Social inequalities were explained as the result of biological and racial differences, or on the basis of the notion that some people or populations, such as white Europeans or Americans, were inherently more valuable or desirable than others.[18]

Eugenics was variously expressed in different national social and political contexts, with measures ranging from so-called positive to negative forms. Examples of positive eugenics are measures to encourage the reproduction of the desirable population, for example, through public education, parental leave, taxation relief for large families and/or child support.[19] Conversely, negative eugenics refers to ways to discourage breeding of the undesirable population, including measures such as sterilisations, marriage restrictions, segregation, euthanasia and killings.[20] Against a backdrop of politically, socially, religiously, and historically favourable conditions, the eugenics movement lent support to sterilisation laws in the US (Indiana as the first state in

[12] See Galton 1883. [13] Weindling 1999: 179. See also Ordover 2003: 59–69.

[14] This is a popular depiction of eugenics. See, for example, Winfield 2012.

[15] Wilson 2018b: 141.

[16] However, the continuity and/or break between present and past discourses of genetics can be discussed. See Koch 2004.

[17] Engs 2005: xvi.

[18] For a critical account on measuring human beings and its oppressive implications, see Gould 1996.

[19] Spektorowski & Ireni-Saban 2014: 154–158.

[20] For the extreme version enacted by the German Nazi regime, see Bock 1983: 414–417.

1907), Vaud (Switzerland) in 1928, Denmark in 1929, Germany in 1933, Norway and Sweden in 1934, Finland in 1935, Estonia and Latvia in 1937, Iceland in 1938 and Japan in 1940.[21]

Although eugenics began to be perceived in a different light after the Second World War, sterilisation remained a popular method for reproductive control of the population throughout the twentieth century, especially considering the lack of other means of effective reproductive management. Paul Weindling considers international sterilisation policies to have occurred in five main temporal phases. The first wave hit the United States of America (US) and parts of Canada; the second, some parts of Europe (most importantly Nazi Germany); the third, the Nordic countries; the fourth, global emerging market economies (such as China, India, Puerto Rico and Singapore); and the fifth, post-communist Eastern Europe in the form of racial measures against Romani groups.[22] Some of these countries – such as the Nordic countries – have legislated and registered the interventions in a transparent and often centralised way, while other countries – such as Slovakia or Japan – have not kept public registers.[23]

Moving on to castration, this scope of the present work is limited to exploring the regulation and use of surgical castration which began to appear at the end of the nineteenth and beginning of the twentieth centuries, primarily in the field of psychiatry.[24] Castration was officially introduced to treat patients with differing pathologies, ranging from 'hysterics' to 'perverts'.[25] Later, it developed as a means to reduce the production of sex hormones (particularly testosterone), intended to mitigate sexual deviance and danger, primarily in reference to sexual criminals.[26]

Sterilisation and castration both became topics of high interest, particularly in medical, psychiatric, criminological and eugenic circles in Europe and Northern America at the end of the nineteenth and beginning of the twentieth centuries. At that time, advancements in medical research had made sterilisation and castration techniques more sophisticated than ever before, and such interventions could be carried out with lower risks to the patient's life.[27] In practice, the interventions targeted a wide range of people, including those

[21] Zaremba 1999: 20–21. [22] Weindling 1999: 186.

[23] As a result, the Nordic countries have high numbers of registered interventions in an international comparison. In Slovakia, by contrast, Romani women had to challenge the lack of access to their own sterilisation files before the ECtHR to get access to them. ECtHR, *K.H. and Others v. Slovakia* (2009). In Japan, some of the sterilisation registries have been destroyed, see The Japan Times 2018. The lack of access is a denial of truth to the victims of involuntary sterilisation, which in turn negatively affects the victims' chances to access other remedies.

[24] Hence, it does not include the long-standing social, religious, punitive, torturous, musical and medical castrations throughout history which have been carried out across different cultures. See Mattila 2002: 6; Bourke 2007: 148–167.

[25] Wessel 2015: 601. [26] See Bourke 2007: 148; Le Maire 1956.

[27] For example, in 1853, the first successful abdominal hysterectomy which did not lead to the death of the patient was carried out by Walter Burnham from Massachusetts. Sutton 2018: 11–12.

considered to be feebleminded, women referred to as hysterical or promiscuous and masturbating men and sexual criminals.

Note that sterilisation and castration are different interventions that have targeted different groups. Sterilisation typically targeted the people whose reproduction was considered undesirable, most typically embodied in the notion of feeblemindedness, while castration targeted the people considered sexually dangerous. At the turn of the century, their use sometimes overlapped regardless. Their somewhat interchangeable character can be seen in the following quote by Swiss psychiatrist Auguste Forel, published in his 1905 book *Die sexuelle Frage*:

> I quite openly admit to agreeing to the castration of a disgusting, psychically ill patient in my hospital, who had complained about a pain in his genitals. He himself wanted this castration *while I clearly thought of it in terms of preventing him from having children rather than treating his condition*. I also allowed the removal of the ovaries of a hysterical 14-year-old girl, whose mother and grandmother were both prostitutes and who gave herself to every boy on the street, because I wished to prevent this misery from being perpetuated. *At that time it was the fashion to use castration to cure cases of hysteria, and I used this pretence although, in reality, it was done purely for social reasons.*[28]

The quote demonstrates how castration, apart from as a means of control over the sexual drive, was also used to control the reproduction of individuals singled out by the expert as being unfit to reproduce. The opposite, that is, when sterilisation was used to treat unwanted sexual behaviour, also occurred in different national contexts. One example was the castration and sterilisation of inmates at the Jeffersonville State Prison in Indiana, carried out by medical doctor Henry Sharp, mainly as a means to treat masturbation.[29] Sharp was an advocate of vasectomy for multiple indications. In a 1902 article, he urged state institutions to 'render every male sterile who passes its portals, whether it be almshouse, insane asylum, institute of the feeble-minded, reformatory or prison'.[30]

Returning to sterilisation, an intervention which has been in wider use globally in comparison to castration, the US provided an early breeding ground for the practices. A famous case which ended up before the US Supreme Court was the sterilisation of Carrie Buck. Buck was a young woman from socially disadvantaged circumstances who was ordered to undergo sterilisation by the authorities and state judicial instances. The underlying motivation for the order was her diagnosis of 'feeblemindedness', largely based on her perceived immorality and sexual promiscuity.[31] In the 1927 ruling of *Buck v. Bell*, the Supreme Court tested the constitutionality of the 1924 Virginia Sterilization Act. The plaintiff argued that the Appellate Court's judgment should be rendered void on the basis of the Fourteenth Amendment, denying her due

[28] English quote appearing in Kuechenhoff 2008: 220. Emphasis added.

[29] Wessel 2015: 593. [30] Quoted in Drake et al 1999: 476.

[31] Nourse 2008: 24. For a detailed account of the case and its context, see Cohen 2016.

process of law and equal protection.[32] In an eight-to-one vote, the Court found that the sterilisation was not unconstitutional, as the public interest weighed heavier than the individual one at stake.[33] The majority opinion delivered by Justice Holmes stated:

> We have seen more than once that the public welfare may call upon the best citizens for their lives. It would be strange if it could not call upon those who already sap the strength of the State for these lesser sacrifices, often not felt to be such by those concerned, in order to prevent our being swamped with incompetence. It is better for all the world if, instead of waiting to execute degenerate offspring for crime or to let them starve for their imbecility, society can prevent those who are manifestly unfit from continuing their kind. [...] Three generations of imbeciles are enough.[34]

The decision crucially lent legitimacy to sterilisation acts of the time.[35] Before the decision, legal question marks surrounded emerging state sterilisation laws, but as eloquently put by Victoria Nourse, '[l]egal doubts, lingering for almost two decades, appeared finally to have been put to rest' after the decision.[36] The judgment led to the establishment of many more US sterilisation laws, and an increase in interventions.[37] Notably, the case has never been overturned,[38] even though the Court established in the 1942 case *Skinner v. Oklahoma* that the right to procreate was 'one of the basic civil rights of man', 'fundamental to the very existence and survival of the race'.[39] *Skinner v. Oklahoma*, which concerned the sterilisation of male prison inmates, was conceptualised differently than *Buck v. Bell*,[40] with the result that coercive sterilisation practices continued to be carried out in the US for a long time after the 1942 *Skinner* decision.[41]

Involuntary sterilisation and castration have also been practised outside of the US. Any introduction of the topic brings to mind Nazi Germany. After the National Socialists' seizure of power, the Government soon introduced regulation on sterilisation through the 1933 Act for the Prevention of Hereditarily Diseased Offspring.[42] The legislation rendered sterilisation possible on the indications of 'hereditary deafness', 'hereditary blindness', 'manic-depressive insanity', 'Huntington's Chorea', 'hereditary dementia', 'schizophrenia', 'feeblemindedness', 'alcoholism' or 'serious hereditary physical deformity'.[43]

[32] See Supreme Court of the United States, *Buck v. Bell* (1927). [33] See Kevles 1999: 436–437.

[34] Supreme Court of the United States, *Buck v. Bell* (1927): 207.

[35] A weighty factor in this legitimacy gaining occurred because it was delivered by Holmes, who was considered to be a progressive justice. Nourse 2008: 31.

[36] Ibid. [37] Nourse 2008: 24–31; Curry 2002: 61. [38] See Silver 2004: 866.

[39] Supreme Court of the United States, *Skinner v. Oklahoma* (1942): 541. See also Curry 2002: 18, 62–65.

[40] Supreme Court of the United States, *Skinner v. Oklahoma* (1942); Silver 2004: 868–869.

[41] Nourse 2008: 158.

[42] Gesetz zur Verhütung erbkranken Nachwuchses [Act for the Prevention of Hereditarily Diseased Offspring] 1933.

[43] Ibid, Article 1.

According to Gisela Bock, sterilisation was depicted as a way to 'clean' the body of the population (*Volkskörper*) of degenerates.[44] She has shown how women were considered to be 'feebleminded' more often than men, and how the evaluation of women's mental health was particularly connected to their work performance inside as well as outside the household.[45]

The earlier-mentioned Weindling identified another important aim underlying the law as its cost-cutting efforts, targeting people depicted as burdens to society, such as people with disabilities.[46] According to Bock, groups particularly vulnerable to the Nazi sterilisation projects were poor people, unskilled workers and their wives, house servants, farmworkers, prostitutes, unmarried mothers, women on welfare, criminals, inmates of institutions, ethnic minorities (such as Romani and Black Germans) and people who broke gender norms.[47] The sterilisation law covered both voluntary and involuntary interventions, but coercion and force were commonly used to make people agree to the interventions.[48] The applications were decided upon by specially established Hereditary Health Courts (*Erbgesundheitsgericht*).[49]

Apart from sterilisation, the Nazi regime was also concerned with castration. The sterilisation legislation was expanded in 1935 to also encompass the voluntary castration of men who had committed a crime caused by their 'degenerate sex drive'.[50] Already in 1933, however, the Act against Dangerous Habitual Criminals and Measures for Protection and Recovery had been enacted, which introduced a possibility in the Penal Code to forcibly castrate people convicted for the following crimes: rape; defilement; illicit sex acts with children; coercion to commit sex offences; public indecency including homosexuality and murder or manslaughter committed to arouse or gratify the sexual drive.[51] According to Geoffrey Giles, most castrations were carried out under the Penal Code rather than the Act for the Prevention of Hereditarily Diseased Offspring.[52] In his theorisation of the practices, Giles has identified a pattern where the castration of sex offenders was seen as a 'security measure rather than a eugenic one'.[53] Castrations were, however, not as widely implemented as sterilisations in Nazi Germany.[54]

[44] Bock 1991: 235. [45] Ibid: 239. [46] Weindling 1989: 441–457. [47] Bock 1983: 414–417.

[48] Giles 1992: 41; Bock 1991: 235.

[49] Gesetz zur Verhütung erbkranken Nachwuchses [Act for the Prevention of Hereditarily Diseased Offspring] 1933, Article 6. No definite numbers exist for how many people were sterilised during the German Nazi regime as many records were destroyed and many interventions went undocumented, such as many of the sterilisations at the concentration camps. Bock has estimated that as many as 400,000 people were sterilised between 1933 and 1945. Bock 1991: 235.

[50] Giles 1992: 45.

[51] Gesetz gegen gefährliche Gewohnheitsverbrecher und über Maßregeln der Sicherung und Besserung [Act against Dangerous Habitual Criminals and Measures for Protection and Recovery] 1933. The provision was regulated in Strafgesetzbuch [German Penal Code] 1871, Section 42k, which was in force until 1946; Grau 1995: 246.

[52] Giles 1992: 46. [53] Ibid.

[54] The total number of registered castrations under the Penal Code was 2,156 for the period between 1934 and 1941. Ibid: 47.

The infamous sterilisations and castrations in the Nazi regime are often popularly depicted as the utmost manifestation of evil and wicked science: 'science gone wrong'. While the Nazi atrocities and the Holocaust can be seen as extremes, it is easy to be blinded by the notion of exceptionalism, making comparison ultimately impossible. This said, a continuity can be traced in many democratic countries during the same period.[55] One example of such continuity is the 'Model Sterilisation Law', developed by the American eugenicist Harry Laughlin in his 1922 book, *Eugenical Sterilization in the United States*,[56] which came to directly or indirectly inspire many a legislator.[57] Its inspirational effect was not only limited to the US states but also reached other countries, including Nazi Germany.[58] Moreover, the eugenics circles of the early twentieth century were an international, cosmopolitan crowd which exchanged ideas about surgical interventions.[59] This complicated the determination of strict, divisional national lines in eugenic expertise, influence and ultimately, implementation.

After the Second World War, 'traditional' eugenic interventions in the name of 'race' experienced a drop in popularity.[60] Sterilisations and castrations nevertheless persisted in a 'reformist' framework rooted in social grounds. Such interventions have continued into the late twentieth and early twenty-first centuries, having targeted among others Romani women in Eastern European countries, indigenous women in Peru and Uyghur women in China.

Castrations and Sterilisations of Trans People

However different in scope and aim, another post-war implementation of the practices is the use of sterilisation or castration as a precondition for amendment of one's legally registered gender. Such sterilisation and castration practices have particularly targeted trans people, in other words, people whose gender identity is not aligned with their birth-assigned gender. I consider these policies to be different from earlier practices of sterilisation and castration, as they specifically targeted a smaller group of people and were explicitly carried out on the basis of gender identity. Yet, I also find a connection to the earlier practices in broad terms, as the interventions constituted public reproductive

[55] An insightful comparison has been performed by Kühl 2002.

[56] The law is presented in Laughlin 1922: 446–451.

[57] In fact, Laughlin's intent was to have the law be designed in such a way that it would 'withstand a U.S. Supreme Court challenge'. Black 2012:113.

[58] The formulation of the 1933 German law has many similarities to the model law developed by Laughlin. Michael G Silver claims that the Nazi sterilisation law was directly inspired by Laughlin's model law. Silver 2004: 870. Ruth Clifford Engs does however not include Germany among the countries which 'adopted' the model law. Engs 2005: 54.

[59] Theories and ideas were discussed, for example, at international congresses. The first international eugenics congress was organised in London in 1912. Hietala 1985: 127.

[60] On the debatable difference between traditional and reformist eugenics, see Roll-Hansen 1999: 201–202.

and sexual control of individuals, which found support in scientific research of the time.

Because of their wish to systematise the normal and abnormal, twentieth-century psychiatry and psychology became increasingly interested in the social and biological categories of man and woman and how to standardise them. With scientifically defined gender boundaries, the 'outliers' would be more clearly defined. These people – such as the intersex, the effeminate man, the butch, the lesbian and the homosexual man – were to be normalised. The psychiatric and medical responses were therefore to 'correct' such deviance.[61]

Simultaneously, advancements in medical and surgical research and technology led to new and improved gender-affirming treatments. With the first 'sex reassignment' surgeries coming to the fore,[62] such as in the famous case of Christine Jorgensen of the 1950s,[63] the topic became one of public debate. The increased possibilities of bodily transformation, often simply referred to as 'changing sex', brought with them new challenges for public administration: Should it be possible for individuals to amend their legally registered gender? How should such amendments be legally regulated? What criteria should apply? Sweden was the first country to legislate the possibility of amending legally registered gender in 1972, with infertility among the listed preconditions. Yet, how did mandatory sterilisation and castration become linked to legal gender recognition?

The connection between sterilisation/castration preconditions and legal gender recognition for trans people is not self-evident. Reviewing the central psychiatric, psychological, sexologist and medical scholarship of the time,[64] such requirements for trans individuals[65] do not appear as a central theme. However, it seems that the medical standardisation of the category 'transsexual' since the 1960s led to a generally accepted notion of a person who permanently wants to assume the physical characteristics associated with the 'opposite' sex in a gender-binary world.[66] Accordingly, this person was assumed to long for access to a fixed set of medical interventions, including genital surgery. Such a

[61] See, for example, the development of a test measuring masculinity and femininity by the psychologists Lewis Terman and Catherine Miles in the 1930s, depicted in Honkasalo J 2016.

[62] 'Sex reassignment' has, during the last decades, been a popular term for referring to surgical interventions such as vaginoplasty, penectomy, orchiectomy, phalloplasty and metoidioplasty. I, however, generally use 'gender-affirming treatment', as I consider this term more respectful of a person's self-identified gender identity.

[63] In the case of Jorgensen's gender-affirming genital surgery, the Danish castration legislation provided a legal ground for the intervention. Honkasalo J 2019: 23–24.

[64] The review most importantly includes the writings of Richard von Krafft-Ebing, Magnus Hirschfeld, Harry Benjamin and Alfred Kinsey.

[65] They were first conceptualised as 'transvestites' and later nuanced with the additional category of 'transsexuals'.

[66] The medical term 'transsexual' has become controversial today, because it views gender variance as a pathology, a 'gender identity disorder' (F64.0 of ICD-10, however not included as a mental and behavioural disorder in ICD-11 of 2018). On the right to depathologisation for trans people under international human rights law, see Theilen 2014.

surgery would also lead to castration or sterilisation/infertility.[67] The legal gender status as a 'man' or 'woman' was understood as connected to such medical interventions. Endocrinologist Harry Benjamin wrote in 1967 that transsexuals 'want a change of their legal status'.[68] Having come into contact with transsexual people in the course of his studies, he had become aware of '[t]heir constant fear of discovery, arrest, and prosecution' which made 'life miserable for them before the operation'.[69] A connection was thus established between legal gender recognition and medical interventions.

Subsequent state regulation resorted to medical expertise, building legislation around the notion of the 'transsexual' who wanted genital surgery when introducing possibilities for legal recognition of gender identity.[70] In doing so, the medical notion went from an element of monitored studies and scientific literature to a legal standard to be implemented on trans individuals' bodies. This step has to be considered in piercing the logics behind sterilisation and castration preconditions which target trans people. In general, such requirements can be regarded as continuous of a discourse where the state has the prerogative to determine what is best for its population, and by extension, to regulate its reproduction and sexuality, a discourse already uncovered in the earlier examples of sterilisation and castration practices.

Coming to the subjects of regulation, as in the people which have been targeted by sterilisation and castration against their will, I suggest that the interventions work by multiple intersecting forms of oppression.[71] Other authors have suggested gender, gender identity, sexuality, ability, class, ethnicity, race and age – or, sometimes, a combination of these categories – as logics or proxies on the basis of which the interventions have been carried out.[72] Personally, I resist the temptation of emphasising one form of oppression over another, but rather emphasise that the interventions have targeted a multiplicity of groups. The governmental logic or ideology behind them has been time and place dependent. An illustrative example of a temporal shift is how pre-war traditional eugenics and its focus on biology gave way to a more flexible focus on culture in the post-war context.[73] As the target groups change, so do the motivations behind the practices. A common theme has been the underpinning alterity of the targeted, often marginalised, individuals and groups which are constructed as disorderly, abnormal and deprived of humanity.

[67] Particularly Benjamin 1966. Castration is depicted as a part of 'the operation' in Benjamin 1967: 120.

[68] Benjamin 1967: 119. [69] Ibid. [70] See, for example, Sørlie 2013.

[71] In the present research, intersectionality is broadly understood as recognising the multiplicities of oppression and discrimination which exist in interaction in the world, for example, gender, race, sexuality, class, age and ability.

[72] See, for example, Runcis 1998; Bock 1983; Tydén 2002; Mattila 1999; Marhoefer 2008; Smith A 2005; Haave 2000a; Curran 2016; Aasen 1989; Björkman 2011; Honkasalo J 2016; Myhre & Thomassen 2014; Sørlie 2016; Stote 2015; Hartmann 2016.

[73] See Repo 2015: 52.

Overview of the Book

After this Prologue, the book commences with Part I on developing rights and wrongs. The first chapter introduces the central research agenda, methodology and scope of the book, centring the concept of grievance formation. The socio-legal meaning of victimhood is addressed and stories are included of physical, reproductive, sexual, emotional and social harm as told by direct and indirect victims. This retelling highlights that the practices have not merely maimed and harmed the individuals coercively sterilised or castrated but also affected their families and broader communities. In this sense, fully comprehending the concept of harm is vital to develop an understanding of appropriate and effective remedies.

Discussing the legal foundations and modalities of remedies in international law, the chapter poses the question of state remedial responsibilities in relation to the passage of time. This is a central question in the globally emerging discussions on whether states ought to remedy sterilisation or castration practices in their past. Furthermore, the chapter lays down the theoretical framework for the book's use of the concept of grievance formation. As employed in social movement theory, this concept describes the process of people starting to address harmful experiences as common grievances. In this chapter, the concept is initially introduced into legal research by linking it with rights mobilisation: how victims of rights violations redefine traumatic experiences as individual or common grievances, rights violations and legal harm to be remedied. As such, the concept offers a theoretical framework to understand how and why some victims of rights violations begin to conceptualise themselves as such and demand state responsibility, while others might not; why victims are publicly and institutionally recognised and redressed to different extents.

After the introductory Part I, Part II engages with four case studies: international law, Sweden, Norway and Finland. The latter's first chapter, Chapter 2, shows how involuntary sterilisation and castration have become problematised in international law. The chapter discusses the rise of international law and human rights in the post-war context. Despite being regarded as international crimes on meeting certain criteria since the Nuremberg trials, the interventions are rarely prosecuted in practice. Efforts to mainstream involuntary sterilisation as human rights violations have been more successful. This development began in the 1990s and has since gone from soft law to binding legal obligations. A few cases have ended up before supranational human rights courts and treaty bodies, such as the European Court of Human Rights (ECtHR), the Inter-American Court of Human Rights (IACtHR), the Inter-American Commission of Human Rights (IACHR), the United Nations Committee on the Elimination of Discrimination against Women (CEDAW Committee) and the Human Rights Committee. The chapter shows that uncertainty prevails regarding the legal and remedial conceptualisation of involuntary sterilisation and castration in international human rights law due to inconsistent and incidental treatment of such cases. Ultimately, the argument is made that international law provides a socio-legal master frame for national legal claims. In the case of involuntary sterilisation and castration, however, this master frame is not sharply defined, effectively impeding investigation and problematisation of the practices in national contexts.

Chapter 3 analyses the Swedish sterilisation laws of 1934 and 1941, castration law of 1944 and sterilisation precondition in the gender recognition act of 1972. More specifically, it considers their establishment, abolition and partial remedy. Exploring both written sources and interviews, the chapter uncovers the processes leading to the compensation acts of 1999 and 2018, and how (particularly trans) victims have mobilised for, and accessed, remedies. The chapter discloses an underlying tension between the limited legal admission of responsibility and the remedies established as *ex gratia* compensation schemes. It compares the unequal remedies given to each different victim group against their diverging degree of mobilisation. In order to understand their dissimilar recognition and redress, the chapter analyses how grievances have formed and been individually, collectively, publicly and/or institutionally recognised for the different groups. In doing so, it illustrates how the victims' claims have aligned with a master frame of rights and achieved legal and sociocultural resonance to diverging degrees.

The fourth chapter presents a historical and socio-legal retelling of how Norway established, implemented and abolished the 1934 and 1942 sterilisation and castration acts. It also engages with the question of how castration was instituted as a precondition for legal gender recognition in the 1970s, and came to be questioned as a human rights violation in the 2010s. It does so through analysing legal primary sources and national scholarship as well as in-depth interviews. The chapter compares the victim groups and explores the reasons why the only group which has received remedies to date, is a small minority, the Romani/*tatere*. It also discusses the difficulties which trans victims of castration face when legally and politically mobilising in order to access remedies. The chapter indicates the limited grievance formation process in Norway where, unlike in Sweden, past sterilisation practices have only been framed as ethnic oppression. This, in turn, results in limited recognition of harm – and accordingly, rights violations and remedies – with respect to other victims of involuntary sterilisation and castration.

The fifth chapter focuses on how the Finnish 1935 and 1950 sterilisation and castration acts were established, implemented and abolished. It also describes the formation of an infertility requirement in the 2002 law which regulated legal gender recognition for trans people until 2023. The chapter also recounts how some victims, mainly trans people and organisations, have mobilised to eliminate the requirement and restructure the law. It compares the mobilisation and non-mobilisation of the groups and the persisting refusal of the Finnish state to acknowledge the violations, accept state responsibility for them and provide related remedies for the victims. In terms of grievance formation, the chapter outlines a stalled process. Therefore, victims have generally refrained from mobilisation due to a missing common identity and sense of wrong to be remedied. The chapter signals a prevailing absence of a socio-cultural rights frame recognising harms of victims and public responsibility in Finland. In this sense, the lack of remedial culture is more evident and the structural impediments to grievance formation are higher in Finland than in its Nordic neighbours.

Part III of the book engages in comparison to analyse the grievance formation process and rights framing at work. Against the background of a three-pronged comparison of cross-national, cross-group and cross-historical elements, Chapter 6 critically discusses the grievance formation process which has led to some victims' harms being regarded as rights violations to be remedied, while other victims' harms remain unchallenged in terms of rights. The chapter scrutinises the socio-legal steps of the grievance formation process adhered to in the present work, from perceiving personal harm and wrong to receiving remedies: personal validation, intra-group validation and external (public and institutional) validation which the victim groups have experienced to different extents. Connecting the grievance formation process to rights, the chapter demonstrates how the three Nordic countries in a globalising world have developed a rights culture and rights reasoning in the twentieth and twenty-first centuries. This development, in turn, has affected the problematisation of intersectional forms of oppression, such as involuntary sterilisation and castration. More importantly, however, the chapter also shows the ultimately fragile and situational nature of rights claims and their public and institutional recognition. In effect, by relating stories rarely told, the present research problematises and complexifies dogmas of Nordic rights development and the universality of rights.

Chapter 7 concludes by offering some brief reflections regarding the utility of grievance formation as a theoretical and methodological tool in socio-legal research in order to understand rights developments in context.

Part I
Developing Rights and Wrongs

1

Victims, Harms and Grievance Formation

This chapter lays the theoretical and methodological groundwork for this work's earlier-stated three main arguments. To repeat, these are, firstly, that the international human rights law framework has provided a weak master frame for the conceptualisation of involuntary sterilisation and castration in the countries investigated, both in a legal and remedial sense. Moreover, apart from as legal instruments, the notion of rights as sociocultural entitlements has been key to victims' formation of individual and group identities and their access to public and institutional recognition. Finally, the concept of grievance formation is helpful to better understand the diverse forms of recognition and remedial responses by states for different victim groups.

1.1 Terminology

At the outset, some central concepts that figure in the work must be determined. The term 'involuntary' is used to express that an intervention has been involuntary from the point of view of the person who was sterilised or castrated, not of the surgeon carrying out the intervention. I have settled on this umbrella term for two main reasons. The first is that it highlights the lack of free will rather than the use of external force. An involuntary intervention is one carried out without the free, full and informed consent of the person in question. It covers a range of terms, from 'forced', 'enforced' and 'coerced', to some forms of 'compulsory' and 'non-consensual' interventions. Such interventions may be characterised by either lack of consent or by formal consent, for example, expressed by a signature, nevertheless obtained under coercive circumstances. The second reason behind the choice of this term is that I am interested in the situations where legal letter or practice has disregarded individual applicants' will and voluntariness, rather than determining if individual interventions have been involuntary or voluntary.

Two other important terms to explain are 'cis' and 'trans'. The former, short for cisgender, is an open category to define people whose gender identity, that is, personal perception of one's own gender, is in line with their birth-assigned gender.[1]

[1] Aultman 2014: 61.

'Trans' is used to cover a range of identities that are not cisgender: people whose gender identity is not in line with their birth-assigned gender. A central group in this volume is people with a strong desire to assume characteristics associated with the 'opposite' sex in a binary world, often referred to as transsexual people.[2] In recent years, trans identities beyond the transsexual have become increasingly visible, particularly through mobilisation. Despite these attempts to clarify 'trans' as a term for explanatory purposes here, I would like to emphasise that this book embraces the open-endedness of trans existences, not confined and situated in relation to 'a destination, a final form, a specific shape, or an established configuration of desire and identity'.[3]

I also consider it necessary to define my use of the words 'gender' and 'sex'. Aware of the interdependency of the two, the work rejects categorical divisions of the former as 'social' or 'cultural' and the latter as strictly 'biological', recognising that they are in constant interaction and are often used interchangeably. I understand sex as connected to hormonal and physical factors, by definition diverse, non-binary.[4] Gender is however often used and portrayed as binary: man and woman. In this view, the law and public administration are primarily concerned with 'gender' rather than 'sex', which aligns with the interests of this research.

Moreover, an important distinction should be made between 'remedies' and 'reparations'. 'Remedy' is broadly understood here as a form of legal recourse, redressing a problem or harm through, for example, compensation or rehabilitation. 'Reparation' rather emphasises state responsibility and public liability as a legal basis.[5] In this monograph, I primarily use the term 'remedies', as many forms of redress to victims of involuntary sterilisation and castration have not been based on legal liability but on other grounds, such as solidarity, instead.

A final terminological issue is the choice between 'victim' and 'survivor'. I have chosen the first over the second. This choice does not seek to undermine the agency of the people victimised, nor their abilities to rebuild their lives, get organised and claim their losses. These narratives are in fact a crucial element of the book.[6] Existing relevant social movements and organisations

[2] The medical term 'transsexual' is controversial however, because it views gender variance as a pathology, a 'gender identity disorder' (F64.0 of ICD-10; no longer included as a mental and behavioural disorder in ICD-11). On the right of trans people to depathologisation under international human rights law, see Theilen 2014.

[3] Halberstam 2018: 4.

[4] This is evident in the many biological variations of sex characteristics outside of 'male' and 'female', often referred to as intersex conditions. See the important contribution by Fausto-Sterling 2000. Intersex 'normalising' surgeries are excluded from the scope of this book, as their aim is not the elimination of reproduction or the sexual drive.

[5] Liable entities related to the sovereign administration of public power are primarily referred to as 'state' in the international legal context, while national legislation often defines them as 'public'. In this book, I use the term 'state responsibility' in a wider sense than the term 'public liability', the latter referring mainly to domestic doctrinal conceptualisations of liability.

[6] On victim/survivor terminology and agency, see Kelly 1988. See also Polletta 2006: 111, who claims that the dichotomy between victimhood and agency is false.

tend to avoid the use of both 'victim' and 'survivor', rather talking about, for example, 'the forcibly sterilised'.[7] For legal clarity, I have chosen to use the word 'victim' nevertheless. International human rights law, international criminal law and national regulations of liability construct their notions of loss and harm around the concept of victimhood.[8] A further reason to use the term 'victim' is that a significant part of the victims' struggles has centred on achieving victim status. In fact, many victims have encountered great difficulties in creating counter-narratives to the dominant ones formulating sterilisation/castration as a voluntary choice, in the best interest of the people affected.[9] The fluidity in determining free will has added to this complexity.[10] In conclusion, 'victim' is a word that highlights the power imbalance between the individual victims and the grantor of rights and remedies: public authorities.

1.2 Methodology

The methodology used in this work builds on a layered, socio-legal approach, where the law is seen as a social construction, contextually embedded. The law is not merely understood as top-down regulation, but rather as ideas and terminology used communicatively to create individual, common and public identities and to provoke state response. Understanding the law as part of a discursive reality – as a tool, an actor and an expression – allows for a wider cultural understanding beyond the letter of the law.[11]

Starting from traditional black-letter legal analysis, a method that can be described as the law's 'inner perspective', the narrative moves towards the margins of the law. Going beyond the law's universal claims, the study historicises and contextualises legal development. Approaching the law's outer reaches, it begins to formulate an 'outsider perspective' where victims either engage with the law or refrain from such engagement. The methodology used can

[7] See, for example, RFSL 2017.

[8] In the UN Basic Principles and Guidelines, determining the right to reparations for victims of gross violations of international human rights law and serious violations of international humanitarian law, the term 'victim' is defined as:

> [...] persons who individually or collectively suffered harm, including physical or mental injury, emotional suffering, economic loss or substantial impairment of their fundamental rights, through acts or omissions that constitute gross violations of international human rights law, or serious violations of international humanitarian law. Where appropriate, and in accordance with domestic law, the term "victim" also includes the immediate family or dependants of the direct victim and persons who have suffered harm in intervening to assist victims in distress or to prevent victimization. A/RES/60/147 (2006), Art 8.

[9] This counter-narrative is used as an act of creating counter-hegemony. See Hunt 1990.

[10] Eivergård & Jönsson 2000 have addressed this.

[11] Discourse is taken to mean the process in which knowledge is produced through 'social practices, forms of subjectivity and power relations which inhere in such knowledges and relations between them'. Weedon 1987: 108, referring to a Foucauldian concept of 'discourse'. See also Niemi-Kiesiläinen et al 2007.

be understood along the lines of Hilary Charlesworth's thoughts on feminist legal methods:

> But when confronted with a concrete issue, no single theoretical approach or method seems adequate. A range of feminist theories and methods are necessary to excavate the issues. In this sense, feminist explorations can be likened to an archaeological dig.[12] There are various layers of practices, procedures, symbols, and assumptions to uncover and different tools and techniques may be relevant at each level.[13]

Accordingly, the overarching way of approaching knowledge can be defined as feminist, emphasising 'conversation and dialogue rather than the production of a single, triumphant truth'.[14] Additionally, in this scholarly context, I understand 'feminism' as critical research perspectives that challenge biologically deterministic, generally accepted 'truths' about the social order, focusing on gender, but embracing intersectionality.[15] This said, the book draws on a wide range of literature, not only on feminist or intersectional. Critically investigating legal development with reference to involuntary sterilisation and castration, I look at which issues are regulated by law and which are not, and the manner in which – if regulated. I use comparative methodology in a dialogic, feminist tradition. On the outskirts of the law, as regards involuntary practices of sterilisation and castration and their victims, stories appear about the law as a means of oppression as well as a hope for emancipation.

More precisely, from the point of departure of black-letter legal analysis, the book firstly queries what rules and principles apply to involuntary sterilisation and castration. This question is raised in particular with reference to the international legal regulation of involuntary sterilisation and castration but also to the national laws in question. The study analyses legal sources issued by states and supranational bodies, taking into consideration their hierarchical position and the doctrinal literature of the countries in question, particularly concerning the interaction between national and supranational law. This stage of the analysis can be depicted as the 'inner' core of the law.

Adding a further layer to the analysis, the work explores how the law has developed. I present and analyse relevant historical laws and decrees, particularly their often-extensive *travaux préparatoires*, and the related legal and political debates on the establishment of these laws. I also engage with secondary legal and historical literature. In doing so, this volume renders visible how

[12] Here, Charlesworth refers to Naffine 1990. [13] Charlesworth 2004: 161. [14] Ibid: 159.

[15] Angie-Marie Hancock describes intersectionality's intellectual project as 'twofold: an analytical approach to understanding between-category relationships *and* a project to render visible and remediable previously invisible, unaddressed material effects of the sociopolitical location of Black women or women of color' (2016: 33). In her book, she attributes particular weight to the writings of Patricia Hill Collins and Kimberlé W Crenshaw. In my monograph, 'intersectionality' is broadly understood as recognising the multiplicities of oppression and discrimination – for example, gender, race, sexuality, class, age and ability – which exist in interaction in the world.

laws and national legal cultures have unfolded in a historical context. This stage of the analysis moves away from the law's insider perspective, emphasising its embeddedness and historical dependency.

A third layer is added to develop the study further. This socio-legal component asks how the law is used and by whom, and correspondingly, how it is not used, and by whom. This reveals the reasons behind national differences in victims' and civil society's legal engagement and mobilisation. The actors of special interest can be divided into three categories: (i) activists and civil society representatives; (ii) state representatives, members of state-appointed investigations and national experts (often employed or appointed by the state); (iii) actors who have contributed to forming public and scholarly debates, that is journalists and academics. Sometimes, these categories may overlap, for example when prominent academics or activists take part in state-appointed investigations, or when academics or journalists speak out on behalf of victims or civil society causes.

The analysis is based on interview material with central actors in all three categories. The underlying objective of including multiple actors is to engage different perspectives in a dialogical, balanced manner, which is in line with the research's aim of contextual understanding. I have interviewed 83 people in total, out of which 23 have been mainly active in the Swedish national context, 27 in the Norwegian, 21 in the Finnish and 12 in an international or non-Nordic context.[16] The interviews have been semi-structured, and the interviewees are all actors who can broadly be defined as key informants.[17] Many of the interviews are of an in-depth character.[18] All cited interviewees have agreed to their names being fully included in the study.

It is important to highlight that I have not sought to interview victims of involuntary sterilisation or castration directly, at least not in their capacity as such.[19] This choice is motivated firstly by the research interest, which

16 Two of the interviewees have been interviewed twice, and five interviews have been carried out in a group format, with two or three people present.

17 I have given the interviewees the opportunity to look at a set of guiding questions a couple of days before the interviews. The guiding questions have been used as a starting point for the conversations. I have mainly conducted the interviews in person, sometimes over the phone or through teleconference calls, and exceptionally, in written format. I have also used electronic correspondence, for instance in order to inquire about administrative procedures or to access centralised statistics.

18 In-depth interviews are preferable for gaining information from key informants. See Della Porta 2014: 229. The length of the interviews has ranged from one to four hours. The interviews have been recorded, transcribed and coded according to central themes, except for when interviewees have not consented to this procedure. While some interviews have been solely beneficial to provide background information for the book, most of the interviewees are referenced in the book.

19 This said, civil society representatives and activists may themselves be victims of involuntary sterilisation or castration, but I have not inquired about personal experiences during the interviews. If such experiences have come up, I have listened and respected the interviewee's wish to talk about them, but neither posed further personal inquiries nor transcribed these narratives.

foregrounds socio-legal development rather than individual experiences of harm and loss, and secondly, by ethical concerns, from a wish to protect the privacy of the people affected.

The themes in the thoughts and experiences that the interviewees have shared with me varied greatly, and therefore provided me with extensive material. Consequently, only a small part of the information is included here. Above all, the interviews have helped me to understand the processes that take place in different actors' decisions to engage with the law through, for instance, civil society rights mobilisation. Understanding the complex underpinnings of, for example, legal mobilisation, primarily through the platforms of civil society organisations, has made me appreciate the importance of factors such as organisational and legal infrastructures. By looking at the weakly resourced groups that have not organised, the absence of such crucial contextual factors renders visible how and why some groups mobilise and organise, while others do not.[20]

A final analytical layer is added to the study by means of comparative analysis. The interest in such analysis lies in revealing any similarities and differences in how the relevant legal regulation and other forms of state reactions have developed in the three countries.[21] Against a backdrop of an ambiguous, developing, patchwork international legal framework, which manifests dissimilarly in the different countries, the book investigates the relevant particulars. The comparative analysis aims to understand, analyse and illuminate the diversities in frame alignment and grievance formation in relation to rights.

1.3 Conceptualising and Redressing Harm

Before diving into the topic of rights and remedies, a few words should be said on harm. Fully taking into consideration the complexities of people's harm and suffering may be an impossible task, but some engagement with the topic is vital for understanding the importance of appropriate, complete and transformative remedies.[22] Keeping in mind Fionnuala Ní Aoláin, Dina Haynes and Naomi Cahn's account of 'feminist methodology', which 'listens to what women say' 'about the forms and nature of harms experienced',[23] I wish to use the (direct and indirect) stories of harm of some people – women, men or non-binary people – directly or indirectly victimised through involuntary sterilisation as an analytical point of departure. Due to a lack of extensive mapping

[20] I understand 'weakly resourced groups' as groups that have little political influence and resources. Chabanet & Royall 2014: 6.

[21] This is in line with Frankenberg's aim of 'distancing and differencing'. Frankenberg 1985: 415.

[22] This should be complemented with a full establishment of the relevant facts, properly identifying the victims and alleged violation(s) and engendering reparations. Rubio-Marín & Sandoval 2011: 1064–1071.

[23] Ní Aoláin et al 2011: 432.

of victims' accounts, particularly regarding the involuntarily castrated,[24] I draw on secondary accounts of victims' stories of involuntary sterilisation as recounted in academic literature, non-governmental organisation (NGO) reports and court cases from different geographical contexts.

Both involuntary sterilisation and castration involve multiple harms. One is the violation of integrity inherent to the intervention being carried out against the free will of the victim. The amount of force, coercion, deception or authoritative persuasion at the time of the intervention may differ. One Romani woman who was involuntarily sterilised in Slovakia retold her story in the following way:

> The doctor told me that if I had a cesarean a third time, then I would die. The doctors and nurses kept repeating this to me. I said that I was young and that I wanted more children. The doctor kept reminding me that when they take me to surgery, they will ligate me. I was in great pain at that time [...] I agreed because I was scared. I had a baby boy at home, my husband works, my mother is ill. I had to make it home. I thought maybe I could have a third child, but then I thought I would die and I cried [...] and thought how could I abandon my boy and my new baby girl.[25]

As seen in her story, the Slovakian woman was presented with false information in a highly stressful situation, depriving her of a free and informed choice. Another woman, sterilised according to historical sterilisation laws in Sweden, retold another kind of coercion, namely the threat of infinite institutionalisation by the authorities: '[I]f I had not signed [the papers], I would have ended up at [a state institution for women considered mentally ill] and never regained my freedom'.[26] A man, belonging to the traveller minority, who was coerced into sterilisation according to the same Swedish historical sterilisation laws, retold the intervention as one of deception by the authorities:

> I got an injection and fell asleep. When I woke up, I was angry. Yes, then I got really angry and said, 'what have you tricked me into'. 'You have signed here', they said. But they never explained what it was. They only said that it is so you can be released. There was a guard there. He was a prison guard and surely a Nazi. He said that 'the race that you belong to should not have children'. That is what he said. And then I understood what would happen to me. But then it was too late.[27]

In other situations that were coercive, the coercion resulted from oppressive legislation rather than pressure by individual civil servants or medical personnel. A trans man in Sweden retold the coercion inherent in the mismatch

[24] Important exceptions exist of breaking the silence and sharing victims' stories, such as Eugenicsarchive.ca or the Quipu Project.

[25] Center for Reproductive Rights et al 2003: 56.

[26] Lomfors 2000: 287. Translated from Swedish.

[27] Ibid: 328. Translated from Swedish.

between legally registered gender and expressed gender identity, forcing him to undergo sterilisation:

> If I had not agreed to the sterilisation, then I would not have been allowed to change my legal gender and then I would have continued to live like some kind of living dead, so to speak. I would probably not have been able to access all the treatment I needed, and I would not have been respected as a man. The state would not have recognised that I existed. The state would have thought that I was a woman. And relatively many in the surroundings who saw my [identity] papers would also have thought that I was a woman. So, they would not have seen me. And you cannot live like that.[28]

The consequences of the intervention can be many. A direct consequence is unwanted infertility which victims experience in various ways, depending on individual, social and cultural circumstances. This can also affect other people than the direct victims, such as their partners and family members. A woman who was sterilised according to Canadian historical sterilisation legislation recounted how her possibilities to enjoy parenting were excluded after the surgery:

> I won't be able to enjoy the children I would have had [...] We don't know these things. But had I had children, I would have loved them, and they would have loved me back, and they would have been a support system and a family [...] I'm missing that. I missed that.[29]

Involuntary infertility is an experience of loss of (future) family relationships, affecting one's life project, by definition incommensurable.[30] Rather than subsiding, the harm of such infertility can take different expressions and intensify during the course of a person's life. Apart from a missing relationship with biological children, infertility can also affect relationships with other people, such as intimate partners. A trans man in Sweden depicted the legislated infertility requirement as a constant impediment, a daily struggle, likely to affect any future relationships:

> I have thought multiple times if [amending legally registered gender] is worth it. Because it is so much, one sacrifices so much. And it will be a bloody difficult life and I constantly have to fight for my rights. It will always be a struggle. For example, having a family. A person who is comfortable in their body and relatively happy with their life can still have a family. I, on the other hand, cannot have a family. And then, depending on whether I meet a man or a woman later, someone who I really want to be together with for a longer period, then I cannot... If it is a man, I cannot have children with him. I cannot adopt because there are a lot of regulations and rules and so on. If it is a girl, she can at least get inseminated and have children that way. In that situation, it is possible, if one

28 RFSL 2015, second personal story in video material. Translated from Swedish.

29 Wilson 2018a.

30 On the notion of harm to life project and its reparation, particularly developed in the jurisprudence of the IACtHR, see, for example, Tonon 2011.

> wants to go down that road. But do you have to choose [between amended legal gender and fertility]? It feels so difficult and I guess that is the part I have been thinking about the most… the social part, families and relationships and so on. Is it worth it?[31]

This account highlights the importance of the social element in the experience of harm. The individual expectations of what constitutes a 'good' or 'normal' life – for example, the desirability of having children and/or a big family – are not just individual but also highly sociocultural. The role of the social context in magnifying the meaning and impact of infertility is addressed in the European Court of Human Rights Case of *V.C. v. Slovakia*:

> [O]wing to her infertility, the applicant experienced difficulties in her relationship with her partner and, later, husband. She indicated her infertility as one of the reasons for her divorce in 2009. […] Owing to her inability to have more children the applicant has been ostracised by the Roma community.[32]

Compound negative effects of infertility were also brought up in my interview with Marta González-Dominguez, legal advisor at the Center for Reproductive Rights. She told me about a Chilean case she was involved with where an HIV-positive woman was involuntarily sterilised in connection to giving birth:

> Different forms of violence act as a circle… so when [the applicant] realised that she could not have more babies, her husband also started to beat her and to mistreat her, because she couldn't have more babies… and this is also very important because it shows how these gender stereotypes […] act. Her role as a woman in society was completely cut. She was very frustrated, she wanted to be a mommy, a young mommy… and it was very difficult for her to accept that she could not have more babies.[33]

Infertility is nevertheless not the only harm. Some victims recount decreased sexual desire and changes in their sexual lives after the involuntary surgery.[34] This also holds true for the involuntarily castrated, for whom the surgery aimed to disrupt sexual drive. The victims' harm and experiences of involuntary castration depend on the socially constructed values and ideas related to sexuality, such as the gendered importance given to men's erectile and penetrative abilities.[35] The European Committee for the Prevention of Torture and Inhuman or Degrading Treatment or Punishment (European Torture Committee) lists the harms of surgical castration as infertility, an increased risk of osteoporosis, mental depression and altered physical appearance – such as diminished body hair, oily skin and the increased formation of breast tissue.[36]

[31] Bremer S 2011: 204–205. Translated from Swedish.

[32] ECtHR, *V.C. v. Slovakia* (2011): Para 118.

[33] González-Dominguez, 5 January 2018.

[34] See, for example, Fodstad 2000: 145.

[35] This is built on differences in social construction between male and female sexuality and reproduction. For the construction of masculinity through, for example, sexuality and fatherhood, see Edwards T 2006; Kimmel et al (eds), 2004.

[36] CPT/Inf (2009) 8: Para 14.

The experience of sexual harm is also affected by the social and cultural context. A woman who was sterilised according to the historical sterilisation laws in Sweden mourned her inability to share her experiences of changed sexual life with her generation due to a general sense of stigma:

> And you get weak in another way. Nowadays they speak so openly about the sexual. The sexual became different in comparison to earlier, if one puts it like that. And one gets sad too, particularly being unable to talk to anyone [about it].[37]

Silence and inability to speak about the surgery, even to spouses, are echoed by other victims. A man sterilised according to historical sterilisation laws in Sweden recounted feelings of shame, limiting his communicative ability in relation to close ones but to authorities as well. This affected his general well-being in turn, such as his access to health:

> Yes, I was ashamed. Even when I was about to get heart surgery and they saw the scar I was ashamed. But I also became hateful. Because they were holding me down. At the time, one could not talk to people from the authorities at all. Nobody cared. This has often come over me. Especially when I have met girls. Because I knew that I could not have children. At these times, it happened that I drank. But it was worst when I was married. Because then I had to lie and say that I had suffered from mumps. But I did not feel good about sitting there lying. So I had to tell.[38]

A general theme of a damaged relationship with authorities, particularly medical ones, appears in victims' stories. Stigmatisation and stereotyping are common, impacting victims' lives beyond the involuntary surgery. One forcibly sterilised Slovakian Romani woman, who only found out that she would be permanently infertile after the surgery, retold her struggle to access healthcare, facing stigmatisation and stereotyping:

> The local gynecologist told me that it would be forever. I was surprised. I wanted to ask the doctor if I could do something to have more children, but I am ashamed to ask because usually gynecologists tell off Romani women for having more children and say that we have children to get [state] benefits. So I was ashamed to ask.[39]

Victims have suffered from physical, mental, emotional, sexual and reproductive harms. One of the few extensive documentations of such harm is nine qualitative interviews with victims of Swedish historical sterilisation practices by Ingrid Lomfors. In the victims' stories, some of the direct physical manifestations of harm are infertility; unattractive, uncomfortable and itchy physical scarring; bleeding; headaches; stress; gastric ulcers; nausea; abdominal pain; decreased sexual pleasure. Some of the psychological, emotional, and social materialisations of harm were destroyed marriages and other intimate relationships, stigmatisation and related psychological problems, a constant fear of public disclosure of the sterilisation, feelings of shame, longing for children and grandchildren, the

[37] Lomfors 2000: 295. Translated from Swedish. [38] Ibid: 330.
[39] Center for Reproductive Rights et al 2003: 62.

need to take psychotropic drugs with side effects, negative effects in sexual life, loss of self-esteem and perceived human dignity, lost opportunities of family life, the feeling of being mutilated, loss of joy and happiness in life, difficulties of engaging in personal relationships, feelings of loneliness and lack of interest in sexual relations. The social stigma regarding sterilisation sometimes led to marginalisation, denied access to adoption services (because of the diagnosis which led to the sterilisation), loss of career and housing opportunities and costs for treatment and therapy with immediate financial effects.[40]

The direct victims also mentioned indirect victimisation of close ones: destroyed relationships, loss of opportunities to have biological children with the sterilised partner or for their children to have siblings. In short, the harms of involuntary sterilisation and castration – and, in most cases, of the inability to access redress – have been manifold and continuous, and impacted a great period of the victims' lives.[41] The accounts tell general life stories of marginalisation, of being considered as less valuable socially.

It is important to take into consideration the multiplicity of harm for remedies to be not only corrective but also transformative.[42] Monetary compensation is often a standard remedy in legal systems. According to Alan Hyde, financial compensation rests on a murky concept of the body as property, where unquantifiable harm is financially valued according to 'notions of social opportunities'.[43] Financial compensation might, for example, increase victims' possibilities of accessing rehabilitation or health services. On its own, it fails to hold any transformative promise, however. Writing primarily on tort law, Leslie Bender has suggested that feminist ethics of care should inform remedies and legal notions of 'responsibility'.

> My suggestion is that we use feminist theory to change the meaning of responsibility in tort – which now means primarily an obligation to make monetary reparations for harms caused – to a meaning rooted in a concept of care. This enriched meaning of responsibility arises out of our recognition of our interconnectedness as human beings and has to do with responding through interpersonal caregiving to the needs of someone who has been injured. It means taking care of. Responsibility as taking care of, rather than solely as paying for, seems completely absent from the law, although it is part of our social understanding of the meaning of responsibility that arises out of our experiences as parents, siblings, lovers, friends, and neighbors. It is time for legal responsibility to include this meaning.[44]

Bender therefore suggests broadening the modalities of redress beyond monetary compensation. Such a broadening exercise also involves understanding the range of victims' harms, including their social aspects. In the case of involuntary sterilisation and castration, one such social aspect is the injury involved when considering a person as a member of a group unworthy of engaging in reproduction or sexual intercourse. In writing on violence against women,

[40] Lomfors 2000. [41] Ibid. [42] See Rubio-Marín 2009b: 382.
[43] Hyde 2003: 63. [44] Bender 1990: 768.

Adrian Howe refers to the collective aspects of harm as 'social injury', pointing to the impact of such violence on not merely individuals, but the whole group.[45] Ruth Rubio-Marín has indicated that the recognition of group-based injuries might be 'useful in contesting the inherited stigmas and hierarchies that often underpin those rights violations in order to build a new democratic order'.[46] Having acknowledged the importance of both the recognition and redress of victims, I now move on to remedies and conceptions of rights as challenging the notion of the state prerogative to decide who is worthy of sexuality and reproduction.

1.4 Rights and Remedies

The world after the great wars has witnessed democratisation efforts, rising individualism and the emergence, and increasing constitutionalisation, of human rights.[47] The idea that people have universal, inherent, inalienable and indivisible rights by virtue of being human is a powerful thought. The post-war international proliferation of rights is manifested, for example, in the increasing number and importance of supranational institutions, conventions and documents regulating human rights.[48] Recognised violations are important for state accountability and responsibility. Developing norms concerning state responsibility and reparations have led to these matters gaining a central role in the international community.[49] From being considered an inter-state phenomenon, realising state responsibility has come to include redress and reparation to individuals and groups.

Indeed, the right to a remedy is a generally accepted principle in international human rights and humanitarian law. In the Convention against Torture and Other Cruel, Inhuman or Degrading Treatment or Punishment (CAT), this right is expressed as the state party's obligation to ensure 'that the victim of an act of torture obtains redress and has an enforceable right to fair and adequate compensation, including the means for as full rehabilitation as possible'.[50] General Comment No. 3 of the Committee Against Torture (CAT Committee) specifies the obligation to provide redress as 'two-fold: procedural and substantive'.[51] The International Covenant on Civil and Political Rights (ICCPR) clearly formulates the obligation of parties to ensure that people

[45] Howe 1991: 156. [46] Rubio-Marín 2009b: 383.

[47] I understand human rights primarily within the international legal framework, taking shape within international organisations in the aftermath of the Second World War, affecting notions of constitutional rights. On the constitutionalisation of international law, particularly human rights, see Klabbers et al 2009; Greer and Wildhaber 2012; Sweet 2009.

[48] On the proliferation of the human rights discourse in the light of human rights mobilisation, see Simmons 2009.

[49] This development is well depicted in Shelton 2015; Crawford 2013.

[50] United Nations Convention against Torture and Other Cruel, Inhuman, or Degrading Treatment or Punishment (1984), Art 14(1).

[51] CAT/C/GC/3 (2012): Para 5.

whose rights have been violated have access to an 'effective remedy'.[52] In 2005, the United Nations General Assembly (UNGA) adopted a resolution on *Basic Principles and Guidelines on the Right to Remedy and Reparation for Victims of Gross Violations of International Human Rights Law and Serious Violations of International Humanitarian Law*.[53] In this document, central international legal principles for the remedy of individual and communal harms were determined. According to the Basic Principles and Guidelines, the modalities of reparations are restitution,[54] compensation,[55] rehabilitation,[56] satisfaction,[57] and guarantees of non-repetition.[58]

[52] United Nations International Covenant on Civil and Political Rights (1966), Art 2(3). Other regulations of the right to remedies are, for example, the Council of Europe Convention for the Protection of Human Rights and Fundamental Freedoms (1950) Art 13 and 41; Inter-American Convention on the Prevention, Punishment and Eradication of Violence Against Women (1994), Art 7(f)–(g); Protocol to the African Charter on Human and Peoples' Rights on the Rights of Women in Africa (2001), Art 4(f), 25.

[53] A/RES/60/147 (2006).

[54] According to the UN Basic Principles and Guidelines, restitution:

> [...] should, whenever possible, restore the victim to the original situation before the gross violations of international human rights law or serious violations of international humanitarian law occurred. Restitution includes, as appropriate: restoration of liberty, enjoyment of human rights, identity, family life and citizenship, return to one's place of residence, restoration of employment and return of property. (A/RES/60/147 (2006), Art 19)

[55] Compensation:

> [...] should be provided for any economically assessable damage, as appropriate and proportional to the gravity of the violation and the circumstances of each case, resulting from gross violations of international human rights law and serious violations of international humanitarian law, such as: a) Physical or mental harm; b) Lost opportunities, including employment, education and social benefits; c) Material damages and loss of earnings, including loss of earning potential; d) Moral damage; e) Costs required for legal or expert assistance, medicine and medical services, and psychological and social services. (A/RES/60/147 (2006), Art 20)

[56] Rehabilitation 'should include medical and psychological care as well as legal and social services'. A/RES/60/147 (2006), Art 21.

[57] Satisfaction:

> [...] should include, where applicable, any or all of the following: a) Effective measures aimed at the cessation of continuing violations; b) Verification of the facts and full and public disclosure of the truth to the extent that such disclosure does not cause further harm or threaten the safety and interests of the victim, the victim's relatives, witnesses, or persons who have intervened to assist the victim or prevent the occurrence of further violations; c) The search for the whereabouts of the disappeared, for the identities of the children abducted, and for the bodies of those killed, and assistance in the recovery, identification and reburial of the bodies in accordance with the expressed or presumed wish of the victims, or the cultural practices of the families and communities; d) An official declaration or a judicial decision restoring the dignity, the reputation and the rights of the victim and of persons closely connected with the victim; e) Public apology, including acknowledgement of the facts and acceptance of responsibility; f) Judicial and administrative sanctions against persons liable for the violations; g) Commemorations and tributes to the victims; h) Inclusion of an accurate account of the violations that occurred in international human rights law and international humanitarian law training and in educational material at all levels. (A/RES/60/147 (2006), Art 22)

[58] Guarantees of non-repetition include:

> [...] where applicable, any or all of the following measures, which will also contribute to prevention: a) Ensuring effective civilian control of military and security forces; b) Ensuring that

Remedial debates have particularly developed in post-conflict settings over the last decades. With radical regime changes, earlier national narratives are challenged and rewritten. Truth and reconciliation commissions and international and national war tribunals often disclose past practices of gross human rights violations.[59] Apart from the criminal legal responsibility of individual wrongdoers, violations often entail international legal state responsibility.[60] With a developing human rights framework, definitions of rights and violations evolve, and the exact nature of state responsibility changes accordingly. This remedial development might evoke criticism of state authority and historical oppression.[61]

The further back the oppression dates, however, the trickier the questions regarding responsibility and remedy. The legal obligations for countries to provide remedies for historical injustices are widely contested. One

all civilian and military proceedings abide by international standards of due process, fairness and impartiality; c) Strengthening the independence of the judiciary; d) Protecting persons in the legal, medical and health-care professions, the media and other related professions, and human rights defenders; e) Providing, on a priority and continued basis, human rights and international humanitarian law education to all sectors of society and training for law enforcement officials as well as military and security forces; f) Promoting the observance of codes of conduct and ethical norms, in particular international standards, by public servants, including law enforcement, correctional, media, medical, psychological, social service and military personnel, as well as by economic enterprises; g) Promoting mechanisms for preventing and monitoring social conflicts and their resolution; h) Reviewing and reforming laws contributing to or allowing gross violations of international human rights law and serious violations of international humanitarian law. (A/RES/60/147 (2006), Art 23)

59 Famous examples of truth and reconciliation commissions in transitional justice settings during the last decades have been, for example, the South African Truth and Reconciliation Commission; the Commission for Reception, Truth and Reconciliation in East Timor; the Argentinian National Commission on the Disappearance of Persons; the Indian Residential Schools Truth and Reconciliation Commission in Canada; the National Truth and Reconciliation Commission in Chile; the Rwandan International Commission of Investigation on Human Rights Violations in Rwanda and the Peruvian Truth and Reconciliation Committee.

60 Such a principle was laid down in *Chorzów factory* case, formulating reparation as 'the indispensable complement of a failure to apply a convention, and there is no necessity for this to be stated in the convention itself'. PCIJ, *The Factory at Chorzów* (1928): 21. The concept of reparations has later developed within international law from an inter-state matter to one which concerns human rights violations of the state against its own citizens. An important milestone for the development of state responsibility is the UN General Assembly's 2010 adoption of a resolution on state responsibility. See A/RES/65/19 (2010). The resolution was intended to become a legally binding treaty, which however never materialised. See Crawford 2013: 42–44.

61 A famous example of such debates is whether reparations for the Atlantic slave trade should be made to the descendants of slaves or to (colonised) countries which have suffered from slavery. So far, these debates have not led to any large-scale reparations apart from individual initiatives and apologies. One important milestone was the UN Durban Declaration and Programme of Action, which recognises that 'slavery and the slave trade are a crime against humanity, and should have always been so' in its preamble. Effective remedies form an integral part of the declaration, see UN 2002.

issue in respect of the passing of time and state responsibility is retroactivity. This particularly concerns historical injustices which would amount to serious violations of international human rights law today but were committed at a time when the state had not ratified relevant treaties, or such treaties not yet existed. In particular, a tension is present in international law between prevailing understandings of the temporality of binding legal norms, on the one hand, and the non-temporality of *jus cogens*, on the other. Particularly important in this respect is the principle of non-retroactivity of treaties, expressed in Article 28 of the Vienna Convention of the Law of Treaties, rejecting state responsibility arising from a treaty concluded before state commitment.[62] As both temporality and non-temporality are generally accepted principles of international law, human rights bodies have attempted to strike a balance between them. The CAT Committee, for example, has given peremptory norms some weight, attributing responsibility to a state for torture and ill-treatment also (immediately) before ratification.[63] Moreover, the ECtHR has considered that pre-ratification responsibility can arise in some cases when there is a 'genuine connection' between the violation and the entry into force of the European Convention for the Protection of Human Rights and Fundamental Freedoms (ECHR),[64] such as when violations happened close to the time of ratification, and the investigation took place after the entry into force of the Convention. The 'genuine connection' rule forms a recognised exception, albeit a limited one, to the principle of non-retroactivity.

Another question concerning the passage of time is that of statutory limitations. This particularly becomes an issue when the injustice was considered a violation of rights at the time it happened, but the victims present their claims when they are time-barred. In this regard, a general principle of international law is to accept domestic rules pertaining to prescription.[65] Illustrated in the Inadmissibility Case of *Thiermann and Others v. Norway* (2007) concerning the maltreatment of German-Norwegian war children in Norway, their failure

[62] 'Unless a different intention appears from the treaty or is otherwise established, its provisions do not bind a party in relation to any act or fact which took place or any situation which ceased to exist before the date of the entry into force of the treaty with respect to that party'. Vienna Convention on the Law of Treaties (1969), Art 28.

[63] This was crucially the case in CAT Committee, *Gerasimov v. Kazakhstan* (2012), where the Committee found the State to have violated the Convention, referring to torture and ill-treatment carried out by law enforcement officers in 2007, one year before the Convention entered into force there.

[64] As established in ECtHR, *Šilih v. Slovenia* (2009): Para 163. It was later reinforced in ECtHR, *Janowiec and Others v. Russia* (2013), see particularly Para 104.

[65] This is seen in the rules on admissibility, expressed in the ECHR, Art 35(1): 'The Court may only deal with the matter after all domestic remedies have been exhausted [...] and within a period of six months from the date on which the final decision was taken'. The same principle is recognised in the American Convention on Human Rights (1969), Art 46.

'to comply with the time-limits laid down in domestic law' was interpreted as a 'failure to exhaust domestic remedies' by the ECtHR.[66] The principle is however not without exceptions. Allowances can be made in some cases, such as when victims of violations have been particularly helpless or vulnerable,[67] or when the harm or violations are ongoing. Regarding enduring harm and the effects of torture, the CAT Committee has stated that 'statutes of limitations should not be applicable as these deprive victims of the redress, compensation, and rehabilitation due to them'.[68] The Committee continued that time does not have a healing effect for many victims, but may in fact increase harms.[69]

While the international legal obligations to provide remedies for historical violations are restricted by non-retroactivity and statutory limitations, remedial debates often broaden their scope from strictly doctrinal arguments to including moral and political considerations. The question of victimhood, that is, who can be deemed a victim, is often a central tenet of such debates. Dinah Shelton has recounted arguments in favour of and against remedies for historical injustices. The main arguments in favour are the illegality of oppressive measures at the time of the actions, earlier unavailability of remedies, continuous inequality between the oppressor and oppressed communities, and the need for recognition of legacies of suffering.[70] Common arguments against remedies are the principle of non-retroactivity, the difficulty of determining causality, questions concerning intergenerational responsibility and caution expressed about promoting 'victim psychology'.[71]

Difficulties in determining state responsibility and effective and appropriate remedies can inevitably be seen in relation to historical sterilisation projects. Remedial debates have awakened in recent decades as such historical practices have become increasingly questioned, and victims have mobilised. Some states have responded to such mobilisation and discussions by establishing remedies. For example, in Virginia, California, North Carolina and Oregon, governors have issued official apologies for past sterilisations.[72] Compensation schemes for victims have been launched in some US states, such as North Carolina (2013) and Virginia (2015).[73] Germany has also remedied victims of Nazi-enforced sterilisations by establishing a special hardship compensation fund in 1980, and a monthly compensation system in 1988.[74] The decisions of the German Hereditary Health Courts were declared a Nazi injustice in 1988.

[66] ECtHR, *Thiermann and Others v. Norway* (2007): 25–26.

[67] See, for example, the Grand Chamber's conclusion in ECtHR, *Mocanu and Others v. Romania* (2014); IACtHR, *García Lucero et al v. Chile* (2013).

[68] CAT/C/GC/3 (2012): Para 40. [69] Ibid. [70] Shelton 2015: 274–275. [71] Ibid: 276.

[72] Silver 2004: 886–888.

[73] The number of victims coming forward has been limited, however. North Carolina instituted a 10 Million US Dollar compensation package which was distributed among approved applicants in 2013–2014. Neuman 2013. Conversely, Virginia compensated each approved applicant with 25,000 US Dollars. Robertson 2015.

[74] Weindling 2014.

In 2007, moreover, the 1933 sterilisation legislation was declared constitutionally invalid by the German Parliament.[75] Japan apologised as well, and established a compensation scheme to victims of eugenic sterilisations in 2019.[76] Furthermore, sterilisation victims have been included in broader national compensation schemes to victims of historical oppression in Switzerland (2016)[77] and Nazi injustices in Austria (1995).[78] Most recently, in 2021, the Czech Republic established a compensation scheme for involuntarily sterilised Roma women.[79] These remedies constitute examples of national attempts to redress oppressive sterilisation histories.

Some victims have taken their case to courts. An internationally exceptional case is *Muir v. Alberta* (1996). In this case, a victim of involuntary sterilisation, Ms Leilani Muir, claimed compensation before national courts for her involuntary sterilisation and 10-year wrongful confinement at a Canadian state institution. Ms Muir was sterilised as a teenager in 1959 without her consent upon the authorities' decision. The province of Alberta declared that the sterilisation had been wrongful, refrained from an objection based on statutory limitations and left it to the court to decide what the damages would amount to. In the judgment, the Alberta Court of Queen's Bench found that the irreversible sterilisation had caused the plaintiff 'catastrophic' physical and emotional damage and permanent suffering. It also found that the damage was 'aggravated by the associated and wrongful stigmatization of Ms Muir as a moron, a high-grade mental defective', which had 'humiliated' her 'every day in her life, in her relations with her family and friends and her employers and has marked her' from when she had been institutionalised 'at the age of 10'.[80] The total amount of damages and interest to the plaintiff for her involuntary sterilisation and wrongful confinement added up to a substantive 740,780 Canadian Dollars. The case demonstrates a judicial attempt to engage with the extensive harm done to an involuntarily and wrongfully sterilised and confined individual, harm which is lifelong and not easily quantifiable. Following the Muir Case, hundreds of other victims of involuntary sterilisation turned to the courts for reparations, claims which the Alberta Government eventually settled with compensations.[81]

[75] However, few victims (around one per cent) have benefited from the reparations, which have been provided at a late stage. Weindling 2014.

[76] See The Japan Times 2019.

[77] Bundesgesetz über die Aufarbeitung der fürsorgerischen Zwangsmassnahmen und Fremdplatzierungen vor 1981 (AFZFG) [Federal Law on the Processing of Compulsory Welfare Measures and Third-party Placements before 1981], 2016. The law entered into force in 2017.

[78] Bundesgesetz über den Nationalfonds der Republik Österreich für Opfer des Nationalsozialismus [Federal Law on the National Fund of the Republic of Austria for Victims of National Socialism] BGBl. 432/1995.

[79] Koslerova 2021. See also Amnesty International 2021.

[80] Alberta Court of Queen's Bench, *Muir v. Alberta* (1996): Paras 1–2.

[81] The compensation amounts depended on the claims at hand. The around 600 lawsuits settled in 1998 were awarded 100,000 Canadian Dollars each. See Dambrofsky 2016.

High-profile cases of individual victims seeking redress from public authorities are exceptional globally, as victims generally remain silent about their harms. Such cases highlight how social development, rights and notions of human dignity have contributed to seeing former state policies of eugenic sterilisation in a different light, raising questions on how the current legal system should approach such practices. Ultimately, they show the incommensurability of the victims' harms and the immense difficulties courts face when engaging with such extensive and complex injuries. Confronted with the insufficiency of legal liability systems, which are built on financial compensation of financial loss, courts deal with the question of how society ought to redress the same individuals which it has long excluded and harmed.

1.5 Rights, Legal Mobilisation and Grievance Formation

Involuntary sterilisation and castration have progressed from being generally accepted to becoming perceived as human rights violations, and being remedied as such in some cases. The interconnection between rights, remedies and mobilisation (or the lack of such) is unfolded borrowing theoretical tools from legal mobilisation and social movement studies, particularly frame analysis and grievance formation. Other key analytical tools in social movement studies, especially resource mobilisation[82] and political/legal opportunities,[83] are given a minor role in the work. Important questions are whether different groups of victims have mobilised, in organised form or individually,[84] to improve their position, the type of mobilisation used and how the state has reacted to it.

Mobilisation shapes the law and the law shapes mobilisation. In the words of Scott Barclay, Lynn C Jones and Anna-Maria Marshall, the law plays a role in 'spawning the initial claims of inequality or injustice, in building movements, and in framing the issues to be challenged'.[85] For social movements, notions of inequality and injustice are often connected to the law and conceptualisations

[82] In order to mobilise socially and legally, the ability to acquire and channel resources is crucial. Resource mobilisation theories primarily focus on social movements' internal elements. See Snow & Soule 2010: 91; Hilson 2002: 240.

[83] There are theories focusing on *political* and/or *legal* opportunities (sometimes referred to as opportunity structures to highlight their structural, rather than contingent, elements). Unlike resource mobilisation theories, opportunity theories focus on the external elements of movements and highlight the importance of context. In Ellen Andersen's account, the law shapes 'the *kinds* of claims that can be made' and the '*persuasiveness* of those claims' (emphasis in original). According to Gianluca De Fazio, legal opportunities consist of 'the features of the legal system which facilitate/hinder social movements' chances to have their grievances redressed through the judiciary'. Andersen 2006: 7, 9–16; De Fazio 2012: 4.

[84] In social movement theory, such mobilisation builds on the 'social' and is often understood as collective, more or less organised. See Bosi 2016: 344. 'Mobilisation', particularly 'legal mobilisation', can also take on a more individual form. The lines between individual and collective are, however, often blurred in social movements. Johnston et al 2009: 8.

[85] Barclay et al 2011: 2.

of 'rights'.[86] In an idealised fashion, rights have been viewed as the means to construct a just social order. Famously theorised by Stuart Scheingold as the 'myth of rights', this vision of emancipatory rights links rights, litigation and remedies.[87] Distinctly connected to the US political context and framed by the traditional American beliefs in individualism, private property and market economy, the myth of rights 'rests on a faith in the political efficacy and ethical sufficiency of the law as a principle of government'.[88] The idea is also firmly established in the US common law cultural background, epitomised in the Blackstonian reassurance that every wrong must have a remedy and reinforced in the liberal classic *Marbury v Madison*,[89] later exported to other parts of the world.[90] While many critical accounts question the empirical truthfulness of the interconnection between rights, litigation and remedies,[91] the legal, social and cultural imaginary of such interconnectedness is, however, an important analytical approach in this context.

Even though the specific link between rights, framing and grievance formation has received minimal attention in scholarship on social movements and legal mobilisation so far, it is important for the emergence and non-emergence, the existence and non-existence, of mobilisation.[92] A large part of the theoretical tradition of social movements conversely builds on existing social movements, groups which are already organised and have access to a wide range of resources. Yet, the paradigmatic analytical frameworks based on such social movements become challenged when addressing out of the ordinary subjects of study, weakly resourced groups, such as the involuntarily sterilised and castrated.[93]

'Grievances' could broadly be defined as a sense of injustice, wrong or harm, individual or collective. Individual grievances are, for example, one person's frustration and sense of harm after undergoing a surgery which they had not given informed consent to. Such grievances become collective when shared with other people, all victimised through similar involuntary interventions, leading to a collective sense of injustice within the group. In investigating collective mobilisation, social movement theory is particularly concerned with shared grievances which 'contribute to the emergence and operation of social movements',

[86] This is true for many 'new social movements', a term which typically refers to social movements that have emerged since the 1970s and includes groups such as women's movements and environmental movements. The term is often used to contrast such movements to 'old social movements', such as workers' movements. See Della Porta 2015: 767.

[87] Scheingold 2004: 5.

[88] Ibid: 17.

[89] Supreme Court of the United States, *Marbury v. Madison* (1803). See D'Souza 2018: 16.

[90] Scheingold 2004: 18; Nader 2007: 118.

[91] See Speed 2007: 178. Also Radha D'Souza has questioned the reliance on rights by social movements and critical legal scholars alike, continuing 'to assume that having rights will provide legal remedies and bring justice'. D'Souza 2018: 17.

[92] See Hilson 2010.

[93] Investigating the mobilisation of weakly resourced groups, Chabanet and Royall highlight the benefits of moving away from the more established models, particularly cost-benefit analysis, in favour of micro-studies and descriptive accounts. Chabanet & Royall 2014: 15, 18.

so-called mobilising grievances.[94] In this work, the concept of grievances is presented as closely connected to rights, as the notions about rights – and violation of rights – shape the 'cultural stock for images of what is an injustice, for what is a violation of what ought to be', as expressed by Mayer Zald.[95]

Grievances are strongly linked to notions of entitlement and identity. As such, they can be recognised and validated by a collective group of victims, courts, other state institutions, mass media or the public. Grievances might also fail to be expressed, since a person, a group, the courts, the state or the public might not perceive certain harms as legally or morally wrong.[96] Judith Butler has written about the normative validation of grievability and the inherent situatedness of such validation. Butler expresses this as follows: '[T]here is no "life itself" at issue [...], but always and only conditions of life, life as something that requires conditions in order to become livable life and, indeed, in order to become grievable'.[97] Linking grievability to framing, Butler contends that 'certain lives are perceived as lives while others, though apparently living, fail to assume perpetual form as such'.[98] The loss of some lives and populations are framed as 'eminently grievable', while others remain 'ungrievable'.[99] Grievances and the individual, collective and public formation of grievances, are inherently connected to the analysis of frames and groups' abilities to align with them.

'Frame analysis' in turn means the analysis of the sociocultural meaning assigned to certain people, populations, institutions or phenomena. Introducing the concept of 'frame' into social movement studies, David Snow and his collaborators explained it as 'borrowed from Goffman [...] to denote "schemata of interpretation" that cognitively enable individuals and groups "to locate, perceive, identify, and label" occurrences within their life space and the world at large'.[100] Hence, frames organise experience and steer individual or collective action by assigning meaning to events or occurrences.[101]

Frame analysis theories emphasise the importance of communication and language in mobilisation, such as in the formation and interpretation of grievances. Snow and Robert Benford underline the essential function of framing:

> [Social movements] frame, or assign meaning to and interpret, relevant events and conditions in ways that are intended to mobilize potential adherents and constituents, to garner bystander support, and to demobilize antagonists.[102]

This creation of meaning is important when it comes to framing grievances as, for example, sexism, racism and discrimination – or more broadly, as rights violations. In this book, rights create an overarching mechanism, a socio-legal 'master frame' of validation, which has bearing on both legal and sociocultural aspects. As such, rights can be either legal or sociocultural instruments

94 Snow & Soule 2010: 24. See also, for example, Nownes 2019: 49–66. 95 Zald 1996: 266.

96 On the personal and intra-group level, the grievance formation process is hence linked to the concept of legal consciousness. See, for example, Chua & Engel 2021.

97 Butler 2016: 23. 98 Ibid: 24. 99 Ibid. 100 Snow et al 1986: 464. 101 Ibid.

102 Snow & Benford 1988: 198.

of entitlement and identity. In their understanding of wrongs, rights violations and in possible mobilisation, actors can align with, or fail to align with, the master frame of rights.[103]

Creation of meaning takes place at both the individual and collective levels. In the 'frame alignment process', individuals or groups mobilise and interact with a frame, identify a problem and propose a solution and call to arms.[104] The existence of grievances does not, however, guarantee mobilisation.[105] Furthermore, in order to be successful, the grievances need to be aligned with existing legal, social and cultural frames.[106] Grievances which fail to do so, gain no resonance. Zald exemplifies this with the slogan 'a woman's body is her own', which 'frames a problem and suggests a policy direction for women in relation to abortion policy and the medical establishment'.[107] However, the slogan only makes sense in a society and 'cultural discourse that highlights notions of individual autonomy and equality of citizenship rights: autonomy because it focuses upon individual choice, equality because it presumes that women are equal citizens'.[108] It would not make sense, for example, in a society where most people were slaves, or believed to belong to their families or the collective.[109] Based on this example, Zald concludes:

> Contemporary framing of injustice and of political goals almost always draws upon the larger societal definitions of relationships, of rights, and of responsibilities to highlight what is wrong with the current social order, and to suggest directions for change.[110]

With reference to rights, framing is explored by Lisa Vanhala in her study of disability rights mobilisation in Canada and the United Kingdom. She highlights that the creation of meaning and the movement's own understanding of its members as rights-holders is crucial for the likelihood of movements to engage in strategic litigation.[111] Framing for social movements means creating meaning and strategically utilising existing cultural frames and aligning with them in order to achieve desired outcomes – pushing 'the right buttons'.[112] Vanhala hypothesises that groups which frame themselves as rights-holders are more likely to pursue their agendas before courts than groups not framing themselves as such.[113] Similarly, Lasse Lindekilde emphasises that 'framing becomes a strategic attempt to guide the activation of particular discourses and repertoires of understanding with the purpose of mobilizing consensus'.[114]

In the frame alignment process, competing frames may be presented and affect people's abilities to form grievances and strategically frame them as rights violations. Competing frames to individual rights can be state prerogative or public order.[115] Another example of competing frames is alternative rights

[103] On the concept of master frames, see Snow & Benford 1992; Markowitz 2009.
[104] Snow & Benford 1988: 199. [105] See Chua 2022: 14. [106] Snow & Soule 2010: 47–63.
[107] Zald 1996: 266. [108] Ibid: 267 [109] Ibid. [110] Ibid. [111] Vanhala 2010: 32.
[112] See Andersen 2006: 8. [113] Vanhala 2010: 32. [114] Lindekilde 2014: 201.
[115] See, for example, Shriver et al 2018; Barkan S 1984.

frames presented by civil society counter-movements. An example of the latter is mobilisation for access to safe abortions, on the one hand, and mobilisation against abortions, on the other. The former generally frames the issue of abortion as one of equal rights to personal autonomy and health for women, while the second aligns its arguments with the right to life of the unborn child.[116] In both these alternative frames, interestingly, rights act as master frames, demonstrating the multifaceted nature of rights. Alternative frames and their resonance and ability to dominate public or legal debate have an effect on mobilisation at all stages: grievance formation, dynamics and outcomes.

In terms of mobilisation, rights have an important discursive value as they carry a normative meaning. Framing an issue as one of 'rights' is a way for actors and movements to create a separate space from 'interests' in legal and political discussions.[117] Ideally, a rights framing prevents the subject matter from being limited by budgetary deficits or other political prioritisations. This type of an idealistic discourse is central to rights, as visible in universal human rights claims. Therefore, rights idealism views rights as neutral and apolitical.[118]

For civil society organisations in the Nordic countries, rights mobilisation has recently become a more popular tool to alter their positions and further their interests. Nordic public authorities in turn increasingly embrace rights and accept rigorous judicial review.[119] This development stands in stark contrast with the countries' earlier culture of state power concentration in parliament. A persistently enhanced profile of the ECtHR and national supreme courts, resolute rights commitments in the international arena, together with the establishment of anti-discrimination and equality legislation, are factors which have worked in unison to promote courts and lower-threshold ombudsman institutions as forums where rights claims can be presented.[120]

Against this background, victims of involuntary sterilisation and castration have – or have not – mobilised. In such mobilisation, the idea of rights as legal and sociocultural instruments comes into play. Accordingly, the idea of rights as legal instruments entails phenomena such as legal regulation, established rights, rights violations, public or individual legal responsibility, liability for harms and access to remedies. As sociocultural instruments, rights entail claims to entitlements, rights-holder status, individual identities, collective identities,

116 See, for example, Siegel 2012: 1059.

117 Alan Hunt has depicted efforts to create counter-hegemony in terms of rights as requiring 'transition from the discourse of "interests" to the discourse of "rights" […] the project of counter-hegemony requires a shift from the plane of the "corporate" to the "universal"'. Hunt 1990: 320.

118 See Merry 2007.

119 Hirschl 2011:450–451; Wind & Follesdal 2009; Karlsson Schaffer 2017.

120 The Nordic ombudsmen present more cooperative, less formalist and often more accessible alternatives of authoritative legal evaluation than the courts, potentially important for the legal mobilisation of disadvantaged and weakly resourced groups. However, with 'softer' legal powers than the courts, often with limited possibilities to order remedies, relying on recommendations and the goodwill of public institutions, an implicit hierarchy exists between courts and ombudsmen. See Hellum 2017: 213–214.

public identities and public images. When mobilising in terms of rights, people and organisations need to conform to and fall in line with already-existing legal, social, historical and cultural understandings of how an intelligible rights claim is made, what it encompasses, and who a rights holder is. The process of grievance formation reveals how some personal experiences of harm and trauma develop into individual, shared, collective and/or public notions of wrong and rights violations, while others do not.

Part II
A Question of Rights?

2

A Master Frame of Rights

Involuntary Sterilisation and Castration in International Law

International law creates binding legal norms, vocabularies, imaginaries and consciousness concerning feasible and valid legal claims. This is not merely true at the supranational level, but also at national and grassroots levels. This chapter depicts how notions of rights and violations of rights in international law – first through international criminal law and then through human rights law – create an opaque and inconsistent socio-legal master frame for involuntary sterilisation and castration. On the one hand, there is a general understanding of the interventions as grave violations of the international normative order since the birth of modern international criminal law and human rights. To this date, on the other hand, an ambiguity remains about how to most appropriately conceptualise and remedy these violations. This vagueness in turn affects the socio-legal status of the international legal norms. To fully comprehend how involuntary sterilisation and castration have been addressed in international law, this chapter has a global scope. This being said, as the European supranational legal framework has more normative relevance for the countries of the case studies later in this work, the chapter has a European focus.[1] The time period investigated is from the emergence of the post-war international community until the end of the 2010s.

2.1 International Criminal Law: Sterilisation and Castration from Nuremberg to Rome

Sterilisation and castration have been part of international criminal law since the Nuremberg trials. International criminal law was developed in response to egregious crimes which extended beyond borders and violated fundamental human values, most clearly manifested in genocide. As such, international criminal law is intimately connected to, and normatively important for, the notion of rights in international law, as international crimes also constitute grave human rights violations. In this sense, international criminal law is relevant for the master frame of rights investigated in this book.

[1] The chapter is particularly focused on Council of Europe institutions, as European Union institutions have rarely addressed the topic.

2.1.1 Nuremberg: Medical Ethics and Genocide

Involuntary sterilisation and castration first appeared in the international criminal legal context in connection to the Nazi atrocities. At the Trials of War Criminals before the Nuremberg Military Tribunals, at which the Nazi German political, military, judicial, medical and economic leadership were tried, sterilisation and castration experiments were among the charges. While such experiments were included in many indictments against Nazi war criminals, one of the most famous cases in which the interventions played a central role was the so-called 'Doctors' Trial', *United States of America v. Karl Brandt et al.*[2] Considered crimes against humanity and war crimes, the medical crimes of sterilisation and castration experiments at Auschwitz and Ravensbruck concentration camps and elsewhere were included in the indictment and the judgment.[3] In *Poland v. Höss,* moreover, the commandant of the Auschwitz concentration camp was found liable for genocide through sterilisation and castration.[4] Moreover, sterilisation was considered an integral part of the charges of genocide in *United States of America v. Greifelt et al.*[5] Among the medical experiments and horrors carried out by the Nazi officials, non-consensual sterilisation and castration were part of the emerging international criminal law in the immediate aftermath of the Second World War.

Even though the Nazi sterilisation and castration projects were challenged at the post-war trials, arguments were limited to their status as medical experiments. The German eugenicists who were tried, were not held responsible for the sterilisations carried out with legislative basis.[6] The defendants on trial were eager to point out the connection between Nazi eugenics and eugenics in other countries as a defence strategy, indicating a common scientific basis. Even the 1927 case *Buck v. Bell* of the US Supreme Court was recited as an example of the legitimacy of eugenic sterilisations.[7] Ignoring such arguments and refraining from comparison, the tribunal consequently conceptualised involuntary sterilisation and castration narrowly as international crimes. This narrative also suited reformist eugenicists, particularly in the United States, who disavowed any connection between Nazi eugenics and eugenicists elsewhere, allowing them to '"forget" their prior support for Nazi eugenic racism'.[8]

The Nuremberg Code, which was published together with the *Karl Brandt et al* Judgment in 1947, is sometimes presented as the modern foundation of human rights in the field of medicine.[9] Drawn up in relation to the Nuremberg trials, the

[2] US Military Tribunal Nuremberg, *United States of America v. Karl Brandt et al* (1946–1947).

[3] This was the case to the extent that the defendants were found guilty of the charges.

[4] The Supreme National Tribunal of Poland, *Poland v. Höss* (1947). See Schabas 2016: 140.

[5] US Military Tribunal Nuremberg, *United States of America v. Greifelt et al* (1947–1948).

[6] I.e. according to Gesetz zur Verhütung erbkranken Nachwuchses [Act for the Prevention of Hereditarily Diseased Offspring] 1933. Kühl 2002: 102.

[7] Kühl 2002: 101. [8] Ibid: 100. [9] See, for example, Ehrenfreund 2007: 149–151.

Code determines some foundational principles of medical ethics.[10] It is based on reports prepared by two American medical expert witnesses, doctors Andrew Ivy and Leo Alexander,[11] regulating the medical ethical foundations for human experiments vitally relying on informed consent.[12] While the Nuremberg Code was not the first medical ethics regulation to emphasise the importance of informed consent,[13] it nevertheless constructed a special regulation of the issue suited to a reality where American prisoners were also subject to medical experimentation, so as not to simultaneously condemn these experiments when denouncing those of the Nazis.[14] In effect, the Code's main point was to condemn Nazi experiments, viewed as the ultimate manifestation of unethical medical research.

The Nazi horrors and the Nuremberg trials became important background models for the codification of international criminal law. The Convention on the Prevention and Punishment of the Crime of Genocide, which was drawn up in the post-war context, was adopted by the UNGA in 1948. The Genocide Convention provides a legal framework in line with which genocide can be investigated and prosecuted. According to its Article II (d), 'imposing measures intended to prevent births within the group' is listed as one form through which the crime of genocide can be perpetrated. In the *travaux préparatoires*, these measures of 'biological genocide' were intended as sterilisation and/or compulsory abortion, segregation of the sexes and obstacles to marriage.[15] Sterilisations – and likely castrations too – are therefore formally a central part of the crime description of genocide.[16]

Like the Nuremberg Code, the Genocide Convention was drafted with the Nazi experiments in mind. Remarkably, the Genocide Convention's entering into force did not mean that global practices of involuntary sterilisation and castration began to be regarded or investigated as genocide. This is demonstrated, for example, by the fact that sterilisation and castration laws – allowing for involuntary forms – continued to be unchallenged in other parts of the world, including by the allied powers, long after the Nuremberg trials.[17]

2.1.2 The Rome Statute of the International Criminal Court

Sterilisation has had a formally unchallenged role in international criminal law since its genesis. Yet, measures challenging sterilisation practices have been largely unimplemented. Over the last decades, gender violence has been

[10] Moreno 1997: 348. [11] Ibid.

[12] Other requirements were qualified medical staff, avoiding unnecessary suffering and injury and basing experiments on previous animal testing. Ehrenfreund 2007: 149. These principles were later completed through the 1964 World Medical Association Declaration of Helsinki which is regularly updated, unlike the Nuremberg principles. See Ghooi 2011.

[13] In fact, the Code bears a high degree of resemblance with the 1931 German Guidelines for Human Experimentation. Ghooi 2011.

[14] Freyhofer 2005: 102–103. [15] E/447 (1947); Tams et al 2014: 91. [16] See Tams et al 2014: 91.

[17] Significantly, the US was among those countries. See Silver 2004; Kühl 2002.

increasingly mainstreamed in international criminal law. Accordingly, in the 1990s, sexual violence – a form of violence disproportionately affecting women – was established as a matter for international criminal law before the International Criminal Tribunals for the Former Yugoslavia and Rwanda, respectively.[18] In both the Statute of the International Criminal Tribunal for Rwanda (ICTR) and the Statute of the International Criminal Tribunal for the Former Yugoslavia (ICTY), rape was listed as a crime against humanity.[19] In the landmark *Akayesu* judgment at the turn of the century,[20] rape was acknowledged as a crime against humanity and genocide.[21] This judgment broadened the gender-sensitive conceptualisation of international, criminally relevant harm, which has traditionally been based on men's experiences of violence.[22] Importantly, however, this acknowledgement of sexual violence has been rather selective and was not translated to other forms of gender violence, such as reproductive violence.[23] Castration was touched upon in passing at the ICTR, in the *Niyitegeka* case, in which an influential Tutsi man was killed and subsequently decapitated and castrated. The acts were considered to constitute crimes against humanity by the Trial Chamber under the heading 'other inhumane acts'.[24] The castration was considered an aggravating factor in the sentencing,[25] but not depicted as a form of sexual violence.[26] The 1998 Rome Statute of the International Criminal Court (ICC) has further increased the international criminalisation of sexual and gender violence.[27] In the Statute, 'enforced sterilisation' is explicitly included as a form of crime against humanity[28] and/or a war crime.[29]

[18] Radical feminist criticism of international law in the 1990s was posed by for example MacKinnon 1994.

[19] Statute of the International Criminal Tribunal for Rwanda (1994), Art 3(g); Statute of the International Criminal Tribunal of the Former Yugoslavia (1993), Art 5(g).

[20] ICTR, *The Prosecutor v. Jean-Paul Akayesu* (2001); ICTR, *The Prosecutor v. Jean-Paul Akayesu* (1998). See Ní Aoláin 2000: 72; Walker 2009: 18; Ambos 2014: 14.

[21] Rape as a crime against humanity has later been reiterated, for example in ICTY, *The Prosecutor v. Dragoljub Kunarac, Radomir Kovac and Zoran Vukovic* (2001). See Edwards A 2006: 384–388.

[22] This is true, e.g., when it comes to torture. See Sifris 2014.

[23] See Grey 2017; Rubio-Marín 2012; A/HRC/14/22 (2010): Para 44.

[24] Statute of the International Criminal Tribunal for Rwanda (1994), Art 3(i); ICTR, *The Prosecutor v. Eliézer Niyitegeka* (2003): Paras 459–467.

[25] ICTR, *The Prosecutor v. Eliézer Niyitegeka* (2003): Para 499(iv).

[26] The lack of recognition of sexual violence against men in criminal law, including castration, is pointed out in Mibenge 2013: 80–82.

[27] See International Criminal Court 2014: 6.

[28] Rome Statute of the International Criminal Court (1998), Art 7(g).

[29] Ibid, Art 8(b, xxii; e, vi). 'Enforced' sterilisation, which the Rome Statute refers to, might however be a narrower concept than 'involuntary' sterilisation. 'Enforced' builds on external use of force rather than the victim's lack of free will, a concept emphasised in 'involuntary'. I recognise here that the terms are not always synonymous, and that all forms of involuntary sterilisation might not legally qualify as 'enforced'. Yet, I nevertheless consider the two to indicate forced or coerced physical interventions. Another important issue is that enforced or involuntary castration is not explicitly included in the Rome Statute. However, given that castration also results in the deprivation of reproductive capacity, I have chosen to interpret 'sterilisation' broadly.

In its definition of the crime of genocide, the Rome Statute upheld a formulation familiar from the 1948 Convention: '[i]mposing measures intended to prevent births within the group'.[30] The 2010 guiding official document 'Elements of Crimes' follows the same structure.[31] Sterilisation and castration are, hence, included in the definition of genocide, depending on the fulfilment of four general criteria. Firstly, the perpetrator has imposed certain measures on one or more persons. Secondly, the victim belongs to a particular national, ethnic, racial or religious group. Thirdly, the measures were intended to prevent births within the group in question. Finally, the conduct was part of a manifest pattern of targeting the group or could itself effect destruction.[32] Apart from these contextual requirements, for an act to constitute genocide, necessary genocidal elements also need to be present – most importantly intent to destroy the group in whole or in part.

Enforced sterilisation as a crime against humanity and a war crime is specified in the same guidelines. For involuntary sterilisation and castration to qualify as a crime against humanity, four elements are necessary. Firstly, the perpetrator has permanently deprived one or more persons of reproductive capacity. Secondly, the intervention was neither medically justified, nor carried out with genuine consent. Thirdly, the conduct was part of a widespread or systematic attack directed against a civilian population. Finally, the perpetrator knew, or intended, the conduct to be a part of such a widespread or systematic attack.[33] For war crimes, the two first elements are identical; the difference lies in that the intervention took place in the context of an international armed conflict of which the perpetrator was aware.[34] This said, a single case of involuntary sterilisation or castration can be enough for an act to qualify as a crime against humanity and/or a war crime, depending on intent and other circumstantial elements.

Involuntary sterilisation and castration being conceptualised as international crimes adds weight to the master frame of rights within which victims of these interventions navigate. This is true in both a legal and a sociocultural sense. Having a crime recognised as an international crime carries important symbolic meaning, signalling legal gravity, moral denunciation and political priority. Furthermore, genocide, war crimes and crimes against humanity are not subject to statutory limitations as violations of peremptory norms as a principle of international law.[35] In addition, the *jus cogens* status of these crimes ultimately weakens any objections invoking non-retroactivity based on

[30] Rome Statute of the International Criminal Court (1998), Art 6(c).

[31] International Criminal Court 2011. [32] Ibid: 3. [33] Ibid: 9. [34] Ibid: 29, 38.

[35] This is manifested in the 1968 Convention on the Non-Applicability of Statutory Limitations to Crimes against Humanity, the 1974 European Convention on the Non-Applicability of Statutory Limitations to Crimes against Humanity and War Crimes and Art 29 of the Rome Statute. According to the 1968 Convention, which covers war crimes, crimes against humanity and genocide, these crimes are imprescriptible 'irrespective of the date of their commission' '[...] even if such acts do not constitute a violation of the domestic law of the country in which they were committed' (Art 1). The Rome Statute similarly states that 'the crimes within the jurisdiction of the Court shall not be subject to any statute of limitations' (Art 29).

the principle of legality.[36] Being recognised as a crime under the Rome Statute, furthermore, means an added legal framework of scrutiny, particularly concerning the ICC's independent status, *ex officio* prosecution and standards of international justice. Such an institutional legal framework is crucial for the realisation of criminal responsibility, which in turn can improve access to remedies for victims.[37] However, no cases of involuntary sterilisation or castration have yet appeared before the ICC, which might challenge these theoretical assumptions of additional scrutiny and improved remedial access.

This said, involuntary sterilisation and castration face a stark paradox in the gap between theory and practice. While interventions in a war context or as a widespread and systematic attack against a civilian population in theory indubitably constitute a crime according to international criminal law, practices of involuntary sterilisation and castration have generally been marked by impunity. Interestingly, as a globally widespread practice, enforced sterilisation has never been prosecuted at international criminal courts or tribunals after Nuremberg. Similarly, forced castration has only been mentioned in passing, and generally ignored.

2.2 Involuntary Sterilisation as a Human Rights Question

Over the last 30 years, involuntary sterilisation – and to some extent, also castration – have been increasingly addressed by the international community as a violation of human rights. Viewing the developing notions of rights as a master frame, involuntary sterilisation has gone from being considered a specific, marginalised issue to becoming viewed as a more general human rights concern. The normative, soft law-based framework surrounding involuntary sterilisation has also solidified in more binding legal obligations. Inconsistencies persist, however, for example, regarding conceptualisation and appropriate redress.

2.2.1 The 1990s: The Specificity of Violence against Women

While voluntary sterilisation was addressed in passing at the UN as a matter of population policy in the 1960s–1980s,[38] involuntary forms were long

Imprescriptibility is a legal obligation for ratifying states. However, through reaching the level of legal principle, imprescriptibility can arguably also bind non-ratifying states. As highlighted by the UN Special Rapporteur on the Promotion of Truth, Justice, Reparation and Guarantees of Non-recurrence in his 2015 report, international jurisprudence has demonstrated many times that the 1968 Convention does not create new rights or obligations, but that 'the principle of imprescriptibility of war crimes, crimes against humanity and genocide is a matter of *jus cogens*'. See A/HRC/30/42 (2015): Para 49. The Special Rapporteur exemplifies case law by referring to a range of cases, among them ECtHR, *Kolk and Kislyiy v. Estonia* (2006); IACtHR, *Gelman v. Uruguay* (2011).

36 A/HRC/30/42 (2015): Para 50.

37 The ICC was the 'first international criminal justice body to which victims of mass atrocities could submit claims for reparations'. Sperfeldt 2017: 351–352.

38 See, for example, E/CN.6/SR.519 (1968): 140.

overlooked by the international community. Involuntary sterilisation was established in the human rights realm through the introduction of violence against women as a matter of international law in the 1990s.[39] This happened mainly on the initiative of the Committee on the Elimination of All Forms of Discrimination against Women (CEDAW Committee). An essential early serious problematisation of the topic in the human rights domain occurred in the 1992 Convention on the Elimination of All Forms of Discrimination against Women (CEDAW) General Recommendation No. 19, addressing violence against women.[40] In this document, compulsory sterilisation was framed as a violation of women's reproductive rights, pertaining to health as well as autonomy.[41] The topic was again included as a reproductive rights matter in the 1994 CEDAW General Recommendation No. 21 on equality in marriage and family relations.[42] Moreover, in the 1995 Beijing Declaration and Platform for Action – one of the most important gender-mainstreaming efforts of the decade – 'forced sterilisation' was included under the title 'violence against women'.[43]

Although other treaty bodies than the CEDAW Committee started to address involuntary sterilisation in the 1990s, it was still mostly treated as a particular, 'women's rights' matter, rather than a general human rights concern. As such, cisgender women were presupposed victims of the violations, and the matter was considered marginal.[44] In 1995, the Committee on Economic, Social and Cultural Rights (CESCR Committee) described involuntary sterilisations of disabled women as a violation of 'the protection of the family and of mothers and children'.[45] Forced sterilisation of women with disabilities,[46] and the lack of compensation for these women, was also addressed by the Human Rights Committee country report on Japan in 1998.[47] In 1999, references to involuntary sterilisation boomed in the UN soft law machinery, signalling an expanding understanding of the topic. As such, it was referred to by the CEDAW Committee,[48] whilst also premiering in reports by the CERD Committee,[49] the Committee on the Rights of the Child (CRC Committee)[50] and the UN Special

[39] This was particularly achieved through the concept of gender mainstreaming since the 1995 Fourth World Conference on women in Beijing. For a critical evaluation of the concept, see Kouvo 2004.

[40] A/47/38 at 1 (1992).

[41] Ibid: Para 22. Involuntary sterilisation was however not mentioned in the subsequent pioneering Declaration of Violence against Women from 1993, see A/RES/48/104 (1993).

[42] Protected under CEDAW, Art 10(h). A/49/38 (1994): Para 22.

[43] UN 1995: Para 115.

[44] On the marginalisation of women in international human rights, see Charlesworth 1995.

[45] E/1995/22 at 19 (1995): Para 31.

[46] The type of disability was not mentioned in the report. Importantly, the law was almost exclusively implemented with regard to women. See Tsuchiya 1997 and Higuchi et al 2019.

[47] CCPR/C/79/Add.102 (1998): Para 31.

[48] A/54/38 (1999): Paras 22, 299, 395.

[49] See, for example, CERD/C/304/Add.69 (1999): Para 19. Allegations of forced sterilisation of indigenous women were included as a 'major shortcoming' in the country report on Peru.

[50] See, for example, CRC/C/15/Add.98 (1999): Para 446. The country report on Austria called for legislation to prevent involuntary sterilisation of disabled children.

Rapporteur on Violence against Women.[51] The reports consistently focused on the victimisation of women, but intersecting categories (e.g., disability or ethnicity) were also included.[52] The newfound interest in involuntary sterilisation was to increase over the decade following.

2.2.2 The 2000s: Generalisation through Soft Law

After a tentative entrance into the human rights domain in the 1990s, involuntary sterilisation gained a more stable position on the working agenda of human rights institutions in the 2000s. Throughout the decade, involuntary sterilisation was addressed as a violation of the prohibition of torture and cruel, inhuman or degrading treatment or punishment, the right to bodily integrity, the right to personal autonomy, the right to private and family life, the right to health and/or the prohibition of discrimination in the general recommendations and reports of various United Nations and Council of Europe institutions.[53] In this evolution of supranational soft law, involuntary sterilisation was increasingly mainstreamed into human rights. This decade also witnessed the appearance of involuntary sterilisation cases before regional human rights courts and international advisory organs. Moreover, apart from problematising sterilisation of ciswomen as a human rights concern, it saw an awakening international human rights discourse concerning sterilisation as a precondition for legal gender recognition.

The first case concerning involuntary sterilisation brought before a supranational organ was *Maria Mamérita Mestanza Chávez v. Peru*, in which the victim had died as a consequence of her sterilisation.[54] National activists took the

[51] See, for example, E/CN.4/1999/68/Add.4 (1999). Special Rapporteur Radhika Coomaraswamy highlighted forced sterilisation as a violation of women's reproductive rights and mentioned the widespread sterilisations of women in Peru and China as examples of such practices.

[52] The attention to involuntary sterilisation in the 1990s developed simultaneously with renewed interest in standardising health care in terms of human rights, manifested in the 1997 CoE Convention on Human Rights and Biomedicine.

[53] Importantly, the UN Human Rights Committee, the CERD Committee, the CEDAW Committee, the CESCR Committee, the CAT Committee, the CRC Committee, the UN Special Rapporteur on Health, the UN Special Rapporteur on Torture; the CoE Commissioner for Human Rights and the European Torture Committee. See, for example, CCPR/C/21/Rev.1/Add.10 (2000): Para 11; CCPR/CO/70/PER (2000): Para 21; CCPR/CO/78/SVK (2003): Para 12; CCPR/C/CZE/CO/2 (2007): Para 10; CCPR/C/CHE/CO/3 (2009): Para 20; A/55/18, Annex V, 152 (2000): Para 2; A/59/18 (2004): Para 12; CERD/C/CZE/CO/7 (2007): Para 14; A/57/38 (2003): Paras 484–485; CEDAW/C/CZE/CO/3 (2006): Paras 23–24; CEDAW/C/CHN/CO/6 (2006): Para 32; CEDAW/C/SVK/CO/4 (2008): Paras 44–45; E/C.12/1/Add.87 (2003): Para 27; E/C.12/1/Add.107 (2005): Paras 36, 100; CAT/C/CR/32/2 (2004): Para 5(k); CAT/C/PER/CO/4 (2006): Para 23; CAT/C/SVK/CO/2 (2009): Para 14; CRC/C/15/Add.268 (2005): Paras 45–46; CRC/C/GC/9 (2007): Para 60; E/CN.4/2004/49 (2004), Paras 25–27; E/CN.4/2005/51/Add.3 (2005): Para 79; A/HRC/4/28/ Add.1 (2008): Para 74; A/HRC/7/3 (2008); CommDH(2003)12; CommDH/IssuePaper(2009)2; CPT/Inf (2007) 32: particularly Paras 153–154.

[54] The case of Chávez is not an isolated incident, as her sterilisation was part of the sterilisation project enacted by the Fujimori regime, particularly during the 1996–2000 Reproductive Health and Family Planning Programme (*Programa de salud reproductiva y planificación familiar*). See Tamayo 1999; Ewig 2006 and 2010; Cáceres et al 2007; Demus 2008 and 2015; Gribble et al 2007.

case to the Inter-American Commission of Human Rights (IACHR), before which a friendly settlement was reached in 2003. Chávez was sterilised on the consent of her domestic partner alone, who later received a payment for the sterilisation.[55] In the 2003 settlement, the Peruvian Government agreed that Chávez's sterilisation and subsequent death constituted violations of the prohibition of discrimination (ACHR Article 1(1)), the right to life (ACHR Article 4), the right to humane treatment (ACHR Article 5), the right to equal protection before the law (ACHR Article 24), and the obligation of states to condemn, prevent, punish and eradicate violence against women (Article 7 of the Belém do Pará Convention).

As a result of these violations, the Government agreed to pay financial compensation to the beneficiaries, the partner and children of Maria Mamérita Mestanza Chávez, and to provide them with psychological rehabilitation treatment, health insurance, free education and a lump sum to buy a house or land.[56] The state also promised to amend laws and policies on reproductive health and family planning in order to eliminate discriminatory approaches and respect women's autonomy. Moreover, it vowed to carry out relevant investigations, punish the people responsible for the forced sterilisation and death of the direct victim, and report to the IACHR about the implementation of the settlement. The Commission's friendly settlement has a lower profile in comparison to a precedent before the Court, but the case can nevertheless be depicted as a ground-breaking first supranational attempt at legally addressing practices of involuntary sterilisation. The case especially demonstrates a broad take on individual and collective remedies for involuntary sterilisations, involving compensation, rehabilitation, satisfaction and guarantees of non-repetition.

The second case on involuntary sterilisation to appear before a supranational body during the 2000s was *A.S. v. Hungary*, decided by the CEDAW Committee in 2006. In the case, a Romani woman had been sterilised when undergoing a Caesarean section in a Hungarian hospital. The applicant signed the consent form, where the word 'sterilisation' appeared in Latin, while in labour. The CEDAW Committee considered the sterilisation involuntary, referring to its General Recommendation 21, regulating the right to specific information on sterilisation and alternative procedures for family planning. The highly stressful and pressing circumstances under which the consent had been obtained, led the Committee to regard the sterilisation as a violation of the right to access information concerning health (CEDAW Article 10(h)).[57] The Committee considered the factors of the short interval between arrival at the hospital and the sterilisation surgery (17 minutes), the applicant's poor health condition, the Latin terminology used on the consent form, and the fact

55 Center for Reproductive Rights 2002: 16; IACHR, *Maria Mamérita Mestanza Chávez v. Peru* (2003).

56 IACHR, *Maria Mamérita Mestanza Chávez v. Peru* (2003).

57 CEDAW, *A.S. v. Hungary* (2006): Para 11.2.

that the applicant asked the doctor when it would be safe to conceive again as sufficient evidence to show that the applicant's right to gender-equal access to appropriate health care services (CEDAW Article 12) had been violated.[58] Moreover, the Committee found that the sterilisation was carried out without the applicant's full and informed consent, had 'permanently deprived her of her natural reproductive capacity' and was therefore a violation of the right to decide on the number and spacing of children (CEDAW Article 16(1e)).[59]

The CEDAW Committee also engaged in remedial responsibilities. The decision emphasised compensation to the primary victim[60] and guarantees of non-repetition with a remedial focus which was both individual and collective. The Hungarian Government was recommended to make sure that medical health staff in public and private hospitals were trained in respect of women's reproductive health and rights, to review domestic legislation, to supervise the practice in order to secure informed consent, to report to the CEDAW Committee, and to translate and distribute the decision in Hungarian.[61] Conceptually and remedially treating the sterilisation as discrimination against women, remarkably, the decision did not point out the intersectional aspects of *Romani* women being particularly vulnerable to the practices.[62]

The ECtHR also anticipated the upcoming jurisprudence of the decade to follow. In the 2009 case *K.H. and Others v. Slovakia*, it granted sterilised Romani women the right to access their medical files.[63] The Court held that the state's failure to ensure access to medical records for the patients themselves and their lawyers was an infringement of the positive right to respect private and family life (ECHR Article 8), without the support of any pressing public interest, resulting in a violation of the Convention.[64] Moreover, the Court considered that full access to the patients' medical records, including photocopying thereof, was crucial for future litigation. Limiting access to them had in effect violated the applicants' access to courts, a vital aspect of the right to a fair trial (ECHR Article 6).[65] Apart from costs and expenses, the eight applicants were awarded 3,500 Euros each for non-pecuniary damages.

In addition to these cases, during the 2000s, the international community also started to question compulsory infertility as a precondition for legal gender recognition, affecting trans people.[66] The issue was first addressed as a human

[58] Ibid: Para 11.3. The CEDAW Committee also made reference to CEDAW General Recommendation No. 24 concerning the interpretation of Art 12 CEDAW.

[59] CEDAW, *A.S. v. Hungary* (2006): Para 11.4. The CEDAW Committee referred to CEDAW General Recommendation No. 29 regarding the interpretation of Art 16(1e) CEDAW.

[60] However, the Committee did not specify an amount for appropriate compensation, or on what grounds it should be evaluated.

[61] CEDAW, *A.S. v. Hungary* (2006): Para 11.5. [62] See Curran 2016.

[63] ECtHR, *K.H. and Others v. Slovakia* (2009). This access was crucial in order to formulate legal claims before the court. See Durbáková, 29 April 2015.

[64] ECtHR, *K.H. and Others v. Slovakia* (2009): Paras 44–58. [65] Ibid: Paras 59–69.

[66] In this decade, important European supranational court case law related to trans people's rights – primarily the right to legal gender recognition and to be equally included and accommodated in the state welfare system – were ECtHR, *Christine Goodwin v. the United*

rights violation in the 2007 advocacy statement, the 'Yogyakarta Principles', initiated by the International Commission of Jurists.[67] The Principles were an attempt to mainstream issues affecting LGBT groups into the human rights framework and should be seen against the background of global, regional and local advancements of (and backlash against) rights relating to sexual orientation and gender identity.[68] According to Principle 3, '[n]o one shall be forced to undergo medical procedures, including sex reassignment surgery [sic], sterilisation or hormonal therapy, as a requirement for legal recognition of their gender identity'.[69] The Principles importantly recommend states to amend legislation and administrative procedures to respect and legally recognise a person's gender identity.[70]

The conceptualisation of sterilisation requirements as a violation of human rights was later picked up by the CoE Commissioner for Human Rights in a 2009 report entitled *Human Rights and Gender Identity*.[71] Recognising that most CoE member states at the time required infertility for legal recognition of gender identity, the Commissioner highlighted that trans people did not always wish to get sterilised.[72] The Commissioner importantly stated that '[i]t is of great concern that transgender people appear to be the only group in Europe subject to legally prescribed, state-enforced sterilisation'.[73] Recommending that states abolish infertility requirements and other compulsory medical treatment of trans people,[74] the Commissioner's report is particularly important as the first supranational institutional policy document to strongly condemn involuntary sterilisation of trans people.[75]

2.2.3 The 2010s: The Time of State Accountability and Inclusion of Trans People?

During the 2010s, binding legal obligations were created for states to materially face up to their responsibility for human rights violations. Simultaneously, a growing number of cases appeared before human rights courts, demanding state accountability for involuntary sterilisation. Furthermore, the Strasbourg

Kingdom (2002); ECtHR, *van Kück v. Germany* (2003); CJEU, *P v. S and Cornwall County Council* (1996); CJEU, *K.B. v. NHS Pensions Agency* (2004); CJEU, *Sarah Margaret Richards v. Secretary of State for Work and Pensions* (2006). These cases helped to pave the way for increasing attention to trans people's situation and rights in Europe.

67 International Commission of Jurists 2007.

68 See O'Flaherty & Fisher 2008. The resistance against the advancement of human rights pertaining to sexual orientation and gender identity was seen in, for example, the denigration campaigns at the UN level against the signatories of the Yogyakarta Principles. Scheinin, 23 October 2017.

69 International Commission of Jurists 2007, Principle 3. 70 Ibid.

71 CommDH/IssuePaper(2009)2. 72 Ibid: 8. 73 Ibid. 74 Ibid: 18.

75 The Commissioner is often the first institution within the Council of Europe to label practices as questionable from a human rights point of view. See Kempf, Lam & Mattioli-Zeltner, 12 October 2017.

Court considered sterilisation requirements for legal gender recognition a violation of the ECHR.[76] As a result, a clearer master frame of rights relating to involuntary sterilisation emerged at the end of the decade, even if not without internal inconsistencies.

During the decade, supranational institutions continued to more consistently include involuntary sterilisation of multiple groups as a human rights violation in their general recommendations, country reports and resolutions. Important thematic resolutions also materialised, such as the 2013 CoE Parliamentary Assembly Resolution 'Putting an End to Coerced Sterilisations and Castrations' and the 2014 UN Interagency Statement 'Eliminating Forced, Coercive and Otherwise Involuntary Sterilizations'.[77] That the interventions target multiple groups and intersecting vulnerabilities was an important highlighted recognition in both documents. Additionally, the 2008 establishment of the UN Committee on the Rights of Persons with Disabilities (CRPD Committee) remarkably contributed to the development of policy documents on involuntary sterilisation (concerning people with disabilities) during the 2010s.[78] Finally, involuntary sterilisation as a human rights violation gained further global recognition through its denunciation by the African Union (particularly concerning HIV positive women).[79] By the end of the decade, emerging supranational policy documents globally treated involuntary sterilisation as a relevant question for human rights.

[76] ECtHR, *A.P., Garçon and Nicot v. France* (2017).

[77] Res 1945 (2013);OHCHR et al (2014). See also, for example, CERD/C/SVK/CO/6-8 (2010): Para 18; CERD/C/CZE/CO/8–9 (2011): Para 19; CERD/C/SVK/CO/ 9-10 (2013); CEDAW/C/CZE/CO/5 (2010): Paras 34–35; CEDAW/C/JOR/CO/5 (2012): Paras 45–6; CEDAW/C/CHL/CO/5-6 (2012): Paras 34–35; CEDAW/C/COL/CO/7-8 (2013): Paras 29–30; CEDAW/C/PER/CO/7-8 (2014): Paras 21–22; CEDAW/C/IND/CO/4-5 (2014): Paras 36–37; CEDAW/C/GC/35 (2017): Para 18; CCPR/C/SVK/CO/3 (2011): Para 13; CRC/C/AUS/CO/4 (2012): Paras 46–47; CRC/C/CHN/CO/3-4 (2013): Paras 67–68; CRC/C/IND/CO/3-4 (2014): Para 65; A/66/254 (2011); A/HRC/17/49 (2011); A/HRC/20/5 (2012); A/HRC/22/53 (2013); A/HRC/26/28/Add.2 (2014): Para 89; A/HRC/29/24 (2015); A/HRC/29/23 (2015); E/C.12/GC/22 (2016): Paras 30, 57–59; CommDH(2011)42: Paras 72–79; Res 2048 (2015): Para 6.

[78] The reporting of the CRPD Committee, which continuously has taken involuntary sterilisation into consideration in its general comments and state monitoring, is particularly important as people with disabilities are among the most vulnerable groups to be subjected to involuntary sterilisations worldwide. See, for example, CRPD/C/PER/CO/1 (2012): Para 34; CRPD/C/HUN/CO/1 (2012): Para 38; CRPD/C/AUS/CO/1 (2013): Paras 39–40; CRPD/C/KOR/CO/1 (2014): Paras 33–34; CRPD/C/GC/1 (2014): Para 31; CRPD/C/LTU/CO/1 (2015): Paras 37–38; CRPD/C/DEU/CO/1 (2015): Paras 37–38; CRPD/C/CZE/CO/1 (2015): Paras 36–37; CRPD/C/GC/3 (2016): Paras 32, 44–45; CRPD/C/GC/5 (2017): Para 83; CRPD/C/GC/6 (2018): Paras 7, 30; CRPD/C/ZAF/CO/1 (2018): Paras 32–33.

[79] Noting the practice of involuntary sterilisation of HIV positive women in several member states, the African Commission on Human and Peoples' Rights (ACHPR) issued a resolution in 2013 (ACHPR/Res.260(LIV)13 (2013)). The Commission has since included the topic in other documents, such as addressing forced sterilisation as a violation of the 'rights to dignity, freedom from torture or ill-treatment, and freedom from arbitrary deprivation of liberty of persons with psychosocial disabilities' in a 2016 resolution (ACHPR/Res.343(LVIII)16 (2016)). See also Supreme Court of Namibia, *Government of the Republic of Namibia v. L.M. and Others* (2014); Nair 2010; Patel 2017.

2.2.3.1 Cases before Supranational Courts and Institutions

More international cases were brought during the 2010s. The UN Human Rights Committee faced its first case of involuntary sterilisation in 2015. In *M.T. v. Uzbekistan*, a female political prisoner had been forcibly sterilised through hysterectomy – and subjected to other forms of torture and ill-treatment – while imprisoned. In respect of the forcible sterilisation and the subsequent denial of justice, the Committee found the state party responsible for breach of the prohibition of torture and ill-treatment, the right to a remedy and the prohibition of discrimination on the basis of sex, as the intervention had particularly targeted the applicant as a woman.[80] It importantly recognised the hysterectomy as a form of torture/ill-treatment as well as one of discrimination.[81] When it came to remedies, the Committee highlighted the obligation of the state to provide effective reparation,[82] carry out impartial, effective and thorough investigations of torture and ill-treatment, launch criminal proceedings, provide the applicant with 'appropriate compensation' and translate and distribute the decision of the Committee.[83] Furthermore, the Committee emphasised the importance of guarantees of non-repetition.[84]

In the inadmissibility decision *J.D. et al v. the Czech Republic* (2019), conversely, the CEDAW Committee struck down a case in which six Romani women had been sterilised without being informed, on being falsely informed that the sterilisation was reversible, or with consent obtained under coercive circumstances. The Committee ruled the case inadmissible since the applicants had failed to exhaust domestic remedies.[85]

Continuing on to supranational courts, the ECtHR also ruled on several cases in the 2010s. The first one concerned the forced sterilisation of a Romani woman in *V.C. v. Slovakia* (2011).[86] *V.C. v. Slovakia* was the first case before the Strasbourg court addressing forced sterilisation of Romani women in Slovakia.[87] The applicant had signed a consent form without understanding the term 'sterilisation' while in labour, after being falsely informed that future childbearing would pose a risk to her life. In the hospital, moreover, she was kept in a segregated room for Romani women and was prevented from using the same washroom facilities as non-Romani women. The fact that the

[80] ICCPR, Art 7, 2(3) and 26. Other violations were also found in the case, albeit not connected to the sterilisation. Human Rights Committee, *M.T. v. Uzbekistan* (2015).

[81] However, the Human Rights Committee only explicitly addressed the case as one of gender/sex-based, rather than intersectional, discrimination.

[82] This is in accordance with ICCPR, Art 2(3a).

[83] Human Rights Committee, *M.T. v. Uzbekistan* (2015): Paras 9–10.

[84] Ibid: Para 9.

[85] CEDAW Committee, *J.D. et al v. the Czech Republic* (2019).

[86] ECtHR, *V.C. v. Slovakia* (2011).

[87] The case was part of a civil society strategic litigation effort to promote remedial access for the many Romani victims of forced sterilisation in Slovakia. In order to get enough information to base litigation on, the lawyers first had to challenge the limited access to the applicants' medical files in ECtHR, *K.H. and Others v. Slovakia* (2009); Durbáková, 29 April 2015. On the legal struggles of involuntarily sterilised Romani women, see also Cahn 2014.

applicant was Romani was stated several times in her hospital records. After the intervention, she suffered from medical and mental harm because of the involuntary infertility: she displayed symptoms of false pregnancy, needed psychiatric treatment for her psychological damage, was ostracised by the Romani community, left by her husband and finally divorced.[88]

The Court found a substantive violation of the prohibition of torture and ill-treatment, asserting that sterilisation without informed consent is a major infringement of reproductive health, dignity, autonomy and physical integrity.[89] It underlined that, contrary to the Slovak Government's claims, the sterilisation had not been motivated by medical necessity.[90] The intervention and the way in which the consent had been obtained provoked feelings of fear, anguish and inferiority, resulting in permanent medical, social and mental suffering.[91] Additionally, the Court found that the involuntary sterilisation was a violation of the right to respect for private and family life (Article 8) as this right also covers reproductive autonomy.[92] This said, the state failed to fulfil its positive obligation to protect the applicant, taking into consideration her vulnerable position as a woman of Romani origin.[93] Regarding the prohibition of discrimination (Article 14), in conjunction with the right to respect for private and family life, the Court reiterated that not enough evidence had been provided to establish that the Slovak doctors had acted in bad faith, that the sterilisation was part of an organised policy or that it was racially motivated.[94] While recognising the vulnerability of Romani women to sterilisation under Article 8, the Court nevertheless thought it unnecessary to investigate whether there had been a violation of the prohibition of discrimination in the case.[95] This choice was criticised by Judge Mijovic in her partly dissenting opinion, which emphasised that discrimination was 'the very essence' of the case; that discrimination means treating differently without an objective and reasonable justification, laid down in previous ECtHR case law.[96]

Other cases of involuntarily sterilised Romani women which came before the Court in the 2010s are *N.B. v. Slovakia* (2012)[97]; *I.G. and Others v. Slovakia* (2012)[98]; *R.K. v. the Czech Republic* (2012)[99]; *Červeňáková v. the Czech Republic* (2012)[100]; *G.H. v. Hungary* (2015).[101] In the three Slovak cases, the Court found violations of the prohibition of torture and ill-treatment (Article 3) and the right

[88] ECtHR, *V.C. v. Slovakia* (2011): Paras 9–20.

[89] Ibid: Paras 100–120. The Court also referred to other human rights documents, such as the Convention on Human Rights and Biomedicine and CEDAW General Recommendation No. 24.

[90] Ibid: Para 113. [91] Ibid: Para 118. [92] Ibid: Para 138. [93] Ibid: Paras 138–155.

[94] Ibid: Paras 176–177.

[95] Ibid: Paras 178–180. The Court also dismissed the applicant's other claims.

[96] Referring to ECtHR, *D.H. and Others v. the Czech Republic* (2007) and *Oršuš and Others v. Croatia* (2010). See also Rubio-Marín & Möschel 2015; Hoyle 2014.

[97] ECtHR, *N.B. v. Slovakia* (2012). [98] ECtHR, *I.G. and Others v. Slovakia* (2012).

[99] ECtHR, *R.K. v. the Czech Republic* (2012).

[100] ECtHR, *Červeňáková v. the Czech Republic* (2012). [101] ECtHR, *G.H. v. Hungary* (2015).

to respect for private and family life (Article 8).[102] For *R.K.*, a friendly settlement was reached, not specifying any violations,[103] and *Červeňáková* and *G.H.* were ruled inadmissible.[104] When it comes to remedies, the Court has opted for compensation of different sums, without specifying the remedial evaluation of the harm. In *V.C. v. Slovakia*, the direct victim was given 31,000 Euros in non-pecuniary damages; in *N.B. v. Slovakia*, the sum was 25,000 Euros. In *I.G. and Others v. Slovakia*, it was 28,500 and 27,000 Euros, respectively.

There have also been cases concerning involuntary sterilisation of non-Romani ciswomen before the ECtHR. One important example was the involuntary sterilisation of women with mental disabilities in the 2012 case *Joëlle Gauer v. France*.[105] The case was litigated with the support of a French advocacy group for people with disabilities and gained international attention, with six international advocacy groups acting as intervening parties.[106] The Court nevertheless declared the case inadmissible on procedural grounds.[107] In another case from 2012, *G.B. and R.B. v. the Republic of Moldova*,[108] a woman had been sterilised without her informed consent during a Caesarean section. The Court considered the intervention to be a 'serious interference' in her private and family life, constituting a violation of ECHR Article 8.[109] In the case, the Court held that the financial compensation provided at the domestic level was not enough to constitute 'sufficient just satisfaction', as it was not in proportion to the 'devastating effect on the first applicant from having lost her ability to reproduce and from the ensuing long-term health problems' which the sterilisation had caused.[110] The Court obliged the state to pay 12,000 Euros in non-pecuniary damages to the direct victim but disregarded the claims of the partner as an indirect victim.[111]

Another case which can be regarded under this header is *Csoma v. Romania* of 2013.[112] In the case, the applicant's life became at risk as the result of medical ill-treatment in connection to an abortion with medical complications, which led to her having to undergo a hysterectomy, excising her ovaries, leaving her permanently infertile. The Court pointed out that the medical malpractice, the failure to seek the applicant's informed consent regarding her treatment and the deficiencies in the national investigation of the doctor's civil,

[102] ECtHR, *V.C. v. Slovakia* (2011); *N.B. v. Slovakia* (2012); *I.G. and Others v. Slovakia* (2012).

[103] ECtHR, *R.K. v. the Czech Republic* (2012).

[104] ECtHR, *Červeňáková v. the Czech Republic* (2012); *G.H. v. Hungary* (2015).

[105] ECtHR, *Joëlle Gauer and Others v. France* (2012).

[106] These were the Irish Human Rights Commission, Center for Reproductive Rights, European Disability Forum, International Centre for the Legal Protection of Human Rights (Interights), International Disability Alliance and Mental Disability Advocacy Center. ECtHR, *Joëlle Gauer and Others v. France* (2012).

[107] ECtHR, *Joëlle Gauer and Others v. France* (2012).

[108] ECtHR, *G.B. and R.B. v. the Republic of Moldova* (2012).

[109] Ibid: Para 32. [110] Ibid.

[111] Ibid. Involuntary sterilisation also appeared as a theme in ECtHR, *L.H. v. Latvia* (2014).

[112] ECtHR, *Csoma v. Romania* (2013).

administrative and criminal liability violated the applicant's private life and the state's positive obligations protected under Article 8 ECHR.[113] As a result, the Court ordered the state to pay 6,000 Euros in non-pecuniary damages.

A final case from the ECtHR to be considered here, even though no sterilisation took place in the case as the applicant persistently refused, is *Soares de Melo v. Portugal*.[114] In the judgment from 2016, the Court stated that rendering custody of the applicant's children conditional on her sterilisation was an impermissible infringement on her integrity. As such, it constituted a violation of Article 8 ECHR.[115]

It is fascinating to note that the ECtHR was unable to find violations of Article 3 in cases in which non-Romani women were involuntarily sterilised, leading to significantly lower amounts of non-pecuniary compensation. This development raises the question whether the Court found involuntary sterilisation of Romani women to be a graver violation of human rights than that of non-Romani women, and, should that be the case, why this is conceptualised as torture/ill-treatment rather than discrimination. Due to the limited case law on the topic so far, no definitive answer can be provided here.

Finally, in the Inter-American context, the important case *I.V. v. Bolivia* was first settled by the IACHR in 2014.[116] In the case, a migrant woman was sterilised while giving birth through Caesarean section. She had neither consented to the sterilisation, nor been informed about the procedure before it was carried out. The national criminal investigations and litigations in the case were shelved, upon which the applicant furthered the case to the supranational level.[117] The Commission found that carrying out a sterilisation on the applicant without her consent was a violation of the right to personal integrity (Article 5(1) ACHR).[118] It also stated that her free and informed consent had not been obtained, which constituted a violation of the right to access to information (Article 13) in matters of reproductive health.[119] Furthermore, the Court considered the sterilisation not to have been in proportion to medical necessity and to violate women's reproductive autonomy as protected under the right to privacy (Article 11(2)) and the right to found a family protected under the rights of the family (Article 17).[120] Moreover, the Commission regarded the insufficient response on the part of the state a violation of the rights to a fair trial and to judicial protection (Articles 8(1) and 25, respectively).[121] Moreover, the obligation of non-discrimination (Article 1(1)) – recognising the particular vulnerability of the applicant as a poor, migrant woman – was considered

113 Ibid: Para 68.
114 ECtHR, *Soares de Melo v. Portugal* (2016).
115 Ibid: particularly Paras 109–111.
116 IACHR, *I.V. v. Bolivia* (2014). The case was litigated with the support of a national NGO called *Derechos en acción [Rights in Action]*. In 2021, furthermore, a friendly settlement was signed before the IACHR in the case *F.S. v. Chile* – a case concerning forced sterilisation of an HIV positive woman.
117 IACHR, *I.V. v. Bolivia* (2014): Para 42.
118 Ibid: Paras 97–107.
119 Ibid: Paras 108–146.
120 Ibid: Paras 147–154.
121 Ibid: Paras 165–174.

breached in conjunction with all the other violations.[122] The Commission concluded that the state obligation to act with due diligence had not been fulfiled, accordingly finding a violation of the duty of the state to refrain from any practice or act of violence against women and the right for women to be free from violence (Article 7 of the Belém do Pará Convention).[123]

The Commission recommended that the Bolivian State provide reparations, including compensation for material and personal/emotional harm and high-quality medical care to the direct victim, investigation and establishment of 'appropriate liabilities and punishments', guarantees of non-repetition, reviewed policies and practices regarding informed consent in hospitals, inclusion of intersectional perspectives in legislative and policy reform, and investigation and reform of the judicial system to secure access to and effective administration of justice.[124] Consequently, the reparations were wide ranging, focusing on redress of individual harm as well as prevention of future collective harm.

The Bolivian Government's subsequent inaction and lack of response to the Commission's recommendations led to the case being brought before the IACtHR. When delivering its judgment in 2016, the Court reiterated many of the points already established by the Commission. It considered that the rights to privacy and personal liberty include fundamental decisions concerning one's identity, personality and dignity, such as the decision to parent.[125] It also pointed out that the right to freedom of thought and expression encompasses health, and that sexual and reproductive health information is particularly important to women as a part of maternal health.[126] Furthermore, it highlighted that the right to raise a family includes the right to procreate.[127] Importantly, the Court underlined that involuntary sterilisation was a grave violation of women's rights,[128] and that the applicant was sterilised as a discriminatory act based on her being female, poor, Peruvian and a refugee.[129] With these motivations, the Court found that the sterilisation of *I.V.* without obtaining her prior, free, full and informed consent was a violation of the right to humane treatment (Article 5(1) ACHR); right to personal liberty (Article 7(1)); right to privacy (Article 11(1, 2)); freedom of thought and expression (Article 13(1)); the right to raise a family (Article 17(2)), in conjunction with a breach of the obligation to respect rights without discrimination (Article 1(1)) and women's right to live a life free from violence (Article 7 Belém do Pará Convention).[130]

Moving along, the Court stated that it is necessary to contextually investigate the violation of integrity in order to appropriately be able to determine the suffering and humiliation caused.[131] When evaluating the harm, the Court highlighted that the applicant suffered from (i) loss of reproductive capacity; (ii) physical negative consequences caused by the involuntary surgical

[122] Ibid, for example, Para 6. [123] Ibid: Paras 175–185, 250–256. [124] Ibid: Para 187.
[125] Ibid: Paras 149–152. [126] Ibid: Paras 156–157. [127] Ibid: Para 153. [128] Ibid: Para 236.
[129] Ibid: Para 242. [130] Ibid: Paras 147–256. [131] Ibid: Para 267.

intervention; (iii) psychological distress, including anxiety, frustration and shame; (iv) emotional anguish caused by the temporary separation from her partner as a consequence of the sterilisation; (v) financial loss due to the medical and legal needs caused by the sterilisation; (vi) feelings of frustration and helplessness due to the lack of access to justice.[132] Moreover, the Court recognised that the immediate family of the applicant, particularly her daughters, had been affected and suffered from a sense of guilt.[133] In its conceptualisation of harm, the Court, hence, demonstrated high sensitivity, acknowledging both direct and indirect victimhood as well as economic, emotional, mental, reproductive and physical harm. Accordingly, the Court confirmed that the involuntary sterilisation constituted cruel, inhuman and degrading treatment (ACHR Article 5 (1.2)) in conjunction with discrimination (Article 1(1)).[134]

Viewing forced sterilisation as a form of violence against women, the Court highlighted that the generic regulations on the right to a fair trial and right to judicial protection should be interpreted in combination with the Belém do Pará Convention and its obligation for states to prevent, punish and eradicate violence against women.[135] Importantly, it also emphasised that forced sterilisation can constitute a war crime, a crime against humanity or genocide according to the Rome Statute, which obliges the state to investigate *ex officio*.[136] The Court concluded that the applicant had been discriminated against through the state's passivity to properly investigate and prosecute her case, finding violations of the right to a fair trial (Article 8(1)) and the right to judicial protection (Article 25), in conjunction with the obligation to respect rights and prohibition of discrimination (Article 1(1)) and the obligation to prevent, punish and eradicate violence against women (Article 7 Belém do Pará Convention).[137]

When it came to remedies, the Court considered it necessary to fully remedy the multiplicity of harm found.[138] In respect of rehabilitation, it ordered free, accessible and specialised medical care tailored to the applicant's psychological, reproductive, sexual and psychiatric needs.[139] It also acknowledged the harm of the indirect victims, the family and the need for them to be included in the therapy.[140] The IACtHR ordered a sum of 50,000 US Dollars to be granted to the direct victim in compensation for monetary and non-monetary damages.[141] What is more, the Court commanded the Bolivian Government to publish the judgment and publicly acknowledge its responsibility as a means of satisfaction.[142] As a guarantee of non-repetition, the Court obliged the state to ensure that consent would always be prior, freely given, informed and full. All Bolivian public and private hospitals were to be provided with a printed

[132] Ibid: Para 268. [133] Ibid: Paras 268, 115. [134] Ibid: Paras 262–270.

[135] Ibid: Paras 295–298. The Court particularly referred to IACtHR, *González et al ('Cotton Field') v. Mexico* (2009); *Velásquez Paiz and Others v. Guatemala* (2015); *Fernández Ortega et al v. Mexico* (2010).

[136] Ibid: Paras 204; 301. [137] Ibid: Paras 288–323. [138] Ibid: Para 325. [139] Ibid: Para 332.

[140] Ibid. [141] Ibid: Paras 354–358. [142] Ibid: Paras 334–336.

information sheet summarising women's sexual and reproductive rights. Moreover, the Court ordered the state to establish permanent programmes on gender stereotyping, gender discrimination/violence and informed consent for medical students and professionals.[143]

Unlike the ECtHR's unwillingness to assess discrimination in *V.C. v. Slovakia*, the Inter-American Court particularly engaged with such claims in *I.V. v. Bolivia.*[144] As such, it recognised that (i) the sterilisation was motivated by prejudice and harmful stereotypes, and (ii) that the state is obliged to prevent such prejudices and stereotypes. The IACtHR's explicit reference to involuntary sterilisation originating in a tradition of men being viewed as decision-makers over women's bodies signals an in-depth assessment of structural gender discrimination and inequalities, affecting reproductive rights.[145]

2.2.3.2 Sterilisation Preconditions for Legal Gender Recognition

Supranational institutions also increasingly explicitly addressed involuntary sterilisation of trans people in the 2010s.[146] After the CoE Commissioner for Human Rights depicted the practice as a human rights violation in 2009, the Parliamentary Assembly of the Council of Europe (PACE) adopted a resolution on discrimination based on sexual orientation and gender identity in 2010, recommending that states issue identity documentation which would reflect 'an individual's preferred gender identity, without any prior obligation to undergo sterilisation or other medical procedures'.[147] Supporting this development, the World Professional Association for Transgender Health (WPATH) importantly released a statement in 2010 declaring that 'no person should have to undergo surgery or accept sterilization as a condition of identity recognition'.[148] Some inconsistencies are, however, present in the master frame of rights, provoking questions on whether involuntary sterilisations of cis and trans people are covered by the same legal norms.

The inconsistencies in the 2011 CoE Convention on Preventing and Combating Violence against Women and Domestic Violence (the Istanbul Convention) reflect these questions. The Convention is the first international treaty to provide a definition of 'gender' as 'the socially constructed roles, behaviours, activities and attributes that a given society considers appropriate

143 Ibid: Paras 340–342. 144 Zampas 2017; Reinsberg & Juaristi 2017. 145 Ibid.

146 Res 1728 (2010); Res 1945 (2013); Res 2048 (2015): Para 6; A/HRC/22/53 (2013); A/HRC/29/23 (2015). Sterilisation preconditions for legal gender recognition were also problematised in thematic reports by EU institutions in the 2010s. See European Union Agency for Fundamental Rights 2014; van den Brink et al 2018.

147 Res 1728 (2010): Para 16.11.2. In 2010, the CoE Committee of Ministers also adopted a recommendation against discrimination based on sexual orientation and gender identity, even if not mentioning sterilisation or castration specifically, but rather recommending that preconditions for legal gender recognition 'should be regularly reviewed in order to remove abusive requirements'. CM/Rec(2010)5: Art 20.

148 WPATH 2010.

for women and men'.[149] Furthermore, the Istanbul Convention contains an obligation for states to criminalise forced sterilisation, here defined as 'performing surgery which has the purpose or effect of terminating a woman's capacity to naturally reproduce without her prior and informed consent or understanding of the procedure'.[150] Despite introducing a notion of 'gender' as socially constructed, the Istanbul Convention is only legally binding as regards violence against 'women', with this term being explained to include 'girls under the age of 18',[151] while it is merely recommendatory when it comes to other forms of (gender) violence. The extent to which trans women are included in the category of 'women' is uncertain as the understanding of the word, particularly in the light of the explanatory report, seems to build on an essentialist conceptualisation of women as exclusively cisgender.[152]

The ECtHR also developed its jurisprudence on involuntary sterilisation of trans people in the 2010s. The European Commission of Human Rights, formerly the institution which decided on the admissibility of individual complaints to the Court, was already faced with the question of sterilisation as a precondition to legal gender recognition in the 1997 case *Roetzheim v. Germany*.[153] Noting that the Court's case law had concerned post-operative transsexual people,[154] the Commission stated that 'the essential nature of transsexualism' resulted in 'extremely complex legal situations'. Finding that Germany had 'in principle taken appropriate legal measures', the Commission dismissed the case as inadmissible.[155] A similar stance was taken by the Court in its 2008 admissibility decision *Nunez v. France*,[156] but concerning requirements of gender-affirming treatment, not sterilisation or castration as such. In the 2015 case *Y.Y. v. Turkey*, the Court *obiter dictum* held that compulsory sterilisation for gender recognition of trans people violates the right to respect for privacy and family life, laid down in Article 8 ECHR.[157]

149 Art 3(c). 150 Art 39(b). 151 Art 3(f).

152 The Istanbul Convention does not clarify whether, for example, trans women are included in this definition. The Explanatory Report to the Istanbul Convention does not provide much guidance on the issue, but stresses that 'categories of individuals such as transgender or transsexual persons, crossdressers, transvestites and other groups of persons that do not correspond to what society has established as belonging to "male" or "female" categories' are covered in the scope of non-discrimination in the Convention (Art 4(3)). However, as regards other paragraphs, it seems that trans people are left outside the hard law dimensions of the Convention, as the Explanatory Report also states that 'Parties may if they wish, extend the interpretation to individuals who are gay, lesbian, bisexual or transgender, who may also face particular forms of gender-related persecution and violence'. Explanatory Report CETS 210 (2011): Paras 53, 313. See Alaattinoğlu 2020.

153 ECmHR, *Roetzheim v. Germany* (1997).

154 The Commission cited ECtHR, *Rees v. the United Kingdom* (1987); *Cossey v. the United Kingdom* (1990); *B v. France* (1992).

155 ECmHR, *Roetzheim v. Germany* (1997). 156 ECtHR, *Nunez v. France* (2008).

157 ECtHR, *Y.Y. v. Turkey* (2015). Nevertheless, as no involuntary sterilisation had actually been carried out in the case, the non-pecuniary damages of 7,500 Euros are not directly comparable to cases in which a sterilisation surgery had taken place.

The *obiter dictum* was developed in the 2017 case *A.P., Garçon and Nicot v. France*,[158] when the Court clearly specified that sterilisation as a precondition for legal gender recognition is a violation of the right to respect for private and family life.[159] The three applicants were all registered as men at birth but self-identified as women: two of them had undergone gender-affirming treatments and one had not. French courts had disapproved all the applicants' requests for legal gender recognition. The ECtHR recognised that the notion of 'private life' in the Convention was broad and included physical and moral integrity and identity such as gender identity or sexual orientation.[160] Moreover, the Court argued that this right implied a right to self-identification.[161] The Court recognised that its jurisprudence had been limited to post-operative trans people, or people wanting to access gender-affirming surgery, thus far.[162] It importantly pointed out that this did, however, not mean that the legal recognition of the gender identity of trans people who did not wish to undergo gender-affirming treatment prescribed by the authorities, was excluded from the scope of Article 8.[163] Quite the contrary: the Court ruled that the French condition of irreversible physical (appearance) transformation, involving sterilisation, was a violation of the right to physical integrity and the right to gender identity.[164] Recognising that the requirements established in French law were an infringement of Article 8, the Court ruled that the French requirement of mandatory infertility did not fall under the narrow margin of appreciation on account of the rights at stake being fundamental to the scope of Article 8.[165] Requiring applicants

[158] ECtHR, *A.P., Garçon and Nicot v. France* (2017).

[159] The Court nevertheless rejected the other claims of the applicants.

[160] Ibid: Para 92. Doing so, the Court referred to ECtHR, *Van Kück v. Germany* (2003); *Schlumpf v. Switzerland* (2009); *Y.Y. v. Turkey* (2015).

[161] ECtHR, *A.P., Garçon and Nicot v. France* (2017): Para 93.

[162] Ibid: Para 94. See ECtHR, *Rees v. the United Kingdom* (1987); *Cossey v. the United Kingdom* (1990); *B v. France* (1992); *Christine Goodwin v. the United Kingdom* (2001); *I v. the United Kingdom* (2002); *Van Kück v. Germany* (2003); *L v. Lithuania* (2003); *Schlumpf v. Switzerland* (2009); *Hämäläinen v. Finland* (2014); *Y.Y. v. Turkey* (2015).

[163] ECtHR, *A.P., Garçon and Nicot v. France* (2017): Para 94.

[164] Ibid: Paras 123–135. Highlighting its doctrine on informed consent and referring to two other cases of involuntary sterilisation, the Court stated that conditioning legal gender recognition on sterilisation was a violation of physical integrity. The cases referred to were ECtHR, *V.C. v.* Slovakia (2011); *G.B. and R.B. v. the Republic of Moldova* (2012).

[165] Ibid: Para 123. The Court admitted however that states can put up other requirements for legal recognition of gender identity. See also Para 71:

> In several of the countries concerned, the abolition of this requirement is the result of recent legal developments (an Administrative Court judgment of 27 February 2009 in Austria; a Law of 15 March 2010 in Portugal; a Federal Constitutional Court judgment of 11 January 2011 in Germany; a Law of 22 May 2013 in Sweden; a Law of 18 December 2013 in the Netherlands; a Law of 11 June 2014 in Denmark; a Law of 1 April 2015 in Malta; a Law of 15 July 2015 in Ireland; a Court of Cassation judgment of 21 July 2015 in Italy; a Law of 17 June 2016 in Norway; and a Law of 12 October 2016 in France). It appears also that a number of member States are currently reviewing or intend to review the conditions for legal recognition of the identity of transgender persons in order to remove any that appear unreasonable [...].

to undergo sterilisation put them in an insoluble dilemma,[166] violating the right to respect for private and family life.[167] The Court also highlighted that European and international opinion on the matter had changed over the preceding years, recognising a tendency to abolish such conditions.[168]

Some unclarities yet remain regarding the Court's conceptualisation of sterilisation in the case, particularly when comparing it to sterilisation cases involving cis women. Firstly, it is unclear why the Court limited itself to finding a violation of the right to respect for private and family life instead of investigating involuntary sterilisation as torture or ill-treatment, as it has in the cases of sterilisation of Romani women.[169] Another unclarity pertains to how the case should be read in terms of remedies. The Court denied the applicants compensation for non-pecuniary damages since it considered its finding a violation of the Convention a sufficient remedy.[170] While such a disparity raises questions about whether the Court intended to create a potentially discriminatory difference based on applicants' gender identity,[171] I shy away from drawing far-reaching conclusions based on only one case, where sterilisation was tried *in abstracto* and national legislation had already been amended.[172]

Following *A.P., Garçon and Nicot v. France*, the European Committee of Social Rights (ECSR) also developed a stance regarding sterilisation requirements for legal gender recognition during the mentioned decade. In 2018, the Committee evaluated the Czech sterilisation requirement for legal gender recognition in a complaint against the Czech Republic by Transgender Europe (TGEU) and International Lesbian, Gay, Bisexual, Trans and Intersex Rights Association (ILGA) Europe. It was found to be unnecessary and effectively to vitiate free consent.[173] As such, the Committee considered the requirement a violation of 'physical integrity' which is 'contrary to the notion of human dignity' and incompatible 'with the right to protection of health' as protected in Article 11(1) of the 1961 European Social Charter.[174]

[166] Ibid: Para 132. The Court has later applied the same reasoning to gender-affirming surgery. See ECtHR, *X and Y v. Romania* (2021).

[167] Ibid: Para 135.

[168] Ibid: Paras 124–125. An important judgment in the European context is particularly Bundesverfassungsgericht [German Federal Constitutional Court], 1 BvR 3295/07, Rn. (1–82) (2011). See also the dissenting opinion by Judge Ranzoni, who highlighted that there was a lack of European consensus on the matter.

[169] This might, however, be due to the claims raised by the applicants. Ibid: Paras 127, 131.

[170] Ibid: Para 164. Nevertheless, the costs and expenses of the applicants were covered (Paras 165–167).

[171] However, the ECtHR did not fully respect the applicants' self-identified gender identity, as seen in the Court's referral to the applicants in the male gender, and its full acceptance of the medicalised, even pathologised, narrative of trans existence. See Dunne 2017; Renz 2017.

[172] See Dunne 2017. While not providing more guidance on appropriate remedies, the State's positive obligation to provide quick, transparent and accessible procedures for legal gender recognition was reiterated in the case ECtHR, *A.D. and Others v. Georgia* (2022).

[173] ECSR, *Transgender Europe and ILGA-Europe v. the Czech Republic* (2018).

[174] Ibid: Para 86. The Committee did not consider discrimination mainly due to procedural reasons, a fact which was nevertheless criticised in the separate concurring opinion of Vice-President Karin Lukas, who considered discrimination to be 'the central matter at stake'.

Outside of the European context, infertility requirements for legal gender recognition were addressed by UN institutions as discrimination, torture/ill-treatment and/or violation of physical integrity.[175] Within the Inter-American context, the IACtHR importantly recognised in a 2017 advisory opinion that requirements of surgical operations and/or hormonal treatments for legal gender recognition are contrary to the right to integrity (Article 5 ACHR), the right to privacy (Article 11.2) and the right to liberty (Article 7), drawing parallels with its recent case law on involuntary sterilisation of a cis woman.[176]

2.3 A Few Words on Involuntary Castration

Groups affected by castration practices have particularly been those depicted as sexually deviant and/or dangerous for society. Once a generally accepted form of treatment, surgical castration has been abandoned in many countries over the last 40 years due to ethical concerns and uncertainty about its effectiveness.[177] However, a global gap remains in data on observed castration practices, reflected in the human rights framework by the few legal and policy documents which conceptualise state-enforced castration as a human rights violation.

One case of involuntary castration, which has been problematised at the supranational level, is the use of surgical castration on imprisoned Czech sexual offenders. Within the CoE framework, the practice has been challenged by the European Committee for the Prevention of Torture and Inhuman or Degrading Treatment or Punishment (CPT). It has pointed out that consent to invasive procedures such as castration should be given in a 'free and informed' manner, and highlighted that the concept is 'hardly reconcilable with a situation in which the options open to an individual are extremely limited: surgical castration or possible indefinite confinement in a psychiatric hospital'.[178] Although a seemingly grave human rights violation, with physical consequences beyond infertility, the CPT has not specified what rights are violated by involuntary castration. The Czech castration practices have also alarmed other CoE institutions, such as PACE, which has, much like the CPT, failed to provide specific guidance on how to legally conceptualise the interventions in terms of human rights.[179]

[175] See, for example, A/HRC/22/53 (2013): Paras 78; 85(3); A/HRC/31/57 (2016): Paras 48–49; 72(e, h); E/C.12/GC/22 (2016): Para 58; CEDAW/C/NLD/CO/5 (2010): Para 46; CEDAW/C/BEL/CO/7 (2014): Paras 44–45; CEDAW/C/FIN/CO/7 (2014): Paras 28–29; CEDAW/C/SVK/CO/5-6 (2015): Para 37; CAT/C/CHN-HKG/CO/5 (2016): Paras 28–29; A/HRC/29/23 (2015): Paras 17; 38; 70; 78(g); A/HRC/35/36 (2017): Paras 14, 57.

[176] Namely, IACtHR, *I.V. v. Bolivia* (2016); OC-24/17 (2017): Para 146.

[177] CPT/Inf (2009) 8: Para 11. [178] CPT/Inf (2007) 32: Para 109.

[179] PACE Report 13215 (2013). The report clearly states that coerced castration constitutes a human rights violation, but does not specify the human rights affected. Pasquier, Kleinsorge & Elveriş, 12 October 2017.

Within the UN, the surgical castration of Czech prisoners was referred to as torture and ill-treatment by the CAT Committee.[180] Other castration practices were also sporadically challenged at the international level in periodic country reports. The CRPD Committee, for example, has noted that people with disabilities are vulnerable to surgical castration practices in the Czech Republic and Lithuania, recommending that the countries abolish the practices.[181]

Although several countries imposed surgical castration of sex offenders in the twentieth century, a lack of discussion persists about rights violations, state responsibility and remedies. This is true even for situations where similar historical violations have been publicly condemned, presenting obvious opportunities for involuntary castration to be addressed.[182]

2.4 An Unclear Picture of Rights and Obligations

There are many lacunas in the international legal master frame of rights relating to involuntary sterilisation and castration, which developed in the post-war international community, particularly since the 1990s. Consequently, no unitary approach has yet crystallised on how the topic is to be legally conceptualised in terms of rights. The violations applicable seem rather to be relatively freely determined by the deciding body. For example, the CEDAW Committee narrowly conceptualised the forced sterilisation of a Romani woman in Hungary as discrimination based on gender.[183] The gender-based discrimination approach was affirmed in a case concerning the forced sterilisation of a female political prisoner before the UN Human Rights Committee.[184] While intersectional discrimination could have been recognised in both of these cases, the only institution which engaged in intersectionality is the IACtHR.[185] Conversely, the Strasbourg Court firmly rejected allegations of discrimination in the cases of involuntary sterilisation before it.[186] Furthermore, most bodies have acknowledged the interventions as torture or ill-treatment, save for the CEDAW Committee and the ECtHR in some cases.[187] Moreover, the deciding

180 CAT/C/CZE/CO/4-5 (2012): Paras 13, 20, 23. See also CAT/C/CZE/CO/6 (2018): Paras 34–35.

181 CRPD/C/CZE/CO/1 (2015): Para 29; CRPD/C/LTU/CO/1 (2015): Paras 37–38.

182 This was the case for the 2017 German law to rehabilitate and compensate victims of post-war criminalisation of male homosexual relations, a group which includes castrated men. See Gesetzes zur strafrechtlichen Rehabilitierung der nach dem 8. Mai 1945 wegen einvernehmlicher homosexueller Handlungen verurteilten Personen und zur Änderung des Einkommensteuergesetzes [Act on Criminal Rehabilitation of People Convicted of Consensual Homosexual Acts after 8 May 1945 and Amendment of the Income Tax Act] 2017; German Government Bill RegE 18/12038 (2017); Kolata 2017; Heim 1980: 50–51; 142–143. Another example are the forcibly castrated Kenyan Mau Mau war veterans, which have not been specifically addressed in the settlement with the British Government. See Elkins 2005; Anderson 2005.

183 CEDAW, *A.S. v. Hungary* (2006).

184 Human Rights Committee, *M.T. v. Uzbekistan* (2015).

185 See IACHR, Maria Mamérita Mestanza Chávez v. Peru (2003); IACtHR, *I.V. v. Bolivia* (2016).

186 Importantly ECtHR, *V.C. v. Slovakia* (2011); *A.P., Garçon and Nicot v. France* (2017).

187 CEDAW, *A.S. v. Hungary* (2006). The ECtHR has also not found a violation of Article 3 ECHR in all cases of involuntary sterilisation before it. However, the findings depend on the facts of the cases and the claims presented before the Court by the applicants.

bodies included references to other rights in the cases, such as the right to family[188] or the ECHR's catch-all right to respect for private and family life.[189] The matter of conceptualisation is important, for example, in order to determine appropriate remedies and because it has implications for whether the interventions are considered *jus cogens* (e.g., as torture) for their prescriptibility.

The type of remedy also varies. The disparity primarily depends on the different deciding forums, with the two regional human rights courts representing two extremes. The ECtHR is the most austere and the IACtHR the most comprehensive.[190] The former pursued a remedial path which called for individual, financial compensation for non-pecuniary damages to the direct victim, seen in *V.C. v. Slovakia*. In doing so, it avoided engaging with the harm of the victims in depth, which might be questionable in respect of the effectiveness and transformative potential of remedies.[191] Nevertheless, given that the CoE system delegates the supervision of the execution of judgments to the Committee of Ministers, guaranteeing non-recurrence, the remedial austerity of the Strasbourg Court can be put into perspective.[192] The San José counterpart went for a further-reaching remedial approach, where it engaged with and addressed both individual and communal, pecuniary and non-pecuniary harm. It did so by focusing on compensating as well as rehabilitating the harm of the individual victims (primarily the direct victim), and through embracing the notion of collective, discriminatory harm, emphasising the importance of preventing future practices of involuntary sterilisation.[193]

Another striking difference can be seen in the conceptualisation and remedial treatment of involuntarily sterilised cis and trans people, respectively. While the involuntary sterilisation of cis people already surfaced as a human rights violation in the 1990s, it took the international community longer to conceptualise the involuntary sterilisation of trans people as such. A difference between the two seems to be based on stereotypical views on trans people as expected to want sterilisation, which can hardly be legally justified.[194] Accordingly, in recent human rights' soft law sources, a turnabout is taking place towards a more unitary normative approach concerning involuntary sterilisation and castration of both trans and cis people.[195]

A further contrast is the difference between the legal regulation of involuntary sterilisation in comparison to castration. While sterilisation was increasingly addressed since the 1990s, castration has remained in the shadows, only incidentally and sporadically investigated by supranational legal institutions. However, with harm that is at least as grave as that of involuntary sterilisation,

[188] IACtHR, *I.V. v. Bolivia* (2016).

[189] See particularly ECtHR, *V.C. v. Slovakia* (2011); *A.P., Garçon and Nicot v. France* (2017).

[190] Nevertheless, the substance of redress depends on various factors, for example, the function of the regional courts in the system. See Shelton 2015: 375, 399–401.

[191] See Rubio-Marín 2009b: 398.

[192] See Committee of Ministers 2018.

[193] See IACtHR, *I.V. v. Bolivia* (2016).

[194] See Lee 2015; Alaattinoğlu & Rubio-Marín 2019.

[195] See, for example, A/HRC/22/53 (2013); Res 1945 (2013).

its lack of codification might be expressive of a general void of historical and legal investigation rather than uncertainty about whether involuntary castration constitutes a violation of international law.

This chapter has shown that the international legal regulation of involuntary sterilisation and castration is in its early stages and rather inconsistent. This fragmented supranational picture might itself be an obstacle to national reception of the international normative framework. Tracing the interaction between the global and the local, I now move on to investigating domestic legal distinctions and disagreements, adding further complexity to an already composite picture.

3

Sweden: Remedies with Limited Legal Recognition of Responsibility

Victims of involuntary sterilisation and castration, who were subjected to interventions between the 1930s and the 2010s, find themselves in different positions in Sweden. Their diverging circumstances are partly explained by a developing and internationalising legal culture but also by how the victim groups have aligned, or failed to align, with existing rights frames. The Swedish example renders visible how changing notions of rights, such as individual integrity, autonomy and equality, have not only played a role as legal instruments but also contributed to changing sociocultural understandings of the interventions, victim groups and state responsibility. Against the background of how Swedish legal culture increasingly embraces rights as legal instruments, this chapter investigates how national sterilisation and castration practices were introduced and how they have been abolished and problematised in remedial terms.

3.1 An Internationalising Legal Culture and the Increasing Importance of Rights

Swedish legal culture witnessed an internationalisation during late twentieth and early twenty-first centuries, challenging domestic legal conventions, particularly concerning rights and judicial review. The official Swedish commitment to international human rights is generally strong.[1] A formal acceptance of central human rights documents and the absence of armed conflict have contributed to the international and domestic picture of Sweden as a state that strongly prioritises human rights.[2] This said, many human rights conventions

[1] The Swedish Government has often been early to sign and ratify international human rights treaties. The country has been a member of the UN since 1946, the CoE since 1949 and the European Union (EU) since 1995. Without any noteworthy reservations or declarations on the topic at hand, it has ratified the ECHR in 1952; CERD, ICCPR and ICESCR in 1971; CEDAW in 1980; CAT in 1986; the CRC in 1990; CRPD in 2008; the European Torture Convention in 1988; the CoE Framework Convention for the Protection of National Minorities in 2000; the Istanbul Convention in 2014. Sweden has signed, but not ratified, the CoE Convention on Human Rights and Biomedicine. The Rome Statute of the ICC was ratified in 2001.

[2] See Karlsson Schaffer & Langford 2018.

have been regarded as abstract guidelines, without obligations of enforcement in practice.[3] An illustrating example is the general lack of domestic incorporation of human rights conventions, with the ECHR[4] and the CRC[5] as important exceptions, intuitively in conflict with the country's formal dualist relationship with international law. Effectively, most treaties do not have the same legal status as domestic legislation and cannot be directly applied by the courts.[6]

The same ambivalent relation to rights also applies to the constitutional level. The first explicit constitutional rights and freedoms catalogue, inspired by international human rights,[7] was introduced in the 1974 Government Act which has constitutional status.[8] This list was, however, not intended for, and consequentially not used by, the courts. Constitutional rights and freedoms were seen as directives for the administration of public power rather than as legal instruments for judicial review.[9] Therefore, the 1974 Government Act has generally not been used in litigation, mainly functioning as an aesthetic element in Swedish law: nice-looking, but with few practical implications.[10] The

[3] See Schultz 2009.

[4] The ECHR was incorporated with ordinary, legislative status in 1994 in preparation for EU membership. Lag om den europeiska konventionen angående skydd för de mänskliga rättigheterna och friheterna [Act on the European Convention for the Protection of Human Rights and Fundamental Freedoms] (1994:1219). See Schultz 2011; Mörk & Hermansson 2008; Erman 2011.

[5] The CRC was incorporated in 2018 as a result of civil society activism. Lag om Förenta nationernas konvention om barnets rättigheter [Act on the United Nations Convention on the Rights of the Child] (2018:1197).

[6] Delegationen för mänskliga rättigheter i Sverige [The Delegation for Human Rights in Sweden] 2010: 149. Currently, constitutionality is not only attributed to domestic constitutional legal norms, but also to those of 'other superior statute', meaning supranational legal norms, yet likely limited to supranational incorporated treaties. Regeringsformen [Government Act] (1974:152), Chapter 11 Section 14. See Cameron 2007. ECHR and EU legislation were the only instruments indicated in Swedish Government Bill Prop. 2009/10:80: 140–145.

[7] International human rights may not have been explicitly mentioned in the *travaux préparatoires*, but the typology of rights, with civil and political rights at the forefront, was evidently influenced by international human rights treaties. See Swedish Government Bill Prop. 1973:90.

[8] Regeringsformen [Government Act] (1974:152). For the historical development of fundamental freedoms and rights, see Justitiedepartementet [The Swedish Ministry of Justice] 1975: 55–87; Nergelius 1996.

[9] Schultz 2009: 315; Åhman 2016. See Swedish Government Bill Prop. 1973:90.

[10] Åhman 2015: 45. See also Swedish Government Bill Prop. 1973:90; Konstitutionsutskottet [The Swedish Parliamentary Constitutional Committee] KU 1973:26; KU 1974:7. In 1982, the Swedish contradiction between resolute rights commitments in the abstract and weak practical allegiance was nevertheless brought to the fore in the 1982 ECtHR Case of *Sporrong and Lönnroth v. Sweden*, in which the state was found guilty of violating the first article of the Convention: the obligation to respect human rights as laid down in the treaty. This case crucially shed light on the gulf between the diverging supranational and domestic images of rights and international commitments. ECtHR, *Sporrong and Lönnroth v. Sweden* (1982). Significantly, Sweden had not formally recognised the ECtHR's jurisdiction before 1966. Nergelius 1996: 610; Swedish Government Bill Prop. 1951:165; Swedish Government Bill Prop. 1966:33.

traditionally weak position of rights in Sweden has been connected to a Nordic legal culture with a restrained emphasis on judicial review, courts and lawyers.[11]

The role of rights and courts is, however, more important today than it was in the twentieth century. The requirements of and challenges posed by European harmonisation have led to a decreasing emphasis on *travaux préparatoires* and an increasing emphasis on courts,[12] particularly the Supreme Court.[13] Legal mobilisation and strategic litigation have emerged in the light of rights becoming more pivotal and courts becoming a plausible avenue for furthering one's interests.[14] A number of anti-discrimination centres and bureaus have been set up in recent decades in order to legally mobilise around rights, rights violations and remedies.[15]

3.2 Sterilisation and Castration: Regulation and Resistance

Against the background of an evolving domestic legal culture which has gone from regarding rights as abstract rhetorical tools to considering them as binding legal instruments, three important sterilisation and castration regulatory frameworks have entered and exited the Swedish legal system over the last century. They provided legal support for interventions controlled by the

[11] National discussions have suggested many factors which may contribute to the weak position of rights, such as the Swedish social democracy and its welfare state project; the strong position of the Parliament; the political use of early twentieth-century Nordic legal realism/ positivism with its rejection of rights; the national culture of consensus. See Modéer 2003: 163–164; Nergelius 1996: 94, 611–613. The notion that state power should be democratically centralised in Parliament held strong in twentieth-century Sweden. Consequently, the role of courts and lawyers was downplayed to technicians, whose ultimate aim was to interpret the law in a manner aligning with the legislator's intention. Modéer 2003. Moreover, only concrete individual cases can be tried constitutionally by the judiciary, preventing it from abstract norm control. The concept of judicial review was legislatively introduced as a measure to strengthen the rule of law – however, not to be used on a regular basis – and customarily has a limited role in Sweden. See Swedish Government Bill Prop. 1978/79:195; Justitiedepartementet [The Swedish Ministry of Justice] 1978; Konstitutionsutskottet [The Swedish Parliamentary Constitutional Committee] KU 1978/79:39: 13; Nergelius 1996: 64–74.

[12] Modéer 2003: 151.

[13] Examples of important rights interpretation are Högsta Domstolen [The Swedish Supreme Court], NJA 2012, s. 400 (2012); NJA 2013, s. 350 (2013); NJA 2012, s. 211 (2012); and NJA 2013, s. 746 (2013). See Åhman 2016: 462–463. Accusations of judicial activism levied against the Supreme Court have intensified national debates about the appropriate role of courts in the division of powers. See Wersäll 2014; Derlén & Lindholm 2016.

[14] Like the other Nordic countries, Sweden lacks a Constitutional Court but it has other forms of norm control than judicial review. Swedish legal norm control de-emphasises courts in favour of early preview of legislation. The Swedish Council on Legislation (*Lagrådet*), for example, legally scrutinises draft bills together with other instances. See Regeringsformen [Government Act] (1974:152), Chapter 8, Sections 20–22. See also Swedish Government Bill Prop. 2009/10:80: 141–144. Swedish law has also traditionally positioned vital control functions in non- or semi-judicial, administrative institutions, such as the system of ombudsmen. In the Swedish system, the ombudsmen are institutionalised, free-of-charge mechanisms for issuing recommendations, mainly based on individual complaints.

[15] Rogalska-Hedlund, 19 September 2016.

authorities, from the introduction of the first sterilisation law in 1934 to the dissolution of the last legal sterilisation requirement in 2013. The discourses relating to sterilisation and castration laws during the twentieth century have changed from state regulatory control of reproduction and sexuality towards an emphasis on individual autonomy.

3.2.1 Reproduction and Sexuality as the Prerogative of the State

Sterilisation and castration practices were built on a wide acceptance of administrative expertise and state prerogative to control the population's reproduction and sexuality. The eugenic and sociopolitical sterilisation laws were seen as the regulatory approval – and limitation – of a new technique to control the reproduction of marginalised groups.[16] The legal regulation of castration was introduced as a humanitarian as well as a criminological measure to control the 'sexually deviant'.[17] Additionally, the infertility requirement for the amendment of legally registered gender was regarded as a way to 'neutralise' people who challenged the legal, gendered system.[18]

3.2.1.1 Sterilisations of the 'Unfit'

Like its contemporary counterparts in other countries, the Swedish eugenics movements at the beginning of the twentieth century were often outspokenly racist, with a fascination for white, Nordic heritage and its 'superiority'.[19] The movements inspired political debates on the introduction of a sterilisation law.[20] Legislation on sterilisation was seen as a way of regulating and establishing the legality of the interventions, similar to the earlier-mentioned US 1927 Case of *Buck v. Bell*.[21] A 1929 Swedish state report on sterilisation reflected the popular thoughts on the preservation of the Nordic race and fear of degeneration.[22] The report focused on the sterilisation of the feebleminded,[23] insane and epileptic. It was in favour of voluntary sterilisation motivated by eugenics but did not recommend sterilisation on social grounds.[24] The report saw

16 See, for example, Socialdepartementet [The Swedish Ministry of Health and Social Affairs] 1929; 1936; Justitiedepartementet [The Swedish Ministry of Justice] 1933.

17 See, for example, Justitiedepartementet [The Swedish Ministry of Justice] 1941a; 1941b; 1941c.

18 See, for example, Justitiedepartementet [The Swedish Ministry of Justice] 1968.

19 An important figure constructing the Nordic race as superior was Swedish eugenicist Herman Lundborg. See Hagerman 2015.

20 The first bill proposing legal regulation of sterilisation of 1922 had multi-party support in Swedish Parliament. Riksdagen [The Swedish Parliament] 1922. See Broberg & Tydén 2005: 101.

21 See *Prologue*.

22 That is, concerns were present about the decreasing 'quality' of the Swedish population material. Socialdepartementet [The Swedish Ministry of Health and Social Affairs] 1929.

23 Feeblemindedness was a term used to describe 'people, in whom hereditary mental defects warrant social surveillance and who cannot get by without similar help'. Socialdepartementet [The Swedish Ministry of Health and Social Affairs] 1929: 26. See Barow 2009.

24 The report was written by medico-legal experts. Socialdepartementet [The Swedish Ministry of Health and Social Affairs] 1929.

sterilisation as a progressive way to grant the weak layers of society access to marriage and a 'more harmonic' life,[25] but it was nevertheless cautiously phrased as non-consensual sterilisation would be a violation of the physical integrity protected in the Swedish Criminal Code.[26] This wariness made experts, most notably those of the medical profession, fiercely criticise the report as overly restrictive.[27] A new sterilisation report and bill were hence commissioned and presented before Parliament in 1934,[28] promoting sterilisation of a more clearly defined group, namely the people considered mentally immature and deprived of legal capacity.[29] These people could not legally consent, so the *travaux préparatoires* reasoned that the sterilisations would fall 'between' voluntary and forced interventions.[30]

The first sterilisation law was enacted in 1934 with minimal parliamentary opposition.[31] The 1934 Sterilisation Act disregarded the individual will of the applicants in broad strokes. It allowed for sterilisation without the consent of the legally incapable if the authorities had reason to believe that the person at hand was 'unable to care for their children' or that they would 'hereditarily transmit feeblemindedness or insanity'.[32] Applications, not necessarily by the patients themselves,[33] were decided by the Swedish Royal Board of Medicine.[34] In the case of feeblemindedness, nevertheless, the consensus of two doctors with written consent by the applicant or their guardian was enough.[35] The 1934 Act was applied relatively narrowly, for example, not on medical indication.[36]

[25] Socialdepartementet [The Swedish Ministry of Health and Social Affairs] 1929: 23. At the time, there were marriage prohibitions for some individuals concerned (such as people with epilepsy). Tydén 2002: 53.

[26] Socialdepartementet [The Swedish Ministry of Health and Social Affairs] 1929: 38–39.

[27] Runcis 1998: 71–75.

[28] The report was authored by the criminal law professor Ragnar Bergendal. Justitiedepartementet [The Swedish Ministry of Justice] 1933; Swedish Government Bill Prop. 1934:103.

[29] Justitiedepartementet [The Swedish Ministry of Justice] 1933; Swedish Government Bill Prop. 1934:103. See also Regeringskansliet [The Government Offices of Sweden] 2014: 115.

[30] Justitiedepartementet [The Swedish Ministry of Justice] 1933: 16; Swedish Government Bill Prop. 1934:103. Simultaneously, two additional investigations were initiated to look further into broadening sterilisation and castration legislation. Runcis 1998: 83–89.

[31] Lag om sterilisering av vissa sinnessjuka, sinnesslöa eller andra som lida av rubbad själsverksamhet [Act on Sterilisation of Certain People who are Insane, Feebleminded or Suffering from Other Mental Disorders] (1934:171). See Broberg & Tydén 2005: 103–104.

[32] Lag om sterilisering av vissa sinnessjuka, sinnesslöa eller andra som lida av rubbad själsverksamhet [Act on Sterilisation of Certain People who are Insane, Feebleminded or Suffering from Other Mental Disorders] (1934:171), Section 1.

[33] The applications could be made by among others doctors or social authorities. Runcis 1998: 178.

[34] The decision was made after hearing the possible spouse, legal guardians, and doctors and directors of institutions if the person was institutionalised. Lag om sterilisering av vissa sinnessjuka, sinnesslöa eller andra som lida av rubbad själsverksamhet [Act on Sterilisation of Certain People who are Insane, Feebleminded or Suffering from Other Mental Disorders] (1934:171), Section 2.

[35] Ibid, Section 3. [36] Ibid, Section 1.

The main criticism of the 1934 Sterilisation Act at the time concerned the newness of the surgical intervention, its uncertain consequences and a concern in the medical community that legislative regulation would limit doctors from sterilising when they found it necessary. Another issue raised was that sterilisation and its possible abuse could be a slippery slope leading to a normalisation of inhuman treatment of the groups concerned.[37] Even if not dominant, a certain notion of humanity and its inherent rights was present in the early political debates on involuntary sterilisation.

While the 1934 Act narrowly focused on people without legal capacity, a state report of 1936 suggested expanding the target group.[38] The report, the subsequent Government Bill[39] and the parliamentary and public debates increasingly framed sterilisation as a socio-economic question rather than a strictly eugenic one,[40] crucial for the well-being of the whole nation, building up to an amendment in 1941.[41]

The broader 1941 Sterilisation Act covered both voluntary and involuntary sterilisation. Its broadened scope included people with 'mental dysfunction' and 'asocial lifestyle'.[42] The view of who was 'asocial' or 'apparently unsuitable to care for children'[43] in the *travaux préparatoires* and the implementation of the openly formulated legislation was influenced by obviously gendered social and moral norms. For women, this meant that the authorities generally focused on their role in the family, particularly as mothers, but also on their sexual behaviour. For men, the general focus was on sobriety and their ability to act as breadwinners.[44] The 1941 Act also regulated sterilisation on a medical, gender-specific indication, namely the consensual sterilisation of ill, disabled or weak women to prevent (further) childbearing if a serious danger for the woman's life or health was present.[45]

The 1934 and 1941 sterilisation laws followed from a broader dominant political discourse which saw population control as a prerogative of public authorities, motivated by the public interests of health, social welfare and hygiene of the population material.[46] Sterilisation was widely believed to be a solution to a number of social problems, such as alcoholism, poverty and other forms of marginalisation. Moreover, the interventions came into force in a society

[37] Following the increased secularisation of Swedish public debate, the religious arguments against sterilisation were undermined. Moreover, Professor of forensic medicine Gunnar Hedrén and Carl Lindhagen of the Socialist Party were among the opponents of the law. See Hedrén 1922; Broberg & Tydén 2005: 103–104.

[38] The report was authored by statistician and politician Nils Wohlin. Socialdepartementet [The Swedish Ministry of Health and Social Affairs] 1936.

[39] Swedish Government Bill Prop. 1941:13.

[40] An important contribution to the debate was Myrdal & Myrdal 1934.

[41] Broberg & Tydén 2005: 105–106.

[42] Lag om sterilisering [Sterilisation Act] (1941:282), Section 1.

[43] Ibid, Section 1(2).

[44] Tydén 2002: 465; Runcis 1998.

[45] Lag om sterilisering [Sterilisation Act] (1941:282), Section 1(3).

[46] See Socialdepartementet [The Swedish Ministry of Health and Social Affairs] 1929; 1936.

where institutionalisation was a common way to treat a wide range of perceived problems.[47] The final decision on whether to undergo sterilisation or not was not made by the applicant. For the legally incapable, consent was not necessary.[48] Furthermore, the legally capable, who on paper had to consent, could in practice often be persuaded or pressured into sterilisation by the authorities through rendering other rights conditional on sterilisation – such as custody of children,[49] access to abortion,[50] social support,[51] marriage[52] and discharge from hospital or institution.[53] The pressure brought to bear on the individual could be immense.

The implementation of the 1934 and 1941 sterilisation laws registered interventions on 62,888 people between 1935 and 1975.[54] This number covers both voluntary and involuntary interventions. It is not possible to determine the number of involuntary sterilisations with certainty, as many applications were formally signed by the applicants themselves.[55] The effect of the at-times coercive application of the sterilisation laws was amplified by the limited possibilities for appeal.[56] Physical force may not have been allowed, but the authority guidelines and the implementation of the laws clearly disregarded the will of the applicants by using the interventions as preconditions to access other rights or services.[57]

Even though tubal ligation is a more invasive intervention than vasoligation, according to the registries, the vast majority – 93 per cent – of the sterilisations were carried out on women.[58] The sterilisations especially affected poor women

[47] See, for example, Engwall 2000.

[48] Consent was not necessary when it came to the legally incapable, but according to the 1941 Sterilisation Act, the authorities could not approve of such interventions unless the legal guardians were given an opportunity to express their opinions. Lag om sterilisering [Sterilisation Act] (1941:282), Section 3.

[49] On the coercive use of deprivation of custody of children, see Runcis 2007.

[50] Lag om sterilisering [Sterilisation Act] (1941:282), Section 6; Justitiedepartementet [The Swedish Ministry of Justice] 1935: 120–121; Lag om avbrytande av havandeskap [Act on Termination of Pregnancy] (1938:318).

[51] Runcis 1998.

[52] Sterilisation as a condition for marriage was not regulated in a law, but in the *travaux préparatoires* of the 1945 amendment of the marriage law. Tydén 2002: 233.

[53] Ibid.

[54] Socialdepartementet [The Swedish Ministry of Health and Social Affairs] 1999: 119.

[55] See Eivergård & Jönsson 2000.

[56] According to the 1934 law, the only possibility to appeal the decision was to the King within 20 days, and in the 1941 law, the possibility to appeal was restricted to decisions where the authorities did not allow for sterilisation. Lag om sterilisering av vissa sinnessjuka, sinnesslöa eller andra som lida av rubbad själsverksamhet [Act on Sterilisation of Certain People who are Insane, Feebleminded or Suffering from Other Mental Disorders] (1934:171), Section 6; Lag om sterilisering [Sterilisation Act] (1941:282), Section 7. For applicants with positive decisions, escaping sterilisation was often only possible through refusing the surgery or not showing up for it. Tydén 2002: 508.

[57] See Kungliga medicinalstyrelsen [The Swedish Royal Board of Medicine] 1939; 1943; 1947; Zaremba 1999: 32.

[58] On the gendered dimensions of the implementation, see Runcis 1998; Hirdman 2000.

from lower social classes, who were single mothers, had many children and/or abusive or alcoholic male partners.[59] Often more dependent on public social and health welfare services in child-bearing and -rearing, women were particularly targeted because of, and affected in, their reproductive roles.[60] A minority of men were also sterilised. Men who were especially vulnerable were those regarded as 'socially irresponsible' or 'asocial': labels which could be used on a heterogeneous group, ranging from disobedient and restless boys to convicted criminals.[61] Ethnicity also featured in the implementation, since Romani/travelling people[62] were at least discursively targeted as unwanted reproducers – the women of these groups in particular.[63] Finally, the sterilisation laws beset people considered to be disabled or mentally ill and other socially marginalised individuals and groups.[64]

3.2.1.2 Castrations of the Sexually Deviant

The discussion of castration legislation in Sweden was partly triggered by the introduction of sterilisation laws.[65] However, the discourses relating to castration were remarkably different. As such, they targeted the 'sexually deviant' aiming to curb danger and criminality from a criminological and psychiatric perspective, rather than controlling unwanted reproduction from the point of view of eugenics and social reform.[66] The interventions were part of a developing medicalisation of sexual nonconformity. Castration concerned a fluid category of people, particularly men, ranging from (sexual) criminals to homosexual men.[67] The *travaux préparatoires* referred to recent international research on castration of male sexual criminals (primarily perpetrators of child sexual abuse) and people labelled as 'constitutionally homosexual',[68] presenting

[59] See Runcis 1998.

[60] This can be perceived in, e.g., the connection between abortion and sterilisation legislation. Tydén 2002: 61–72; Runcis 1998. As crucially observed by Björkman, fatherhood had a limited role in the evaluation of superiority or inferiority in Swedish eugenic circles, while motherhood was crucial. Björkman 2011.

[61] See Tydén 2002; Björkman 2011: 111–112.

[62] This group was often referred to as 'tattare', a group different from modern understandings of Romani people in Sweden. Regeringskansliet [The Government Offices of Sweden] 2014: 100.

[63] Ibid: 97–138; De Los Reyes 2012; 2013. This becomes particularly apparent from the language in authority reporting, even though numerical overrepresentation of Romani is not a settled matter. See Runcis 2016.

[64] Bukowska-Jacobsson et al 2000.

[65] See Broberg & Tydén 2005.

[66] The positive aspects of castration were pointed out by multiple actors in the criminological and medical professions. See Broberg & Tydén 2005: 132–133.

[67] The establishment of castration as a control of the sexually deviant homosexual can be seen as a monumentally Foucauldian example of a shift from criminalisation to medicalisation. Even though a person engaging in same-sex sexual acts with adults was no longer subject to criminalisation after 1944, the person was pathologised and risked institutionalisation and castration. Homosexuality was registered as a mental disorder in Sweden until 1979. See Foucault 1990; Rydström 2000; 2007a.

[68] At the time, a difference was made between the 'constitutionally homosexual' and the 'pseudo-homosexual' in medico-social sciences. See Rydström 2003; Nilsson 2001; Rydström, 14 September 2016.

castration as a new, more humane way of controlling sexual danger and deviance in comparison to imprisonment or indefinite institutionalisation.[69]

Castration became legislatively regulated in Sweden in 1944.[70] The intervention was allowed upon two indications. The first was criminological, justifying castration of a person 'on account of his sexual drive reasonably presumed to commit a crime which inflicts serious danger or harm on another'.[71] The second was described as a humanitarian indication, referring to the castration of a person whose sexual drive caused 'severe mental suffering or other serious inconvenience' 'because of the abnormal orientation or strength thereof'.[72] The legally capable formally had to consent to the intervention and the legally incapable could be castrated without their consent.[73] A recommended minimum age of 23 years was also included in the legislation, a stipulation lacking in the sterilisation legislation.[74] Even though the possibility of castrating a person without their consent was legislatively expressed as exceptional, the *travaux préparatoires* highlighted persuasion tactics and the option to render discharge from institutionalisation conditional on castration.[75] Like sterilisation, the final decision about castration was made either by the state's Royal Board of Medicine[76] or two doctors,[77] not the applicant.

Unlike the sterilisation laws, the 1944 Castration Act was rarely used. The law was most frequently used at its introduction, falling rapidly in application afterwards.[78] While the law officially remained in force until 2013, the implementation had changed at the end of the 1960s when the law became used as a legal basis for gender-affirming genital surgery.[79] According to Jens Rydström, 463 people (almost exclusively men) were castrated, on criminological or

[69] Justitiedepartementet [The Swedish Ministry of Justice] 1941b: 23–24; Swedish Government Bill Prop. 1944:14. See also Justitiedepartementet [The Swedish Ministry of Justice] 1941a; 1941c.

[70] Lag om kastrering [Castration Act] (1944:133). See also Rydström 2007b.

[71] Lag om kastrering [Castration Act] (1944:133), Section 1(1). [72] Ibid, Section 1(2).

[73] Ibid, Section 2. However, along similar lines to as was the case for sterilisation, the legal guardians of the legally incapable had to be given the opportunity to provide a statement (Section 4).

[74] Lag om kastrering [Castration Act] (1944:133), Section 3.

[75] Justitiedepartementet [The Swedish Ministry of Justice] 1941b.

[76] The Board acted upon criminal indication. Lag om kastrering [Castration Act] (1944:133), Section 4(1).

[77] The two doctors could act upon humanitarian indication. Lag om kastrering [Castration Act] (1944:133), Section 4(2).

[78] This information is based on the annual reports on approved applications by the Swedish Royal Board of Medicine. The instance for appeals was changed from the King to the administrative courts in the 1970s, effectively improving the applicant's access to justice. Lag om kastrering [Castration Act] (1944:133), Section 7; Swedish Government Bill Prop. 1971:30: 61

[79] This is visible in authority statistics, where the registered gender is no longer clearly expressed since 1967. 1969 is the first year when the report explicitly states that all castrated people were 'transsexual'. Kungliga medicinalstyrelsen [The Swedish Royal Board of Medicine] 1967: 123; 1969: 119.

humanitarian grounds, during the period 1944–1979.[80] In comparison to the sterilisation laws, a lack of systematic research exists concerning the implementation of the 1944 Castration Act.

3.2.1.3 Compulsory Sterilisation to Eliminate Threats to Family Relations

The compulsory sterilisation of people who wished to amend their legally registered gender was introduced in the 1970s in Sweden.[81] With traditional views on gender roles and sexual relations becoming more openly questioned during the sexual revolution of the 1960s, the first Swedish trans club *Transvestia* was established in 1962 and the first Swedish trans association *FPES* (Full Personality Expression Sweden) in 1966.[82] Later, in 1980, *Club Benjamin* was founded, with transsexual people as the main target group,[83] within the scope of what is today referred to as the Swedish Federation for Lesbian, Gay, Bi, Trans, Queer and Intersex (LGBTQI) Rights RFSL.[84] With greater visibility, the concerns of trans people began to appear on the political agenda. In 1966, a state investigation was launched to look into the situation of 'the intersexual', a term used to refer to intersex as well as trans (mainly transsexual) people. The investigation results published in 1968 led to legislation allowing for conditional legal gender recognition.[85]

As the first gender recognition law in the world, the 1972 Swedish Gender Recognition Act preconditioned change of legally registered gender on the applicant being sterilised or otherwise infertile, a Swedish citizen, over 18 years and unmarried.[86] Moreover, the applicant had to have identified with 'the other gender' from their youth, have acted accordingly 'for a considerable time', and was expected to also act gender-conformingly in the future.[87] When established, the law was considered cutting-edge, later inspiring the introduction of similar regulation in other countries, among others Germany, the Netherlands and Finland. Remarkably, apart from infertility, no other medical requirements, such as hormonal treatment or surgery, were made.[88]

[80] Rydström 2003: 175. 152 of the castrations were carried out on criminological grounds, 137 on humanitarian grounds and 174 on a combination of the two. No centralised statistics exist regarding the frequency of the implementation. Socialdepartementet [The Swedish Ministry of Health and Social Affairs] 1999: 23.

[81] In Sweden, the legal gender is registered in the state population register, and visible in the passport and the personal identity number.

[82] Siverskog 2016: 68. [83] Rydström 2007a: 171.

[84] The original name of RFSL was *Riksförbundet för sexuellt likaberättigande*, which can be translated as the 'Federation for Sexual Equality'.

[85] See Justitiedepartementet [The Swedish Ministry of Justice] 1968; Swedish Government Bill Prop. 1972:6.

[86] Lag om fastställande av könstillhörighet i vissa fall [Act on Legal Gender Recognition under Certain Circumstances] (1972:119), Sections 1, 3.

[87] Ibid, Section 1.

[88] The Swedish infertility requirement was however extensively interpreted as an absolute prohibition on preserving gametes for later fertility treatment. JK, Decision No. 4243-13-40 et al (2014); RFSL 2015.

The *travaux préparatoires* of the 1972 law highlighted the socio-legal gender binary and the difficulties it posed for the daily lives of non-conforming individuals.[89] Instead of suggesting a de-gendering legislative accommodation in relation to the non-conforming subject, the state authorities preferred an adjustment of the non-conforming subject to the existing gender order.[90] The argumentation behind the infertility requirement was three-pronged, motivated by: (i) a fear of administrative gender disorganisation, (ii) prevailing heteronormativity and (iii) an exclusive reliance on medico-legal expertise.

Regarding the first point, the infertility requirement was considered necessary to 'completely eliminate the risk of confusion in family relations'[91] and to avoid that 'one who officially has the male gender becomes a mother and one who officially has the female gender becomes a father'.[92] The preparatory state report admitted that individual interests spoke against compulsory infertility, but that these were outweighed by the best interest of the child coupled with the public order in the structure of family relations.[93] The same report did however not explain further how or why these interests would be threatened by reproduction crossing traditional gender boundaries.[94] Rather than going into detail, the *travaux préparatoires* settled for an abstract notion of 'chaos' looming on the horizon. Implicitly assuming the rightness of the heterosexual nuclear family, the *travaux préparatoires* found transparents to fall too far outside the parental (hetero)norm, leading to disapproval.[95]

Secondly, in a country only allowing marriages between two people registered with different genders, high requirements for change of legally registered gender were considered necessary. The *travaux préparatoires* highlighted the need to prevent 'disloyal' and 'homosexual' people from changing legal gender.[96] Surprisingly, this logic was upheld for a long time: While civil partnership for same-sex couples was legally introduced in the mid-1990s,[97] and marriage in 2009,[98] the precondition for applicants to be unmarried was maintained until 2012.[99]

Thirdly, the dominant perspective in the *travaux préparatoires* was that of the state and the (psychiatric) expert, with the voices of trans people notably absent.[100] The compulsory, potentially coercive, nature of sterilisations was not taken into consideration, as amended legal gender and genital surgery were seen as intrinsically connected and the trans subject was assumed to want both. Regarding trans people's wishes to become parents, a brief statement

[89] Justitiedepartementet [The Swedish Ministry of Justice] 1968: 33–34.
[90] Ibid; Swedish Government Bill Prop. 1972:6. See Alm 2006.
[91] Swedish Government Bill Prop. 1972:6: 50. [92] Ibid: 49.
[93] Justitiedepartementet [The Swedish Ministry of Justice] 1968: 52.
[94] See Justitiedepartementet [The Swedish Ministry of Justice] 1968. [95] See Edenheim 2005.
[96] See Justitiedepartementet [The Swedish Ministry of Justice] 1968: 45; Edenheim 2005: 141.
[97] Lag om registrerat partnerskap [Act on Civil Partnership] (1994:1117).
[98] Through the amendment SFS 2009:253. [99] See Swedish Government Bill Prop. 2011/12:142.
[100] Justitiedepartementet [The Swedish Ministry of Justice] 1968; Swedish Government Bill Prop. 1972:6.

acknowledged that cases of transsexual people giving birth occurred, but that such pregnancies had 'not primarily been a consequence of the will to fulfil original gender roles in sexual life, but rather an involuntary sexual contact under the influence of alcohol or other momentary circumstances'.[101] With these words, trans people's reproductive concerns were disqualified.

Between 1972 and 2013, the period that the law was in force, around 1,000 people amended their legally registered gender according to the Swedish Gender Recognition Act requiring infertility.[102] No official statistics exist concerning how many of these people underwent sterilisation or castration surgery and how many of them were already infertile for other reasons.[103] Much like the earlier sterilisation and castration laws, the 1972 Gender Recognition Act was an expression of a state prerogative discourse, as infertility was a condition for legal recognition of gender identity which could only be granted by the state.[104]

3.2.2 The Power of Ideas: Equal Citizenship, Individual Rights and Civil Society

Sweden long presented a Janus-face, where rights were acclaimed in the international arena but given less importance in the domestic legal system. Yet, in the case of involuntary sterilisations and castrations, notions of rights and individual autonomy became increasingly important in creating sociocultural and legal scepticism towards these practices. Social engagement with individual control of reproduction has challenged state control over time. The 1970s marked the beginning of legal change, being the decade when Sweden ratified central human rights conventions,[105] and introduced a new Government Act[106] and a new Liability Act.[107] This shift was motivated by a burgeoning rights master frame, growing rights awareness and increased pressure from civil society, eventually affecting (some) victims of involuntary sterilisation and castration.

3.2.2.1 Free Sterilisation: The Individual Right to Fertility Control

Only a couple of years after the introduction of the 1972 Swedish Gender Recognition Act, the 1941 Sterilisation Act was abolished through the introduction of the 1975 Sterilisation Act.[108] The sterilisation laws which had been adopted with minimal opposition in the 1930s and 1940s began to attract opponents over decades of implementation. Four essential, high-profile points of critique, engaging with the rule of law and rights to individual autonomy and equality, can be recounted here. Firstly, in 1947, the Parliamentary

[101] Justitiedepartementet [Swedish The Swedish Ministry of Justice] 1968: 52.
[102] Socialdepartementet [The Swedish Ministry of Health and Social Affairs] 2017a: 53.
[103] See Socialdepartementet [The Swedish Ministry of Health and Social Affairs] 2017b: 19.
[104] See Burman & RFSL 2013.
[105] CERD, ICCPR and ICESCR were ratified in 1971.
[106] Regeringsformen [Government Act] (1974:152).
[107] Skadeståndslag [Liability Act] (1972:207).
[108] Steriliseringslag [Sterilisation Act] (1975:580).

Ombudsmen (JO) criticised the arbitrariness and opaqueness of the implementation of the law, applied outside its letter, as a condition to be discharged from institutionalisation.[109] Secondly, in the mid-1950s, a complaint was raised in Parliament that the legislation was too difficult to access as a voluntary birth control method for women.[110] Thirdly, in the 1960s, the legislation was decried in Parliament for discriminatingly targeting vulnerable women.[111] Finally, in the 1960s and 1970s, medical doctor Karl Grunewald condemned the arbitrary and discriminatory implementation of the sterilisation laws, particularly on young girls.[112] Moreover, following highly critical mass media reporting on the state care of institutionalised people, as well as growing civil society activism regarding people with disabilities, the 1950s and 1960s came to embrace an approach which was increasingly reproving of institutionalisation.[113]

This criticism was echoed in a 1974 review of the sterilisation law. Marking a clear discursive break, the investigation stated that the 1941 Sterilisation Act was 'based on different values and conditions than the ones governing today's society'.[114] The investigation stressed that this statement was particularly true for 'eugenic and social indications',[115] emphasising that a guiding principle for the law should be the right for every person to decide over their own body.[116] Sterilisation should therefore only be permitted with the informed consent of the individual.[117] According to the following 1975 Sterilisation Act, which is still in force at the time of writing, only individual interests are accepted as grounds for sterilisation,[118] and an application can only be initiated by adult applicants themselves.[119] With the 1975 Act, the decision-making power was thus taken out of the hands of the authorities and put into the individual's. When the new legislation was introduced, an explosion of the number of people undergoing sterilisation as a form of voluntary contraception occurred,[120] which should be seen in the light of the failure of the former sterilisation legislation to be accessible as such, particularly for men.[121] Tubal ligation being a more invasive

109 Riksdagens ombudsmän [The Swedish Parliamentary Ombudsmen] 1947: 189–214.

110 Runcis 1998: 242–243.

111 Ibid: 246–251.

112 Grunewald 1962, 1970a, 1970b; Andrén, 21 September 2016.

113 This can be perceived in the public outrage in the 1950s and 1960s with regard to the treatment of the patients at Vipeholm Mental Hospital. Björkman 2011: 190. The same decades also marked the rise of civil society organisation for people with disabilities, such as FUB. See Andersson 2002.

114 Justitiedepartementet [The Swedish Ministry of Justice] 1974: 17.

115 Ibid.

116 Steriliseringslag [Sterilisation Act] (1975:580), Section 5; and Justitiedepartementet [The Swedish Ministry of Justice] 1974: 9.

117 Justitiedepartementet [The Swedish Ministry of Justice] 1974; Swedish Government Bill Prop. 1975:18.

118 Justitiedepartementet [The Swedish Ministry of Justice] 1974: 9.

119 Steriliseringslag [Sterilisation Act] (1975:580), Sections 2–3; Justitiedepartementet [The Swedish Ministry of Justice] 1974: 9.

120 According to the Swedish Board of Health and Welfare, the numbers doubled for women and increased by a factor of four for men. Jacobsson, 18 April 2017.

121 Persson, 20 September 2016.

intervention than vasectomy, the 1975 Act contributed to promoting the latter as a permanent birth control method.

A rise of individual rights, reproductive rights and gender equality was behind the introduction of the 1975 Sterilisation Act. The almost simultaneous 1974 adoption of the new Government Act and the 1971 ratification of central human rights instruments (CERD, ICCPR and ICESCR), introducing the first catalogue of rights, is another manifestation of increasing recognition of individual rights and personal autonomy.[122] Even though constitutional or human rights were not directly referred to in the state reports introducing new legislation on sterilisation, recent rights developments were reflected in a new discourse which underlined individual rights rather than state prerogative. As such, the 1970s symbolised a new era in the relationship between the individual and public authorities.

Reproductive autonomy, sexual reform and women's organisations played a role in changing the relationship between the state and the individual.[123] In the first half of the twentieth century, the interventions were seen as a means of permanent contraception, revolutionary for family planning – for women in particular.[124] Towards the second half of the century, women's political engagement with the sterilisation laws nevertheless developed into a criticism of men's administration and control of the laws.[125] The concept of autonomy gained prominence as feminist and women's movements advanced the idea that control over women's sexuality should only be conditioned on their own free will.[126] During the 1960s and 1970s, like many other parts of Europe and North America, Swedish society liberalised its views on sexuality,[127] resulting in legislative reforms concerning topics such as birth control pills,[128] abortion[129] and free sterilisation.[130] Significantly, the sexual revolution took place at the same time as the wider struggle for women's liberation, with Swedish women's movements successfully pushing through social and welfare reforms.[131]

122 Regeringsformen [Government Act] (1974:152).

123 An earlier prohibition on spreading information about contraception was abolished in 1938, a move which allowed a blend of different sections of Swedish society – workers, anarchists, eugenicists, women's movements – to organise around sexual liberalisation, in which sterilisation played a role. A leading figure in this debate was the Swedish-Norwegian feminist sex educator and journalist Elise Ottesen-Jensen (1886–1973), who founded RFSU, the Swedish Association for Sexuality Education, in 1933. See Lennerhed 2002; 2000.

124 The broader eugenics movement provided a main forum for (feminist and non-feminist) women's political organisation in the twentieth century, meaning increased access to birth control and state-financed care reforms. See Tydén 2002: 541–544.

125 See Broberg & Tydén 2005: 124; Runcis 1998: 242–243.

126 See Broberg & Tydén 2005: 124.

127 On this development, see for example Herzog 2011.

128 This happened in 1964, because of pressure exerted by women's movements and the media. See Dagens Nyheter 2010.

129 See Abortlag [Abortion Act] (1974:595).

130 Steriliseringslag [Sterilisation Act] (1975:580). The Swedish sexual revolution was pursued less through judicial litigation than in for example the US. See Supreme Court of the United States, *Griswold v. Connecticut* (1965); *Roe v. Wade* (1973). See Siegel 2012; Case 2009.

131 One important reform was Lag om jämställdhet mellan män och kvinnor i arbetslivet [Act on Equality between Men and Women in Working Life] (1979:1118); Swedish Government Bill Prop. 1978/79:175; Arbetsmarknadsdepartementet [The Swedish Ministry of Employment] 1978.

Along with social movements for gender-equal citizenship and reproductive autonomy, a developing concept of individualism and individual rights – interconnected with notions of modernity – played an important role in the rhetorical shift as regards sterilisation. This is reflected in the *travaux préparatoires* of the 1975 Sterilisation Act,[132] in which reproductive control and bodily integrity were formulated as individual interests which public interests necessarily yielded to in a modern society.[133] Modern society was portrayed as one where reproduction was governed by the individual, while a state where public interests governed reproductive interventions was considered history. The changing conceptualisation of sterilisation was however sociopolitical rather than legal,[134] and the focus on individual autonomy was restricted to questioning state interests in sterilisation. As such, the new focus on individual rights did not extend to problematising the Gender Recognition Act or the Castration Act. The much later abolishment of these laws exemplifies the political and sociocultural situatedness of the legal balancing of individual and public interests in discussions on sexual and reproductive interventions.

3.2.2.2 Castration: Forgotten and/or Abandoned?

In comparison to the 1941 Sterilisation Act, the 1944 Castration Act did not spark major social opposition during its implementation. Even if individuals raised resistance to the latter,[135] no organised social movements for its abolition materialised. After a series of legislative delays, the Act was repealed through an amendment which came into force in 2013.[136] The law had presumably been long forgotten by the general public, but not abandoned by the legal system, and was repeatedly amended between the 1960s and the 2000s.[137] During this time, rights argumentation was generally absent from the legal and political discussions relating to castration. The main reasons for why the Castration Act was not abolished earlier were legislative delays and limited implementation, along with a lack of activism and political pressure to abolish it.

The abolition of the Castration Act was sporadically discussed between the 1980s and the 2010s.[138] Yet, not until the sterilisations of trans people became

[132] See Justitiedepartementet [The Swedish Ministry of Justice] 1974; Swedish Government Bill Prop. 1975:18.

[133] Ibid.

[134] This is clear from the lack of specific references to rights or treaties in the *travaux préparatoires*.

[135] Individual accounts of resistance are sporadically found. See Rydström 2003: 289–291.

[136] Amendment SFS 2012:455.

[137] It was amended fourteen times between 1964 and 2012. The amendments concerned procedural regulations, material specifications of who could be castrated, confidentiality and changes in connection to other acts.

[138] In 1989, the Swedish National Board of Health and Welfare tabled the topic, perceiving the legislation to be outdated and obsolete. The issue was also raised in a 1993 Government Bill, which moved the legal regulation of genital gender-affirming surgeries from the Castration Act to the Gender Recognition Act. The Bill nevertheless concluded that the legal implications would have to be more thoroughly investigated. In 1996, a Government Bill was prepared

a more pressing political concern did castration legislation begin to be thoroughly questioned. Its abolition was advocated for on the basis of human rights, finally leading to the abrogation of the law.[139] More specifically, in the 2012 Government Bill to abolish the law, surgical castration, particularly the possibility to castrate people against their will, was questioned in the light of the prohibition against forced physical intervention in the Swedish Government Act.[140] In further pondering the justification and proportionality of the law,[141] the Government considered that the Castration Act did not live up to the individual rights requirements imposed by modern society.[142]

Note the complete lack of organised opposition to the law.[143] Possible reasons for this silence are stigmatisation; the weak social position of the victims at the time, being sexual offenders and homosexual men; the law's relatively infrequent application and the fact that organised homosexual men wanted to distance themselves from child molesters and other sex offenders.[144] In the implementation of the Castration Act, the two categories were closely intertwined. Bosse Lindquist, who was the first person to interview victims of involuntary sterilisation for mass media,[145] indicated the stigma surrounding castration, still persisting in the 1990s:

> [The Castration Act] was something one did not talk about [...] but it was considered more shameful than the sterilisation legislation. And there was some kind of stigma of violence, and well, criminality – which was absent in [the sterilisations].[146]

Lindquist's statement symbolises the ambiguous victim status of the involuntarily castrated, connected to criminal policy rather than eugenics. This status has affected the outset of mobilisation for, and access to, justice and remedies for the victims. A similar silence echoes at the supranational level.[147]

The implementation of the 1944 Castration Act and the 1941 Sterilisation Act developed differently, which explains why the former could be abolished

to abolish the Castration Act, but it was never presented before Parliament. In 1999, the similarities between the castration legislation and the sterilisation laws of 1934 and 1941 were highlighted by a national sterilisation investigation, which recommended the abolition of the Castration Act. Yet, this failed to result in any legal action. The Swedish authorities repeated the wish in 2007 – again, without results. Swedish Government Bill Prop. 1992/1993:197: 10; Socialdepartementet [The Swedish Ministry of Health and Social Affairs] 1999: 73, 149–150; Socialdepartementet [The Swedish Ministry of Health and Social Affairs] 2007.

139 Swedish Government Bill Prop. 2011/2012:142.

140 Regeringsformen [Government Act] (1974:152), Chapter 2 Section 6.

141 Ibid, Chapter 2 Sections 20–21.

142 Swedish Government Bill Prop. 2011/2012:142: 64.

143 A telling example is that no information concerning the implementation of the 1944 Castration Act, nor possible mobilisation against it, can be found in the archives of the prominent earlier-mentioned LGBT+ organisation RFSL (founded in 1950). Petersson, 17 September 2016.

144 'These possible reasons were discussed with' Rydström, 14 September 2016.

145 Lindquist 1991.

146 Lindquist, 13 September 2016. Translated from Swedish.

147 As depicted in the previous chapter.

38 years later than the latter. The aims of the Castration Act became regarded as old-fashioned soon after its introduction. Instead of its original purposes, the law started to become used to provide legislative support for voluntary genital surgery during the 1960s and continued to be implemented as such for decades. In comparison, the 1941 Sterilisation Act did not change as radically in implementation and concerned a larger group of people. Moreover, contrary to the Castration Act, movements were pushing for the abolition of the 1941 Sterilisation Act, and for increased individual access to sterilisation as a form of voluntary contraception. While the laws had different longevities, both interventions changed in implementation, moving towards emphasising individual autonomy rather than state prerogative.

3.2.2.3 Involuntary Sterilisation as a Rights Violation

Even though organisations for trans people have been active in Sweden since the 1960s,[148] organised opposition to the infertility requirement is relatively recent.[149] The aforementioned national LGBTQI organisation RFSL officially put the abolition of the infertility requirement on their agenda in 2004, and increased its priority in 2010.[150] The prioritisation was the decision of then-President Ulrika Westerlund, from a wish to broaden RFSL's publicly visible work beyond its campaign for marriage equality.[151] With the new millennium witnessing more organised movements advancing trans rights – supported by international NGOs such as ILGA and TGEU – political organisation and campaigning have added weight and resources to the activism.[152] The domestic Swedish development matches and interconnects with the supranational, where rights for trans people, including the challenge of infertility/castration conditions,[153] have only advanced in more recent years. In Sweden, the activism to abolish the sterilisation requirement was multi-level: before the executive power, the legislator and the judiciary. At all levels, rights were used as advocacy tools.

In 2007, Swedish authorities investigated a possible renewal of the Gender Recognition Act.[154] Little engaged with human rights and relying heavily on

[148] Trans people were included in the RFSL charter in 1983; in the 1990s, they were omitted from it, as no trans people were active in the RFSL any longer; they were reinserted in it in the 2000s. Rydström 2007a: 171–172.

[149] Ulrika Westerlund underlined that activism for the abolition of the sterilisation requirement had started earlier than 2010, albeit in less organised forms. One example of this is an (unsuccessful) application to the Swedish Chancellor of Justice by an individual trans person, without legal representation, as early as in the 1990s. Westerlund, 16 September 2016.

[150] Westerlund, 16 September 2016.

[151] Ibid. Particularly in recent years, the living conditions and rights of trans people have been brought to public awareness and put on the political agenda, leading to reforms in discrimination law, state registration of pathologies, naming laws and amendment of the Gender Recognition Act.

[152] See Westerlund, 16 September 2016.

[153] See, for example, ECtHR, *A.P., Garçon and Nicot v. France* (2017); *Y.Y. v. Turkey* (2015); A/HRC/22/53 (2013).

[154] Socialdepartementet [The Swedish Ministry of Health and Social Affairs] 2007.

medical experts, the report did not recommend the abolishment of the sterilisation requirement.[155] Informed by national trans organisations such as Harry Benjamin and RFSL, the investigation conceptualised the trans existence through a post-operative transsexual narrative, adhering to a binary vision of gender. In my interview with the main investigator, Lars Göran Abelson, he highlighted that the Swedish Gender Recognition Act was in line with many other countries' regulation at the time.[156] Furthermore, taking supranational developments into consideration, the topic was only beginning to become conceptualised as a human rights violation.[157] However, Abelson highlighted that the dominant idea of a 'biological sex' began to be increasingly legally challenged when the report was published in 2007.[158]

Three years later, in 2010, the state response was strikingly different, saliently on account of emerging supranational and transnational developments in the field. Another state investigation was published, recommending the abolition of the requirements of infertility and the unmarried state.[159] Its tone marks a clear break from the 2007 report, which had remained anxious about the familial order: proposing castration instead of sterilisation, assuming that 'most transsexuals want their gonads removed'.[160] The shift towards a more inclusive rights discourse in the 2010 state report should be seen against the backdrop of increased social mobilisation around trans rights and increased attention to the topic in the European human rights arena.[161] The 2010 report directly cited human rights soft law,[162] included several statements from involuntarily sterilised trans people,[163] highlighting that 'it is a fundamental principle that every human being has an absolute right to decide over her body'.[164] Furthermore, at the press conference on the release of the report broadcast on national television, investigator Karin Lindell told the Swedish Government that it should be ashamed that it had practised involuntary sterilisation in the twenty-first century, referring to the country's history.[165]

The subsequent 2011 Government Bill, promoting the removal of the sterilisation requirement, was clearly informed by human rights. It stated that the international development of trans people's rights suggested a likely future scenario in which the ECtHR would find sterilisation requirements contrary to the respect for private life in Article 8 ECHR.[166] While the ECtHR had focused

155 Ibid. 156 Abelson, 20 September 2016. 157 See the second chapter of this book.

158 Abelson, 20 September 2016.

159 Socialstyrelsen [The Swedish National Board of Health and Welfare] 2010.

160 Socialdepartementet [The Swedish Ministry of Health and Social Affairs] 2007: 183.

161 See CommDH/IssuePaper(2009)2.

162 The documents quoted were the 2007 Yogyakarta Principles and the 2009 CoE Commissioner for Human Rights' report, both recommending the abolition of sterilisation preconditions for legal gender recognition. See Socialstyrelsen [The Swedish National Board of Health and Welfare] 2010: 29–30.

163 Socialstyrelsen [The Swedish National Board of Health and Welfare] 2010: 20, 26–27, 30, 32, 54.

164 Ibid: 29. 165 Lindell, 15 September 2016.

166 This later happened in ECtHR, *A.P., Garçon and Nicot v. France* (2017). See Swedish Government Bill Prop. 2011/12:142: 55.

on post-operative transsexual people,[167] and not taken a stance against sterilisation requirements at the time, the Government nevertheless sensed an increasing trans-inclusiveness in supranational rights.[168] A connection was made between developing human rights, trans-inclusiveness, internationalisation and modernity as the Government emphasised its desire to be at the international forefront of ensuring the 'right to physical integrity and rule of law for transsexuals'.[169] However, the abolishment of compulsory sterilisation proposed in the Bill was not immediately approved and met with resistance in Parliament.[170]

This resistance was countered by activism. The aforementioned RFSL President at the time, Westerlund, indicated January 2012 as an intense moment when trans civil society tried to turn the political tides on the infertility requirement, for example, by using an international petition and campaigns on social media.[171] An open letter from Human Rights Watch to the Swedish Prime Minister pointed out how '[t]he Swedish law causes anguish for transgender people who choose not to have the required surgery, involving an invasive medical procedure, for various reasons such as out of a wish to one day become parents'.[172] In my interview with her, Westerlund recalled how RFSL utilised the parliamentary opposition to voice critique of the law:

> January 18, the reason that we chose that day was that there was a debate between the party leaders in the Parliament [...] 8 a.m. in January, it was very dark then and freezing cold – but there were maybe 400 people [...] and that is relatively many people for a manifestation. And we had a wide range of speakers, different parties [...] and later the same day, when there was the debate – this came up, of course, both the Green Party and the Left Party brought it up, because it was a great opportunity to kick the Government, it was a shame, 'how could you do this?', so it was an open target.[173]

The campaign proved effective. An important turn in the debate came about when the party leader of the Christian Democrats, Göran Hägglund, officially changed his position in a newspaper article, referring to the matter as a question of individual rights; in his view, this argumentation built on Christian tradition.[174] Before Parliament decided to abolish the sterilisation requirement, however, the issue appeared before the courts in a case concerning a trans plaintiff who wanted legal gender recognition without sterilisation. The case was furthered as strategic litigation by lawyer Kerstin Burman and the Uppsala Anti-Discrimination Agency. The final decision was delivered by the Stockholm

[167] See most importantly ECtHR, *Christine Goodwin v. the UK* (2002).
[168] Swedish Government Bill Prop. 2011/12:142: 55. [169] Ibid.
[170] Opposition originated in primarily the right-wing Swedish Democrats and the Christian Democratic Party. Socialutskottet [The Swedish Parliamentary Committee on Health and Welfare] 2012/13:SoU23; 2012/13:SoU24.
[171] Westerlund, 16 September 2016. [172] Dittrich 2012; Huffington Post 2012.
[173] Westerlund, 16 September 2016. Translated from Swedish. [174] Hägglund 2012.

Administrative Court of Appeal in December 2012.[175] Interestingly, while the prohibition to preserve reproductive cells in the light of the sterilisation precondition had been dealt with – and approved – by the same court some years earlier,[176] it came to recognise the infertility precondition as a violation of constitutional and international human rights.

The lead lawyer, Burman, described her engagement with rights as a conscious choice:

> This was the first case I litigated based on the ECHR, and then I had previously worked in court, and there, one was taught that everyone invoking the ECHR were querulants. You could not take [them] seriously – so we [...] discussed whether we could invoke it – because there is a risk that one dilutes these rights, if one uses them out of context, without substantiation, or in questions that are pulled too far. But we thought that this was such a grave infringement, so here it was evident that we should invoke both the ECHR and the Government Act. [...] one has to make a proper legal investigation so that one really can connect it to the Convention. And that is probably the limitation, there are not that many decisions on trans rights, for example, but then one has to argue for parallels or comparisons.[177]

Being a public interest lawyer specialised in gender identity and sexual orientation, Burman was aware of the relevant legal developments and traditional scepticism to rights arguments in Sweden, as well as knowledgeable on how to navigate this tricky territory. Her expert engagement can be seen as a crucial resource for the victim group.

The final decision by the Stockholm Administrative Court of Appeal considered the requirement to be a violation of three rights: (i) the prohibition of forced physical interventions in the Swedish Government Act,[178] since the grave physical intervention of sterilisation was a condition of access to legal benefits or rights; (ii) the right to respect for private and family life in Article 8 ECHR, as the intervention was an unjustified and irrevocable limitation of the right and (iii) the prohibition of discrimination in Article 14 ECHR, as the sterilisation requirement 'only targeted transsexual people'.[179] In addition, the Court used its constitutional mandate to disapply the infertility requirement in the Gender Recognition Act.[180] Soon after the final court judgment, legislation was passed to officially erase the requirement.[181]

175 Kammarrätten i Stockholm [Stockholm Administrative Court of Appeal], 1968-12 (2012). See also Förvaltningsrätten i Stockholm, 45723-10 (2012).

176 Kammarrätten i Stockholm [Stockholm Administrative Court of Appeal], 3413-04 (2005). The Swedish Supreme Administrative Court rejected the petition for a writ of certiorari in 2008. Regeringsrätten [The Swedish Supreme Administrative Court], 2751-05 (2008).

177 Burman, 8 September 2016. Translated from Swedish.

178 Regeringsformen [Government Act] (1974:152), Chapter 2 Section 6.

179 Kammarrätten i Stockholm [Stockholm Administrative Court of Appeal], 1968-12 (2012). In the first instance, ECHR Article 14 was not considered. Förvaltningsrätten i Stockholm, 45723-10 (2012).

180 Regeringsformen [Government Act] (1974:152), Chapter 11 Section 14. Kammarrätten i Stockholm [Stockholm Administrative Court of Appeal], 1968-12 (2012).

181 Swedish Government Bill Prop. 2012/13:107; SFS 2013:405.

The strategic litigation should be seen in the context of the developing Swedish legal system, where courts, constitutional and international human rights and judicial review have become more important.[182] It should also be seen as a result of rights mobilisation and a more inclusive conceptualisation of constitutional and human rights. The 2012 judgment cites a wide range of recent international human rights sources – both within and outside traditional legal source hierarchies – without engaging with them in much detail however. By referring to ECtHR practice (particularly *Christine Goodwin v. the UK*),[183] the Yogyakarta Principles,[184] the EU Charter, WPATH[185] and the CoE Commissioner for Human Rights,[186] a general theme of trans rights development appeared. According to this interpretation, upholding sterilisation requirements became more difficult to defend.

3.3 State Responsibility, Responsiveness to Rights Claims and Remedial Standards

Having explored the Swedish practices of involuntary sterilisation and castration, the time has come to address the victims' struggles for remedies, and the state response to such struggles.

3.3.1 State Responsibility and the Marginalised

In 1997, journalist Maciej Zaremba published a series of articles in a major Swedish newspaper,[187] initiating a large public debate about the sterilisations in the period 1935–1975.[188] Prior to this, the sterilisation laws were no secret, but in fact critically researched and reported.[189] What sparked the great debate in 1997 was the connection between the oppressive practices and the legacy of the Swedish social democratic welfare state, seemingly so contradictory to the

[182] A reference to judicial review (though limited to concrete cases) was explicitly introduced in Swedish legislation in 1980. Judicial review had long been addressed in jurisprudential and political debates, making the concept not entirely new at the time, but the 1980 reform formalised a constitutional obligation for courts to abstain from applying ordinary legislation when in apparent conflict with the constitution. The requirement that the conflict had to be 'apparent' was removed in 2010, when the Government Act was reformed to include a more extensive rights catalogue. As this example suggests, the entrenchment of rights and judicial review have gone hand in hand in Swedish constitutional reform. See Swedish Government Bill Prop. 1978/79:195; Justitiedepartementet [The Swedish Ministry of Justice] 1978; Högsta domstolen (HD) [The Swedish Supreme Court], NJA 1964, s. 471. A famous debate on judicial review took place in the mid-twentieth century in *Svensk juristtidning*. See, for example, Petrén 1956; Undén 1956; Bindreiter 2009.

[183] ECtHR, *Christine Goodwin v. the United Kingdom* (2002).

[184] International Commission of Jurists 2007. [185] WPATH 2012.

[186] CommDH/IssuePaper(2009)2. [187] Zaremba 1997a; 1997b. [188] Liljeborg 2009.

[189] See, for example, Tidningarnas Telegrambyrå 1986a; 1986b; 1987a; 1987b; Broberg & Tydén 1991; Dahlgren 1986; Lindquist 1991; Sprengel 1987; Sprengel & Dahlgren 1986.

country's excellent international reputation.[190] In the words of the main investigator of the subsequently appointed Sterilisation Committee, Carl-Gustaf Andrén, the Swedish (Social Democratic) Government of 1997 faced a difficult situation in terms of negative international publicity:

> [B]ut then *The Times* dealt with it, and made the occasion almost a bit of a triumph… 'look at Sweden, which is so nice, look at what they have done… these Social Democrats'… And then [the news] spread over the world […] and then journalists worldwide started to get interested. And came to Stockholm. And then [the Swedish Government] finally had a meeting […] because they had all of these journalists who were supposed to get an answer: 'Is it true? How will you manage this?' And then the old Swedish model is: make a state investigation.[191]

The immense attention called for action. In 1997, the Government established an independent investigation team to report on the implementation of the 1934 and 1941 sterilisation laws.[192] A Compensation Act was created in 1999.[193] Moreover, as additional satisfaction for the victims, two public apologies were issued in 1999 and 2000, one general and one specifically focusing on the vulnerability of Romani/travelling people.[194]

A parallel development to the newfound interest in the Swedish sterilisations was the awakening human rights engagement with involuntary sterilisation at the international level. The CEDAW Committee, followed by other UN treaty bodies, had started to pay attention to involuntary sterilisation as violence against women in the early 1990s.[195] It is fascinating to note the lack of supranational human rights interventions, recommendations or commentaries regarding Sweden despite the scrutiny at that time. The absence of such international remarks should however be viewed in the light of the Swedish Government's swift response to the 1997 scandal, the lack of organised activism and a consequential dearth of, for example, shadow reports to supranational bodies.

The establishment of the 1999 Compensation Act was the outcome of limited public liability with reference to the historical sterilisation practices. In fact, the concept of public liability was not introduced until 1972, when the Liability Act entered into force non-retroactively.[196] Before this date, only individual liability

[190] Andersson 1997; Axelsson 1997; Broberg & Tydén 1998. This was also mentioned by Persson, 20 September 2016; Andrén, 20 September 2016; Lindquist, 13 September 2016; Zaremba, 13 September 2016.

[191] Andrén, 21 September 2016. Translated from Swedish.

[192] Socialdepartementet [The Swedish Ministry of Health and Social Affairs] 1999; 2000a; 2000b.

[193] Lag om ersättning till steriliserade i vissa fall [Act on Compensation to Sterilised People under Certain Circumstances] (1999:332). Compensation was considered the main remedy already at the outset of the investigation. Socialdepartementet [The Swedish Ministry of Health and Social Affairs] 1999: 10.

[194] Persson, 20 September 2016. See also Swedish Government Letter Skr. 2000/01.

[195] See the second chapter of this book.

[196] Swedish Government Bill Prop. 1972:5; Skadeståndslag [Liability Act] (1972:207). On public liability, see also Bengtsson 1996; Justitiedepartementet [The Swedish Ministry of Justice] 2010.

for damages was regulated in national legislation.[197] Victims of involuntary sterilisation could nevertheless not claim public liability in court based on the Sterilisation Act as wrongful parliamentary decision-making before the law was abolished.[198] For the 1941 Sterilisation Act, this meant that such claims for damages, if they were not already time-barred,[199] could not be presented before 1975.

Despite existing legal possibilities,[200] victims of involuntary sterilisation have not presented liability claims in court.[201] Instead of turning to the courts, possibly due to statutory limitations, liability restrictions or limited legal knowledge, some people directed their claims to the Government. Between 1980 and 1999, the Government received 38 applications for compensation from people who had been sterilised.[202] In 16 of these cases, that is, less than half, the state provided compensation *ex gratia* – as an expression of moral, rather than legal, obligation.[203] The compensation was based on tort practice 'for similar damages',[204] generally around 50,000 Swedish Kronor (around 5,000 Euros) in 1999.[205] Compensation was paid only in cases in which a formal error was found: most commonly, where the signature of a legally capable person was missing.[206] *Ex gratia* compensation was hence paid in cases in which the law had been clearly violated, in other words, cases which could have been presented as viable legal claims for damages at the time of the intervention as well.[207]

[197] Socialdepartementet [The Swedish Ministry of Health and Social Affairs] 1999: 67–82. Therefore, legal claims could only be based on individual authority representatives for wrongful application of the sterilisation legislation – for example, through forging signatures. Mild coercion was however encouraged in authority guidelines. See Kungliga medicinalstyrelsen [The Swedish Royal Board of Medicine] 1939; 1943; 1947.

[198] Skadeståndslag [Liability Act] (1972:207), Chapter 3 Section 2.

[199] According to the general rule, claims for damages have to be presented within 10 years after the grounds for the claim appeared. This time is counted from when the tortious act was committed, i.e., the surgical intervention. Preskriptionslag [Statutory Limitations Act] (1981:130), Section 2. The law is retroactively valid. See Socialdepartementet [The Swedish Ministry of Health and Social Affairs] 1999: 81–82.

[200] For a long time during the twentieth century, moreover, there were no rules about strict liability in health care, negatively affecting the possibilities of claiming liability for malpractice or abuse in medical settings.

[201] The same tendency is also visible when it comes to other types of widespread historical abuse in Sweden, such as the maltreatment of children in foster homes and state institutions during the twentieth century. See Socialdepartementet [The Swedish Ministry of Health and Social Affairs] 2011; Swedish Government Bill Prop. 2011/12:160; Socialutskottet [The Swedish Parliamentary Committee on Health and Welfare] 2012/13:SoU3; Lag om ersättning på grund av övergrepp eller försummelser i samhällsvården av barn och unga i vissa fall [Act on Compensation for Abuse or Negligence in State Social Care of Children and Youth under Certain Circumstances] (2012:663).

[202] Socialdepartementet [The Swedish Ministry of Health and Social Affairs] 1999: 188.

[203] See Bengtsson 2009.

[204] Socialdepartementet [The Swedish Ministry of Health and Social Affairs] 1999: 188.

[205] Ibid. [206] Ibid.

[207] In the general lack of court cases, one exception is present: one applicant, dissatisfied with the *ex gratia* compensation amount, claimed a higher amount before the administrative courts. Tidningarnas telegrambyrå 1987a; 1987b. The void of subsequent media reports nevertheless suggests that the case was rejected.

Aforementioned Zaremba, the journalist who brought Swedish sterilisations to the attention of international media, described the relationship between victims and public authorities prior to the 1997 scandal in words that highlight the contemporary void of a rights consciousness:

> [A] Swede does not take the state to court. Now they do, but then it was almost unthinkable. They went to the Government. [...] and [the Government] rejected a couple of these compensation claims with the argument that 'this happened in the name of the law, it was a democratically made decision, and a democratic decision that leads to a certain law, cannot, so to say, by definition lead to compensation'. That is how they thought then.[208]

The 1999 sterilisation report was authored against this background. It considered the possibilities for victims to present legally viable claims of public liability to be limited, particularly because of statutory limitations and the late, non-retroactive introduction of the concept of public liability in the domestic legal order.[209] Remarkably, the investigative team did not draw a line between the sterilisations which were permissible by contemporary legislation and those which were not. The investigation did not ponder either whether the sterilisations were violations of international law, and what implications this would have for prescriptibility. The investigation furthermore made comparisons to remedial practices regarding historical injustices in other countries – Norway, Denmark and Canada –[210] but found little guidance in the wide range of national compensation practices.[211] Motivated by the difficult situation which the victims were in – as existing possibilities for the victims to access compensation were legally restricted, unreliable, costly and lengthy – the Government decided that *ex gratia* compensation legislation was warranted.[212] According to the Government, the law was only to be applied to victims of involuntary sterilisation, not to be considered

[208] Zaremba, 13 September 2016. Translated from Swedish. Lindquist, who met victims through his research and helped some of them to write letters to the Government at the beginning of the 1990s, reported similar attitudes among the authorities. Lindquist, 13 September 2016.

[209] Socialdepartementet [The Swedish Ministry of Health and Social Affairs] 1999: 139.

[210] The report investigated Norwegian compensation practices to victims of eugenic sterilisations, lobotomies and radiation damages, the Danish cases of eugenic sterilisations and one court case of compensation for sterilisation as a result of medical malpractice, as well as the Canadian practices of eugenic sterilisation in Alberta, the court case *Muir v. Alberta*. See Socialdepartementet [The Swedish Ministry of Health and Social Affairs] 1999: 94–101; Alberta Court of Queen's Bench, *Muir v. Alberta* (1996).

[211] Socialdepartementet [The Swedish Ministry of Health and Social Affairs] 1999: 144.

[212] According to the state investigation, an alternative to a compensation law could have been that victims claimed public liability in general courts, with the state abstaining from referring to the liability claims as statute-barred. However, the investigation team considered this alternative problematic on the following grounds: legal insecurity concerning public liability; difficulties relating to evidence requirements; financial risks and costs for legal assistance and lengthy legal processes. Hence, a legislated compensation scheme was considered a better alternative, as it would be faster, cheaper and involved a more certain outcome. Socialdepartementet [The Swedish Ministry of Health and Social Affairs] 1999: 139. Truth-telling in the form of cross-examination can be painful for victims of violence in disadvantaged positions. See Rubio-Marín 2009a: 5; A/HRC/14/22 (2010): Paras 34–35.

a precedent for other groups; as such, it would not substantially change Swedish liability law.[213]

A compensation scheme was legally established in 1999.[214] According to the law, all direct victims who were alive and could prove that they had been involuntarily sterilised under the 1934 or 1941 sterilisation laws, or before 1976 without legal ground, were entitled to financial compensation. The sterilisation was considered involuntary if the applicant: (i) was a legal minor or legally incapable at the time of sterilisation; (ii) had not signed the sterilisation application or consented to it; (iii) was institutionalised at the time of sterilisation; (iv) was sterilised on the grounds of being mentally ill, feebleminded or epileptic; (v) was sterilised as a requirement by the authorities to enter into marriage, to have an abortion, or to receive other public support and (vi) consented to sterilisation because of general negligence or inappropriate influence of public authorities.[215] These categories were established to minimise the burden of proof for the applicants who, in order to access compensation, had to fill in a form indicating where and when they were sterilised to authorise administrative officials to find their medical journals. The journals were then used as the main evidence.[216]

The remaining part of the aforementioned sterilisation investigation historically mapped and evaluated ethical principles to avoid similar practices in the future.[217] Moreover, an exhaustive historical study[218] and a special issue of the *Scandinavian Journal of History* were published.[219] These publications can be understood as 'verification of the facts and full and public disclosure of the truth', being a form of satisfaction,[220] but were as such disconnected from the design and implementation of the compensation scheme.[221]

Essentially, the victims remained unorganised, even though the investigation provided them with depictions of common grievances and reports which could have formed a basis for further mobilisation and litigation. Officially,

213 'The proposition to compensation presented hence involves significant departures from current legal principles of public liability. The proposition can therefore in the future not be invoked by other groups who might claim liability of the state'. Swedish Government Bill Prop. 1998/99:71: 9.

214 Lag om ersättning till steriliserade i vissa fall [Act on Compensation to Sterilised People under Certain Circumstances] (1999:332); Swedish Government Bill Prop. 1998/99:71.

215 Ibid, Section 2.

216 Persson, 20 September 2016; Socialdepartementet [The Swedish Ministry of Health and Social Affairs] 1999.

217 Socialdepartementet [The Swedish Ministry of Health and Social Affairs] 2000a; 2000b. The reports included analyses of the sterilisation files, the access to contraception, sterilisation and abortion in the relevant period, the implementation of the sterilisation laws and interviews with sterilisation victims.

218 See Socialdepartementet [The Swedish Ministry of Health and Social Affairs] 2000a; Tydén 2002.

219 Socialdepartementet [The Swedish Ministry of Health and Social Affairs] 2000b.

220 A/RES/60/147 (2006), Article 22(b).

221 Socialdepartementet [The Swedish Ministry of Health and Social Affairs] 2000b.

moreover, the voices of the victims were only included in the investigation through annexed interviews which were not further analysed in the report.[222] That is not to say that victims went entirely unheard by the investigative team. The main investigator, aforementioned Andrén, and the secretary, Leif Persson, had personal contact by means of telephone and letter exchange with hundreds of victims (300–400 each) to hear their stories and answer questions and concerns. Persson's words are illustrative of the feelings of shame and stigmatisation which many victims had to overcome to contact the authorities. Moreover, they provide insight into the reasons behind their lack of organisation:

> So, when the investigation was made, when there was more information about it, [the victims] called and asked, and were scared to death that it would become official. And many said that 'I don't dare to apply for compensation if this will become [public]... because I have not told anyone... How do you do with the compensation? Do you send a letter home?' 'Yes, we send an anonymous letter' [...] We were very careful with the compensation, it was a regular, white envelope. And the compensation, how it was paid, was up to the individual to decide: if they wanted it anonymously on an account, they could get it. Because many did not have the courage, they did not want to tell their relatives that this had happened to them, they were ashamed. And [...] that was the reason why we made everything confidential.[223]

The quote renders visible how feelings of shame affected the grievance formation of individual victims and hindered them from conceptualising themselves as rights-holders.

The compensation was a fixed sum of 175,000 Swedish Kronor (approximately 17,400 Euros) for non-pecuniary damages.[224] The compensation was individual to the direct victims and could not be transferred to successors, spouses, children or other possible indirect victims.[225] The sterilisation investigation concluded that the compensation should amount to *at least* the compensation given to victims of involuntary infertility according to insurance schemes for disability compensation, which at the time amounted to 110,000 Swedish Kronor (around 10,900 Euros). The investigative team considered it necessary to increase this amount for bodily harm to further compensate the

[222] Lomfors 2000; Lomfors, 8 September 2016.

[223] Persson, 20 September 2016. Translated from Swedish.

[224] This amount was also similar to that claimed by most sterilisation victims who had turned to the Government, or directly to the investigation team after the public debate, generally a sum between 50,000 and 200,000 Swedish Kronor. Socialdepartementet [The Swedish Ministry of Health and Social Affairs] 1999: 147–148.

[225] In case of death of the direct victim, the compensation could only be granted to the estate if the decision had been communicated to the applicant before their death. Lag om ersättning till steriliserade i vissa fall [Act on Compensation to Sterilised People under Certain Circumstances] (1999:332), Sections 3(3) and 3(4). No pecuniary damages for loss of income or other financial harm were taken into consideration, as the investigation assumed sterilisations generally not to have affected the work and career possibilities of the sterilised, even though victims' stories suggest otherwise. See Lomfors 2000.

subjective suffering which the sterilisation victims experienced on account of the often-arbitrary application of the sterilisation laws.[226] A symbolic need was also present to show that the state did not share the values on which the historical sterilisation laws had been based.[227]

The 1999 Compensation Act was established on the basis of political goodwill rather than legal obligation. The sterilisation investigation did not engage with questions of rights or state responsibility.[228] When asked about the lack of engagement, members of the investigation team Bertil Bengtsson and Gunnar Broberg emphasised the exceptionality of the compensation scheme, the consensus among the team that compensation should be paid and the late development of rights discourses in Sweden, as possible reasons.[229]

The reluctance to engage with international legal obligations or domestic rights should be understood against the backdrop of the Swedish legal culture of limited recognition of public liability and rights.[230] The authorities feared opening a 'Pandora's box' of possible extensive responsibility. Recognising rights violations would not only challenge the public image of the state but also identify the victims as rights-holders and legal subjects capable to claim public liability. State engagement with a rights framework might in other words facilitate grievance formation among direct victims of sterilisation, which could in turn affect the grievance formation of other victims of historical oppression.

226 The laws' application often exceeded their letter. Socialdepartementet [The Swedish Ministry of Health and Social Affairs] 1999: 147–148.

227 Socialdepartementet [The Swedish Ministry of Health and Social Affairs] 1999: 145–148. The investigative team thought that this additional amount should be comparable to non-pecuniary compensations in serious crimes and somewhat higher than the ordinary non-pecuniary damages for aggrievement in court cases of rape at the time, at 50,000 Swedish Kronor (5,000 Euros). See Bengtsson's attached statement on the difficulty of determining fair compensation for the victims, Socialdepartementet [The Swedish Ministry of Health and Social Affairs] 1999: 181. When asked about the comparison, three of the members of the investigation team – Andrén, Persson and Bengtsson – all indicated that both involuntary sterilisation and rape were serious violations of personal integrity. Persson highlighted that, apart from this similarity, the former was seen as more serious, given its permanent consequences. Andrén, 21 September 2016; Bengtsson, 1 October 2016; Persson, 20 September 2016.

228 The report made reference to human rights treaties which 'might have had an importance'. An external researcher was contracted for this treaty description, effectively marginalising in-depth discussions on rights and state responsibility within the investigation team. Constitutional rights were not discussed either. Socialdepartementet [The Swedish Ministry of Health and Social Affairs] 1999: 106; Persson, 20 September 2016.

229 Bengtsson, 31 August 2016; Broberg, 20 September 2016.

230 This held true for both supranational and constitutional rights violations. However, the situation changed during the 2000s and 2010s. See Högsta domstolen [The Swedish Supreme Court], NJA 2003, s. 217 (2003); NJA 2005, s. 462 (2005); NJA 2007, s. 584; NJA 2014, s. 323; and NJA 2014, s. 332. See Skadeståndslag [Liability Act] (1972:207), Chapter 3 Section 4. Swedish Government Bill Prop. 2017/18:7; Konstitutionsutkottet [The Swedish Parliamentary Committee on the Constitution] KU 2017/18:12; Justitiedepartementet [The Swedish Ministry of Justice] 2010.

The applications for compensation were heard by a specially established Sterilisation Compensation Committee, active from 1999 to 2002.[231] The Committee received applications from 2,042 individuals, of which 1,591 received compensation according to the 1999 Compensation Act.[232] Considering that the number of people who had been sterilised according to the 1934 and 1941 laws was high – 62,888 – the number who received compensation was considerably lower (a mere 2.5 per cent). However, 1,521 women and 521 men filed applications.[233]

Why did so few victims apply for compensation? The Sterilisation Compensation Committee posited that reasons for the low number of applications could lie in the death of the direct victims, old age and illness, emotional distress and trauma, lack of access to information about the compensation scheme (despite nation-wide information campaigns) or lack of knowledge concerning how to file compensation claims.[234] Moreover, the prevalence of involuntary interventions might have been overestimated in the first place.[235] Other possible reasons for the low number are distrust in public authorities, manifested in fear of the official nature of the procedure or of sharing personal details with the authorities, and feelings of humiliation. Applying for compensation from the state was an experience of recognition and relief for some victims,[236] but one of pain and shame for others.[237]

3.3.2 State Responsibility and the Sexually Dangerous

According to the 1944 Castration Act, involuntary castrations were outlawed through the abolition of the law in 2013. This group has received no remedies and an equal lack of civil society attention. Similar to the sterilisation victims, many castration victims were likely dead, old and/or ill in the early decades of the new millennium, which explains eliminated or decreased possibilities for them to engage in remedial struggles. An additional factor was severe social and personal stigma: being labelled as deviant and suspected of possibly having

[231] Applications after 2002 were handled by the Swedish Ministry of Health and Social Affairs. Persson, 20 September 2016.

[232] Socialdepartementet [The Swedish Ministry of Health and Social Affairs] 2004. Some people filed several applications, as no appellate instance existed.

[233] Socialdepartementet [The Swedish Ministry of Health and Social Affairs] 2004: 7. This means that 74 per cent of the applicants were women and 26 per cent were men. Around 80 per cent of the applications by female victims and around 73 per cent by male victims were approved. Effectively, around 9 per cent of sterilised men were compensated and around 2 per cent of sterilised women.

[234] Socialdepartementet [The Swedish Ministry of Health and Social Affairs] 2004: 6–7.

[235] Ibid.

[236] Socialdepartementet [The Swedish Ministry of Health and Social Affairs] 1999: 149.

[237] These thoughts were expressed by individual victims in their communication with historian Maija Runcis, 7 May 2015.

been convicted.[238] Victims' experiences and harms have not been documented as the topic has been given little attention in Swedish public, political and legal discussions.

While the aforementioned sterilisation investigation highlighted similarities between the use of coercion in historical sterilisation and castration practices,[239] the 1999 compensation scheme nevertheless excluded victims of involuntary castration according to the 1944 Castration Act.[240] This Act was abolished as a potentially rights-violating law in 2013,[241] but questions concerning public responsibility for the practices have never officially been raised.

To date, no liability claims have been brought to court about involuntary castrations in Sweden, possibly due to the limited possibilities to present claims before the Castration Act was abolished. No cases of victims of involuntary castration turning to the authorities with compensation claims are known either.[242] Moreover, no civil society organisation has raised the question of access to justice and remedies for the victims of involuntary castration.

Unlike in the case of its historical sterilisation laws, Sweden has not been internationally or nationally reproached for the 1944 Castration Act. As the castrations have not been publicly addressed as oppressive or as violations of human or constitutional rights by the state, international organisations or mass media, the castration victims have not been framed as rights holders either. This lack has also affected victims' opportunities to form and align grievances in terms of rights and to conceptualise themselves as rights-holders: individually, collectively and publicly.

3.3.3 State Responsibility and Trans People

Compensations for victims of involuntary sterilisation according to the 1972 Gender Recognition Act were a contested issue in Sweden in the 2010s. Many victims, who had been young when they underwent the required sterilisation, later expressed the wish to have biological children.[243] The sterilisation precondition also brought other harm for trans individuals, as some refrained from achieving legal gender recognition because they did not wish to comply with the sterilisation requirement, causing multiple difficulties in their daily lives. The problems caused by the sterilisation requirement were voiced by victims and activists in the 2010s, gaining space in mass media and public debates.[244]

[238] This stigmatisation can be likened to the stigmatisation of, e.g., victims of sexual violence. See Rubio-Marín & De Greiff 2007: 322–323; Walker 2009: 43.

[239] Socialdepartementet [The Swedish Ministry of Health and Social Affairs] 1999: 23.

[240] The law only granted compensation to victims of the 1934 and 1941 sterilisation laws, and people who were sterilised by the authorities before 1976 *without legal ground*. Lag om ersättning till steriliserade i vissa fall [Act on Compensation to Sterilised People under Certain Circumstances] (1999:332), Section 1.

[241] Swedish Government Bill Prop. 2011/12:142.

[242] See Ågren, 26 November 2015; Vilenius, 26 November 2015.

[243] Westerlund 2015.

[244] See Lundberg 2013; Sveriges Radio 2013; RFSL 2015.

A legal possibility to claim public liability for damages caused by the infertility requirement in the 1972 Gender Recognition Act appeared in 2013, when the requirement was abolished.[245] An active civil society engagement ensured that, as soon as liability claims were viable, they were brought before the Chancellor of Justice – a simplified, semi-judicial process for public liability claims.[246] The plaintiffs originally numbered 142, increasing to 161 later. They were supported by civil society organisations RFSL and the Uppsala Anti-Discrimination Agency, later joined by trans activist organisations RFSL Youth, KIM and FPES.

Albeit a relatively weakly resourced group, trans victims hence benefited from a completely different outset in comparison to the other victim groups: An organised civil society platform with international networks was driving the issue and a conscious decision had been taken to legally mobilise in terms of rights and state responsibility. The movement also benefited from the increasing importance of rights in the domestic legal culture along with supranational legal developments in the field, particularly during the 2010s, such as emerging soft law and regional developments.[247] Vitally, the victims were also aware of these legal frameworks and able to conceptualise their harms and formulate their claims accordingly.

Before the Chancellor of Justice, the applicants claimed 300,000 Swedish Kronor (approximately 29,800 Euros) for non-pecuniary damages caused by involuntary infertility and the violation of physical integrity. The sum was based on references to the compensation scheme for victims of historical sterilisations,[248] and ECtHR cases of forced sterilisation of Romani women.[249] Some applicants also claimed additional damages for the unnecessary removal of internal organs. According to the applicants, the sterilisation requirement lacked justifiable grounds and amounted to a violation of the prohibition of torture and inhuman or degrading treatment or punishment under Article 3 ECHR. Moreover, they considered it to violate the right to respect for private

[245] According to the 1972 Liability Act, public liability claims based on legislation cannot be made while the legislative norms in question are still in force. When legislation has been abolished or amended, such claims can however also be made retroactively. The reasons for this limitation lay in the believed inappropriateness of the distribution of public funds and fears that a possibility to hold the government or parliament liable for damages would be abused for political purposes. With growing domestic recognition of supranational norms, this exception from public liability nevertheless began to be criticised. Skadeståndslag [Liability Act] (1972:207), Chapter 3 Section 7; Justitiedepartementet [The Swedish Ministry of Justice] 2010: 90–91; Swedish Government Bill Prop. 2017/18:7; Konstitutionsutkottet [The Swedish Parliamentary Committee on the Constitution] KU 2017/18:12; Bengtsson 2016: 46.

[246] See Förordning om handläggning av skadeståndsanspråk mot staten [Decree on the Administration of Liability Claims against the State] (1995:1301) Section 3; Lambertz 2008: 204.

[247] See the second chapter of this book.

[248] Lag om ersättning till steriliserade i vissa fall [Act on Compensation to Sterilised People under Certain Circumstances] (1999:332). The sum in this earlier law was nominally lower, but the sums are comparable when taking into account inflation and consumer index developments.

[249] Particularly ECtHR, *V.C. v. Slovakia* (2011); *N.B. v. Slovakia* (2012); *I.G. and Others v. Slovakia* (2012).

and family life under Article 8 ECHR, and the prohibition of discrimination under Article 14 ECHR, along with the prohibition of forced physical intervention under Chapter 2, Section 6, Government Act. The applicants considered the liable acts of the state to be wrongful decision-making (the establishment of the sterilisation requirement) and the inaction of the legislator (the failure of the state to abolish the requirement) in the face of continuous evidence that the requirement was comparable to coercion.[250]

In her decision, the Chancellor of Justice recognised that involuntary sterilisation can qualify as torture or inhuman or degrading treatment under Article 3 ECHR, but that the sterilisations of trans people were carried out with informed, even if not entirely free, consent. In her view, the sterilisations were not comparable to the ECtHR cases invoked, as the coercive elements were different. Accordingly, she found no violation of Article 3. The Chancellor also stated that the sterilisations had been a limitation of the applicants' private and family lives (Article 8 ECHR), yet justified, as the motive behind the law had been to protect the rights and freedoms of their children.[251] Taking into consideration the dynamic interpretation of the Convention, and the margin of appreciation together with the international legal principle of non-retroactivity, the Chancellor concluded that, while the amendment of the law was welcome,[252] the sterilisation requirement had not violated Article 8 when it was in force.[253] In addition to this, the comparator referred to by the applicants – people undergoing medical treatment who were given possibilities to save their reproductive cells – was legally unviable according to the Chancellor. As such, she found a violation of neither Article 14 ECHR, nor the constitutional prohibition of forced physical intervention.[254] Finally, she stated that the 1999 Compensation Act was extraordinary, not precedentary, and could not be used as grounds for compensation claims by other groups.[255] Accordingly, the Chancellor rejected all the applicants' compensation claims.[256]

Having lost the case before the Chancellor, the applicants were preparing to bring the battle for compensation to the general courts.[257] However, before a lawsuit was filed, the Swedish Government decided to pay compensation to the

[250] Burman & RFSL 2013.

[251] Through 'avoiding the complications that could follow if a child had a biological mother, who after amended gender status legally was a man, or a biological father, who legally was considered a woman'. JK, Decision No. 4243-13-40 et al (2014).

[252] See Kammarrätten i Stockholm [Stockholm Administrative Court of Appeal], 1968-12 (2012).

[253] This was also highlighted during my interview with Skarhed, 14 September 2016.

[254] Here, the Chancellor of Justice simply stated that '[…] of the same reasons that have been stated regarding the European Convention, a violation of the Government Act cannot be regarded as having taken place when the sterilisation requirement of the Gender Recognition Act has been implemented on the applicants'. JK, Decision No. 4243-13-40 et al (2014).

[255] Swedish Government Bill Prop. 1998/99:71: 9. The Chancellor also stated that claims concerning arbitrary interpretation by health care authorities should be directed to the county councils or municipalities.

[256] JK, Decision No. 4243-13-40 et al (2014).

[257] Burman, 8 September 2016; Westerlund, 16 September 2016.

victims: a result of continuous, simultaneous civil society awareness-raising campaigns and lobbying.[258] The 2018 Act on State Compensation to People who Have Obtained Legal Gender Recognition under Certain Circumstances provides a legislative symbolic compensation based on *ex gratia* for the victims of involuntary sterilisation according to the 1972 Gender Recognition Act.[259] According to the Act, individual compensation of 225,000 Swedish Kronor (approximately 22,400 Euros)[260] was to be paid to applicants: (i) who had applied for amendment of legally registered gender before 30 June 2013[261] and (ii) whose application was confirmed – that is, people who had undergone sterilisation or been rendered infertile otherwise.[262] Compensation was paid to all applicants who fulfilled these criteria, and who applied between May 2018 and April 2020.[263] The compensation was also paid to those who were infertile for other reasons (for instance age) and people who willingly underwent sterilisation.[264] In this sense, the compensation did not take into consideration individual applicants' subjective experiences. The compensation was administered by the Swedish Legal, Financial and Administrative Services Agency,[265] the decisions of which could be appealed in administrative courts.[266]

The *travaux préparatoires* of the law engage with the harm suffered by the direct victims and mention the ECtHR cases *Y.Y. v. Turkey* (2015),[267] and *A.P., Garçon and Nicot v. France* (2017).[268] They particularly highlight the similarity between the elements of coercion in the implementation of the 1972 Gender Recognition Act and the earlier sterilisations laws. The preliminary investigation for the preparation of the compensation scheme included meetings with trans civil society representatives, and the investigators watched films of interviews with the victims.[269] This victim group was therefore officially more included in the preparation of the compensation scheme than the victims of historical sterilisation laws.

258 Ibid.

259 Socialdepartementet [The Swedish Ministry of Health and Social Affairs] 2017a; 2017b; Swedish Government Bill Prop. 2017/18:64. See Alaattinoğlu & Rubio-Marín 2019.

260 Lag om statlig ersättning till personer som har fått ändrad könstillhörighet fastställd i vissa fall [Act on State Compensation for People who Have Obtained Legal Gender Recognition under Certain Circumstances] (2018:162), Section 2.

261 That was the period when the law was in force.

262 Lag om statlig ersättning till personer som har fått ändrad könstillhörighet fastställd i vissa fall [Act on State Compensation for People who Have Obtained Legal Gender Recognition under Certain Circumstances] (2018:162), Section 1.

263 Ibid, Section 6.

264 Socialdepartementet [The Swedish Ministry of Health and Social Affairs] 2017a: 64.

265 Lag om statlig ersättning till personer som har fått ändrad könstillhörighet fastställd i vissa fall [Act on State Compensation for People who Have Obtained Legal Gender Recognition under Certain Circumstances] (2018:162), Section 6.

266 Ibid, Section 8.

267 ECtHR, *Y.Y. v. Turkey* (2015); Socialdepartementet [The Swedish Ministry of Health and Social Affairs] 2017a: 46.

268 ECtHR, *A.P., Garçon and Nicot v. France* (2017); Socialdepartementet [The Swedish Ministry of Health and Social Affairs] 2017b: 15; Swedish Government Bill Prop. 2017/18:64: 15.

269 Socialdepartementet [The Swedish Ministry of Health and Social Affairs] 2017a; Sandegård, 15 September 2016; and Sundkvist, 3 October 2016.

While mentioning the European human rights framework, the *travaux préparatoires* carefully avoided the question of whether the 1972 Gender Recognition Act and its implementation amounted to violations of international or domestic law.[270] In fact, the *travaux préparatoires* emphasised that compensation was *not* paid for violation of rights, repeating the position of the Chancellor of Justice, pointing out that an *ex gratia* compensation is not the same as compensation based on public liability for damages.[271] The 2018 Compensation Act consequently contains elements of redress without recognising state responsibility for violation of rights.[272]

The *travaux préparatoires* furthermore assign some importance to the evolving domestic *ex gratia* compensation tradition – involving, aside from the 1999 Compensation Act, compensations for abuse or negligence in state social care of children and youths (2012) and for people suffering from narcolepsy after certain pandemic vaccination (2016); yet, they highlight the non-binding character of the tradition.[273] The *travaux préparatoires* make two points here: (i) that the compensation amount should be comparable in size to the 1999 Compensation Act and (ii) that the amount should not be higher than the one given to maltreated children (250,000 Swedish Kronor, approximately 24,900 Euros), as compensation in these cases was only given in the gravest cases of maltreatment, involving serious physical and sexual abuse.[274]

This law was the first in the world to grant compensation to people who had to undergo sterilisation to amend their legally registered gender.[275] Trans rights activists welcomed the scheme which provided facilitated access to remedies as compared to court procedures, for example. However, they expressed a wish for a compensation scheme which would provide a higher amount and would be more inclusive,[276] along with a public apology.[277]

[270] Socialdepartementet [The Swedish Ministry of Health and Social Affairs] 2017a; 2017b; Swedish Government Bill Prop. 2017/18:64.

[271] Ibid. [272] Alaattinoğlu & Rubio-Marín 2019: 730–731.

[273] Socialdepartementet [The Swedish Ministry of Health and Social Affairs] 2017a: 71–72. See also Socialdepartementet [The Swedish Ministry of Health and Social Affairs] 2017b: 11; Swedish Government Bill Prop. 2017/18:64: 11. Lag om ersättning till steriliserade i vissa fall [Act on Compensation to Sterilised People under Certain Circumstances] (1999:332); Lag om ersättning på grund av övergrepp eller försummelser i samhällsvården av barn och unga i vissa fall [Act on Compensation for Abuse or Negligence in State Social Care of Children and Youth under Certain Circumstances] (2012:663); Lag om statlig ersättning till personer som insjuknat i narkolepsi efter pandemivaccinering [Act on State Compensation for People Suffering from Narcolepsy after Vaccination for Pandemic] (2016:417). On the emerging tradition, see Arvidsson 2016.

[274] Socialdepartementet [The Swedish Ministry of Health and Social Affairs] 2017a: 71–2; 2017b: 11; Swedish Government Bill Prop. 2017/18:64: 11.

[275] Alaattinoğlu & Rubio-Marín 2019. The law has provided inspiration for a similar compensation scheme, albeit with a considerably smaller compensation amount, in the Netherlands, there coupled with a public apology. Schaps 2020.

[276] RFSL 2017; FPES 2017. [277] RFSL 2017: 6.

During the two-year application period, a total of 573 people applied for compensation, with a majority of the applications (530) being approved.[278] Put in relation to the earlier-estimated number of victims (1000), the number receiving compensation can be considered relatively high (53 per cent). This is particularly true in comparison to the victims of historical sterilisation practices, a group of which only a small minority of the victims applied for and accessed compensation.

Three main conclusions can be drawn here. Firstly, the trans group has been more active in mobilising, framing their harms as rights violations and applying for compensation, particularly in comparison to the two earlier groups. The group has benefited from the support of international networks, human rights organisations and legal experts – all important resources. Secondly, Swedish trans activism has taken advantage of the transnational and supranational normative rights developments regarding gender identity, seen in the continuous reference to important policy documents such as the 2007 Yogyakarta Principles. Finally, the struggle of this group is indicative of an emerging, increasingly complex and strained, national compensation tradition in the face of developing notions of rights and responsibility, expanding the notion of *ex gratia* while simultaneously avoiding questions of public liability.

3.3.4 Cross-Group Comparison

Remedies to victims, and differences between different victim groups, come to the fore in the Swedish case. Table 3.1 sums up the situation:

The dissimilar remedial treatment of the victims shows that the Swedish state has redressed the harm of different victim groups differently. For the first and third victim groups, it has depreciated the practices and provided remedies, with compensation as the central modality of redress. Crucially, the Government has not recognised rights violations or state responsibility. With an emphasis on solidarity rather than liability, the reason behind the victimisation of the groups becomes obscured. Regarding the second group, the state has not recognised any harm or violations, let alone state responsibility.

The provision of remedies in the Swedish case is accessible. With its relaxed evidence requirements and lack of cross-examination, the compensation scheme recognises victims' harm and the need to redress them on both symbolic and material levels. Issuing legislation with clear, transparent and openly framed criteria also increases remedial access. Moreover, benefiting from the *ex gratia* compensation scheme does not

[278] 43 applications were rejected. Törngren, 9 October 2020.

Table 3.1 Remedies to castrated and sterilised people in Sweden

	Group 1: Victims of involuntary sterilisation (1935–1975)	Group 2: Victims of involuntary castration (1944–2013)	Group 3: Victims of involuntary sterilisation according to the Gender Recognition Act (1972–2013)
Restitution	N/A	N/A	N/A
Compensation	*Ex gratia* upon application (175,000 Swedish Kronor; approximately 17,400 Euros)	N/A	*Ex gratia* upon application (225,000 Swedish Kronor; approximately 22,400 Euros)
Rehabilitation	N/A	N/A	N/A
Satisfaction	Public apologies, published state investigations	N/A	Limited state investigation
Guarantees of non-repetition	N/A	N/A	N/A

prevent victims from claiming compensation based on public liability in court.

The Swedish *travaux préparatoires* also do not differentiate between cis and trans people in the assessment of involuntary sterilisation. Doing so, they highlight that sterilisation was used inappropriately as a precondition to access rights in both cases, and that neither group had 'in practice' 'a real choice' to be sterilised or not.[279] On the basis of this reasoning, the *travaux préparatoires* conclude that the two groups are 'not different from each other in any decisive manner that should affect the compensation amount to a notable extent'.[280] This equal understanding of harm and 'equal and effective access to justice',[281] indiscriminately of gender identity, is in line with the most trans-inclusive global human rights developments in the 2010s.[282]

A comparison between the compensation amounts nevertheless raises some questions. In the 1999 Compensation Act, the starting point was based on prevailing insurance schemes for medical malpractice. Nevertheless, because of changing compensation practices, the sums provided to victims of involuntary

[279] Socialdepartementet [The Swedish Ministry of Health and Social Affairs] 2017a: 70–71.
[280] Ibid: 71. [281] A/RES/60/147 (2006), Article 11(a). See also Article 25.
[282] Such as OC-24/17 (2017). See the second chapter of this book.

sterilisation due to medical malpractice have increased since then.[283] Hence, even though the 1999 compensation scheme was designed to provide a higher compensation to the victims of systematic state policies than victims of individual errors in medical practice, the increasing insurance compensations in the 2000s have resulted in the opposite. This becomes particularly problematic in the 2018 Compensation Act, as the compensation amount is substantially below contemporary standards for compensation for victims of medical malpractice. This problem was also picked up by RFSL, which claimed that the compensation amount should be higher, referring to current compensation standards and that the sterilisation requirements violate the ECHR.[284] The Government has countered this claim by repeatedly highlighting the *ex gratia* character of the compensation, warranting a different standard than compensation based on public liability.[285]

Grounding compensation in *ex gratia* has given the Government a possibility to redress victims without holding the state liable, seemingly making everyone happy. From a remedial perspective, however, the crucial question of state responsibility is circumvented. This raises questions concerning victim recognition, which is both symbolically and materially important for access to remedies. It also raises questions concerning the future of the proliferating, increasingly complex *ex gratia* compensations in Sweden, mushrooming in the restrictive regulation and recognition of public liability.

3.4 Discussion

The Swedish case demonstrates a changing and globalising rights culture where rights have recently achieved a more prominent position, particularly through more active courts and judicial review. This development has gone hand in hand with an evolving national liability culture, through courts recognising public liability for rights violations and an emerging *ex gratia* compensation tradition. The changing rights culture has provided not only legal but also sociocultural rights instruments. Actors interacting with rights as master frames have been chiefly victims, civil society organisations, state representatives and mass media.

Rights as legal instruments have, however, not played a crucial role in the Swedish case. This can be observed in for instance the state's limited recognition of rights violations and legal liability, the non-retroactivity of

[283] An example of monetary compensation for complete infertility for a 30-year-old person was 363,100 Swedish Kronor (approximately 36,100 Euros) in 2016. This example is based on an applicant who is considered to have 30 per cent disability and who is able to work after the infertility. The example was included in Socialdepartementet [The Swedish Ministry of Health and Social Affairs] 2017a: 23; Karlbom, 30 November 2015 and 19 September 2016.

[284] RFSL 2017. See also Alaattinoğlu 2017.

[285] See, for example, Socialdepartementet [The Swedish Ministry of Health and Social Affairs] 2017b: 11, 14; Swedish Government Bill 2017/18:64: 11, 14.

emerging supranational and constitutional rights and the fact that many of the rights instruments referenced and utilised – such as the Yogyakarta Principles – are not legally binding. Moreover, a lack of distinction between hard and soft law is present in the referencing of supranational norms, which contributes to the impression that rights as legal instruments are not perceived as binding.

Instead, a broader, changing legal culture and an emerging tradition of compensations based on solidarity lie at its basis. According to historical laws, the involuntarily sterilised were the first group to benefit from *ex gratia* compensation, adopted in reaction to public and international outrage, as an effort by the state to amend violations in a context where public liability for damages was limited. Despite their more recent victimisation, trans victims have been similarly conceptualised by the state: as victims of historical oppression. This victim recognition and redress was not however addressed *ex officio*, but was preceded by public debate and mobilisation. Yet, a changing rights culture does not in itself lead to remedies for and reconciliation with past oppression, as evidenced by the involuntarily castrated, who have not received any recognition or redress.

Changing notions of rights, personal integrity, non-discrimination and equality have also contributed to the creation of individual, collective and public identities. The only Swedish victims who have mobilised and framed themselves collectively as rights-holders have been the trans victims. This group has successfully aligned with the recently emerging frame of supranational rights norms pertaining to sexual orientation and gender identity. Domestically, they have also repeatedly evoked the national memory of the historical practices of involuntary sterilisation and underscored the similarities between the two groups as victims of state oppression. Furthermore, their access to resources such as civil society organisations, legal expertise and international contacts has facilitated the creation of a collective identity and grievance formation in terms of rights. For the two other groups, the absence of such networks, resources and general rights frames has hindered individual and collective identity creation.

When it comes to general perceptions of victims as rights-holders, victim groups encompass among others unmarried mothers, people with disabilities and trans people – groups which have benefited from changing sociocultural notions of them as rights-holders during the twentieth and twenty-first centuries. Mass media has particularly contributed to framing sterilisations as oppressive and unjust, which has strengthened the public identity of the groups as victims. The media scandalisation of the historical sterilisations in 1997 acted as a major remedial catalyser, especially taking into consideration that victims of historical sterilisation laws generally refrained from mobilising. Regarding the involuntarily castrated, conversely, mass media has generally avoided the topic. Public views may not have changed significantly regarding the rights-holder status and victim status of the group, often portrayed as sexual offenders. As such, this group largely fails to align with sociocultural frames of rights-holders and victims.

Unlike castrations, sterilisations have been used in framing the public identity of the state. Historical and contemporary sterilisation practices have been used by media and political opposition to pressure the Government. Swedish Governments have, in turn, framed their responses to such pressure as positive developments, in particular with reference to the trans victims of sterilisation. In other words, abolishing and remedying the practices presented Governments with the opportunity to create a positive, inclusive and human rights-friendly public identity for the state.

4

Norway: 'Ethnic Cleansing'?

Like Sweden, Norway is a country which has awarded remedies for past injustices in the light of an increasing embrace of human rights. The groups subjected to sterilisation and castration practices in Norway are also similar to those in the Swedish case. Yet, the state responses to the policies are divergent in the two nations. This chapter analyses how the 1934 and 1942 Norwegian sterilisation and castration acts were established and implemented in the context of a developing rights culture, and how they were later problematised as ethnic oppression of the Romani/*tatere* minority (hereinafter the Romani).[1] Remedies for this group have nevertheless not been precedentary for other involuntarily sterilised or castrated groups. In other words, the ethnic framing did not facilitate the grievance formation process for other mobilising victims, chiefly trans people. For the latter group, the transnational element of the Swedish compensation scheme seems to have had a greater influence than national legal tradition.

4.1 Rights and Responsibilities in the National-International Web

In order to understand the domestic context surrounding involuntary sterilisations and castrations, Norwegian legal culture should first be perused, particularly as regards developing notions of rights and state responsibility. Importantly, Norway has a legal culture which embraces the Constitution[2] as

[1] Currently often understood as an ethnic belonging mostly based on self-ascription, the Romani people are an indigenous Norwegian minority, not to be confused with the Roma minority. Norwegian Romani have traditionally been craftspeople pursuing a travelling lifestyle. See Kommunal- og moderniseringsdepartementet [The Norwegian Ministry of Local Government and Modernisation] 2015a; Romanifolkets landsforening [The Romani People's Association of Norway] 2000.

[2] 17 May, the celebration of the 1814 Constitution, is the main national holiday in Norway. The Constitution is proudly the second-oldest constitution still in force in the world (after the US), the oldest one in Europe; it has paved the country's way for sovereignty: first creating a national identity separate from Denmark, subsequently securing regional autonomy and independence from Swedish rule (1814–1905), and later symbolising national resistance during the Nazi occupation (1940–1945). While having been in force for over two centuries, the Constitution has been amended over the years. Wiklund 2008: 168–169; Smith E 2003a.

well as international commitments.[3] The country has also received relatively few condemning judgments from the ECtHR. Much like in Sweden, national and international law were nevertheless long regarded as two separate worlds in Norway.[4] With more and more Norwegian cases appearing before the Strasbourg Court in the 1990s,[5] however, the normative tension between direct effect and lack of incorporation started to become a legal and political issue.[6]

The first time that international human rights were officially inserted into national legislation was through a 1994 constitutional amendment introducing a responsibility for the state to 'respect and ensure human rights'.[7] The 1999 Human Rights Act[8] incorporated the ECHR, the ICCPR and the ICESCR,[9] and later also the CRC, the CEDAW and some of their additional protocols.[10] In case of conflict between the incorporated human rights instruments and national legislation, the former should prevail; the instruments consequently assume a 'semi-constitutional status'.[11] Human rights actually appear to have

[3] Norway has been a member of the UN since 1945 and the CoE since 1949. Norway may not be an EU member state, but it is party to the European Free Trade Association (EFTA) and the European Economic Area (EEA). Like Sweden, Norway has typically been early to sign and ratify international human rights treaties. Within the UN human rights framework, the CERD was ratified in 1970; the ICCPR and the ICESCR in 1972; the CEDAW in 1981; the CAT in 1986; the CRC in 1991; the CRPD in 2013. In addition, the Rome Statute of the International Criminal Court was ratified by the Norwegian Government in 2000. Regionally, the ECHR was ratified in 1952; the European Torture Convention in 1989: the CoE Framework Convention for the Protection of National Minorities in 1999; the CoE Convention on Human Rights and Biomedicine in 2006; the Istanbul Convention in 2014. In ratifying these international instruments, the country has not made any relevant reservations with regard to this work.

[4] See Vik & Skage 2018; Bruzelius 2008.

[5] The jurisdiction of the ECtHR was not accepted until 1964. Vik & Skage 2018: 307. See also Norwegian Government Bill St.prp.nr. 83 (1951).

[6] Two of the early cases are ECtHR, *E v. Norway* (1990); *G and E v. Norway* (1983). Even though the ECtHR did not find a violation of the Convention in any of these cases, the cases were not ignored by national authorities. See also Andenæs & Bjørge 2012: 79–128; Bruzelius 2008: 32.

[7] Kongeriget Norges Grundlov [The Constitution of the Kingdom of Norway] 1814, Section 110c. This was done through Amendment No. 675, 1994. See also Kontroll- og konstitusjonskomiteen [The Norwegian Parliamentary Committee on Scrutiny and Constitutional Affairs] 1994; Justis- og politidepartementet [The Norwegian Ministry of Justice and Public Security] 1993.

[8] Lov om styrkning av menneskerettighetenes stilling i norsk rett [Act on Strengthening the Position of Human Rights in Norwegian Law], No. 30, 1999.

[9] See Justiskomiteen [The Norwegian Parliamentary Committee on Justice] 1999; Justis- og politidepartementet [The Norwegian Ministry of Justice and Public Security] 1993; Kontroll- og konstitusjonskomiteen [The Norwegian Parliamentary Committee on Scrutiny and Constitutional Affairs] 1994; Norwegian Government Bill Ot.prp.nr. 3 (1998–1999).

[10] More precisely, ECHR Protocols Nos. 1, 4, 6, 7, and 13; the first and second Optional Protocols of the ICCPR; the CRC Optional Protocols on involvement on children in armed conflict and sale of children, child prostitution and child pornography; the CEDAW Optional Protocol. See Justiskomiteen [The Norwegian Parliamentary Committee on Justice] 2003, 2009; Norwegian Government Bill Ot.prp.nr. 45 (2002–2003); Norwegian Government Bill Ot.prp.nr. 93 (2008–2009). See also Hellum 2013.

[11] The rights protected by the 1999 Human Rights Act have substantial legal importance in practice, even though the Act itself does not formally have the same legal status as the Constitution. Broch 2003: 248.

taken centre stage in modern Norwegian legal culture. The Norwegian Supreme Court refers to the ECHR more and more.[12] In 2012, human rights became a constitutionally protected, foundational value[13] through the proclamation that the Constitution 'shall ensure democracy, a state based on the rule of law and human rights'.[14] In recent decades, the small dualist country has come closer to international legal normative frameworks.

As in other Nordic countries, Norwegian courts are not the only venues for ensuring rights in practice.[15] Parliamentary review of legislation is crucial.[16] Other instances to be taken into consideration are among others the ombud institutions, which have developed at pace with evolving discrimination legislation.[17] Unlike the other countries compared in this work, Norway has a long tradition of judicial review in concrete cases,[18] however restrictively implemented, leaving constitutional amendments to the Parliament.[19]

With the Norwegian Supreme Court increasingly referring to the ECHR, public liability based on human rights violations have eventually become a topic of debate among Norwegian lawyers.[20] Despite the lack of a longstanding domestic tradition of public liability for rights violations, or perhaps exactly because of this, Norway provides extra-judicial, easily accessible compensation for individual suffering outside the scope of the 1969 Compensation Act.[21]

12 See Smith C 2005. 13 Amendment No. 522, 2012.

14 Kongeriget Norges Grundlov [The Constitution of the Kingdom of Norway] 1814, Section 2. Official English translation.

15 Rights are also regulated in legislation and through budgetary means. Smith E 2015: 346.

16 Kongeriget Norges Grundlov [The Constitution of the Kingdom of Norway] 1814, Section 66; Stortingets forretningsorden [The Norwegian Parliamentary Proceedings Act], No. 518, 2012, Section 14 Point 9. See Sejersted 2002.

17 The Gender Equality Act was established already in 1978, the Act on Prohibition of Discrimination on the Grounds of Ethnicity, Religion, Etc in 2005, and protection against discrimination was further expanded through the 2008 Act on Prohibition of Discrimination on the Ground of Disability and the 2013 Act on Prohibition of Discrimination on the Grounds of Sexual Orientation, Gender Identity and Gender Expression. In 2017–2018, the discrimination legislation was gender-neutralised and unified in the 2018 Act on Equality and Prohibition of Discrimination. On the development of anti-discrimination legislation for sexual and gender diversity, see Hellum 2021.

18 Norwegian courts have carried out judicial review since the early nineteenth century, but the concept was not specifically mentioned in the Constitution before 2014. See Kongeriget Norges Grundlov [The Constitution of the Kingdom of Norway] 1814, Section 89; Kierulf 2016; Smith E 2003b. The Supreme Court has stated that the power to review the constitutionality of laws is grounded in established constitutional customary law, in Høyesterett [The Norwegian Supreme Court], Rt. 1976 s. 1 (Kløfta). See Smith E 2015; Wiklund 2008.

19 A former obstacle for judicial review in respect of international law was the doctrine of the 'clarity requirement'. See Andenæs & Bjørge 2012: 97; Høyesterett [The Norwegian Supreme Court], Rt. 1994 s. 610 (Bølgepappkjennelsen); Rt. 2000 s. 996 (Bøhlerdommen).

20 The issue has for example been discussed in reference to the case Høyesterett [The Norwegian Supreme Court], Rt. 2013 s. 588 (Besøksforbud); Hjelmeng 2016.

21 These systems render compensation more easily accessible to protected groups through measures such as lower evidence requirements, stricter liability standards, or *ex officio* obligations for authorities to investigate. See, e.g., Lov om erstatning ved pasientskader mv. [Act on Compensation for Patient Injuries etc.], No. 53, 2001; Lov om produktansvar [Act

An institutional form of individual financial *ex gratia* compensation called *rettferdsvederlag* was launched in Norway in 1814.[22] It is used in cases in which people have suffered harm and no other legal possibilities for compensation exist. It neither aims to cover the full amount of the financial loss nor is it a compensation *stricto sensu*; rather, it is a small remedy for wrongs inflicted by the public.[23] There have also been a number of extraordinarily established *ex gratia* compensation schemes for groups since the 1990s, among others for people subjected to lobotomy (1994–1995),[24] women damaged by radiation treatment at *Radiumhospitalet* (1998–1999),[25] victims of confiscation of Jewish property (1999),[26] Norwegian war prisoners in Japan (2001)[27] and national minorities and war children (2004).[28] Even though these compensations were not based on public liability in the legal sense, their establishment temporally coincided with an increasing emphasis on rights culture in the country.

4.2 Sterilisation and Castration: Legislation and Practice

The first sterilisation and castration regulations in Norway were established during the first half of the twentieth century. In contrast to eugenic and sociopolitical sterilisation and criminological and psychiatric castration, castration of trans people long remained legally unregulated. In the following section, I set out these disparate laws and practices, paying particular attention to the legal, social and political arguments utilised for introducing and abolishing the practices.

4.2.1 Sterilisation and Castration: A Means to Shape the Population?

Norwegian regulation of sterilisation and castration was first introduced under the pretext of eugenics, social policy and crime control. Other than in Sweden, sterilisation and castration were regulated under the same normative framework in Norway. The analysis in the following nevertheless investigates

on Product Liability], No. 104, 1988; Lov om erstatning fra staten for personskade voldt ved straffbar handling m.m. [Act on State Compensation for Personal Injury Due to Punishable Act Etc.], No. 13, 2001.

22 This compensation is approved either directly by the Norwegian Parliament or by the Parliamentary Committee for *Ex Gratia* Payments, depending on its amount and nature. See Nordvik 2015: 692–693.

23 Applications for compensation are evaluated in relation to the openly formulated 'standards of the time' on the basis of 'reasonableness'. Kommunal- og regionaldepartementet [The Norwegian Ministry of Local Government] 2003.

24 Sosialdepartementet [The Norwegian Ministry of Social Affairs] 1992; Tømmerås 2002: 58–60.

25 Norwegian Government Bill St.prp.nr. 3 (1998–1999); Tømmerås 2002: 55–58.

26 Tømmerås 2002: 50–52.

27 Norwegian Government Bill St.prp.nr. 67 (2000–2001).

28 Justis- og politidepartementet [The Norwegian Ministry of Justice and Public Security] 2004; Justiskomiteen [The Norwegian Parliamentary Committee on Justice] 2004.

sterilisation and castration separately, since these interventions had different objectives and targeted different groups.

4.2.1.1 Eugenic and Sociopolitical Sterilisation

In Norway, eugenics gained popular support during the early twentieth century. Norwegian eugenics movements were supported by various actors with different aims and interests from the whole political spectrum.[29] Many arguments used in the sterilisation discussions of the time adopted and found common ground in eugenic discourse.[30] The interventions were already being practised when the first official state initiative to legally regulate sterilisation (and castration) was introduced in a state report of 1932.[31] The proposal built on the concept of voluntary sterilisation if the applicant had 'respectable' (*aktverdig*) 'grounds'.[32] The proposal also allowed for interventions without the consent of the applicant if they were permanently considered 'insane'[33] or suffered from 'inadequately developed mental faculties'.[34] According to the report, the intervention was however always to be approved by the authorities.[35] The report advised a careful approach, considering that great scientific insecurity still surrounded the topic;[36] among its authors were experts who were critical of the interventions.[37]

Both social and individual interests motivated regulation. The 1934 Government Bill highlighted the need for legislation of 'sexual interventions', a phrase used to cover both sterilisation and castration, as these were considered important to prevent hereditary illnesses and disabilities from spreading.[38] The Bill referred to a transnational trend: the established Danish and German sterilisation legislation, and the pending legislative proposals in Sweden, Finland and the UK.[39] When the Norwegian Parliamentary Committee on Justice discussed the Bill, it recognised the 'seriousness' of the intervention but emphasised the interest of the public and the coming generations in limiting the reproduction of 'inferior and weakly-equipped individuals' who would create costs for society.[40] Apart from such public interests, sterilisation was also

[29] On the importance of analysing the relationship between science and politics when investigating eugenics or human reproductive technology, see Roll-Hansen 2017. Roll-Hansen, 13 December 2016.

[30] Yet, not all people supportive of eugenic ideas endorsed (involuntary or voluntary) sterilisation. Similarly, not all advocates of sterilisation were necessarily motivated by eugenics. See Haave 2000a; Haavie 2003.

[31] Justis- og politidepartementet [The Norwegian Ministry of Justice and Public Security] 1932.

[32] Ibid: 3. [33] Ibid.

[34] Ibid. This was considered to be the mental level of a nine-year-old. See Medisinaldirektoratet [The Norwegian Directorate of Medicine] 1938.

[35] Justis- og politidepartementet [The Norwegian Ministry of Justice and Public Security] 1932: 3–4.

[36] Ibid.

[37] For example psychiatrist Ragnar Vogt was critical of coerced interventions, rejecting the idea of prioritising societal interests over individual ones. Haave 2000a; Haavie 2003.

[38] Norwegian Government Bill Ot.prp.nr. 17 (1934): 2–3. [39] Ibid.

[40] Justiskomiteen [The Norwegian Parliamentary Committee on Justice] 1934: 52.

motivated by the individual interest to prevent unwanted pregnancies.[41] The Bill was approved by Parliament in 1934.[42]

The 1934 Sterilisation Act was openly formulated and allowed for sterilisations on 'respectable grounds' in line with the *travaux préparatoires.*[43] The word 'respectable' was chosen from a desire to implement the law in keeping with public morals – not, for example, as a voluntary birth control method for prostitutes and 'promiscuous' women.[44] Three categories of consent requirements were created in the law. Voluntary applications were the point of departure.[45] Minors and people thought to be *temporarily* mentally incapable needed to give consent themselves, but they also needed the approval of a legal guardian.[46] People regarded as permanently mentally incapable could however get sterilised without their own consent.[47] According to the law, it was only the permanently mentally incapable who could get sterilised against their will. According to the 1934 Sterilisation Act, all sterilisations and castrations were to be approved by the Chief Medical Officer or the expert Sterilisation Council.[48]

One intervention which was left completely outside legal regulation was sterilisation on medical indication. Motivated by risk for health or life, these interventions were thought to fall under the legal regulation of emergency[49] to be decided by medical professionals (doctors), and not to be bureaucratically restricted.[50] Such sterilisations were supposedly carried out to decrease risks connected to childbirth, targeting women in their capacity as child bearers.[51] In practice, medical doctors did not only evaluate this indication based on medical emergency but also on other grounds – such as social and economic circumstances.[52]

In 1940, six years after the first Sterilisation Act was established, Norway was occupied by Nazi Germany. The Norwegian NS (*Nasjonal Samling,* National Union) Government enacted a new Sterilisation Act in 1942 which, unlike the previous law, did not build on free will.[53] Rather, it highlighted state interest and targeted people with a hereditary illness or defect (often referred to as feebleminded).[54] Moreover, the law ordered that people who were sentenced to prison and showed 'pronounced antisocial tendencies',[55] along with those

[41] See Justis- og politidepartementet [The Norwegian Ministry of Justice and Public Security] 1932; Justiskomiteen [The Norwegian Parliamentary Committee on Justice] 1934.

[42] Lov om adgang til sterilisering m.v. [Act on the Access to Sterilisation etc.], No. 2, 1934.

[43] Ibid, Section 3, first sentence. [44] See Haave 2000a: 84, 97.

[45] Lov om adgang til sterilisering m.v. [Act on the Access to Sterilisation etc.], No. 2, 1934, Section 3, first sentence.

[46] Ibid, Section 3, second sentence. [47] Ibid, Section 4. [48] Ibid, Sections 5–6.

[49] Regulated in the Penal Code. Almindelig borgerlig Straffelov [Penal Code], No. 10, 1902, Section 47.

[50] Haave & Giæver 2000; Justis- og politidepartementet [The Norwegian Ministry of Justice and Public Security] 1932.

[51] See Haave 2000a: 280–288. [52] Haave 2000a: 283–288; Haave & Giæver 2000: 18–25.

[53] Lov til vern om folkeætten [Act for the Protection of the Population Ancestry], No. 1, 1942.

[54] Ibid, Section 2. [55] Ibid, Section 9.

who were sentenced several times for violating the Vagrancy Act,[56] had to be examined by the authorities to determine whether sterilisation or castration was recommendable.[57] This inspection was part of the NS Government's policy to 'solve' the 'vagrancy issue', particularly targeting the Romani. While such policies against the Romani were not completely new and had also existed before the occupation, they were further centralised and emphasised during this time.[58]

Heredity was more clearly articulated in the 1942 Act than in the earlier law, making the Act more traditionally eugenic, similar to the German Nazi Sterilisation Act of 1933.[59] Yet, possibilities to sterilise on social grounds were largely missing, signalling an important difference between the laws.[60] The regulations on consent were completely removed from the 1942 Act; the more strictly defined categories of people targeted could be deprived of their reproductive abilities on the say of the Norwegian Chief Medical Officer alone.[61] The 1942 Act authorised police assistance if the applicant opposed the intervention, introducing legal permission for the authorities to use physical force.[62] Despite its officially more coercive character, however, the Act also introduced some new procedural safeguards: an absolute minimum age of 21 years,[63] and a possibility to appeal the decision of the Chief Medical Officer before the National Expert Council.[64] As such, while the 1942 Act invited the use of more force in comparison to earlier legislation, it contrastingly included regulations to prevent abuse by the authorities. In 1945, the war was over. With the Nazi occupation of Norway coming to an end, the Sterilisation Act of 1942 was annulled. Almost as if nothing had happened, the 1934 Sterilisation Act came back into force, grammatically unaltered and remained in force until 1977.

The 1934 and 1942 laws were actively implemented. According to Per Haave, a total of 44,477 sterilisations were officially registered during the period 1934–1977 – 30,509 (around 69 per cent) on women and 13,968 (around 31 per cent) on men.[65] Moreover, medical sterilisations, being legislatively unregulated and

[56] Lov om løsgjengeri, betleri og drukkenskap [Act on Vagrancy, Mendicancy and Drunkenness], No. 1, 1918.

[57] Lov til vern om folkeætten [Act for the Protection of the Population Ancestry], No. 1, 1942, Section 9.

[58] Haave 2015a: 642.

[59] See Gesetz zur Verhütung erbkranken Nachwuchses [Act for the Prevention of Hereditarily Diseased Offspring] 1933; see *Prologue*.

[60] See Aasen 1989; Haave & Giæver 2000; Haave 2000a.

[61] Lov til vern om folkeætten [Act for the Protection of the Population Ancestry], No. 1, 1942, Section 4(1).

[62] Ibid, Section 4(2). See Have 2000a: 133–134.

[63] Lov til vern om folkeætten [Act for the Protection of the Population Ancestry], No. 1, 1942, Section 3.

[64] Ibid, Sections 7–8. According to Section 8 of the law, the Expert Council consisted of two medical doctors, one eugenicist, one judge and one woman.

[65] Haave 2000a: 153.

exclusively carried out on women, were not centrally registered.[66] In his extensive research, Haave has nevertheless estimated that the total number of medical sterilisations between 1934 and 1977 could be around 42,000.[67] Together with the registered sterilisations, this amounts to an estimated total number of 86,477 interventions, of which around 72,000 (around 83 per cent) were performed on women.[68]

Whether individual sterilisations were involuntary or voluntary is difficult to determine on the basis of medical journals, as authoritative coercion and active persuasion were used to extract signatures.[69] The voluntariness of the interventions varied, with some applicants opting for sterilisation on their own initiative, others approving the social and health authorities' suggestion of sterilisation and yet some others giving in to authoritative pressure.[70] The use of coercion changed over time, and overt forms gave way to more covert methods of persuasion after the Second World War.[71] Particularly during the first 30 years of implementation, many of the sterilisations were likely not actually voluntary but the result of authority pressure[72] by making several matters conditional on sterilisation, such as discharge from an institution, marriage and abortion.[73]

With changing sociocultural attitudes regarding sexuality, reproduction and individual rights during the 1960s and 1970s, sterilisation became increasingly often used as a form of birth control, whereby emphasising voluntariness.[74] Simultaneously, there was an increase of men accessing sterilisation. Unlike in Sweden, where less flexible legislation made it difficult for men to access sterilisation as voluntary birth control, Norway had a relatively high figure of male (voluntary) sterilisations, particularly in the 1960s and 1970s. By contrast, many Norwegian women were sterilised during the earlier years of implementation, when the level of coercion was higher.[75] This said, the implementation of *involuntary* sterilisation was focused on women in Norway.

People particularly targeted by sterilisation practices were women, Romani, people who were poor and marginalised, people with mental disabilities, and individuals who broke social and sexual norms.[76] Female victims of

[66] The precise number of sterilisations can only be discovered by going through individual medical journals in all hospitals and medical clinics performing sterilisations between 1934 and 1977. See Haave 2000a: 276–299.

[67] These numbers are estimated based on medical journals from a few selected hospitals. Haave 2000a: 279.

[68] Ibid. This estimate indicates that, from the 1930s until the 1970s, Norwegian sterilisations were more prevalent than the Swedish ones, but that the latter more frequently affected women.

[69] Formal consent was sometimes given by the patients, even though they did not necessarily know what their signature meant or they were pressured into signing. See Ericsson 1997; Fodstad 1999.

[70] Haave 2003. [71] Haave 2000a: 348–380. [72] Ibid: 182–193. [73] Ibid: 371–380.

[74] See Haave 2000a: 371–380; Roll-Hansen 2005: 177. [75] Braun et al 2014: 209; Haave 2000a.

[76] See Haave 2000a, 2000b; Haave & Giæver 2000.

sterilisations were working-class, 'worn-out' mothers, and girls seen as promiscuous and naïve.[77] Men were also targeted when they failed to fulfil social expectations on acting as breadwinners.[78]

4.2.1.2 Castrations of the Deviant and Dangerous

Unlike in Sweden, sterilisation and castration were regulated under the same legislation in Norway. While both were referred to as 'sexual interventions', castration more clearly targeted unwanted sexual behaviour than sterilisation, which focused on reproduction.[79] Castration targeted the 'sexually deviant' and 'dangerous'; as such, it was supported by diverse groups, including women's movements, at its introduction.[80] The *travaux préparatoires* discussed the possibility of the introduction of forced castration, but opted for a procedure where individuals applied for the surgery themselves, building on free will.[81] Nevertheless, a constant conflict was present between involuntariness and voluntariness in the law and its implementation. This was brought to the fore with the adoption of the 1934 Act. Unlike for sterilisation, the matter of castration was debated in Parliament. A fierce voice of opposition came from the Social Rights Party's MP, Gjert Edvard Bonde,[82] who argued that a law allowing for involuntary castration was 'one of the most dangerous law proposals that have ever come to light in this country'.[83] Significantly, his critique was not directed at eugenics or invasive surgery in general, but limited to the use of forced castration on sexual offenders. He saw the latter as 'barbaric and medieval', ignoring more modern treatment methods such as psychoanalysis.[84] The criticism was countered by other MPs, indicating what they saw as Bonde's misunderstanding of the law: that it did not allow for forced castration in general, but

77 See Ericsson 1997: 59–75; Helsedirektoratet [The Norwegian Directorate of Health] 1950; Haave 2000a: 333–343.

78 This is exemplified in a 1950 court case, where a man successfully challenged his legal guardianship to escape forced sterilisation. Interestingly, the Court's evaluation of whether the plaintiff was legally capable largely depended on his socio-economic position, as well as his fulfilment of the role as a responsible citizen and breadwinner, also illustrative for the implementation of the Sterilisation Act:

> It is clear that he has, despite his small means and limited knowledge, always been able to take good care of himself. He is clean and careful with regards to himself and his clothes and does not abuse alcohol. He has reportedly disposed over his limited incomes with care and concern, even though he has used them primarily for clothes and tobacco. He does not have any noteworthy finances and no prospects of inheritance. […] He is fully informed that marriage is a serious business which can bring about responsibility and obligations. […] All things considered, the Court of Appeal does not find grounds to assign him a legal guardian.

Frostating Lagmannsrett [Frostating Court of Appeal], Appeal No. 97/1949 (1950): 490.

79 See Haave 2000a. 80 One advocate was Aas 1932.

81 Haave 2000a: 136; Norwegian Government Bill Ot.prp.nr. 17 (1934), Annex I.

82 See Haave 2000a: 106; Roll-Hansen 2005: 175; Ericsson 1997: 61; and Hassenstab 2014: 132.

83 This quote comes from a translation by Roll-Hansen 2005: 175–176. Stortinget [The Norwegian Parliament] 1934: 157–162.

84 Haave 2000a: 106.

only for non-consensual castration of the mentally incapable, who could not consent in any case.[85] Their argumentation is a good example of how castration became conceptualised as 'treatment' rather than 'punishment'. By placing the question in a different context, the meaning of 'free will' was replaced by 'best interest', warranting different standards of scrutiny.

According to the subsequently established 1934 Act, castration aimed to 'extinguish' a person's 'sexual drive'.[86] The target group of castration was relatively openly formulated in the legislation. A person could get castrated upon their own application, on invoking 'respectable grounds'.[87] In some cases, it was possible for the legal guardian or a specially appointed counsellor to apply for castration on behalf of the immediate applicant without their consent. This was the case if applicants were considered mentally ill or had severe mental disabilities and were presumed to be at risk of committing a sexual offence because of their 'abnormal sexual drive'.[88] Moreover, when the applicant was considered to have a severe mental disability, it was also possible for the local chief police constable or the manager of an institution if the applicant was detained there, to file an application on behalf of the applicant with the approval of the legal guardian or the specially appointed counsellor.[89] The final decision-making power was entrusted to the Chief Medical Officer if the applicants were legally capable and filed their own application;[90] if the applicant was a minor or had a mental illness or disability, the decision was made by the expert Sterilisation Council.[91]

Castration received further emphasis in the later 1942 Sterilisation Act, which allowed for coercion using physical force.[92] In the renewed Act, the intervention clearly targeted sexual criminals,[93] people with 'abnormal sexual drive' and people thought to be likely to carry out sexual offences.[94] Moreover, the law dictated that people who had been sentenced to prison and showed 'pronounced antisocial tendencies', ought to be examined by the authorities to determine whether castration (or sterilisation) was recommendable.[95] This examination was a measure to enhance the control over sexual criminals through castration, which did not attach importance to individual consent.[96]

When it came to the implementation of the 1934 and 1942 legislation, considerably fewer castrations than sterilisations were performed in Norway. Haave has concluded that a total of 359 castrations were registered under the

[85] Ibid.

[86] Lov om adgang til sterilisering m.v. [Act on the Access to Sterilisation etc.], No. 2, 1934, Section 1.

[87] Ibid, Section 3. [88] Ibid, Section 4(1). [89] Ibid, Section 4(2). [90] Ibid, Section 2(1).

[91] Ibid, Section 2(2).

[92] Lov til vern om folkeætten [Act for the Protection of the Population Ancestry], No. 1, 1942, Section 1.

[93] Ibid, Section 3(1). [94] Ibid, Section 3(2). [95] Ibid, Section 9.

[96] The final decision was to be made by the Chief Medical Officer. Lov til vern om folkeætten [Act for the Protection of the Population Ancestry], No. 1, 1942, Section 4(1).

1934 Sterilisation Act, and 56 under the 1942 Sterilisation Act.[97] Castration was mostly used during the period 1934–1956, with a peak in the late 1940s.[98] The total number of castrations was 415, constituting only 0.9 per cent of the total number of registered 'sexual interventions' between 1934 and 1977. 370 castrations (89 per cent) were carried out on men, and 45 castrations (11 per cent) on women.[99] Hence, even though castrations generally targeted men as (presumed) sexual offenders, a significant number of interventions were also performed on women, particularly in the form of hysterectomies to treat 'hysterical' women in psychiatric wards.[100] Interestingly, moreover, despite rarely being regarded as a criminal threat and prosecuted accordingly, homosexual men were subjected to castration as sexual deviants, similar to the Swedish case.[101] Even though sexual offenders were targeted in the *travaux préparatoires*, and formally in the legislation as well, castration was thus also effected on other grounds, beyond the strict scope of criminality.[102]

No statistics exist on how many castrations were voluntary or involuntary, but the majority of the applications lacked the applicants' formal consent.[103] Similar to the sterilisations, some castration applicants signed the application forms under coercive conditions: for example, when the intervention was used as a condition to be released from a psychiatric institution.[104]

4.2.1.3 Accommodation through Castration? The Case of Trans People

The existence of people whose gender identity did not match their legally registered gender became of particular interest to the medical community in the latter half of the twentieth century.[105] When the sterilisation legislation was revised in 1977, the medical faculty at the University of Oslo pointed out that 'castration in connection to transsexualism' was 'not mentioned at all' in the draft law.[106] In response, national expert medical doctors Jørgen Herman

97 Haave 2000a: 137, Table 5.1. 98 Ibid: 139. 99 Ibid: 138. 100 Ibid: 137.

101 However, no research regarding the extent of this practice has yet been undertaken. Some examples are recounted in Bremer J 1958. See also Haave 2000a: 142. The Norwegian case sheds light on the complex relationship between castration and the medicalisation and criminalisation of sexuality and sexual behaviour as sexual deviance and danger. An interesting example is homosexual men, who discursively fell between criminality and medicalisation. While same-sex sexual acts between men (not women) were criminalised until 1972, these acts were generally not found to pose a great threat to public security and were rarely prosecuted. Almindelig borgerlig Straffelov [Penal Code], No. 10, 1902, Section 213 (abolished in 1972). Halsos 2007.

102 Have 2000a: 137–140. A particularly targeted group was patients at psychiatric hospitals, who were not necessarily guilty of any crime, but regarded as 'sexually troublesome'.

103 According to the 1934 Sterilisation Act, 60.0 per cent of women's, and 80.5 per cent of men's, castration applications lacked the applicant's consent. According to Haave, the last castration of a woman from which formal consent was missing was carried out in 1952; the last intervention on a man without formal consent occurred in 1968. Haave 2000a: 138.

104 Ibid: 140.

105 See the Prologue of this book. On the development in Norway, see Sandal 2021.

106 Norwegian Government Bill Ot.prp.nr. 46 (1976–1977): 10.

Vogt and Per Anchersen were consulted, recommending that 'these interventions should take place on pure medical indications, and should therefore be kept outside the legislation in question'.[107] As a result, practices of castration in connection to gender-affirming surgery remained legally unregulated, even though the intervention was used as an administrative precondition for amending one's legally registered gender. The possibility to amend the gender identifier in the personal identification number had already been legislatively introduced in 1979, albeit without specifying the preconditions for such legal gender recognition.[108]

The administrative practice presented a narrow road to legal gender recognition for trans people.[109] Recognition long depended on clearance from one single institution: the Oslo University Hospital. Since its commencement of gender-affirming treatment in the early 1960s,[110] the hospital only accepted a fragment of the number of trans people for treatment, namely people diagnosed to be transsexual by a specialist team.[111] This meant that the trans people who did not pass the admission test could not access gender-affirming treatment or legal gender recognition.[112] Conversely, the people approved were subjected to a fixed set of gender-confirming treatments, referred to as 'real sex reassignment', including surgical removal of reproductive organs.[113] As the castration precondition was never legislatively regulated, no *travaux préparatoires* exist which would render its motivation or justification visible. Nevertheless, the 1979 letter from chief psychiatrist Per Anchersen at Oslo University Hospital to the Norwegian Government reflects some considerations prevalent among medical experts of the time:

107 Ibid.

108 The personal identification number is needed for people who work and/or reside in Norway. See Lov om folkeregistrering [Act on Population Registration], No. 1, 16 January 1970, Section 4. See Forskrifter om føringen og ordningen av folkeregistrene [Decree on the Administration of the Population Registration], No. 9, 1979; Forskrift om folkeregistrering [Decree on Population Registration], No. 161, 1994; Foreskrift om folkeregistrering [Decree on Population Registration], No. 1268, 2007. See Sørlie 2015: 360; 2013: 36. Lov om folkeregistrering [Act on Population Registration], No. 1, 1970.

109 See Amnesty International 2014; Sørlie 2013.

110 According to Tone Maria Hansen at the Norwegian Harry Benjamin Resource Centre, the first gender-affirming surgery was performed at Oslo University Hospital in 1963. Hansen, 12 December 2016.

111 The categories in question, F64.0 and F64.2, were classified as gender identity disorders according to the International Classification of Diseases. Amnesty International 2014: 71.

112 Amnesty International 2014: 71. The lack of access to health care for trans people not fitting within the Norwegian authorities' category of 'transsexualism' is criticised from a right to health perspective in Sørlie 2018. People who had undergone privately financed gender-affirming surgery abroad were only able to get their registered gender changed through confirmation by Oslo University Hospital until 2013, when the Norwegian Directorate of Health took over this task. See Lohne 2013.

113 See Amnesty International 2014: 71–74.

> As far as women are concerned, I have presented the reasons for recommending castration, since without this, there is *at least a theoretical possibility* to be converted into a *menstruating man*. And to only conduct a simple sterilisation (which may be unsuccessful) one could *in the worst case become a man who can become a mother*. Such a […] calamity would create *unsolvable legal complications* and discredit the whole treatment procedure for transsexuals.[114]

The above quote runs along similar lines to the related Swedish *travaux préparatoires*: representing fear of reproduction crossing traditional gender boundaries, epitomised by the man who gives birth.[115] The Norwegian administrative practice was even more invasive of bodily integrity than the Swedish legislation, requiring castration instead of sterilisation.[116] What is particularly interesting is that the Norwegian *legislation* did not mention the words sterilisation or castration, only referring to 'changed gender status'.[117] The invasive, mandatory surgical intervention was therefore never subjected to the political scrutiny of parliamentary review to which legislation is subject. Instead, the precondition was governed by medical expertise.[118]

Despite scientific, social and legal developments, the Norwegian administrative practice for amendment of legally registered gender remained unaltered for four decades.[119] When the administration of gender-affirming medical treatment was brought up in Parliament in 2000,[120] however, MP Olav Gunnar Ballo from the Socialist Left Party criticised Norway for not having legislation 'connected to transsexuals', which a number of European countries had already instituted at the time.[121] The Health Minister rejected the comment as outside of the scope of the debate, leaving the question hanging.[122] Apart from this incident, the castration requirement and the lack

114 Quote included in Helsedirektoratet [The Norwegian Directorate of Health] 2015: 65. Translated from Norwegian. Emphasis added.

115 On this reasoning, see also Sørlie 2016; Sandal 2021: 57.

116 However, Swedish administrative practices are also claimed to have encouraged more invasive surgeries than required by legislation, such as castration and gender-affirming surgeries. See Burman & RFSL 2013.

117 Forskrift om folkeregistrering [Decree on Population Registration], No. 1268, 2007, Sections 2-2 and 2-5.

118 This made the practice particularly questionable in the light of Art 8 ECHR. See Sørlie 2013. The lack of legislative transparency was emphasised by Van der Ros, 2 January 2017.

119 The practice of amendment of legally registered gender between the 1970s and the 2010s was based on a medicalised understanding of the 'transsexual' prevalent in 1960s psychiatry. See Sørlie 2013.

120 This came up in relation to the dissolution of the Gender Identity Disorder Clinic. Frydenlund, 10 December 2016.

121 Stortinget [The Norwegian Parliament] 2000: 2059. Frydenlund, 10 December 2016.

122 Ibid.

of legislation were generally not topics for political or public discussion until more recent years.[123]

An estimated 500 people were castrated because of the administrative requirement between the 1970s and 2016.[124] There are however no official numbers on how many people underwent the treatment at Oslo University Hospital, that is, who were castrated as a condition for legal gender recognition, before the practice was changed in 2016.[125]

4.2.2 Criticism and Abolition

4.2.2.1 Sterilisation

The 1934 and 1942 laws by and large received no public criticism. The legislation was uncontroversial among the political elites, with its implementation being surrounded by a wall of silence and secrecy regulations.[126] After the end of the German occupation, sterilisations continued to be carried out, as they were viewed as different from Nazi practices. The incessant push for sterilisation of the feebleminded by the Norwegian Director of Health Karl Evang in the 1950s implies that sterilisation was essentially uncontentious.[127] The accession of Norway to the ECHR in the 1950s neither had a direct impact on how sterilisation/castration practices were viewed nor were these laws questioned in the accession process.[128] While no broader or collective attempts were made to challenge the 1934 or 1942 laws in the 1950s or 1960s, some exceptional individual resistance has been documented. These acts of defiance were not only

[123] See Lindvik, 7 December 2016; Frydenlund, 10 December 2016; Paulsrud, 7 December 2016. An interest group to guard the rights of patients at the Oslo University Hospital Gender Identity Disorder Clinic was established in 2000 under the name of the Norwegian Federation for Transsexuals *(Landsforeningen for transseksuelle)*. This organisation later changed its name to the Harry Benjamin Resource Centre and cooperated with the hospital. The hospital's monopoly position and the mutual support between the patient organisation and the hospital – both narrowly understanding the interest group as people with gender incongruence, often avoiding the term trans – are among the reasons for the long lack of organised trans activism challenging the administrative practice.

[124] The number 500 is used as an informal reference by civil society as well as authorities in Norway, since no official statistics exist. See Myrberg, 3 and 13 February 2017.

[125] None of the authorities which have access to the sensitive information in question, i.e., the Oslo University Hospital and the Norwegian Tax Administration, nor the patient interest organisation Harry Benjamin Resource Centre, have kept anonymised statistics. Duurhuus, 29 November 2016; Hansen, 12 December 2016. The number of patients referred to the Gender Identity Disorder clinic at Oslo University Hospital was 115 in 2011, of which 30 were denied treatment; in 2012, this number was 152 (60 denied); in 2013, 179 (43 denied). Helsedirektoratet [The Norwegian Directorate of Health] 2015: 37.

[126] Fodstad 1999; 2000.

[127] See Helsedirektoratet [The Norwegian Directorate of Health] 1950.

[128] This is reflected in the lack of reservations regarding sterilisation and lack of legal amendments of the Sterilisation Act in connection to the accession. Kommunal- og moderniseringsdepartementet [The Norwegian Ministry of Local Government and Modernisation] 2015a; Ekeløve-Slydal, 7 December 2016.

committed by the victims themselves, but also by others, such as people working at institutions.[129]

The implementation of the 1934 Sterilisation Act changed over time. Like in Sweden, alternative forms of contraception became increasingly available in Norway in the 1960s and 1970s.[130] Additionally, medical research on heredity and genetics evolved, slowly leading to a change in public views on the role of sterilisation and how the intervention should be regulated and administered. Another important influence on these changed public views was Norwegian women's movements for increased gender equality and free abortion,[131] together with changing views on institutionalisation and individual rights.

A new Sterilisation Act was introduced in 1977. It was motivated by a growing amount of applications, a need to introduce possibilities for appeal and most of all because the other Nordic countries had recently introduced more liberal sterilisation legislation, emphasising individual agency.[132] The Government Bill establishing the law highlighted that people who wanted to get sterilised should first be given information about the procedure and other forms of contraception.[133] The proposal was that people with 'mental illnesses' should however not be sterilised unless the authorities had approved of such sterilisation.[134] The *travaux préparatoires* imply the awakening of a reproductive rights discourse, conceptualised under the notion of privacy: 'The right to decide for oneself if one wants to have children, and how many, appears for more and more people as a personal matter'.[135] Such statements indicate a break from earlier public views on reproduction as a matter for state authorities.

Unlike the Swedish legislative reform in 1975, which clearly distanced itself from earlier laws, the Norwegian legislation is characterised by continuity.[136] While the *travaux préparatoires* pronounced individual rights, the legislative regulation nevertheless remained relatively similar. The Norwegian 1977 Sterilisation Act is still in force at the moment of writing. Much like its Swedish counterpart, the Norwegian law has a general age limit of 25 years.[137] The legislation

129 Psychologist Gori Gunvald, working at the institution Bjerketun for girls, was someone who was actively trying to raise the scores of the IQ tests for the girls at the institution in order for them not to be sterilised. Ericsson 1997: 60; Ericsson & Papendorf, 8 December 2016.

130 The most important were contraceptive pills, which were introduced in Norway in 1967. Nesheim 2018.

131 For a more detailed account on women's changing role in Norwegian twentieth-century society and the regulation of birth control, see Andresen & Elvbakken 2018.

132 The Government Bill referred to new legislation in Sweden, Denmark and Iceland, according to which people above 25 years of age had the autonomous right to decide if they wanted to get sterilised, suggesting a similar legislative development in Norway. Norwegian Government Bill Ot.prp.nr. 46 (1976–1977): 3.

133 Norwegian Government Bill Ot.prp.nr. 46 (1976–1977): 6. 134 Ibid.

135 Ibid. See also Sosialkomiteen [The Norwegian Parliamentary Committee on Social Affairs] 1977.

136 Roll-Hansen 2005: 176. See Steriliseringslag [Sterilisation Act] (1975:580).

137 Lov om sterilisering [Act on Sterilisation], No. 57, 1977, Section 2.

still allows for interventions which are not based on the applicant's request in exceptional cases,[138] such as when the applicant has permanent severe mental illnesses or disabilities and is unable to make an informed, free choice.[139] The lack of distinct rhetoric change might be traced back to the more open-worded formulation of the Norwegian eugenic and sociopolitical sterilisation legislation in comparison to the Swedish one, in practice having already left more space for voluntary choice before the revision of the law in the 1970s.[140]

4.2.2.2 Castration in Modern Norway?

Unlike sterilisation, castration was controversial even before its legislative introduction.[141] Later, in the 1950s, the therapeutic efficiency of the interventions became increasingly questioned by medical experts and crucially by the national Sterilisation Council as well.[142] Karl Evang, the aforementioned Norwegian Director of Health who advocated for sterilisations of the feebleminded in the same decade, was highly critical of castration. He particularly decried the use of castration on sexual offenders in exchange for more lenient punishments, viewing such practices as coercive.[143] This contemporary criticism of castration practices does not merely problematise the unscientific or unmodern character of the interventions; conceptualising their coercive circumstances as impermissible also signals an implicit rights consciousness.

Despite the successive abandonment of the practice in the 1960s and 1970s, castration was maintained in a relatively unaltered form in the 1977 Sterilisation Act. The intervention is permitted if applicants have an 'abnormal sexual drive'

[138] The indications for sterilisation have to be one of the following: when pregnancy or childbirth might lead to significant danger for the female applicant's physical or mental health; when taking care of a child might put the applicant in a particularly difficult situation; when there is a risk for serious hereditary disease or defect in the child; when the applicant is unable to take satisfactory care of a child because of mental illness or mental disability. For the two last indications, sterilisation is to be considered the best method of preventing childbirth. See Lov om sterilisering [Act on Sterilisation], No. 57, 1977, Section 3 and 5(2).

[139] Lov om sterilisering [Act on Sterilisation], No. 57, 1977, Section 4(3). The people in question can be sterilised upon application by their legal guardians, with the approval of a regional Sterilisation Committee. The Committee's decisions can be appealed to the national Sterilisation Council according to Section 5(2) of the same law. The legislation was amended in 2006 to bring it in line with the CoE Convention on Human Rights and Biomedicine, emphasising that all interventions should be based on the applicant's best interest. Norwegian Government Bill Ot.prp.nr. 63 (2005–2006). Even though the current Norwegian law allows for more invasive interventions than the Swedish one, where only the applicants themselves can apply for sterilisation – even in cases where they have a legal guardian – this is not generally considered to lead to coercive interventions in practice. This perception is reflected in a lack of mobilisation around the topic among Norwegian disability rights organisations. Ekberg, 27 October 2016; Hansen, 7 November 2016; Sørlie-Rogne, 26 October 2016; Syse, 25 October 2016. See Syse 2001.

[140] This was discussed in my interview with Roll-Hansen, 13 December 2016.

[141] See Norwegian Government Bill Ot.prp.nr. 17 (1934): Annex I.

[142] Haave 2000a: 139–143. A vital medical study on castration, which is critical of the effects of the intervention, is Bremer J 1958.

[143] Haave 2000a: 143.

and they are likely to commit sexual offences as a result.[144] The point of departure is the applicant's own request,[145] but in cases in which the applicant suffers from a severe mental illness or disability, the decision can also be made by the legal guardian or the regional police officer in chief.[146] Accordingly, a growing emphasis on individual rights, reproductive autonomy and medical advancements were reflected in the changing implementation, rather than the text, of the law with regard to both sterilisation and castration in Norway.

4.2.2.3 Legal Recognition of Gender Identity: Criticism and Legislation

More expression forums for trans issues in Norway have been created in recent decades through increasing and more inclusive activism. Trans activism has become visible in the aftermath of other successful LGBT+ rights struggles, among which are the introduction of registered partnerships in 1993 and marriage equality in 2008/2009.[147] More visibility has also led to more vocal resistance against injustices affecting trans people, such as questioning preconditions for legal gender recognition. Important milestones have been the establishment of a national trans political committee; the official inclusion of trans on the agenda of the Norwegian Association for Gender and Sexuality Diversity (FRI, previously called LLH);[148] a change in approach of the Norwegian Association for Trans People (FTPN), becoming more outwardly oriented;[149] the active engagement of Amnesty International in LGBT questions in Norway through local trans rights activists.[150] The domestic trans community has also become increasingly connected to international and foreign LGBT+ organisations.[151]

In the light of these expanding socio-organisational resources, the preconditions for legal gender recognition became scrutinised in terms of rights in the 2010s. In 2010, the earlier mentioned organisation FRI/LLH sent a letter to the Norwegian authorities, claiming that the Norwegian preconditions were contrary to CoE recommendations, recalling the previous developments where the Commissioner for Human Rights and PACE had condemned legal

144 Lov om sterilisering [Act on Sterilisation], No. 57, 1977, Section 8(1). 145 Ibid.

146 Ibid, Sections 4(3); 8(2); 9. With the intervention being considered invasive and unusual and not to be used for contraception, the Norwegian Sterilisation Council always has to approve castration applications before the intervention can be carried out. The current legislation, which theoretically leaves the door open to involuntary castration, might however paint an unrealistic picture of reality. According to the Norwegian Directorate of Health, no castration applications have occurred for several decades, mirrored by a lack of civil society activism around castration.

147 Lov om registrert partnerskap [Act on Registered Partnership], No. 40, 1993 was abolished through a 2008 amendment, which introduced marriage equality.

148 Originally, it focused on the interests of gay men and lesbian women. Frydenlund, 10 December 2016.

149 For a long time, FTPN had been an organisation which was internally-oriented, with its members being afraid of visibility mainly due to transphobia. Lindvik, 7 December 2016.

150 Frydenlund, 10 December 2016; Kaatee, 6 December 2016.

151 Such as TGEU and ILGA. See Frydenlund, 10 December 2016; Lindvik, 7 December 2016.

gender recognition preconditioned on surgical requirements.[152] Attentive to the conceptualisation of rights furthered by the activists, the Norwegian Directorate of Health released a preliminary report in 2011 which was written from a rights-based perspective.[153] Referring to international policy documents such as the 2009 report of the CoE Human Rights Commissioner, the 2010 CoE Committee of Ministers Recommendation against Discrimination on the Ground of Sexual Orientation and Gender Identity and the Yogyakarta Principles,[154] the report relevantly stated that the requirements for surgical intervention and castration were contrary to the respect for a person's physical integrity under the ECHR.[155] The activism thus phrased its criticism of the law in line with emerging supranational soft law around trans rights, which led to an institutional response. As such, the authority's reaction to the rights terminology demonstrates frame alignment.

The draft report and its rights framing nevertheless received a mixed response among stakeholders, which led to its reformulation. While organisations like LLH and FTPN generally supported the initiative to abolish castration requirements, the report was harshly criticised as unscientific and misleading by the Oslo University Hospital and the Harry Benjamin Resource Centre patient organisation, referring to medical literature on transsexualism.[156] As this criticism came from the only national hospital treating trans people and the only official patient-interest organisation, it was taken very seriously by the Directorate of Health, which 'considerably restated' its narrative.[157] In the 2012 final report, the human rights-based criticism of the earlier draft was evidently downplayed. Instead of a rights violation, castration was framed as an integral part of the 'medical treatment of transsexuals'.[158] However, a slight criticism of the concept of 'real sex conversion' in the treatment was upheld. Further investigation was indicated to be necessary.[159]

Later the same year, however, the Stockholm Administrative Court of Appeal handed down the judgment where it considered the Swedish infertility/sterilisation requirement to be a violation of constitutional and human rights.[160] In this context, the Norwegian LGBT civil society organisations LLH, Skeiv Ungdom and FTPN, together with Amnesty International, stepped up their activism.[161] The campaign consisted of active use of human rights rhetoric, lobbying and a petition to abolish the surgical preconditions for legal

152 Helsedirektoratet [The Norwegian Directorate of Health] 2011: 15; CM/Rec(2010)5.

153 Helsedirektoratet [The Norwegian Directorate of Health] 2011.

154 CoE Commissioner for Human Rights 2009; CM/Rec(2010)5; and International Commission of Jurists 2007.

155 Helsedirektoratet [The Norwegian Directorate of Health] 2011: 17.

156 See FTPN 2011; LLH 2011; HBRS 2011; Oslo University Hospital 2011. See also Sørlie 2016.

157 Helsedirektoratet [The Norwegian Directorate of Health] 2012: 1.

158 Ibid: 16.

159 Ibid: 16–17.

160 See Kammarrätten i Stockholm [Stockholm Administrative Court of Appeal], 1968-12 (2012) and Chapter 3 in this work.

161 Amnesty International Norway 2012.

gender recognition, chiefly castration.[162] Patricia Kaatee, Policy Advisor at the national department of Amnesty International, described the campaign in the following words:

> How you present questions conditions how the receiver understands the seriousness in what you are saying. [...] the weight, and the strength in Amnesty, is that at the moment we, in our research [...] document that this is [...] about rights violations, then – at least in the Nordic countries – we are listened to. So, I think that we did not say anything that others had not said before us, but we put it in another story then, another narrative... we said, 'this is about rights, and Norwegian authorities are breaking what they have committed to protect'.[163]

With these words, Kaatee highlighted the importance of framing the question as one of rights, as well as of the organisational and political weight of Amnesty International in the civil society campaign. Noticeably, the campaigns focused on the castration practices above other administrative requirements.[164] The Norwegian castration requirement was often referred to as 'irreversible sterilisation' rather than castration, possibly influenced by the simultaneous Swedish civil society campaign.[165] Media and academia also picked up on the activism, helping to raise public awareness.[166]

In 2014, Amnesty included Norway in a report on the situation of trans people in Europe,[167] which coincided with its international human right campaign focusing on John Jeanette Solstad Remø, a trans woman not allowed to amend her legally registered gender because of her reluctance to undergo castration.[168] Trans rights activist Stein Wolff Frydenlund, who played a decisive role in including Norway in the 2014 Amnesty report and campaign, described the pressure which the campaign put on the Norwegian Government in the following words:

> A public focus was created, because the campaign for John Jeanette was massive [...] and it was very visible that there was something wrong here... and Amnesty had a great weight [...] Amnesty does not criticise Norwegian authorities particularly often, at least not to the extent that was done then.[169]

162 Ibid. 163 Kaatee, 6 December 2016. Translated from Norwegian.

164 According to Anniken Sørlie, this was also the requirement which many people thought was the gravest interference. Sørlie, 7 December 2016.

165 The cooperation of, and transnational influence between Swedish and Norwegian trans rights activists were highlighted by Frydenlund, 10 December 2016. The relevance of the Swedish legal developments was underlined by Sørlie, 7 December 2016, and Paulsrud, 9 December 2016.

166 See Lohne et al 2013; Akre 2013. An important contemporary documentary series that followed trans people which was broadcast on national television was *Født i feil kropp [Born in the Wrong Body]* (2014). In 2013 and 2014, the Norwegian administrative practices for changing legal gender were closely scrutinised nationally, most importantly in Van Der Ros 2013; Sørlie 2013; 2014.

167 The other countries covered in the report were Denmark, Finland, France, Ireland, Belgium and Germany. Amnesty International 2014.

168 Kaatee, 6 December 2016. See Amnesty International 2015.

169 Frydenlund, 10 December 2016.

The Amnesty-led campaign for John Jeanette was strengthened by the outcome of the decision in her case before the Norwegian Equality and Anti-discrimination Ombud, delivered in 2014. The legally non-binding, but influential decision scrutinised the mandatory requirements for legal gender recognition: diagnosis and hormonal and surgical treatment, involving irreversible sterilisation (castration).[170] The decision found that these requirements were a violation of the domestic legislative prohibition of discrimination on the grounds of gender identity and expression.[171] The preconditions indirectly placed trans applicants in a worse position than other people through different legal treatments.[172] The applicant could therefore not fully express her gender identity, making such different treatment unlawful discrimination. The decision particularly focused on the requirement of irreversible sterilisation/ castration. The Ombud supported her decision on the basis of emerging supranational and transnational sources regarding trans rights: ECtHR practice,[173] international soft law[174] and recent developments in other countries,[175] particularly the Swedish court decision.[176] A key development in the domestic sphere was the 2013 Act on Prohibition of Discrimination on the Grounds of Sexual Orientation, Gender Identity and Gender Expression,[177] expanding the legal recognition of discrimination of trans people.[178]

Sensing the political controversy and emerging legal tensions,[179] the Government appointed an expert group to investigate the preconditions for

170 See Langseth & Falch, 6 December 2016. Likestillings- og diskrimineringsombudet [The Norwegian Equality and Anti-discrimination Ombud], Decision No. 14/840 (2014).

171 Lov om forbud mot diskriminering på grunn av seksuell orientering, kjønnsidentitet og kjønnsuttrykk [Act on Prohibition of Discrimination on the Grounds of Sexual Orientation, Gender Identity and Gender Expression], No. 58, 2013, Section 5.

172 Likestillings- og diskrimineringsombudet [The Norwegian Equality and Anti-discrimination Ombud], Decision No. 14/840 (2014).

173 ECtHR, *Van Kück v. Germany* (2003): Para 69; *Christine Goodwin v. the United Kingdom* (2002); and *I v. the United Kingdom* (2002). The Ombud also referred to *Y.Y. v. Turkey*, but the ECtHR had not yet handed down a judgment in the matter at the time. See ECtHR, *Y.Y. v. Turkey* (2015).

174 International Commission of Jurists 2007, Principle 3; CommDH/IssuePaper(2009)2; WPATH 2010.

175 Sweden, Denmark, Iceland, Germany, Argentina and the United Kingdom.

176 Kammarrätten i Stockholm [Stockholm Administrative Court of Appeal], 1968-12 (2012). Questions about compensation falls outside of the competences of the Ombud. Likestillings- og diskrimineringsombudet [The Norwegian Equality and Anti-discrimination Ombud], Decision No. 14/840 (2014).

177 Lov om forbud mot diskriminering på grunn av seksuell orientering, kjønnsidentitet og kjønnsuttrykk [Act on Prohibition of Discrimination on the Grounds of Sexual Orientation, Gender Identity and Gender Expression], No. 58, 2013. See also Hellum 2016.

178 Langseth & Falch, 6 December 2016. However, the castration requirement was not mentioned in the law's *travaux préparatoires*. Norwegian Government Bill Prop. 88 L (2012-2013). In order to demonstrate its importance, mention should be made of the fact that a case identical to the 2014 case was dismissed by the Ombud in 2012, as no domestic law was in place yet to recognise such preconditions as discriminatory. Likestillings- og diskrimineringsombudet [The Norwegian Equality and Anti-discrimination Ombud], Decision No. 12/650 (2013).

179 See Helsedirektoratet [The Norwegian Directorate of Health] 2012.

legal gender recognition in 2013.[180] Moreover, the Norwegian Minister of Health at the time, Bent Høie from the Conservative Party, was pressed on the topic during a debate at the Oslo LGBT Pride Festival in 2014, and prematurely promised a legislative change.[181] Subsequently, the appointed expert group published its final report in 2015, recommending the abolishment of all surgical preconditions.[182] In the report, especially the right to non-discrimination, the right to private life and the right to health care were emphasised as human rights negatively affected by the administrative practice.[183] Much like the Swedish Government Bill,[184] the Norwegian report highlighted the international developments in the field, stating that the ECtHR could potentially find the Norwegian practice to violate the Convention.[185]

Following the institutional framing of the administrative practice as potentially rights-violating, the ensuing legislative process did not encounter any obstacles. The Bill to introduce the Act on Amendment of Legal Gender built on the same rights argumentation presented by the expert group, that is, focusing on the right to non-discrimination and protection of private life.[186] It was passed by Parliament without further ado. The 2016 Norwegian Act on Amendment of Legal Gender, which makes it possible to amend legal gender simply through 'ticking a box', has been depicted as cutting-edge because of its accessibility, receiving worldwide attention.[187] It only has two preconditions: the first is that the applicant is a Norwegian resident or citizen of Norway;[188] the second is that the applicant declares that they identify with 'the other gender',[189] rather than the one documented in the population register.[190] In the months after the law entered into force, hundreds of people applied for legal gender recognition.[191]

To sum up, the activism to abolish castration and the other preconditions for legal gender recognition in Norway was able to effectively operationalise emerging supranational soft law norms concerning the rights of trans people.

180 Helsedirektoratet [The Norwegian Directorate of Health] 2015.

181 Paulsrud, 9 December 2016.

182 Helsedirektoratet [The Norwegian Directorate of Health] 2015.

183 Ibid: 70–78. The report referred to the Norwegian Constitution, Sections 98 and 102; ECHR Articles 8 and 14; ICCPR Articles 2(1), 17 and 26; ICESCR Article 12; and CRC Article 2(1).

184 See Swedish Government Bill Prop. 2011/12:142.

185 Helsedirektoratet [The Norwegian Directorate of Health] 2015: 77.

186 Norwegian Government Bill Prop. 74 L (2015–2016): 10–11.

187 See Knight 2016. See also Lindvik, 7 December 2016.

188 Forskrift om endring av juridisk kjønn for norske statsborgere bosatt i utlandet [Decree on Amendment of Legal Gender for Norwegian Citizens Residing Abroad], No. 1565, 2016.

189 Norwegian legislation currently only recognises two options: male or female.

190 Lov om endring av juridisk kjønn [Act on Amendment of Legal Gender], No. 46, 2016, Section 2. The general age limit is set to 16; other rules apply to younger children. See Section 4(1–3).

191 190 people applied for amendment of legal gender within the first month after the law was passed; by the end of November 2016, over 400 applications had been made. Duurhuus, 29 November 2016.

Amplified by transnational developments, importantly the Swedish strategic litigation and subsequent legislative change, together with effective resource mobilisation, this rights alignment soon provoked an institutional response. The alignment, in other words, led to the adoption of legal gender recognition based on self-ascription.

4.3 Remedies?

After having examined the establishment and abolishment of past sterilisation and castration practices, I here investigate victims' mobilisation for remedies. I first discuss redress to Romani victims, who were among those most vulnerable to sterilisations. Members of the group have actively mobilised, effectively becoming the focal point of the Norwegian debate on remedies. I then focus on remedies for other victim groups, including that of trans people, and compare the differences.

4.3.1 Remedies for Romani People

In Norway, many remedies for sterilisation victims have been directed at Romani people. Subjected to discrimination throughout Norwegian history, the group was oppressed through organised, abusive assimilation policies during the twentieth century,[192] which included child abduction, involuntary sterilisation, bullying, registration and the prohibition of Romani language and lifestyle.[193] The mistreatment was perpetrated by the state and the Mission, a private religious organisation with strong ties to the state.[194] Since the 1990s (after the church Mission was abolished),[195] the topic of involuntary sterilisation has been predominantly framed as state oppression of the Romani minority.[196]

192 See Fodstad 1999; 2000; Haave 2000b; 2000a; 2007; 2015a; 2015b; Kommunal- og moderniseringsdepartementet [The Norwegian Ministry of Local Government and Modernisation] 2015a. See also Hvinden 2000a.

193 This occurred in particular through the use of Lov om løsgjengeri, betleri og drukkenskap [Act on Vagrancy, Mendicancy and Drunkenness], No. 1, 1918. See Kommunal- og moderniseringsdepartementet [The Norwegian Ministry of Local Government and Modernisation] 2015a.

194 See Haave 2000a; Fodstad 1999.

195 The church Mission was abolished in 1986. Romanifolkets landsforening [The Romani People's Association of Norway] 2000: 9.

196 In 1973, the state television NRK broadcast Vibeke Løkkeberg's documentary *Tatere* about the abuse and ill-treatment of the inhabitants at a working colony for Romani people. The documentary evoked some national debate. In 1975, Norwegian Socialist Left Party MP Torild Skard made an interpellation in Parliament, asking about the conditions of the Romani in Norway. As a consequence of the criticism, the state investigated the assimilation policies. At the time, however, no reference was made to sterilisation or castration. See Hvinden 2000a: 12; Romanifolkets landforening [The Romani People's Association of Norway] 2000: 9; Sosialdepartementet [The Norwegian Ministry of Social Affairs] 1980; Den Norske Helsingforskomite [The Norwegian Helsinki Committee] 2009: 49; Sosialkomiteen [The Norwegian Parliamentary Committee on Social Affairs] 1977; Norwegian Government Bill Ot.prp.nr. 46 (1976–1977).

The minority however also mobilised against oppression. In the 1990s, Romani mobilisation included the foundation of organisations for Romani people,[197] and the publication of literature on abuse against the minority.[198] In the mid-1990s, the question of remedies for the Romani for past abusive policies was raised in Parliament by the Workers' Communist Party MP Erling Folkvord.[199] In his intervention, Folkvord used the powerful term 'ethnic cleansing' – a term also used by some of the actively mobilised Romani – bringing to mind genocide and international criminal legal discourse.[200] Moreover, being approached by a few Romani activists in 1993, the Norwegian Helsinki Committee (a domestic human rights NGO) turned to the Ministry of Social Affairs to apply for research funding to investigate past assimilation policies.[201] Even though this request was denied, the Ministry initiated a greater research project on the topic two years later.[202]

The publicly funded research project was finalised and published in 2000.[203] It included an extensive historical report on sterilisation and castration policies and practices,[204] and an interview-based study of sterilisation practices.[205] The investigation showed that while Romani people – and women in particular[206] – were vulnerable to sterilisation practices, they were not victims of a systematic state policy of ethnic extermination.[207] The claims of systematic 'ethnic cleansing' were therefore dismissed, but the remedy discussion remained on the political agenda.[208]

Remedies for Romani victims have been affected by the advancement of supranational and domestic legal norms regulating ethnic minority protection, mainly in the 1990s. The most crucial events were the ratification of supranational minority rights instruments,[209] and the official recognition of the Romani minority and their inclusion in the Government Human Rights Action Plan.[210] These developments created a legal rights frame for minorities to further their claims. Some Romani people have actively used such opportunities

[197] Such as Romanifolkets landsforening, established in 1995. Halvorsen 2000: 202.

[198] See Bastrup & Sivertsen 1996; Schlüter 1993; Tranøy 1995.

[199] Justiskomiteen [The Norwegian Parliamentary Committee on Justice] 1996: 3.

[200] Ibid. See also Braun et al 2014: 214.

[201] Kommunal- og regionaldepartementet [The Norwegian Ministry of Local Government] 2003: 8; Ekeløve-Slydal, 7 December 2016.

[202] See Ekeløve-Slydal, 7 December 2016.

[203] See Hvinden 2000a.

[204] Haave 2000a.

[205] Fodstad 1999.

[206] Among the 128 interventions on Romani people registered, 112 affected women and 16 men. Haave 2000a: 388.

[207] See Haave 2000a: 387–390.

[208] Reparations to the Romani is still subject to political debate in Norway. See Haave, 5 December 2016; Plesner, 14 December 2016.

[209] The European Charter for Regional and Minority Languages (1993) and the CoE Framework Convention for the Protection of National Minorities (1999). The 1990 ratification of the International Labour Organization's Indigenous and Tribal Peoples Convention has also strengthened Norway's commitment to ethnic minority rights.

[210] This occurred in 1998 and 1999 respectively. See Utenriksdepartementet [The Norwegian Ministry of Foreign Affairs] 1999.

and mobilised before supranational instances[211] or national authorities, framing their claims in terms of rights.[212] The levels of mobilisation nevertheless vary greatly within the heterogeneous Romani group(s).[213] While some have been highly rights conscious, others have not; many have remained unorganised. The Romani sterilisation victims, mainly old women by now, have been particularly quiet and their grievances have been seldomly publicly voiced.[214]

4.3.1.1 Compensation Ex Gratia

Looking into the issue of compensation to Romani victims of past oppression in 2000, the Norwegian Government concluded that few possibilities for compensation were accessible to victims. Statutory limitations excluded the option to claim legal liability in courts.[215] The report further determined that the *ex gratia* compensation system was difficult to access in practice.[216] An additional state report in 2001 scrutinised the evidence requirements and conditions for individual *ex gratia* payments and recommended an amendment with respect to national minorities.[217] In the report, the 1999 Swedish Compensation Act to victims of involuntary sterilisation was discussed as a potential model for compensation legislation to improve remedial access, demonstrating a transnational influence.[218]

When remedies for victims of involuntary sterilisation were politically discussed in Norway in the early 2000s, the topic was largely framed as a social justice question related to former ethnic oppression. A Romani civil society organisation approached the Government in the beginning of the decade, asking

211 See CRI(2000)33; CRI(2004)3.

212 See Kommunal- og regionaldepartementet [The Norwegian Ministry of Local Government] 2003; Thune & Stiftelsen romanifolket/taterne 2003.

213 Haave, 5 December 2016; Ekeløve-Slydal, 7 December 2016; Vigardt, 1 February 2017.

214 This observation was emphasised in particular by Drefvelin & Skotvedt, 9 December 2016.

215 Kommunal- og regionaldepartementet [The Norwegian Ministry of Local Government] 2000. However, the policies were not questioned as possible violations of international criminal law or *jus cogens*, which would have raised different questions regarding prescriptibility.

216 Kommunal- og regionaldepartementet [The Norwegian Ministry of Local Government] 2000. Despite a lack of official statistics, Norwegian authorities have documented that at least one Romani woman received compensation in 2001 for her sterilisation according to the 1934 Sterilisation Act which proved to be ethnically motivated. In his extensive historical research, Haave has also found an early case of *ex gratia* payment to a minor Romani woman in the 1960s whose sterilisation was carried out according to the NS-enacted 1942 Sterilisation Act without obtaining her parents' consent. The Norwegian authorities highlighted that the sterilisation was ethnically motivated and that the 1942 Act allowed forms of sterilisations not possible under the 1934 Sterilisation Act, clearly distancing themselves from NS sterilisation policies. Noticing few reported cases of individual *ex gratia* compensation, such compensations have likely been uncommon. See Aasen, 23 November 2016; Tystad, 19 October 2016; Haave 2000a: 344–346.

217 Kommunalkomiteen [The Norwegian Committee on Local Government and Public Administration] 2001: 18.

218 Ibid: 18–19. See Lag om ersättning till steriliserade i vissa fall [Act on Compensation to Sterilised People under Certain Circumstances] (1999:332).

for a special *ex gratia* compensation scheme with lower evidence requirements and higher compensation amounts.[219] It indicated the published research, the treatment in respect of remedies for other minorities,[220] and the supranational human rights framework for national minorities,[221] indicating possible future litigation as well.[222] Simultaneously, the matter of compensation was raised in Parliament by Christian Democrat MP Ivar Østberg.[223] Around the same period, moreover, the supranational CoE Advisory Committee on the Framework Convention for the Protection of National Minorities recommended that the Norwegian Government assist abused minorities, specifically pointing out the need for sterilised Romani people to access compensation and the evidentiary difficulties which they would encounter in the process.[224]

These developments put pressure on the Norwegian Government, which soon appointed a working group to evaluate Romani people's access to financial compensation.[225] The results were published in 2003, according to which special legislation along the lines of the Swedish model was deemed unnecessary. Instead, the report recommended lowering the evidence requirements in the individual *ex gratia* compensation system.[226] Consequently, the Government proposed to establish a special compensation scheme for predefined, abused minorities, requiring as evidence, firstly, the applicant's own story, and secondly, documentation of surgical intervention for the involuntarily sterilised.[227] The compensation amount for Romani victims of involuntary sterilisation was set to a comparatively high 150,000 Norwegian Kroner (around 14,500 Euros), which highlighted the seriousness of the violation.[228] The amount was also similar to the Swedish compensation sum, to which the Government made comparisons.[229] The compensation scheme was adopted by Parliament in 2004.[230]

219 Thune & Stiftelsen romanifolket/taterne 2003.

220 The Norwegian Jewish minority whose assets were confiscated by the state during the Second World War. See Vollebæk & Plesner 2014: 183; Thune & Stiftelsen romanifolket/taterne 2003: 4.

221 Particularly the 1994 Council of Europe Framework Convention for the Protection of National Minorities.

222 Thune & Stiftelsen romanifolket/taterne 2003.

223 Stortinget [The Norwegian Parliament] 2002: 2280–2281. See also Kommunal- og regionaldepartementet [The Norwegian Ministry of Local Government] 2003: 5.

224 ACFC/INF/OP/I(2003)003 (2003): Para 33; Kommunal- og regionaldepartementet [The Norwegian Ministry of Local Government] 2003: 7.

225 Kommunal- og regionaldepartementet [The Norwegian Ministry of Local Government] 2003: 5.

226 Ibid: 27.

227 Justis- og politidepartementet [The Norwegian Ministry of Justice and Public Security] 2004: 58. This was confirmed by Tonning, 13 March 2018.

228 Justis- og politidepartementet [The Norwegian Ministry of Justice and Public Security] 2004: 37, 59, 84. Quite interestingly, and without explanation, the Government looked to the Norwegian Supreme Court's compensation practice for sexual offences for guidance on appropriate compensation amounts for involuntary sterilisation, along similar lines to the Swedish sterilisation investigation.

229 Ibid: 53–56. See Lag om ersättning till steriliserade i vissa fall [Act on Compensation to Sterilised People under Certain Circumstances] (1999:332).

230 Justis- og politidepartementet [The Norwegian Ministry of Justice and Public Security] 2004; Justiskomiteen [The Norwegian Parliamentary Committee on Justice] 2004. According to the

Few involuntarily sterilised Romani people have applied for compensation. According to a 2015 government report, no more than 15 applications were filed, of which seven were approved.[231] Thirteen of the applicants were women, and two men.[232] Remarkably, the number of applications was much lower than for instance those based on bullying, for which 1,231 Romani people applied and 1,220 were compensated.[233] Assuming the numerical correctness of Haave's research on sterilisations of Romani – with registered ones amounting to 128 in the period 1934–1977[234] – and that many of the interventions were coercive, many victims can be deduced not to have applied for *ex gratia* compensation.

Reasons for the low number of applications suggested by the authors of the 2015 report and the interviewees of this study are that the compensation scheme was introduced a long time after the interventions took place and that many victims have died, are old and/or ill; that sterilisation is perceived as stigmatising;[235] that accessing old medical files is difficult and traumatic; that the application procedure is difficult.[236] It is also possible that some victims were unaware of the compensation schemes, particularly the ones who were unorganised.[237] Moreover, many Romani people were unsure about how to apply for compensation, and what harm could be compensated.[238] According to the President of the Secretariat of the aforementioned 2015 report, Ingvill Thorson Plesner, negative experiences of rejected applications were discussed in Romani communities, which might have impacted negatively on victims' decisions to apply.[239] Romani activist Kai-Samuel Vigardt, who has assisted various applicants, recounted an incident where he tried to convince a woman

scheme, applications do not need to follow a certain format, but a standard form to facilitate the procedure is provided by the Norwegian Civil Affairs Authority. The form contains questions about to what kind of abuse the applicant was subjected. The categories are school bullying, internment at the Svanviken work colony, forced sterilisation and the more openly formulated 'ill-treatment by authorities'. Remarkably, the form is only available in Norwegian (*bokmål* and *nynorsk*), not in the Romani language, which might impede remedial access. Statens sivilrettsforvaltning [The Norwegian Civil Affairs Authority], *Søknadsskjema [Application Forms]*.

231 Kommunal- og moderniseringsdepartementet [The Norwegian Ministry of Local Government and Modernisation] 2015a.

232 Nordvik 2015: 696. Of the applications which were approved, six were made by women and one by a man.

233 Kommunal- og moderniseringsdepartementet [The Norwegian Ministry of Local Government and Modernisation] 2015a: 92. In contrast to sterilisation, the only evidence required for compensation on account of bullying was the applicant's own story.

234 Haave 2000a: 388.

235 The stigmatisation of the intervention might be worsened by its underlying reason. Additionally, the importance attached to children and large families in the Romani community might have worsened the victims' stigmatisation. Haave, 5 December 2016. On the stigmatisation of victims of sexual and reproductive violence, see Rubio-Marín 2012: 75–76.

236 The applicants who used legal counselling had to pay for it themselves. Nordvik 2015: 695.

237 Haave, 5 December 2016; Plesner, 14 December 2016. Information about the compensation scheme was published in several newspapers. Nordvik 2015: 694.

238 Nordvik 2015: 695.

239 Plesner, 14 December 2016.

who had been sterilised to apply for *ex gratia* compensation. The woman had told very few people about her sterilisation and consistently rejected encouragements to apply, unwilling to accept payment from the state.[240] Her decision, which may well not be unique in the group, reveals another issue: deep and persistent mistrust of state authorities.[241] This example demonstrates how the existence of a compensation scheme does not guarantee *per se* that victims conceive of themselves as rights-holders or have the resources to engage in remedial procedures. Furthermore, there is no guarantee that they will gain access to remedies.

4.3.1.2 Other Remedies

The Romani people were also granted remedies other than compensation, particularly collective and symbolic ones. Abuse against the Romani has been investigated relatively thoroughly on the initiative of Norwegian authorities. The first significant project was the earlier-mentioned historical research project which covered research on assimilation policies.[242] The report constitutes a symbol of truth-finding efforts, a possibility of rewriting national history and a potential basis for remedial claims.[243] Continued Romani civil society mobilisation moreover led to the Government's commencement of an additional investigation from a human rights-based perspective in 2011.[244] In order to secure representation, Romani voices were included through victim interviews as well as the inclusion of two Romani members in the investigative group.[245]

Published in 2015, the final report made a distinction between human rights in the legal and moral sense.[246] It concluded that the involuntary sterilisations carried out pursuant to the 1934 and 1942 laws were morally regrettable, and that involuntary sterilisation was currently a violation of the right to be free from torture and ill-treatment and the right to private and family life, guaranteed under Articles 3 and 8 ECHR.[247] Nevertheless, in the context of the late legal development of ECtHR case law on involuntary sterilisation,[248] the report remained unsure whether involuntary sterilisation could be considered a human rights violation in the legal sense before 1977, when the

[240] Vigardt, 1 February 2017.

[241] This mistrust was also highlighted by Plesner, 14 December 2016.

[242] This was the final report of the project, see Hvinden 2000a.

[243] At the time of publication, the Government also published a general report on past minority policies covering the five officially recognised national minorities, in which it recognised historical abuse, including the involuntary sterilisation of Romani. Kommunal- og regionaldepartementet [The Norwegian Ministry of Local Government] 2000.

[244] See Kommunal- og moderniseringsdepartementet [The Norwegian Ministry of Local Government and Modernisation] 2015a.

[245] See Kommunal- og moderniseringsdepartementet [The Norwegian Ministry of Local Government and Modernisation] 2015b; 2015a.

[246] Kommunal- og moderniseringsdepartementet [The Norwegian Ministry of Local Government and Modernisation] 2015a: 13.

[247] Ibid: 78.

[248] This implied a reference to ECtHR, *V.C. v. Slovakia* (2011). Ibid: 78.

new law was established.[249] According to Plesner, the moral/legal differentiation of human rights was however made in order to expand, rather than limit, state responsibility:

> [...] to show that Norwegian authorities had a responsibility, even then, even though it was not legally sanctioned, in the way it is today, and the contents of the norms were not clarified precisely [...] not least when it comes to such serious forms of abuse and so obvious violations of human rights as castration and sterilisation [...].[250]

In her response, Plesner referred to castration and sterilisation as 'obvious' violations of human rights. While the violations were not recognised in a legal sense, the moral accountability of public authorities for past oppression was generally accepted, even though the legislation built on voluntary interventions. As such, questions regarding whether involuntary interventions were a result of authoritative abuse by individual civil servants or oppressive legislation, or what characterised involuntariness at the individual level, were not brought up in the report.

Between 1998 and 2015, the Norwegian Government officially apologised for past oppression of the Romani minority three times.[251] These apologies were important symbolic remedies, aiming at the collective, acknowledging facts and accepting state responsibility.[252] None of the apologies were however broadcast, rendering their 'public' character and ultimate symbolic nature questionable.[253] The Norwegian state church has also apologised thrice to the Romani, apologies which are important given the role of the Mission in carrying out the practices.[254]

Other forms of collective remedies were monuments and exhibitions with the aim to symbolically commemorate victims, marking a break with the past, and to inform current societies about the violations. The exhibition *Latjo Drom* at Glomdal Museum is a permanent exhibition of Romani culture established by the state.[255] The 'Stone of Shame' monument in Oslo at Ris graveyard is another state-initiated memorial to the victims of the Norwegian assimilation policies.[256] Finally, another form of collective remedy is a public fund established in 2004.[257]

[249] See Kommunal- og moderniseringsdepartementet [The Norwegian Ministry of Local Government and Modernisation] 2015a: 78.

[250] Plesner, 14 December 2016. Translated from Norwegian.

[251] In 1998, 2000 and 2015.

[252] Braun et al 2014: 206, 214; Nordvik 2015: 688; Kommunal- og regionaldepartementet [The Norwegian Ministry of Local Government] 2000; Zondag 2015.

[253] Nordvik 2015; Zondag 2015.

[254] Nordvik 2015: 689–690.

[255] The first official initiative for an exhibition was mentioned in Parliament by MP Folkvord in 1996 already, but it took until 2006 to establish a permanent exhibition. See Nordvik 2015: 690.

[256] The people in the grave under the monument are however predominantly non-Romani. See Haave 2015b.

[257] Justis- og politidepartementet [The Norwegian Ministry of Justice and Public Security] 2004: 45.

In conclusion, the Norwegian efforts with regard to remedies for the Romani minority have been relatively extensive over the last decades. There is nevertheless cognitive dissonance between the amount of state responsibility accepted in the symbolic remedies – such as apologies in which the violations, and state responsibility for them, are accepted – and the principle of *ex gratia* rather than legal liability underlying the compensation. Increasingly adopting a discourse of rights, the state has accepted a moral, albeit not legal, responsibility for past violations, demonstrating an institutional response to and sociocultural acceptance of the rights claims advanced by the mobilising minority.

4.3.2 What about the Others?

In contrast to the remedies awarded to the Norwegian Romani, remedies for other victims of involuntary sterilisation and castration are lacking. The groups presented here are the non-Romani victims of involuntary interventions according to the 1934 and 1942 Acts, and the trans people who had to get castrated to amend their legally registered gender.

4.3.2.1 Other Victims of Involuntary Sterilisation and Castration before 1977

From 1934 until 1977, most sterilisations and castrations were performed on people who were non-Romani.[258] However, this larger group of people which was sterilised or castrated, some of the them against their will, has generally not mobilised, resulting in little public debate and very few remedies. It is remarkable that the non-Romani victims have not mobilised, even in the aftermath of the Swedish 1999 Compensation Act and the compensation scheme for Norwegian Romani victims, mass media attention and general minority mobilisation. These events could potentially have spurred grievance formation, which could have transformed their experiences of reproductive harm into legal claims for remedies.

The lack of mobilisation can be seen in the light of the difficulty to access remedies. Theoretically, two possibilities exist for non-Romani victims to access compensation. The first is to claim public liability for pecuniary and non-pecuniary personal damage according to national compensation legislation;[259] such legal claims are however likely to fall under the Statute of Limitations.[260] The second possibility to access remedies is to apply for individual *ex gratia*

[258] Officially, 128 Romani were registered as sterilised during the time period 1934–1977. This corresponds to approximately 0.3 per cent of the total number of registered sterilisations. Haave 2000a: 388.

[259] Lov om skadeserstatning [Compensation Act], No. 26, 1969, Chapter 3, Sections 1 and 2.

[260] Lov om foreldelse [Statute of Limitations], No. 18, 1979, Section 9. This was also the conclusion of the 2003 report, which considered damages before 1986 to fall under the Statute of Limitations. Kommunal- og regionaldepartementet [The Norwegian Ministry of Local Government] 2003: 26.

compensation.[261] When applying, applicants have to demonstrate that they have been sterilised/castrated with medical files[262] and provide official documentation that this intervention was involuntary, since their personal stories do not suffice as evidence.[263]

The general silence around the non-Romani victims has been broken by a few notable exceptions.[264] Here, I particularly recall the case of a woman who took her case of involuntary sterilisation to court in 1950. While she was ultimately unsuccessful in obtaining compensation, her legal struggle conceptualises the involuntary interventions as harm in legal terms and exemplifies the practical difficulties in navigating such legal claims. Moreover, as a challenge to state sterilisation practices, the litigation came to have an impact on the law's subsequent implementation.[265]

In 1950, a woman filed a lawsuit against a medical doctor and the Norwegian Ministry of Social Affairs on the matter of her sterilisation, which she claimed had been processed and approved on grounds of gross negligence and was therefore unlawful.[266] She was sterilised in 1942 pursuant to the 1934 Sterilisation Act, which allowed for sterilisation without the patient's consent.[267] The woman was a legal minor at the time, with only her father having provided his consent. The doctor had considered the mother's consent to be unnecessary given the latter's history of mental illness.[268] The doctor believed that the applicant suffered from hereditary, permanent and severe mental deficiencies.[269] She had never been informed about the sterilisation, being under the impression that she was undergoing surgery to relieve her menstrual pain.[270] Before the Court, she challenged the grounds for the medical evaluation of her intelligence.[271] Moreover, the applicant highlighted procedural errors, as several members of

[261] This applies only to the generally available one, not the 2004 scheme.

[262] Kommunal- og regionaldepartementet [The Norwegian Ministry of Local Government] 2003.

[263] Tonning, 13 March 2018. Such documentation can be medical files which indicate that the intervention was involuntary, or that it was carried out illegally – i.e., without fulfilling the legislative conditions. Some non-Romani victims may have applied for individual *ex gratia* compensation, but the lack of official statistics leaves this a mystery. Aasen, 23 November 2016; Tystad, 19 October 2016.

[264] There are also other exceptions. Another case is that of a Finnish woman who was involuntarily sterilised in 1975. Her legal claims of compensation were dismissed as subject to statutory limitation by the Norwegian court in 1985. Yet, the court pointed out that she might be eligible for *ex gratia* compensation. Tana og Varanger Herredsrett [Tana and Varanger Court of First Instance], Case No. 36/1985 A (1985).

[265] Haave 2000a: 363–369.

[266] Eidsivating Lagmannsrett [Eidsivating Court of Appeal], Appeal No. 43/1954 (1956).

[267] Lov om adgang til sterilisering m.v. [Act on the Access to Sterilisation etc.], No. 2, 1934, Section 4. Haave 2000a: 363; Eidsivating Lagmannsrett [Eidsivating Court of Appeal], Appeal No. 43/1954 (1956).

[268] Eidsivating Lagmannsrett [Eidsivating Court of Appeal], Appeal No. 43/1954 (1956): 10.

[269] Haave 2000a: 363.

[270] Ibid: 364. Eidsivating Lagmannsrett [Eidsivating Court of Appeal], Appeal No. 43/1954 (1956).

[271] She referred to a later intelligence test showing that her IQ was high enough for her consent to be required by law. With a letter from her employer, showing that she was responsible

the Sterilisation Council – including the Norwegian Chief Medical Officer – had been absent when her application was approved. She claimed 100,000 Norwegian Kroner in compensation for her unlawful sterilisation, which was a substantial sum at the time.

The Court of First Instance found that the doctor had committed no error in her evaluation of the applicant's intelligence. The Court recognised the fact of all members of the Sterilisation Council not having been involved in the decision-making process as a procedural error. Regardless, dismissing that this would have had an impact on the factual or legal outcome of the case, the Court found no liable error in the actions of the authorities or the individual doctor.[272]

Having lost in the first instance, the applicant appealed. On losing in the second instance with a 5-2 division among the judges, she tried to take the case to the Supreme Court, where it was rejected.[273] The final judgment of the Court of Appeal confirmed the ruling of the first instance, even though it found multiple procedural flaws: particularly that the applicant had not consented to, or even been duly informed about her sterilisation, and that the Chief Medical Officer had not participated in the decision-making process. Along similar lines to the first instance, the Court of Appeal pragmatically ruled that the outcome would likely not have differed with the presence of the Chief Medical Officer; doing so, it rejected the applicants' claims. Nonetheless, it also ruled that the applicant did not have to carry the costs and expenses of the respondent, implying a certain recognition of the applicant's claims.[274]

Before the courts, the applicant's lawyer illustratively formulated the applicant's reproductive harm as rights violations:

> The intervention has caused Ms NN a lifelong and irreversible aggravated bodily injury which has deprived her not only of a woman's most valuable right, namely the right to have children, but which has also significantly reduced her possibilities to enter into marriage and thereby be [financially] supported. This is not merely a violation of the Sterilisation Act, but also of the Conventions about Human Rights to which Norway has acceded.[275]

This excerpt from the final 1956 judgment demonstrates the lawyer's awareness, however rudimentary, of Norway's commitment to international human rights in the mid-1950s, and that 'the right to have children' fell under these rights. The Norwegian Constitution was interestingly not invoked in the case, indicating its perceived irrelevance.

The majority nevertheless bluntly dismissed the human rights arguments, stating that '[i]t [was] obvious that Ms NN cannot invoke the human rights

and could take care of her tasks at work, she further challenged the doctor's evaluation. See Eidsivating Lagmannsrett [Eidsivating Court of Appeal], Appeal No. 43/1954 (1956): 8–9; 20.

272 Haave 2000a: 365. 273 Ibid: 367. 274 Ibid: 366.

275 Eidsivating Lagmannsrett [Eidsivating Court of Appeal], Appeal No. 43/1954 (1956): 4. Translated from Norwegian.

declarations in this case'.[276] Pointing out the impossibility of this rights claim, the majority highlighted that the sterilisation had taken place before Norway acceded to the 'Convention about these declarations', and that the Government had found no reason to amend the 1934 Sterilisation Act when it ratified the Convention, implying a lack of normative conflict.[277]

Even though the unsuccessfully litigated case did not challenge the letter of the 1934 Sterilisation Act, only its wrongful implementation, Haave has demonstrated that the Sterilisation Council was affected by the challenge in court. The applicant's lawyer was in direct contact with the Norwegian Director of Health at the time, Karl Evang; the case was distributed to and discussed by the national Sterilisation Council. It was also reported in media. According to Haave, the Council adopted a more careful approach in 'difficult cases' in the period following the case, ultimately marking a turning point in national sterilisation policies.[278] As such, the exceptional case showed how an individual litigation attempt formulated in terms of rights, unsuccessful in outcome but accompanied with efforts to also mobilise the administrative decision-making organs, was able to introduce a notion of rights, and ultimately affect the implementation of the sterilisation law.

4.3.2.2 Trans People

The mobilisation for remedies for castrated trans people has centred on individual litigation in Norway. Inspired by Swedish civil society and the subsequent 2018 Compensation Act, discussions have taken place about litigating collectively, primarily in order to access compensation. Yet, such discourses have not translated into filing a collective lawsuit.[279] Former FRI Advisor on Gender Diversity, Luca Dalen Espseth, emphasised that when discussing this issue within the organisation in the mid-2010s, it was difficult to find people who were ready to come out and to publicly address their harms, as the topic was generally perceived 'painful and traumatic' among victims.[280] Furthermore, he signalled more structural hurdles to legal mobilisation, such as that these types of collective litigations are unusual in Norway, and that FRI as a general LGBT+ organisation has limited resources when it comes to trans-specific questions.[281] Another structural legal hurdle to collective litigation is that each case would nevertheless need to be individually evaluated by the courts.[282]

Despite hurdles, two trans people decided to take their cases to court to claim compensation for the castration precondition – albeit unsuccessfully. The court cases concerned the impact of the castration precondition to access legal gender recognition in two different ways: the first plaintiff having avoided castration and the second having undergone it.

[276] Eidsivating Lagmannsrett [Eidsivating Court of Appeal], Appeal No. 43/1954 (1956): 7.
[277] Ibid. [278] Haave 2000a: 363–369. [279] Frydenlund, 10 December 2016.
[280] Espseth, 4 January 2022. [281] Ibid.
[282] Ibid. This was also pointed out by Jentoft, 20 December 2021.

The first litigant was a transwoman who had postponed her application for legal gender recognition until the 2016 law was established, as she did not wish to undergo medical interventions. The resulting lack of legal gender recognition had led to many problems in her daily life. The plaintiff requested a compensation of 75,450 Norwegian Kroner (approximately 7,500 Euros) for the pecuniary and non-pecuniary damages which she had incurred due to the active enforcement of castration and genital surgery by the Norwegian public authorities. As a result of the requirement, which had never been legislated, the public authorities had failed to recognise her legal gender in line with her gender identity. She claimed that these actions amounted to a violation of the principle of legality (Sections 92 and 113 of the Norwegian Constitution); her personal integrity and right to respect for private and family life (Article 8 ECHR and Section 102 of the Norwegian Constitution), and her right not to be discriminated against (Article 14 ECHR, Section 98 of the Norwegian Constitution and Section 5 of the 2013 Act on Prohibition of Discrimination on the Grounds of Sexual Orientation, Gender Identity and Gender Expression).[283] The public authorities in question, the Ministries for Health and Finance, contested all the claims.[284]

The Oslo Court of First Instance rejected the claims regarding a violation of the plaintiff's right to integrity and respect for private and family life. The Court based its interpretation on the principle of non-retroactivity of legal norms in combination with the dynamic interpretation of the ECHR, the margin of appreciation and ECtHR practice. Consequently, it did not consider an obligation for the state to repeal the surgical preconditions to have been present before 2016, when the law based on self-identification was established. It held that the 2017 case of *A.P., Garçon and Nicot v. France* was the case which had recognised such an obligation.[285] The Court nevertheless ruled that the applicant had been placed in an unfavourable position in comparison to ciswomen, and that she was indirectly discriminated against in a way which was contrary to national discrimination legislation.[286] Regardless, the Court did not find public liability for pecuniary or non-pecuniary damages in the case, rejecting the plaintiff's claims of compensation.[287]

283 The plaintiff also claimed that the actions were in violation of personal data legislation. Lov om behandling av personopplysninger [Act on Processing Personal Data], No. 31, 2000, Sections 2 and 8.

284 Oslo tingrett [Oslo Court of First Instance], Case No. 17-146470 TVI-OTIR/04 (2018).

285 The Court referred to the inadmissibility decision of the ECtHR, *Nunez v. France* (2008), to demonstrate that the latter had not yet problematised such requirements in 2008.

286 Lov om forbud mot diskriminering på grunn av seksuell orientering, kjønnsidentitet og kjønnsuttrykk [Act on Prohibition of Discrimination on the Grounds of Sexual Orientation, Gender Identity and Gender Expression], No. 58, 2013, Section 5. Oslo tingrett [Oslo Court of First Instance], Case No. 17-146470 TVI-OTIR/04 (2018), 18.

287 The Court either did not investigate, or rejected the plaintiff's other claims. Oslo tingrett [Oslo Court of First Instance], Case No. 17-146470 TVI-OTIR/04 (2018).

In the appeal of the case, all the plaintiff's claims were rejected. The Borgarting Court of Appeal did not consider a different treatment of the plaintiff to amount to unlawful discrimination, as it considered the registration of legal gender in line with the gender registered at birth according to 'medical' and 'biological' definitions of sex to be reasonable.[288] The plaintiff appealed to the Supreme Court, which rejected the case.[289] The case was appealed to the European Court of Human Rights, where it was soon ruled inadmissible.

In the second case, the plaintiff had undergone gender-affirming treatment at the Oslo University Hospital in the 2000s in order to amend his legal gender from female to male. This treatment included mandatory castration, in the case referred to as irreversible sterilisation, despite the applicant's reservations. The plaintiff claimed that he had been subjected to 'inhuman and degrading treatment' through 'an unnecessary physical intervention' which led to permanent suffering and which was 'not based on free and informed consent', amounting to a violation of Article 3 ECHR.[290] Moreover, he held that the European Court of Human Rights had established a positive obligation for the state to legally recognise trans people's gender identity,[291] and a negative obligation not to require sterilisation for legal gender recognition within the scope of Article 8 ECHR.[292] He argued that the Norwegian procedure for amending legal gender amounted to a violation of the right to respect for privacy and family life.[293] The plaintiff also claimed that the irreversible sterilisation amounted to discrimination according to Article 14 ECHR and the domestic (former) Gender Equality Act of 1978,[294] as he was treated differently than (i) other (cis) men, who could get legal gender recognition without sterilisation and (ii) post-operative trans people, as they were granted legal gender recognition after sterilisation.[295] In conclusion, the claim for compensation was supported by referring to the right to effective remedy under Article 13 ECHR. In comparison, the plaintiff mentioned the amount provided to Romani victims of sterilisation, the *V.C. v. Slovakia* case of the ECtHR and the 2018 Swedish Compensation Act.[296] The state refuted these claims.[297]

[288] Borgarting lagmannsrett [Borgarting Court of Appeal], Case No. LB-2018-154220 (2020).
[289] Høyesteretts ankeutvalg [The Appeals Committee of the Norwegian Supreme Court], Case No. HR-2020-1486-U (2020).
[290] Jacobsen 2018: 7.
[291] He referred particularly to ECtHR, *Christine Goodwin v. the United Kingdom* (2002), where this principle was established. Jacobsen 2018: 13.
[292] He referred to ECtHR, *A.P., Garçon and Nicot v. France* (2017), and the Swedish *travaux préparatoires* for the 2018 Compensation Act. Socialdepartementet [The Swedish Ministry of Health and Social Affairs] 2017a; Jacobsen 2018: 14.
[293] Jacobsen 2018: 11, 17.
[294] Lov om likestilling mellom kjønnene [Gender Equality Act] No. 45, 1978, Section 3.
[295] He referred particularly to Norwegian Government Bill Prop. 88 L (2012–2013). Jacobsen 2018: 21.
[296] Jacobsen 2018: 22–23.
[297] Regjeringsadvokaten [The Office of the Attorney General of Norway] 2017.

The Court of First Instance rejected all the plaintiff's claims, highlighting that he had consented to the irreversible sterilisation and that 'there were medical indications for the intervention',[298] referring to his gender dysphoria diagnosis. Evaluating whether the intervention amounted to torture or ill-treatment as protected under Article 3 ECHR, the Court considered that *V.C. v. Slovakia* was largely incomparable to the situation at hand as the consent in question 'was obtained well before the intervention, which provided [the applicant] with the opportunity to reflect on the intervention and also to retract his consent'.[299] Moving on to Article 8, the Court held that requiring irreversible sterilisation for legal gender recognition was 'a view that today is outmoded',[300] while underscoring that Norway was not the only country which had enforced such requirements.[301] Recognising supranational developments such as the 2007 Yogyakarta Principles and the 2009 CoE Commissioner for Human Rights report on gender identity, the Court emphasised that a development had taken place in respect of 'the rights of transsexuals',[302] which had provoked the recent Norwegian legal amendment and the ECtHR judgment *AP, Garçon and Nicot v. France.* Similarly to the first case, the Court pointed out that the plaintiff's irreversible sterilisation had taken place in 2009, when the matter still fell within the state's margin of appreciation, manifested in cases such as the inadmissibility decision *Nunez v. France* of 2008. In conclusion, the Court found that the sterilisation had not violated Article 8.[303]

When it came to discrimination according to the 1978 Gender Equality Act,[304] which had been in force at the time of the intervention, the Court discarded the comparability to cis men based on the fact that the requirement was only directed at trans people.[305] The Court acknowledged that trans people received disparate treatment but it considered the practice to have a legitimate reason. Accordingly, 'that the practice of registering gender is inconvenient for some citizens – namely for those who do not identify with their biological gender – can, according to the Court, not motivate viewing the practice as such as a disproportionate intervention'.[306] The Court went on to point out that it did not agree with the legal reasoning of the 2014 Norwegian Equality and Anti-discrimination Ombud decision, as it did not consider a comparison between trans and cis people possible.[307]

When appealing the case to the second instance, the Borgarting Court of Appeal also rejected all the plaintiff's claims. Particularly pondering the principle of non-retroactivity, and whether the Norwegian legal developments

[298] Oslo Tingrett [Oslo Court of First Instance], Case No. 17-132417TVI-OTIR/08 (2018): 18.

[299] Ibid: 19. [300] Ibid: 20. [301] Ibid. [302] Ibid: 22. [303] Ibid: 22–23.

[304] Lov om likestilling mellom kjønnene [Gender Equality Act] No. 45, 1978, Section 3.

[305] Oslo Tingrett [Oslo Court of First Instance], Case No. 17-132417TVI-OTIR/08 (2018): 25.

[306] Ibid: 25.

[307] Ibid. Likestillings- og diskrimineringsombudet [The Norwegian Equality and Anti-discrimination Ombud], Decision No. 14/840 (2014).

complied with international legal standards in the light of the right to respect for private and family life (Article 8 ECHR), the Court stated that:

> the development in Norway in this field was set in motion in 2010. This corresponds well to what is observed internationally. After this the conclusion that the sterilisation precondition was problematic and ought to be discontinued was reached relatively promptly, but it took some time before this process ended with the legal amendment in 2016.[308]

The case was appealed to the Supreme Court, which rejected said appeal.[309] Moreover, this case has been appealed to the European Court of Human Rights, which has not yet reached a conclusion at the moment of writing. The two individual plaintiffs were supported by trans human rights defenders, that is, the sexual and gender diversity organisation FRI and the Norwegian Patient Organisation for Gender Incongruence PKI.[310] Additionally, Amnesty International and the Norwegian Department of the International Commission for Jurists (ICJ-Norge) supported the plaintiffs' claims through *amicus curiae* briefs.[311]

In my interview with the plaintiffs' lawyer, Maria Hessen Jacobsen, she pointed out that the support from civil society was vital, as it provided her clients and the stakeholder group with

> momentum[. T]hey were two individuals who took a very strenuous fight and a great financial risk on behalf of very many people, and they did not feel like they were alone. It also gave us, as legal representatives, good support.[312]

Through the collective support, a common identity as rights holders was created among the victim group. Jacobsen highlighted that her decision to represent the plaintiffs in the case was partly motivated by the impending judgment of the ECtHR in the matter of *A.P., Garçon and Nicot v. France*, as this moment presented a chance to get a 'judicial evaluation of the Norwegian practice'.[313]

The cases were initiated by the individuals themselves, but they were actively monitored and supported by civil society organisations.[314] Campaigning around the cases was careful, however, particularly as one of the plaintiffs wished to remain anonymous.[315] While unsuccessful in outcome, the court procedures prompted a broader political and public discussion on remedies.[316]

308 Borgarting lagmannsrett [Borgarting Court of Appeal], Case No. 18-190131ASD-BORG/02 (2021): 21. Translated from Norwegian.

309 Høyesteretts ankeutvalg [The Appeals Committee of the Norwegian Supreme Court], Case No. HR-2021-1392-U (2021).

310 Alvheim & Hansen Advokatfirma 2017.

311 Amnesty International Norway 2018; ICJ-Norge 2020.

312 Jacobsen, 16 December 2021. Translated from Norwegian.

313 Ibid.

314 Jentoft, 20 December 2021; Espseth, 4 January 2022.

315 Jentoft, 20 December 2021.

316 See Lied 2020; Rosef 2020. Yet, a broader discussion is impaired by a difficulty to frame the question of remedies as separate from the establishment of the present law. Espseth, 4 January 2022.

Civil society has mainly organised meetings with the Government and state authorities, authored open letters, involved mass media and supported the individual plaintiffs financially.[317] In acknowledgement of their struggle, the plaintiffs were awarded the trans pride award in 2021.[318]

The idea of establishing a compensation scheme similar to the Swedish one, and issuing an official apology on the part of the state, has been raised repeatedly, not only by civil society,[319] but also by the Norwegian Equality and Anti-discrimination Ombud.[320] In a letter to the Ministry of Justice and Public Security, the Ombud pointed out that a compensation scheme ought to be established, even though it 'will not change the serious consequences of irreversible sterilisation, and will for many not be a satisfactory remedy'.[321] A compensation would however constitute 'a recognition that Norway for many years enforced a highly regrettable practice which meant that many lost the opportunity to live a full life and to raise a family'.[322] In addition to this, an official apology, a state recognition of wrongdoing together with a guarantee of non-repetition 'would for many be worth more than money' according to FRI Advisor on Gender Diversity, Christine Marie Jentoft.[323] Furthermore, in a parliamentary initiative by three MPs from the Socialist Left Party, the need for a compensation scheme was repeated.[324] The MPs also stressed that the Government should apologise to trans people for its past practice regarding the amendment of legally registered gender.[325] However, these actions have not led to any remedial developments, as the initiative was voted down; the letter from the Ombud has not led to any concrete political action at the moment of writing.

The struggle for remedies by castrated trans people illustrates how international developments have created a master frame within which remedial claims are navigated in both a narrow legal, and a broader sociopolitical sense. The furthering of remedial claims through mainly individual litigation has emphasised legal obligations, resulting in a rejection of the claimants as rights-holders as regards remedies, particularly on the basis of the principle of non-retroactivity. An unexpected impact of the litigation mentioned by Espseth, is that it has mainstreamed a legal conceptualisation of responsibility and affected political discussions. In effect, many politicians erroneously conflate the legal processes and the political establishment of remedies, rejecting any non-legal – such as moral or sociopolitical – notion of state responsibility.[326]

[317] Jentoft, 20 December 2021; Espseth, 4 January 2022.

[318] Engesbak 2021; Jentoft, 20 December 2021.

[319] FRI 2020. The civil society organisations working together are the LGBT+ organisations FRI, Salam, Skeiv Ungdom, Skeiv Verden, Skeivt kristent nettverk, PKI, and Forbundet for transpersoner i Norge. See also Alaattinoğlu & Sørlie 2019.

[320] Likestillings- og diskrimineringsombudet [The Norwegian Equality and Anti-discrimination Ombud] 2020.

[321] Ibid: 3–4. [322] Ibid: 4. [323] Jentoft, 20 December 2021.

[324] Stortinget [The Norwegian Parliament] 2020.

[325] Ibid. It also raised the need for a third gender category. [326] Espseth, 4 January 2022.

Table 4.1 Remedies to castrated and sterilised people in Norway

	Group 1: *Tatere*/Romani victims (1934–1977)	Group 2: Non-Romani victims of involuntary sterilisation/castration (1934–1977)	Group 3: Trans victims (–2016)
Restitution	N/A	N/A	N/A
Compensation	*Ex gratia* upon application (150,000 Norwegian Kroner, approximately 14,900 Euros)	N/A	N/A
Rehabilitation	N/A	N/A	N/A
Satisfaction	- Museum exhibition - Cultural fund - State investigations - Official apologies (by the Government and the State Church)	N/A	N/A
Guarantees of non-repetition	N/A	N/A	N/A

4.3.3 Cross-Group Comparison

The measures with respect to remedies vary for the victims of involuntary sterilisation and castration. Table 4.1 summarises the state remedies which are provided to victims.

Except for the lack of restitution and rehabilitation for all groups, the remedies for the different groups are remarkably dissimilar. Only one group, the Romani, has the possibility to apply for compensation from an extraordinary, specially established scheme. The only group which benefits from other means of satisfaction is that of the Romani as well. The remedies formally indicate that the state has acknowledged the violations and its responsibility and has declared its willingness to reconcile with the past in order to move forward. However, the limited access to some of the remedies, particularly compensation, has sparked criticism regarding the genuineness of the state's commitment to redress Romani victims.[327] In comparison to other national remedial standards, most relevantly compensation for sterilisation due to medical malpractice, the compensation scheme for Romani victims is notably lower in amount and more difficult to access.[328] The difference in treatment between

[327] Haave, 5 December 2016; Ekeløve-Slydal, 7 December 2016; and Vigardt, 1 February 2017.

[328] Victims of medical malpractice can access special legislation and bodies with relaxed evidence requirements and different liability standards; they are entitled to individually determined non-pecuniary damages. As an illustrative example, a woman who was 30 when she became infertile through a loss of ovaries as the result of medical malpractice, received a compensation of 350,000 Norwegian Kroner (approximately 34,500 Euros) in 2016. Forskrift om menerstatning ved yrkesskade [Decree on Compensation for Permanent Occupational Injuries], No. 373, 1997; Grammeltvedt, 8 December 2016.

the Romani victims and the other groups compared in this chapter is also striking, revealing the latter's marginalisation in Norwegian discussions on remedies.

Norway and Sweden have favoured *ex gratia* solutions for (some) victims of involuntary sterilisation, in accordance with which national guilt is determined in political/moral, rather than legal and courts-based terms. The current situation sheds light on the complex legal and sociocultural relationship between recognised rights violations, state responsibility and remedies, where one is not necessarily dependent on the other(s).

4.4 Discussion

While Norway can be considered to have a stronger constitutional culture than Sweden, supranational rather than constitutional rights have created master frames for victims of state oppression in both countries. Discussions on the implications of developing rights and past and present injustices for state accountability have awakened in Norway as well; a number of *ex gratia* compensation schemes for certain groups have been established since the 1990s. The only group which has benefited from this development as regards remedies among the involuntarily sterilised and castrated was the involuntarily sterilised Romani people. Using the existing developing framework of supranational rights instruments, and the recent national recognition of ethnic minorities, members of the minority have organised and successfully formulated grievances as rights claims in tandem with other human rights organisations. These grievances have in turn been recognised in subsequent state investigations. Such truth-finding efforts have paved the way for *ex gratia* compensation, official apologies and other remedies.

Trans rights activists have collectively mobilised to amend the administrative practice requiring castration for legal gender recognition. The successful mobilisation owed much to formulating the harm of mandatory castration in terms of rights violations and rendering the practice visible to the general public. So doing, trans rights activists have utilised recent supranational policy developments when framing their claims to abolish the practices.

Unlike for its Swedish counterpart, the Norwegian struggles for remedies emphasised individual litigation. This form of mobilisation centred on the personal situation of the litigants and warranted a more careful approach to campaigning by the supporting organisations, as they wished to protect the privacy of the plaintiffs. The individual litigation has also warranted an institutional response which narrowly conceptualises rights as legal instruments, rather than sociopolitical commitments. In the mobilisation outside of the courtroom, transnational influence of the Swedish Compensation Act from 2018 is evident. Meanwhile, the national remedies for Romani victims of involuntary sterilisation have generally not provided a precedent for trans victims, most likely due to their ethnic framing.

In respect of the public perception of victimhood, the Norwegian case is similar to the Swedish one, particularly when it comes to the involuntarily castrated – a group generally surrounded by silence and not portrayed as victimised. Contrastingly, mass media framing of oppressive policies against the Romani minority and trans people has provided an external verification of their rights claims at times, contributing to shaping public opinion on these groups' victim status.

In Norway too, the public identity of the state is affected by the responses to some of the victim groups. The establishment of legislation on legal gender recognition based on self-ascription in 2016 was actively publicised as a positive rights development, one with which Norway became a leader of the European rights development. This framing has in fact been formulated as victim satisfaction, a type of remedy, which in this case also has affected the sociocultural standing of the other remedial claims advanced by the group. Similarly, the remedies for Romani people have also been framed by the state as positive for its public identity: a redress for a dark history, marking a break from past oppression, and legitimising the modern nation.

5

Finland: Silence

This chapter foregrounds the legal regulation of sterilisation and castration in Finland during the twentieth and twenty-first centuries, focusing on involuntary interventions. It first describes the internationalising Finnish legal culture with its developing notions of rights and public liability. Subsequently, it moves on to investigating the introduction of legislation on sterilisation and castration in Finland, the criticism of the practices, the liberalisation of the legislation and victim mobilisation. This chapter compares the varying degrees of mobilisation among the victims and the state's continuing failure to acknowledge the violations, to accept state responsibility for them and to provide remedies for the victims. As such, the Finnish example demonstrates an austere remedial culture with a stalled grievance formation process, in which victims have generally refrained from mobilisation, lacking a common identity as well as a sense of wrong to be remedied.

5.1 Developing Rights: Looking Forward, Not Back

The youngest nation in the comparison, Finland has sometimes been described as having a deep-rooted constitutional culture resembling that of Norway, which is linked to the very identity of the nation.[1] Today, Finnish Parliament carries a lot of weight in the constitutional power division, much like in the other Nordic countries.[2] Along similar lines to Sweden and Norway, rights have a much more pronounced role in today's Finnish legal culture than they did in the beginning of the twentieth century.[3] With the growing internationalisation of the national political and legal culture from the latter half of the

[1] See, for example, Husa 2011. The main Finnish constitutional document drafted after its independence in 1917 was the Government Act of 1919. See Suomen Hallitusmuoto [Finnish Government Act] 94/1919.

[2] However, uniquely Finnish is the more pronounced, semi-judicial role of the Parliamentary Constitutional Law Committee, which not only performs abstract constitutional preview but also issues binding legal opinions. Husa 2010: 108; Scheinin 1996: 260.

[3] See Perustuslakivaliokunta [The Finnish Parliamentary Constitutional Law Committee] PeVM 25/94: 3. In the 1919 Finnish Government Act, only a sweeping reference was made to the protection of life, honour, personal freedom and property. Suomen Hallitusmuoto [Finnish Government Act] 94/1919, Section 6.

twentieth century, human and constitutional rights have generally become more important.[4]

The 1990s was an important decade for Finnish rights culture in terms of internationalisation.[5] This development can be understood in the light of the fall of its neighbour in the east, the Soviet Union, ultimately resulting in Finland becoming freer to form alliances in the international arena and to transform its geopolitical isolation into infatuation with Europe. Apart from its late joining in the European human rights framework,[6] the dualist country's record of formal international human rights commitment is similar to Sweden and Norway's: eager and resolute. Over the mentioned years, Finland's supranational rights dedication also affected the constitutional domain. In 1995, existing sparse constitutional rights references were expanded to a full catalogue.[7] Four years later, the previous constitutional documents were converted into a new Finnish Constitution, which entered into force at the dawn of the new millennium.[8]

With its increased dedication to rights, the new Constitution also pronounced the role of the courts by introducing concrete judicial review in a narrow sense, limited to *apparent* conflicts.[9] This reference broke with the earlier legal tradition, according to which judicial review was prohibited.[10] Similarly to Sweden and Norway, constitutional reform in Finland remained a matter for the national parliament, not the courts. While the Finnish legal system traditionally does not assign a strong role to the courts, an important Nordic

4 Criticism of Finnish constitutionalism and fundamental rights has nevertheless been a recurring theme in right-wing populism since the 2000s.

5 Finland has ratified international treaties earlier than European ones. The country has been a member of the UN since 1955 and the CoE since 1989. Finland ratified the CERD in 1970; ICCPR and ICESCR in 1975; CEDAW in 1986; CAT in 1989; CRC in 1991; and CRPD in 2016. Finland was also among the first states to ratify the Rome Statute of the ICC in 2000. At the accession to these instruments, Finland did not make any relevant reservations regarding the topic of this work.

6 Having long avoided joining the Council of Europe, Finland did not ratify the ECHR until 1990. In the same year, the European Torture Convention was ratified; in 1994, the European Charter for Regional or Minority Languages; in 1997, the CoE Framework Convention for the Protection of National Minorities. In 1995, Finland and Sweden both upgraded their European commitment from being EFTA members to joining the EU. Moreover, the CoE Convention on Human Rights and Biomedicine was ratified in 2009; the Istanbul Convention in 2015.

7 Amendment 969/1995. Finnish Government Bill HE 309/1993; Perustuslakivaliokunta [The Finnish Parliamentary Constitutional Law Committee] PeVM 25/94, PeVM 3/95. See Salminen 2014:48.

8 Suomen perustuslaki [The Constitution of Finland], 731/1999. See mainly Finnish Government Bill HE 1/1998; Perustuslakivaliokunta [The Finnish Parliamentary Constitutional Law Committee] PeVM 10/1998; PeVM 1/1999.

9 Suomen perustuslaki [The Constitution of Finland], 731/1999, Sections 106 and 107.

10 The 1919 Government Act only explicitly allowed for courts to review lower-level decrees, which came to be interpreted as a prohibition of judicial review of legislation in practice. Suomen Hallitusmuoto [Finnish Government Act] 94/1919, Section 92; Perustuslakivaliokunta [The Finnish Parliamentary Constitutional Law Committee] PeVM 25/94: 3; Husa 2011: 160.

feature in the protection of citizens' interests and rights is the several ombudsman institutions.[11]

Finland's supranational legal commitments, primarily its EU membership and ECtHR record, have also led to more attention for the topic of state responsibility.[12] On account of the increase of rights violations found and growing awareness of the European human rights system in the legal community, national public liability tradition has begun to change.[13] However, like its Nordic neighbours, Finnish legal culture traditionally builds on the assumption that public liability is grounded in the wrongdoing of individual civil servants, rather than rights-violating legislation.[14] Unlike the Swedish Supreme Court, the Finnish Supreme Court has largely escaped criticism for basing public liability on constitutional and human rights violations without explicit legislative support.[15]

In comparison to Norway and Sweden, Finland also has a weak tradition of questioning and remedying oppression in its modern history.[16] One existing compensation tradition – even if neither based on public liability nor explicitly *ex gratia* – is that which is focused on war-related individual harm, particularly for soldiers for physical injuries and illnesses.[17] However, when it comes to

[11] Such as the Parliamentary Ombudsman, the Non-discrimination Ombudsman or the Ombudsman for Equality. These institutions might not possess 'hard' legal power, but their recommendations, reports and investigations have practical importance for the realisation of rights and non-discrimination.

[12] This is particularly the case in the *Francovich* doctrine holding member states liable for failing to implement a directive. See CJEU, *Andrea Francovich and Danila Bonifaci v. Italian Republic* (1991); Wilhelmsson 2001: 300–304. Since the country's accession to the CoE, the Strasbourg Court has found Finland in violation in a vast amount of cases. Significant cases in which violations have been found, are among others: ECtHR, *M.P. v. Finland* (2016); *Ristamäki and Korvola v. Finland* (2013); *Grönmark v. Finland* (2010); *Backlund v. Finland* (2010); *Eerikäinen and Others v. Finland* (2009); *Juppala v. Finland* (2008); *K.U. v. Finland* (2008); *Johansson v. Finland* (2007); *Muttilainen v. Finland* (2007); *Vilho Eskelinen and Others v. Finland* (2007); *Hokkanen v. Finland* (1994).

[13] Hakalehto-Wainio 2008: 112–123. See Finnish Government Bill HE 159/2014; Laki valtion vahingonkorvaustoiminnasta [Act on the Administration of State Liability] 978/2014. ECtHR practice has also brought about change with its relatively diverse and inclusive conceptualisation of harm to be compensated. This holds especially true for non-pecuniary damages, which Finnish liability law rarely compensates, as it has traditionally presupposed material, quantifiable harm, and been inherently sceptical towards compensation for emotional, psychological, social, sexual or reproductive harm. Hakalehto-Wainio 2011: 240–241; Sisula-Tulokas 1995.

[14] The Finnish Liability Act of 1974 was the country's first law to systematically regulate public responsibility for damages. Hakalehto-Wainio 2008: 29–30. Public liability legislation was originally introduced as a result of Nordic harmonisation. See Bill HE 187/1973; Wilhelmsson, 5 September 2017; Sisula-Tulokas, 8 September 2017; Vahingonkorvauslaki [Liability Act] 412/1974.

[15] See Korkein oikeus [The Finnish Supreme Court], KKO:2008:10. In its judgment, the Supreme Court based public liability for suffering as non-pecuniary damages on both the ECHR and the Constitution, referring to the normative and social development of liability law without explicit legislative support in the Liability Act. See Hakalehto-Wainio 2011: 241.

[16] In fact, there is no academic debate around *ex gratia*, seen in a lack of scholarship and confirmed by Wilhelmsson, 5 September 2017; Sisula-Tulokas, 8 September 2017.

[17] Thomas Wilhelmsson sees the war-related compensation tradition in Finland as different from the other Nordic countries' *ex gratia* payments, as 'no expression of

historical injustices outside the immediate war context, Finland has so far been more remedially austere than its Nordic neighbours. No remedies have been granted to the lobotomised, the children sent away from their families during the war, Romani/travellers, the involuntarily sterilised or castrated, or other mistreated minorities. Nevertheless, a changing legal and remedial culture seems apparent in some recent examples, such as an investigation and public apology for the maltreatment of children in substitute care facilities,[18] and the appointment of a truth commission on past oppressive assimilation policies targeting Sámi people in Finland.[19]

5.2 Sterilisation and Castration: From Force to Free Choice

At its introduction, much like that of its Nordic neighbours, Finland's legislation on sterilisation and castration – and also legal gender recognition to some extent – has emphasised public interest and expert knowledge rather than individual will. Yet, an increasing amount of emphasis has come to be placed on individual will in later decades.

5.2.1 Sterilisation and Castration Legislation: Controlling Practice

The first sterilisation and castration laws were introduced in Finland as a result of the perceived urgency of regulating such interventions. Introducing legislation governing the amendment of legally registered gender was the result of mobilisation, mainly by trans activists themselves, on account of a long period of unregulated practices. As its Nordic neighbours, Finland preconditioned such amendment with an infertility requirement. This section investigates the introduction and abolition or preservation of sterilisation and castration regulations in Finland, and their underlying motivations.

5.2.1.1 Legislation on Sterilisation

Much like in Norway and Sweden, the first Finnish sterilisation laws were connected to eugenics. Appearing around the turn of the twentieth century,

moral responsibility' is included with these compensations. Wilhelmsson, 5 September 2017. During the twentieth century, the Finnish Government introduced pension and compensation schemes to war veterans and their dependents. In recent decades, the limited conceptualisation of war harm to be remedied has expanded. In 1997, rehabilitation was legislatively prescribed to men and women in certain services related to the wars – such as demining, health care, education, and evacuation of cattle. In 2003, a state compensation scheme was established for people who fell ill as a result of Soviet partisan attacks between 1939 and 1945. In 2014, an apology was issued, and a compensation scheme was established, for civilians having been interned in post-war prison camps. Many war-related harms, such as that caused by sexual violence during the civil war or assault of dissenters still remain unaddressed. See Liukkonen 2017; Näre 2008; Kirves 2008.

[18] Sosiaali- ja terveysministeriö [The Finnish Ministry of Social Affairs and Health] 2016a; 2016b.

[19] See Remes et al 2018; Valtioneuvoston kanslia [The Finnish Prime Minister's Office] 2021.

and fed by a growing fear of degeneration,[20] the Finnish eugenics movements were similar to contemporary international ones.[21] The fear of degeneration was manifested in an increasing attention for the feebleminded. In 1906, psychiatrist Adolf Björkman published a study on the feebleminded in Finland, which revealed that a surprisingly high amount of people in the country could be classified as such.[22] With medical professionals and politicians increasingly alarmed by the prevalence of feeblemindedness, and the lack of state response, the administration of public care was brought up in the Finnish Parliament.[23] In 1926, a medico-legal committee was established to investigate the possibility of introducing legislation on sterilisation, a practice as yet unregulated by law at the time.[24] On the publication of the investigation results in 1929, the same year that the eugenically inspired Matrimonial Act was adopted, sterilisation was widely discussed in the Finnish Parliament.[25]

The 1929 report recommended sterilisation of the feebleminded. It emphasised that the permanent and invasive procedure would be carefully supervised by the authorities, and dismissed the likelihood of it leading to rising promiscuity among the population. The report recommended legislation which formally lacked gender identifiers. The feebleminded imagined in the report were, however, particularly women, whose potential psychological and emotional harm by (involuntary) sterilisation was disregarded, as they 'rarely longed for motherhood'.[26] The report concluded that it was still in their best interest not to have children even should they want them.[27] The report referred to sterilisation legislation and discussions in other countries,[28] highlighting that it saw no

[20] Mattila 1997a: 21.

[21] However, uniquely Finnish is that one of the main eugenics supporters was a linguistic and ethnic minority: the Swedish-speaking Finns. Well established in Finland since the years of Swedish rule, its representatives increasingly became anxious about threats to their position and privileges by Finnish speakers. Eugenics – and more specifically, claimed racial superiority – became a rhetorical weapon in the hands of the minority. Augmented by further opposition during the ideologically motivated 1918 civil war, the conservative 'whites', to which the Swedish-speaking minority mainly belonged, often downgraded the socialist 'reds' in not only ideological but also racial/eugenic terms. Mattila 1998: 117; 1999: 100–105; Spektorowski & Ireni-Saban 2014: 78–79; Mattila 2016.

[22] Mattila 1999: 20. At the 1912 Nordic Conference on the Welfare of the Handicapped, organised in Helsinki, the topic of sterilisation was raised. Mattila 1997b: 11.

[23] Mattila 1999: 276.

[24] Komitea, joka on asetettu harkitsemaan tylsämielisten y.m. sterilisoimista koskevaa kysymystä [The Finnish Committee appointed to Consider the Question of Sterilisation of the Feebleminded etc.] 1929: 1.

[25] Mattila 1997a: 24–25.

[26] Komitea, joka on asetettu harkitsemaan tylsämielisten y.m. sterilisoimista koskevaa kysymystä [The Finnish Committee appointed to Consider the Question of Sterilisation of the Feebleminded etc.] 1929: 41. See also Mattila 1999: 299.

[27] Ibid.

[28] The countries referred to in the report are the US, Norway, Sweden, Denmark, Switzerland, Estonia and Germany. Komitea, joka on asetettu harkitsemaan tylsämielisten y.m. sterilisoimista koskevaa kysymystä [The Finnish Committee appointed to Consider the Question of Sterilisation of the Feebleminded etc.] 1929: 16–19.

need to ponder balancing when public and individual interests would collide, as the former categorically trump the latter.[29] It stated that sterilisation constituted physical assault even with the applicant's consent, and that it was therefore at first glance a violation of Finnish criminal law.[30] In some cases, however, the great benefits of sterilisation were considered to outweigh the initial legal problems. Legislation could regulate when such interventions would be permissible.[31] Yet, the report did not promote forced sterilisation, recommending voluntary forms.[32] There was thus a certain incongruity in discourse between the conclusion that individual concerns always subjugate to social ones, on the one hand, and that the interventions should not be coerced, on the other.

The tension between involuntariness and voluntariness in the 1929 report was addressed by criminal legal scholar Brynolf Honkasalo, who prepared a Government Bill covering both sterilisation and castration. The Bill was presented before the Finnish Parliament in 1934, and included interventions on eugenic, medical, social and humanitarian indications.[33] It attached comparatively little importance to the will of the individual, reaffirming that a pressing public interest would justify the interventions, even if they violated individual personal autonomy.[34] Moreover, medical necessity and care concerns were believed to legitimise the intervention, with the latter aspect being carefully phrased to avoid the negative connotation of punishment. The Bill's target group was conceptualised as medically well defined and restricted, a formulation considered to justify a more invasive intervention. Consent was described as unnecessary, since the people in question would be unable to understand the social benefits of the intervention and were therefore likely to oppose it.[35] Along similar lines, the consent of the guardian of the legally incapable was regarded as equally unnecessary,[36] as Honkasalo referred to formal regulations on consent to 'satisfy the liberal viewer' as disingenuous.[37] The possibility of future abuse of the law was rejected, as the well-trusted Finnish Board of Health was vested with the decision-making authority.[38] To sum up, the Bill proposed a law which strongly emphasised state prerogative.

The first Finnish Sterilisation Act was established in 1935. It was supported by experts and adopted with the great majority of Parliament.[39] As Markku Mattila has shown, there was some resistance in Parliament; regardless, none of the parliamentarians criticised the interventions *per se* as violations of any legal or moral order. Rather, socialists feared classist bias in the implementation of the law in a capitalist society; Christian Democrats resisted the interventions because of their possible effects on sexual morality;[40] others criticised the law's restrictive

[29] Ibid: 14. [30] Ibid: 20–21. [31] Ibid: 21. [32] Ibid: 43–49.
[33] Finnish Government Bill HE 112/1934: 2.
[34] Ibid: 18–21. This was also highlighted in Honkasalo B 1935: 119–120.
[35] Finnish Government Bill HE 112/1934: 19. [36] Ibid. [37] Honkasalo B 1935: 116–117.
[38] Finnish Government Bill HE 112/1934.
[39] 144 MPs were in favour; 14 against; 6 abstained; 35 were absent. Mattila 1997a: 26.
[40] Mattila 1999: 320–322.

character.[41] Nevertheless, the vast majority thought that the establishment of a Sterilisation Act was acutely needed and should be adopted despite its flaws, as Finland lagged behind its Nordic neighbours in instituting measures.[42]

According to the 1935 Sterilisation Act, a person could be ordered to undergo sterilisation, or allowed to get sterilised if there was reason to believe that they would produce 'defective' 'offspring'.[43] Applications could be filed by directors of institutions for mentally ill people or alternatively by applicants themselves.[44] Additionally, school inspectors had an obligation to inform health authorities of decisions to exempt children from compulsory education because of feeblemindedness, so that they could be considered for sterilisation.[45] The Board of Health was to approve or reject sterilisation or castration applications as they saw fit.[46] If possible and applicable, the Board should provide the spouse or the legal guardian with an opportunity to make a statement before it would make a decision.[47] The Act included a possibility to appeal the decision of the Board to the Supreme Court. The appeal was to be made within thirty days after receiving the decision, and the Supreme Court was to give such appeals urgent consideration.[48] The legislation did not include guidelines on how the authorities were to act, should the applicant refuse sterilisation or castration. Yet, physical force could not be used.[49]

The 1935 Sterilisation Act was criticised by civil society even before it entered into force. Mattila has indicated that some of the most vocal criticism was published in the liberal-socialist magazine *Tulenkantajat*, especially by its editor-in-chief, Erkki Vala, and his sister, Katri Vala.[50] The journal even published a letter written by a woman who had been sterilised before the 1935 Act came into effect, in which she condemned the intervention as a 'big and bad surgery, which one could easily die from'.[51] Among experts, anatomist and chair of the newly founded Finnish League for Human Rights, Väinö Lassila, was a strong opponent of the Sterilisation Act, considering it inappropriate, scientifically unfounded, financially unnecessary and a grave human rights violation.[52] This rights criticism is noticeable, particularly taking into account the lack of supranational rights instruments at the time and the limited constitutional rights recognition. Indeed, the criticism was based on moral reasoning rather than legal sources.[53] Individual doctors also opposed and resisted the legislation.[54] Such criticism was nevertheless weak in comparison to the legislation's strong, vocal support in media and among experts.[55] This being said, the infrequent application of the 1935 Act might suggest a silent disapproval of or caution towards the law among the authorities and the medical profession.[56]

[41] Ibid. [42] Ibid: 322–325. [43] Sterilisoimislaki [Sterilisation Act] 227/1935, Sections 1–2.
[44] Ibid, Sections 2 & 4. [45] Ibid, Section 7. [46] Ibid, Section 3. [47] Ibid, Section 5.
[48] Ibid, Section 8. [49] This was not legislatively regulated. Mattila 1999: 325–327.
[50] Mattila 1999: 327–334; Elmgren 2018. [51] Cited in Mattila 1999: 333. [52] Ibid: 332.
[53] According to Ainur Elmgren, the criticism was similar to Catholic criticism of eugenic sterilisation in the US in the 1930s. Elmgren 2018: 54.
[54] Mattila 1999: 333. [55] Ibid: 334. [56] Ibid: 335. See also Elmgren 2018.

The infrequent implementation was soon problematised by enthusiasts and authorities. In 1943, a recently established expert organisation, the Family Federation of Finland (*Väestöliitto*), published a report recommending that the execution of the sterilisation legislation be rendered more effective.[57] The report led to a Government investigation and two Government Bills,[58] which were passed as legislation in 1950.[59] The legislative revision regulated sterilisation and castration in separate acts, being the Sterilisation Act and Castration Act, for legal-technical reasons,[60] as the aims and the target groups of the two interventions were different.[61]

In the 1950 Sterilisation Act, the indications for voluntary sterilisation were expanded to eugenic, social and medical ones.[62] Another significant amendment was that doctors were given increased competences to initiate sterilisation applications.[63] The 1950 legislation thus widened the target group and increased its application. Similar to the Swedish 1941 Sterilisation Act, the Finnish 1950 Sterilisation Act introduced more possibilities for voluntary sterilisation, developing the legislation's scope from population control in the strict sense into one including voluntary contraception.[64] The 1950 Finnish legislation, while experiencing a shift towards voluntariness, still emphasised social interests over individual ones, and did not build on free will. A manifestation of this focus was that the right to appeal was abolished as unnecessary to guarantee the applicant's right to due process, an argument which was supported by the complete lack of appeals under the previous law.[65]

When it comes to the implementation of the laws, sterilisation surgeries had already been carried out, for example, in state institutions,[66] before the first Sterilisation Act entered into force in 1935. At the time, the interventions were conceptualised as extra-legal, or outside the law, meaning that no records were collected nationally. Sterilisation statistics thus only exist from the introduction

[57] Mattila 1999: 337. See also Leppälä 2014: 56.

[58] Lainvalmistelukunta [The Finnish Preparatory Legislative Committee] 1947; Finnish Government Bills HE 58/1948; HE 59/1948.

[59] Talousvaliokunta [The Finnish Parliamentary Commerce Committee] TaVM 5/1949, TaVM 4/1949; Suuri valiokunta [The Finnish Parliamentary Grand Committee] SuVM 97/1949; SuVM 96/1949.

[60] Sterilisoimislaki [Sterilisation Act] 83/1950.; Kastroimislaki [Castration Act] 84/1950.

[61] Finnish Government Bills HE 58/1948: 1; HE 59/1948: 1. Mattila, 1 September 2017.

[62] Sterilisoimislaki [Sterilisation Act] 83/1950, Sections 1–2. See also Finnish Government Bill HE 59/1948: 2.

[63] Sterilisoimislaki [Sterilisation Act] 83/1950, Sections 4–6. See also Finnish Government Bill HE 59/1948: 4.

[64] Finnish Government Bill HE 59/1948: 2.

[65] Sterilisoimislaki [Sterilisation Act] 83/1950, Section 9. See also Finnish Government Bill HE 59/1948: 3.

[66] That was the case at the state-owned Perttula Training School for the Feebleminded, which sterilised 19 inmates between 1912 and 1922. The interventions were considered permissible as the decision-making power was allocated to the legal guardian of the inmates, which was often the institution itself. Mattila 2002: 2.

of the first Sterilisation Act.[67] Of the 996 people sterilised pursuant to the 1935 Sterilisation Act, around 83 per cent were women.[68] With the more inclusive indications of the 1950 Sterilisation Act, the implementation increased. Among the new possibilities for interventions was that of medical indication,[69] targeting overfatigued mothers.[70] The number of sterilisations on eugenic indications was relatively high in the 1950s; sterilisations based on social indications increased at the beginning of the 1960s.[71] Towards the end of the 1960s, almost all sterilisations were performed on medical indication.[72]

The total number of sterilisations predominantly consists of sterilisations of women. During the period 1951–1970,[73] a total of 53,132 (involuntary and voluntary) sterilisations were carried out.[74] 99 per cent of these interventions were performed on women. Together with the sterilisations according to the 1935 Sterilisation Act, a total of 54,128 sterilisations were registered in Finland between 1935 and 1970, of which sterilisations on women were also 99 per cent.[75] In Sweden and Norway, the large majority of people sterilised may also have been women, but Finland almost exclusively focused its interventions on women.

The sterilisations were performed either by order or permission of the Board of Health. However, coercion occurred or pressure was applied under various circumstances,[76] including in situations where the applications had been formally signed by the applicants themselves. Categorically assuming that interventions formally registered as permissions were voluntary and those registered as orders involuntary would therefore be too simplistic. In broad terms, the growing number of sterilisations on medical indication towards the end of the 1960s corresponds to an increase in voluntary sterilisations as contraception.[77] Nevertheless, coercive implementation of the legislation also occurred.[78] Much like in Sweden and Norway, eugenic sterilisations were often used as preconditions to access abortion on eugenic grounds in Finland.[79] Sterilisations were

[67] Mattila 2002. [68] Borgström 1958: 49; Hietala 2005: 234–235. [69] See Lahti 1970: 88.
[70] Hietala 2005: 240. [71] Ibid; Mattila 1999: 392. [72] Hietala 2005: 240.
[73] The precise period ended on 31 May 1970.
[74] Mattila 1999: 392; Lahti 1970: 88; Heino, 10 August 2017.
[75] See Mattila 1999: 392; Lahti 1970: 88.
[76] This was noted with the renewal of the legislation. See Lahti 1972: 32.
[77] This was highlighted by Mattila, 1 September 2017.
[78] It was, for example, a condition for getting married.
[79] Mattila 2003: 2–3. A major change which heavily affected the implementation of the sterilisation legislation was the adoption of legislation on abortion in 1950. Many women were sterilised in Finland in connection to abortion. Before 1950, abortions were officially criminalised in Finland. The increasing amount of illegal abortions and women harmed, sometimes lethally, was alarming, and the legalisation on abortion became an intensively discussed political topic in 1940s Finland. The 1950 Act on Termination of Pregnancy was established with strict indications to keep the number of abortions to an absolute minimum. These indications were referred to as humanitarian, social and eugenic. Already in the *travaux préparatoires*, the connection between sterilisation and abortion based on eugenic indication was highlighted. In fact, the *travaux préparatoires* stressed that sterilisation should be performed in cases of eugenic abortions in order to avoid future

performed not only on unmarried women but also on married women with multiple children.[80] A particular vulnerability to coercive practices can be observed among people identified as feebleminded, the institutionalised, the imprisoned, the poor, people with disabilities or those who were dependent on public welfare, and also traveller/Romani women.[81] Unlike in its Nordic neighbours, the number of eugenic and social sterilisations – often containing elements of coercion – increased in Finland after the Second World War, while it was decreasing in Norway and Sweden.[82]

5.2.1.2 Castration: Controlling Sexual Offenders

Castration was first legally regulated in Finland in the 1935 Sterilisation Act. The law did not differentiate between the interventions sterilisation and castration, constantly referring to 'rendering a person incapable of reproduction', reflecting a general confusion of the interventions among some of the early advocates.[83] In the 1935 Act, however, a distinction was made between the target groups.[84] Castration was described as a surgery performed on sexually dangerous men in order to prevent sexually motivated crimes.[85] Said intervention was considered to be more harmful than sterilisation, warranting more pressing grounds.[86] While the latter was conceptualised as mere deprivation of reproductive capacity, castration was thought to weaken the sexual drive and capacity.[87] Castration was, however, never framed as a punishment, but rather as a form of treatment.

The *travaux préparatoires* of the 1935 Sterilisation Act portrayed castration as an intervention for criminals whose 'unnaturally strong or unnaturally oriented' sexual drive needed to be rendered 'harmless'.[88] The 1934 Government Bill highlighted that castration should be considered when addressing sexual crimes against minors, targeting child sex offenders.[89] However, same-sex sexual acts between adults, which were criminalised at the time, did not trigger the Act.[90] In fact, Honkasalo, the drafter of the law, wrote in a contemporary article that adult consensual homosexual acts were not to be regarded as a 'danger

abortions, unless special circumstances precluded sterilisation or rendered it unnecessary. See Laki raskauden keskeyttämisestä [Act on Termination of Pregnancy] 82/1950; Finnish Government Bill HE 60/1948; Talousvaliokunta [The Finnish Parliamentary Commerce Committee] TaVM 3/1949; Lakivaliokunta [The Finnish Parliamentary Legal Affairs Committee] LaVL 4/1948; Suuri Valiokunta [The Finnish Parliamentary Grand Committee] SuVM 95/1949; Valtion Väestöpoliittinen komitea [The Finnish Population Policy Committee] 1941.

[80] Mattila 2003. [81] See Mattila 2006. [82] See Mattila 2003: 2–3.

[83] See Sterilisoimislaki [Sterilisation Act] 227/1935, Section 3. Women's movements, for example, fiercely advocated for both sterilisation and castration of sexual offenders, probably aiming for the latter. Mattila 1999: 178; Mattila, 1 September 2017.

[84] Sterilisoimislaki [Sterilisation Act] 227/1935, Section 1.

[85] Finnish Government Bill HE 112/1934: 2. [86] Ibid: 23. [87] Ibid: 1.

[88] Ibid: 20–23. Sterilisoimislaki [Sterilisation Act] 227/1935, Section 1.

[89] Finnish Government Bill HE 112/1934: 6, 20.

[90] Finnish Government Bill HE 112/1934; Mattila, 1 September 2017.

for another person'.[91] Yet, he continued by stating that if a person engaged in homosexual conduct 'in order to lead minors astray', this could qualify as 'danger' according to the legislation.[92]

According to the 1935 Sterilisation Act, a person, who had committed a crime or was 'prone to commit crimes' because of their sexual drive, could be ordered or allowed to undergo castration by the Finnish Board of Health.[93] People who fell under this category could apply for castration themselves.[94] However, if the person was incarcerated in a penal establishment, the director of the institution, the bailiff, the head of the local police department or the public prosecutor could file an application.[95] If possible and applicable, the Board was required to ask the spouse or the legal guardian for a statement before a decision was made.[96] People considered to be sexually dangerous and found guilty of a crime or attempted crime in court could be castrated;[97] Alternatively, a person with full legal capacity could be castrated for special reasons if they consented to it.[98] Furthermore, castration had a minimum age requirement of 21 years, which did not apply to sterilisation.[99] Interestingly, while the Finnish regulation here officially attached less importance to the individual will of the applicant than the Swedish or Norwegian one, it was also more clearly connected to the criminal process, acquiring additional procedural safeguards, such as due process and evidence requirements.

As mentioned above, there was some resistance to the 1935 Sterilisation Act in Finland, particularly that expressed in the magazine *Tulenkantajat*. Its writers not only opposed sterilisation but also castration. They reported the first castration performed on a sexual offender, publishing an interview with a doctor who had been asked to carry out the surgery, but refused on account of insufficient medical grounds.[100] Being an attempt to frame the practices as unfounded and oppressive, such critical journalism was essential for making the law and the practices known to a broader audience, yet without much societal or institutional response.

Castration was regulated in a separate act in 1950.[101] In order to increase the number of interventions, the 1950 Castration Act included more possibilities for voluntary castration.[102] Moreover, the Board of Health was given the authority to prescribe the use of force in case the applicant refused to submit to castration.[103] An additional measure to increase the number of castrations was to restrict the right to appeal to only include orders and decisions where the

[91] Honkasalo B 1935: 126 [92] Ibid.

[93] Sterilisoimislaki [Sterilisation Act] 227/1935, Sections 1–2, 3, 6. [94] Ibid, Section 2.

[95] Ibid, Section 4(2). [96] Ibid, Section 5.

[97] However, they did not need to be sentenced. Salmiala 1951.

[98] Sterilisoimislaki [Sterilisation Act] 227/1935, Section 6.

[99] Sterilisoimisasetus [Sterilisation Decree] 228/1935, Section 5(2). [100] Mattila 1999: 332–333.

[101] Finnish Government Bill HE 58/1948.

[102] Kastroimislaki [Castration Act] 84/1950, Sections 1–2; Finnish Government Bill HE 58/1948: 3–4.

[103] Kastroimislaki [Castration Act] 84/1950, Sections 9(1), 11; Kastroimisasetus [Castration Decree] 233/1950, Section 8. See Salmiala 1951: 164.

Board had not been unanimous.[104] A final change to render the implementation more effective was the introduction of an obligation for the authorities to always consider castration of criminals in correctional facilities who had been found guilty of certain serious sexual offences, such as sexual abuse of children and rape.[105] The focus of the 1950 Act lay on forced castration of sexual criminals, primarily child sex offenders.[106]

The castration laws were not extensively used. Secondary literature suggests that the total numbers of castration orders and permissions by the Finnish Board of Health was 63 for the period 1935–1950.[107] Even without confirmation of how many of these orders were eventually carried out, the number is significantly lower than for sterilisations.[108] Between 1950 and 1968, moreover, 90 castrations were recorded.[109] Together with the castration permits according to the 1935 Sterilisation Act, a maximum number of 153 – involuntary and voluntary – castrations were conducted in Finland between 1935 and 1968. The number is considerably lower than that of Sweden and Norway. Most, if not all, castrations were performed on men.[110] The newly introduced obligation to *ex officio* consider certain people for castration resulted in an increase in castration applications.[111] Nevertheless, the Finnish Board of Health continued to apply a restrictive and careful approach; after 1958, castration applications were no longer approved. This limited application was a result of the increasing medical contestation of the efficiency of castration as a method to abolish sexual drive,[112] and criticism of the intervention as a forced, inhuman physical intervention: considered old fashioned at best, inhumane at worst.[113]

Much like sterilisation, no clear distinction was present in practice between involuntary and voluntary castrations before 1970. An example of the obscure line between free will and force in the application of the 1950 Castration Act can be seen in an article written by Finnish legal scholar Toini Honkanen in 1954, in which she denounced 'castration carried out using force' by applying police assistance as undesirable, being 'more in line with the Law of Moses than with modern criminology'.[114] She continued by arguing that the Castration Act offered 'a more humane alternative' for cases in which applicants objected to

104 Kastroimislaki [Castration Act] 84/1950, Section 12; Finnish Government Bill HE 58/1948: 5.
105 Kastroimislaki [Castration Act] 84/1950, Section 5.
106 Finnish Government Bill HE 58/1948; Talousvaliokunta [The Finnish Parliamentary Commerce Committee] TaVM 4/1949.
107 The number of castrations carried out might be lower. Salmiala 1951: 150. For castrations, no centralised statistics are available for this period. Heino, 18 August 2017.
108 Which were 996 in the period at hand.
109 Based on Hietala 2005: 242; Lahti 1970: 96. See also Sorainen 2005: 5.
110 The uncertainty regarding implementation is the result of a lack of centralised statistics.
111 The number of applications was annually between 123 (1968) and 211 (1962) for the period 1951–1968. Hietala 2005: 242; and Lahti 1970: 88.
112 This was highlighted by Salmiala 1951.
113 See Salmiala 1951; Lahti, 8 September 2017; Mattila, 1 September 2017.
114 Honkanen 1954: 44.

castration, which was to 'postpone the intervention indefinitely and forcibly institutionalise' them in order to make them 'voluntarily agree to castration'.[115]

Even though castrations were not explicitly intended to control consensual, same-sex sexual conduct, a few cases of castration of 'sodomites' were reported.[116] Same-sex acts were criminalised for both women and men until 1971.[117] Due to criminalisation, it seems that homosexual men were targeted as possible sexual deviants and offenders by the law. Moreover, the different age limits for consent for same- versus different-sex sexual relations discriminated against those who engaged in the former. Specifically, homosexual people were indirectly conceptualised as child sexual offenders, a group which was in fact explicitly targeted by the legislation.[118]

5.2.1.3 Trans People: Conditioned Legal Recognition

Even though castration became a dated intervention on sexual offenders in the late 1950s, the law was viewed as a potential legal justification for genital surgery. More specifically, between 1959 and 1969, four people applied for voluntary castration as a way to access genital gender-affirming surgery, based on that their gender identity was not in line with their registered gender. This motivation fell outside the original scope of the 1950 Castration Act,[119] which caused the Board of Health to reject their applications.[120]

In the middle of the twentieth century, large parts of Finnish society and institutions were uninformed about the existence of trans people. The 1970s was a decade which marked a small change in Finnish trans awareness among civil society, authorities and medical experts.[121] The foundation of the sexual diversity organisations *Psyke* in 1969 and *Seta* in 1974, which mainly focused on the situation of homosexual men and women, were important milestones,[122] challenging biologised gender binaries and heteronormativity in Finland.[123] At the time, authorities hardly differentiated between legal and medical questions relating to trans people, then conceptualised as 'transsexual'.[124] The lack of relevant medico-legal standards was highlighted by the Psychiatric Clinic at the

115 Ibid: 45.

116 Five homosexual men were forcibly castrated between 1935 and 1948, according to Erkkilä 1948: 75.

117 According to the 1889 Finnish Penal Code. See Mustola 2007.

118 The age of consent remained different for different-sex and same-sex sexual relations in Finland until 1999; Amendment 563/1998. See Mustola 2007: 238.

119 Pimenoff 2008: 19.

120 Ibid; Pimenoff 2006: 24. There was no legal obligation for the Board to provide reasons for its decision and equally no right to appeal. Kastroimislaki [Castration Act] 84/1950, Section 12.

121 The first Finnish psychiatric studies on transsexualism were published in 1972. They included eight individuals, who had undergone genital surgery in Finland or abroad, despite rejections from the Board of Health. Alanko & Achté 1971. See Pimenoff 2006: 24.

122 See Eriksson P 2017: 11.

123 With same-sex sexual acts having been decriminalised in 1971, homosexual communities could organise more freely than before. Especially cross-dressers found a place within homosexual men's movements and gained visibility during the 1970s. Wickman 2001: 94.

124 Ibid.

Helsinki University Hospital in 1972, which asked the Board of Health whether transsexual people should be given access to castration since this was seen as appropriate legal grounds for allowing surgical removal of healthy gonads, as part of genital gender-affirming treatment.[125] The Board did not, however, provide an official answer; the *travaux préparatoires* of the 1970 Castration Act did not mention the issue at all.[126] In the 1970s, moreover, personal identification numbers – the ultimate marker of legally registered gender in Finland – were relatively new and regionally administered.[127] During this period, some municipal registries approved amendments of personal identification numbers and first names on an *ad hoc* basis.[128]

In the 1980s, several steps were taken to unify the medical and legal treatment of transsexual people in Finland. The Board of Health decided to apply the 1970 Castration Act procedure to give people access to gender-affirming genital surgery.[129] Amendment of registered gender was nevertheless made impossible when the registration of personal identification numbers was centralised in the Finnish Population Register Centre, which did not allow for such amendments.[130] For instance, a genitally post-operative trans woman could not be legally recognised as a woman, but only as a (castrated) man.

The 1980s also produced more Finnish trans rights activism. In 1984, the first official national organisation for transsexual people, *Trasek*, was founded.[131] Its primary aim was not only to assist and represent transsexual people so that the members of the group could access medical treatment, but it also intended to raise public awareness.[132] Increasingly visible activism criticised the lack of legal recognition. In 1987, a trailblazer activist, a post-operative trans woman and her partner, protested by marrying in their registered legal gender – male and female – contrary to their gender expression (and gender identity) – female

[125] Rastas 1992: 39.

[126] Finnish Government Bill HE 106/1969; Talousvaliokunta [The Finnish Parliamentary Commerce Committee] TaVM 17/1970. See also Pimenoff 2008: 21. Nevertheless, the first case of an approved castration on these grounds was likely from 1971. See Lääkintöhallitus [The Finnish Board of Health] 1971.

[127] Wickman 2001: 82.

[128] However, the lack of central records prevents conclusions on how many people were able to amend their personal identification numbers, let alone what preconditions were implemented. Rastas 1992: 7; Pimenoff 2008: 23. The recommendation by a physician was often a condition for amendment. See Wickman 2001: 82; Pimenoff, 5 September 2017.

[129] Lahti 2006: 186. The criteria for permission to get castrated, as laid down by the Finnish Board of Health, were as follows: (i) medically certified transsexualism; (ii) sexual attraction to the opposite sex; (iii) sufficient psychiatric investigation; (iv) stable mental health; (v) positive prospects for recovery; (vi) mental and hormonal preparation; (vii) castration being viewed as the only way to alleviate the person's 'grave mental suffering'; (viii) unlikelihood of future problems. See Finnish Government Bill HE 56/2001: 5.

[130] Pimenoff 2008: 23. This position is also expressed in Väestörekisterikeskus [The Finnish Population Register Centre] 1987.

[131] Pimenoff 2008: 24; Bremer P 1991. Nowadays, the organisation is a sex/gender diversity organisation.

[132] Eriksson P 2017: 11–12; Wickman 2001: 98; Pimenoff 2006: 24.

and female – in a nationally televised wedding.[133] Such pioneering activism seems to have been effective, as the Finnish Ministry of Social Affairs and Health appointed a working group to review the legislative regulation on gender recognition in the same year.[134]

Before the authorities created any legislative proposals, however, the aforementioned trans activist had appealed the Finnish Population Register Centre's rejection to alter her legally registered gender before the Finnish Supreme Administrative Court. She referred to a section in the 1970 Population Registry Decree, which allowed for the amendment of one's personal identification number if the date of birth or the gender identifier was 'wrong'.[135] The Court was pragmatically accommodating. As the section in question did not specify in what situations the gender identifier could be considered 'wrong', and the local authorities had already approved the applicant's name change in 1986, the Court saw no obstacle to altering the legal gender accordingly.[136] Hence, the decision by the Finnish Population Register Centre was overturned by the Court, returning it to the Centre with the instruction to approve the application for a female personal identification number.[137] The brief decision neither included legal argumentation about the public interest behind legal gender registration and the applicant's rights, nor did it state what the preconditions should be for legal gender recognition of trans people.[138] Regardless, the court's ruling meant a change in administrative procedure. After the decision, other people turned to the Population Register Centre to amend their legally registered gender.[139]

At the end of the 1980s and beginning of the 1990s, there were supra- and transnational tendencies to view legal gender recognition – be it conditional – as a matter of individual rights. In 1989, the Council of Europe Parliamentary Assembly vitally recommended that member states permit 'transsexuals, particularly those who have undergone an operation, to have civil status amendments made to take account of their appearance, external morphology, psychology and social behaviour'.[140] The recommendation stirred up debate about the lack of legislative regulation on the matter in the new member state Finland, which was eager to meet European standards.[141] In 1991, Finnish Parliamentary Ombudsman Jakob Söderman wrote a letter to the Finnish Ministry of Social Affairs and Health, suggesting that legislation on legal recognition be adopted.[142] He wrote that

[133] Rastas 1992: 42; Wickman 2001: 84. The wedding was televised on 17 May 1987 by the private TV channel MTV under the title *Toisenlaiset häät [Another Kind of Wedding]*; Seta 1987.

[134] Sosiaali- ja terveysministeriö [The Finnish Ministry of Social Affairs and Health] 1987.

[135] Väestökirja-asetus [Population Registry Decree] 198/1970, Section 6; Korkein hallinto-oikeus [The Finnish Supreme Administrative Court], KHO:1988-A-46.

[136] Ibid.

[137] Korkein hallinto-oikeus [The Finnish Supreme Administrative Court], KHO:1988-A-46.

[138] Ibid. [139] Pimenoff 1993. [140] Rec. 1117 (1989), Art 8. See Chapter 2 of this work.

[141] See Finnish Government Bill HE 56/2001: 8.

[142] Eduskunnan oikeusasiamies [The Finnish Parliamentary Ombudsman] 1991; Pimenoff 2008: 26.

the effects of such legislation were likely to be negligible for society, but that regulation might mean 'relief of years of suffering and facilitated social integration' for the individuals concerned.[143] This initiative led to the Ministry of Social Affairs and Health appointing a working group to prepare a legislative proposal. An extremely strict one was soon drawn up, containing the following requirements for legal amendment: Finnish citizenship, irreversibly infertility, no previous children, no previous marriage and a minimum age of 20 years.[144] Furthermore, anxious about the unregulated trans-specific health care, the proposal severely restricted the availability of hormone treatment.[145]

Already during its preparation, the proposal was criticised on the basis of its potential violation of the ECHR by Martin Scheinin, who was invited to legally evaluate the proposal.[146] In his opinion, CoE member states were recommended to render legal recognition of trans people's gender identity possible, but they retained the right to apply preconditions for such recognition.[147] However, he pointed out that these preconditions could not violate individual rights as protected in the Convention.[148] Bringing up ECtHR practice,[149] he highlighted that the draft law was questionable, primarily in the light of the right to private and family life (Article 8 ECHR), but also the right to a fair trial (Article 6 ECHR), the right to an effective remedy (Article 13 ECHR) and the prohibition of discrimination (Article 14 ECHR).[150] Scheinin emphasised that the suggested precondition of the applicant never having been married or having had children, went 'too far' and violated the right to private and family life.[151] Furthermore, he criticised the suggested constraints on hormonal treatment, prohibition of appeal, requirement of Finnish citizenship and criminalisation of doctors who provided gender-affirming treatment outside the scope of the law, as well as the inexact and potentially offensive terminology.[152] However, in his thorough criticism of the draft law, he did not address the infertility precondition. In my interview with him, he highlighted that this precondition was not considered legally controversial at the time, probably because of a medicalised conceptualisation of trans people among public authorities and experts.[153] In other words, applicants were assumed to want gender-affirming treatment which would result in infertility. Therefore, Scheinin did not then think of the infertility precondition as coerced sterilisation but rather as a medical conceptualisation of

[143] Eduskunnan oikeusasiamies [The Finnish Parliamentary Ombudsman] 1991: 2.
[144] Sosiaali- ja terveysministeriö [The Finnish Ministry of Social Affairs and Health] 1991.
[145] Doctors prescribing hormones were criminalised unless regulated. Sosiaali- ja terveysministeriö [The Finnish Ministry of Social Affairs and Health] 1991.
[146] Pimenoff 2008: 26–27; Eriksson P 2017: 17–18. Scheinin, 23 October 2017.
[147] Scheinin 1992: 2. [148] Ibid.
[149] Particularly ECtHR, *Dudgeon v. the United Kingdom* (1981); *Norris v. Ireland* (1988); *X and Y v. the Netherlands* (1985). Other examples of legal gender recognition cases referred to were ECtHR, *Van Osterwijk v. Belgium* (1980); *Rees v. the United Kingdom* (1986); *Cossey v. the United Kingdom* (1990).
[150] Scheinin 1992: 1. [151] Ibid: 2–3. [152] Ibid: 3–5. [153] Scheinin, 23 October 2017.

the applicants' own requests.[154] In addition, infertility was a precondition for legal gender recognition in many countries at the time.

The heavy criticism strangled the legislative effort in its cradle.[155] The 1990s saw a continued lack of regulation.[156] In 1993, the authority to amend registered legal gender was again decentralised to the local magistrates,[157] which applied differing, unstandardised preconditions.[158] The incoherence was criticised by the organisation Trasek and its president, Santeri Ilola, before the Finnish Deputy Parliamentary Ombudsman at the end of the 1990s.[159] This activism, problematising the lack of legislation as a matter of rights, made the Finnish Ministry for Social Affairs and Health appoint a working group to investigate the medical, social and legal needs of transsexual people.[160] When the working group published its results in 2000, it concluded that the ECtHR had laid down an obligation for member states 'to recognise people's gender identity in public administration where gender matters, for example in registries and personal identity documents'.[161] Guiding Strasbourg practice was reported to signal an increased social acceptance of transsexual people, requiring recognition, particularly of 'the ones who have had genital correction surgery'.[162] Gender identity was stated to fall under the protection of private and family life of the 'transsexual, their partner of the opposite gender and their child'.[163] Nevertheless, the report considered that the state could decide how to strike a balance between the individual and the public interests at stake because of the great differences in state practices, implying a wide margin of appreciation.[164]

The working group criticised the use of the 1970 Castration Act as the foundation for gender-affirming treatment, as the health care needs of transsexual people required better expertise and more refinement.[165] The abolition of the Act was an issue at the heart of the trans activism at the time, highlighted in

154 Ibid. 155 Pimenoff 2006: 25.

156 The Finnish Ministry of Social Affairs and Health, however, published a report about the living situation of transsexual people in Finland in 1992, which highlighted the importance of legal recognition. Rastas 1992.

157 Väestötietolaki [Population Information Act] 507/1993; Eduskunnan apulaisoikeusasiamies [Finnish Deputy Parliamentary Ombudsman] 1998: 4.

158 Preconditions ranged from six months' hormonal treatment and a psychiatric diagnosis of transsexualism to requiring castration, a certificate of genital surgery or a statement from the National Board of Health. Sisäasiainministeriö [The Finnish Ministry of the Interior] 1999. In 1994, the medical treatment of transsexualism was nationally unified through authority guidelines. Stakes [The Finnish Centre for Research and Development on Health and Welfare] 1994.

159 Ilola, 30 October 2017; Eduskunnan apulaisoikeusasiamies [Finnish Deputy Parliamentary Ombudsman] 1998.

160 Sosiaali- ja terveysministeriö [The Finnish Ministry of Social Affairs and Health] 2000.

161 Ibid: 32. The cases referred to were ECtHR, *Rees v. the United Kingdom* (1987); *Cossey v. the United Kingdom* (1990); *Sheffield and Horsham v. the United Kingdom* (1998); *B v. France* (1992); and *X, Y and Z v. the United Kingdom* (1997).

162 Sosiaali- ja terveysministeriö [The Finnish Ministry of Social Affairs and Health] 2000: 1.

163 Ibid. 164 Ibid: 33. 165 Ibid: 4.

my interview with previously mentioned Ilola, a member of the working group behind the 2000 report:

> [The authorities] referred to the Castration Act… which had nothing to do with the issue… and I had dug out all the old laws from decades back and their reasoning, and the basis for the decision was something like 'the strength of the sexual desire' or something like that… and I said that this is not the case here, that they cannot refer to this …and the Board of Health at the time said that they did not have any other section to refer to… and I said that then they do not have a right to make decisions, if there is no law… then they found themselves between a rock and a hard place, when this revealed their problem.[166]

The *travaux préparatoires* imagined the future applicants of legal gender recognition to be 'transsexual',[167] yet with different health care needs.[168] While surgical interventions were not always considered medically motivated,[169] infertility was considered a necessary precondition for legal recognition.[170] A castration requirement was considered unnecessary and possibly in violation of the medical principle of the patient's autonomy.[171] The public interest behind the required infertility was not considered or discussed at length.[172] Similar to the Swedish and Norwegian motivations, the report imagined dawning gender chaos in the absence of infertility requirements, as situations could occur where 'legally registered women would impregnate, and legally registered men would become pregnant'.[173]

The subsequent 2001 Government Bill suggested a specific law on legal gender recognition, which included an infertility precondition.[174] Legislation and practices of other countries – Sweden, Germany, Italy, Turkey, the Netherlands, France, the UK, Norway, Switzerland and Denmark – were compared in the Bill, highlighting that they had similar sterilisation/castration requirements.[175] Other preconditions in the Bill were a diagnosis of transsexualism and that the

[166] Ilola, 30 October 2017. Translated from Finnish.

[167] The term 'transgender' occasionally appeared, since some activists at the time used it. See Sosiaali- ja terveysvaliokunta [The Finnish Parliamentary Social Affairs and Health Committee] 2002a; 2000b; 2000c.

[168] Involving gender-affirming surgery, hormonal treatment, further surgical treatment and other medical and social support services. Sosiaali- ja terveysministeriö [The Finnish Ministry of Social Affairs and Health] 2000: 6–9.

[169] Ibid: 1. [170] Ibid: 16. [171] Ibid.

[172] Psychiatrist Pimenoff, who was a member of the working group, highlighted that she problematised the infertility requirement based on practical reasons: that parenthood after medico-legal transition would be rare and that applicants were able to have children before legal recognition, effectively causing a disalignment of gender legal status and mother-/fatherhood. She emphasised, however, that requiring surgery or infertility was in line with supra- and transnational medico-legal standards at the time. The trans activist representative Ilola did not problematise the precondition, neither did the working group focus its discussions on it. Pimenoff, 5 September 2017; Ilola, 30 October 2017; Söderlund, 4 September 2017.

[173] Sosiaali- ja terveysministeriö [The Finnish Ministry of Social Affairs and Health] 2000: 37. See also Repo 2019.

[174] Finnish Government Bill HE 56/2001. [175] Ibid: 6–8.

person in question be 18 years or older, be a Finnish citizen or resident, and not be in a registered partnership or marriage.[176] Around the same time, registered partnership between same-sex couples was introduced in Finland.[177] If applicants were married or in a registered partnership, the approval by their partners was necessary for the amendment, turning the partnership into a marriage or vice versa.[178] The Bill considered the legal gender recognition important for promoting the individual rights of the people concerned, such as rights to personal autonomy and privacy, family life and prohibition of discrimination as protected by the ECHR,[179] as well as the constitutional protection of personal life.[180] How a legislative infertility precondition would affect these rights was nevertheless neither contemplated in the Bill nor discussed in Parliament.[181] When the 2002 Act on Gender Recognition of Transsexuals was adopted, the infertility precondition was formally identical to the Swedish one: requiring the applicant to be sterilised or otherwise infertile.[182] Yet, the implementation has differed, since the Finnish infertility requirement is interpreted as met through hormonal treatment, with surgical sterilisation not actually being required (as long as the applicant undergoes hormonal treatment).[183]

How many people have changed their personal identification numbers and therefore been subjected to the infertility precondition? There appears to be a lack of centralised statistics. Nevertheless, according to Statistics Finland, between 2006 and 2016, around 600 people amended their legally registered gender in Finland, fulfilling the infertility precondition at least in terms of hormonal treatment.[184]

[176] Ibid: 16.

[177] Ibid: 13–14. See Finnish Government Bill HE 200/2000; Pimenoff, 5 September 2017.

[178] Laki transseksuaalin sukupuolen vahvistamisesta [Act on Gender Recognition of Transsexuals] 563/2002, Section 2. According to the rule, which was amended in 2016, the partner had to be heard in person by the authorities.

[179] ECHR Articles 8; 12 and 14. Finnish Government Bill HE 56/2001: 8–12.

[180] Suomen perustuslaki [The Constitution of Finland], 731/1999, Section 10; Finnish Government Bill HE 56/2001: 10.

[181] There were, however, some attempts by conservative MPs to restrict the possibilities for amendment of legally registered gender, such as requiring an age limit of 30 years, or that the applicant not be the caretaker of children under 16 years of age. This criticism resulted in an amendment of the draft, demanding that the applicant show that their state of transsexualism was 'permanent'. Sosiaali- ja terveysvaliokunta [The Finnish Parliamentary Social Affairs and Health Committee] StVM 7/2002:9.

[182] Laki transseksuaalin sukupuolen vahvistamisesta [Act on Gender Recognition of Transsexuals] 563/2002, Section 1 Point 1.

[183] The requirement has, nevertheless, been central. According to Antti Karanki, former President of Trasek, the infertility precondition was most central in the legal transition process, manifested by a general insensitivity towards trans people's reproductive rights among health care staff. Karanki, 6 September 2017.

[184] The exact number of 595 is limited to applicants who were at least 8 years old in 2006 and had been born in Finland. This number is therefore approximate and incomplete. Rapo, 9 November 2017. The Finnish Institute for Health and Welfare reported to me in October 2017 that no surgical sterilisations had ever been registered in the national sterilisation registry based on the Act on Gender Recognition of Transsexuals. Indicated in Steriloimislaki

5.2.2 Criticism Coming to the Fore

Like the two other Nordic countries investigated in this book, Finland witnessed social change and an increased emphasis on individualist values in the 1960s and 1970s. In these new times, the earlier sterilisation and castration laws, which had been amended as recently as 1950 to allow for more interventions to be carried out and more force to be used, came to be seen in a different light.

5.2.2.1 Sterilisation as Voluntary Contraception

With Finnish society going through an international wave of reformist thought, anti-psychiatry movement and sexual revolution, many earlier views were subject to challenge and change.[185] When a social democratic government came to power after the parliamentary elections in 1966, many legislative changes regarding sexual and reproductive policies hung in the air.[186] A specially appointed expert group published a state report on the need to review the Finnish abortion legislation in 1969. The expert group represented a new generation of experts on law, medicine and sociology.[187] It was headed by the first Finnish female professor of criminal law, Inkeri Anttila, who had written her doctoral thesis on the criminal legal regulation of consent two decades earlier.[188] The 1969 report, informed by a certain ethos of individual rights, recommended a reform of the strict abortion legislation, also in addition to an abolition of forced sterilisation and castration.[189] The recommendation indicated that contemporary social conceptions of justice did not support forced physical interventions, proclaiming that there was no important public interest supporting the performance of sterilisations and castrations against the will of the individual.[190]

New acts on sterilisation, castration and termination of pregnancy were all established in 1970.[191] The Finnish legislative amendment was the earliest of the neighbouring countries compared in this work.[192] In comparison to the radical Swedish review of abortion and sterilisation legislation in the mid-1970s, preconditioning all interventions on individual free will, the Finnish reform was more careful and restrictive. While a newfound emphasis on individual will

[Sterilisation Act] 283/1970, Section 1 Point 7; Heino, 23 October 2017. This can be interpreted as an indication that hormonal treatment has been favoured over surgical sterilisation among applicants and/or that surgical sterilisations have not been duly registered.

185 A pivotal book of the era was *Pakkoauttajat* [Helpers by Force], edited by Lars Eriksson, criticising the use of forced health and social care and institutionalisation in Finland. The criticism provoked change at the legislative level. Lahti, 8 September 2017; Eriksson L (ed) 1967; Lahti 1980; 1982.

186 Lahti, 8 September 2017.

187 Mattila, 1 September 2017; Lahti, 8 September 2017.

188 Anttila 1946. See also Lahti (ed), 2016; (ed), 1996; 1986.

189 Aborttikomitea [Abortion Committee] 1969: 60.

190 Ibid.

191 Kastroimislaki [Castration Act] 282/1970; Steriloimislaki [Sterilisation Act] 283/1970; and Laki raskauden keskeyttämisestä [Act on Termination of Pregnancy] 239/1970.

192 However, Nordic harmonisation of abortion legislation was a contested topic at the time. Nordiska rådet [The Nordic Council] 1969; Andersen et al 1969; Lahti, 8 September 2017.

was present in the Finnish *travaux préparatoires*, the approval of the National Board of Health was still considered necessary on account of the intervention being permanent.[193] As such, a certain degree of paternalism prevailed.[194] The access to sterilisation as a voluntary birth control method was accentuated in the 1970 Sterilisation Act, which should also be seen against the backdrop of emerging new research, contraception methods and changing sexual and reproductive policies in the light of individual rights.[195] In contrast to earlier legislation, the topic of gender equality in sterilisation politics was also picked up in the *travaux préparatoires* of the 1970 Act, highlighting that women carried an unequal burden of reproductive responsibility and that the number of vasectomies should increase.[196]

Despite stressing voluntary interventions, the legislation still allowed for interventions on the legally incapable with the sole approval of the legal guardian.[197] The 1970 Sterilisation Act was later altered to improve patients' rights, with the possibilities for sterilising the legally incapable being further restricted in order to secure their informed consent.[198] Nowadays, people

[193] See Finnish Government Bill HE 105/1969; Steriloimislaki [Sterilisation Act] 283/1970, Section 4; Finnish Government Bill HE 106/1969; Kastroimislaki [Castration Act] 282/1970, Section 4; Finnish Government Bill HE 104/1969; Laki raskauden keskeyttämisestä [Act on Termination of Pregnancy] 239/1970, Section 6. According to the 1970 abortion legislation, only exceptional cases were, however, to be decided by the National Board of Health.

[194] The laws may have been inspired by Anttila's doctoral thesis, which had suggested that, while the consent of the individual was crucial, it was not enough in some cases of serious infringement. Anttila 1946.

[195] Contraception pills were first sold in Finnish pharmacies in the 1960s.

[196] Talousvaliokunta [The Finnish Parliamentary Commerce Committee] TaVM 16/1970: 3; Lahti 1985: 1813. Already in 1971, 270 male sterilisations were carried out, compared to 12 in 1969. Heino, 10 August 2017. This pragmatic point on gender equality in respect of reproductive responsibility was made 16 years before any law on gender equality was adopted. Finland was late to adopt a law on gender equality prohibiting discrimination based on gender (1986) in comparison to Sweden (1975) and Norway (1978). Laki naisten ja miesten välisestä tasa-arvosta [Act on Equality between Women and Men] 609/1986.

[197] Steriloimislaki [Sterilisation Act] 283/1970, Section 2. This approval was, however, considered to be in line with the wishes of the legally incapable person. See Lahti 1973: 313. In a 1985 article, Raimo Lahti cited a difficult case before the National Board of Health from 1977, when a legal guardian had applied for the sterilisation of a person who had long suffered from schizophrenia. The Board rejected the application on the grounds that the patient appeared to understand what sterilisation meant (i.e., a permanent inability to have children) and crucially opposed the surgery. By rejecting the application, the Board went against the recommendation of not only the legal guardian but also the expert doctors consulted. This decision, specifying the meaning of informed consent in difficult cases, became precedentary. In my interview with him, Lahti highlighted that the Board's threshold to approve sterilisations upon request of the legal guardian was high in practice. Lahti 1985: 1812; Lääkintöhallitus [The Finnish Board of Health] 1979; Lahti, 8 September 2017.

[198] Legal amendment 329/2001. This change was primarily substantiated through references to the constitutional protection of inviolable human dignity and personal autonomy; the ECHR and ICCPR's protection of the right to liberty and security of person; the regulation of informed consent in the European Convention on Human Rights and Biomedicine. See Suomen perustuslaki [The Constitution of Finland], 731/1999, Sections 1(2) and 7(1); ECHR Article 5 and ICCPR Article 9; Convention on Human Rights and Biomedicine, Article 5. See Finnish Government Bill HE 207/2000: 2–3.

who are permanently unable to understand the meaning of sterilisation due to illness can only be sterilised upon application by their legal guardian under certain circumstances.[199] However, some concerns prevail that the possibility to sterilise people on the consent of the legal guardian alone leads to abuse of the law and endangers the personal integrity of the people concerned.[200]

5.2.2.2 Castration: Harshly Criticised

In the middle of the twentieth century, castration began to be criticised. Just one year after the 1950 Castration Act was established, legal scholar Bruno Salmiala criticised how forced castration could be carried out as a consequence of a crime. He particularly condemned that the intervention could be performed without a hearing, completely disregarding the wishes of the individual.[201] In the absence of contemporary supranational legal standards, his evaluation relied on medical critique of the efficiency of castration, the rule of law, humanist principles and comparative legal examples.[202] He referred to Sweden, Norway and Switzerland, where the legislation built on voluntary castration; to Denmark, where forced castration was allowed in theory, but not applied in practice, and to Germany and some states in the US, where forced castration had been abolished as a rights violation.[203] Remarkably, Salmiala did not mention Finnish constitutional rights. This lack of reference might be indicative of the modest position of constitutional rights in 1950s Finnish legal culture, as well as that constitutional rights were not interpreted as encompassing reproductive and sexual concerns.[204] Salmiala argued that forced castration had to be abolished for humanity's sake.[205] Similarly, the 1969 *travaux préparatoires* also saw castration as harmful and ineffective.[206] Nevertheless, the intervention was still maintained in the 1970 Castration Act because of its potential therapeutic effect for people whose sexual drive caused them grave mental suffering or other serious harm.[207]

[199] The exceptional circumstances are the following: if pregnancy would endanger the life or health of the person in question; if there is reason to believe that their offspring would have or develop a severe illness or disability; if the person is unable to take care of children; if compelling reasons support sterilisation. Steriloimislaki [Sterilisation Act] 283/1970, Section 2. The application is made to the Finnish Supervisory Authority for Welfare and Health. Steriloimislaki [Sterilisation Act] 283/1970, Section 4(1) Point 3.

[200] See CEDAW/C/FIN/CO/7 (2014): Para 28. In my interview with Lisbeth Hemgård and Mikael Lindholm at Inclusion Finland FDUV, an NGO working with people with intellectual disabilities and their close relatives, they highlighted that, in their experience, pressure from relatives rather than authorities is often the problem in practice, which might lead to involuntary interventions. Hemgård & Lindholm, 7 September 2017.

[201] Salmiala 1951. [202] Ibid. [203] Ibid: 140–141; Lahti 2006: 185–186.

[204] This was also highlighted by Lahti, 8 September 2017. [205] Salmiala 1951: 165.

[206] Finnish Government Bill HE 106/1969; Talousvaliokunta [The Finnish Parliamentary Commerce Committee] TaVM 17/1970.

[207] Finnish Government Bill HE 106/1969. In practice, the law was, however, only used as legal grounds for allowing genital gender-affirming surgery.

The possibility to perform interventions on the legally incapable with the sole approval of the legal guardian was preserved for sterilisation but not for castration, creating an essential difference between the two laws from 1970 on.[208] The Castration Act contained an explicit prohibition of the castration of legal minors and people with severe mental disabilities or illnesses.[209] As such, the boundaries between involuntary and voluntary interventions were significantly defined for castration, but kept more fluid for sterilisation.

As mentioned in the context of sterilisation, the 1970s saw changing values in Finnish society and legal culture. The prominent Finnish constitutional legal scholar Paavo Kastari brought up the past practice of forced castration in his seminal book on civil rights in 1972,[210] using it as an example of interventions which violated the constitutional protection of personal freedom.[211] Kastari raised the question of how such forced interventions had been introduced through ordinary legislation without even considering constitutional rights.[212] In his explanation on why this had happened, he attached importance to forced castration having been conceptualised as a form of care rather than punishment, and that the right to decide over one's own body not having been given fundamental importance when the laws were established.[213] Kastari concluded that social values and understandings of justice had changed since then, altering public views on forced physical interventions – also noticeable in the fact that forced castration had not been applied since 1958.[214] Kastari's analysis of the interventions should be seen as a manifestation of a shift in Finnish legal opinion in the 1970s, an awakening of a rights culture, particularly regarding interventions in a criminological context.[215] The 1970 Castration Act was nevertheless not abolished until 2002 with the establishment of legislation on legal gender recognition.[216]

5.2.2.3 Trans: Working for Change

The 2002 Act on Gender Recognition of Transsexuals, often referred to as the Trans Act, became an object of human rights criticism in the 2010s. According to trans rights activist Antti Karanki, former president of Trasek, the criticism of the infertility precondition did not immediately arise after the adoption of the law, as many trans people and activists welcomed legislation

[208] Steriloimislaki [Sterilisation Act] 283/1970, Section 2. See Lahti 1973: 313.

[209] Kastroimislaki [Castration Act] 282/1970, Section 2. [210] Kastari 1972.

[211] Suomen Hallitusmuoto [Finnish Government Act] 94/1919, Section 6.

[212] Kastari 1972: 157. [213] Ibid: 159.

[214] Ibid: 158. Forced sterilisation was not criticised in the same manner, however. On the contrary, it was only mentioned in passing as a phenomenon of the past without problematising that it remained legally possible in some cases.

[215] The problematisation of forced castration was a sign of the development of the right to physical integrity in Finnish legal culture. See Lahti 2007.

[216] From then on, the law no longer served as legal grounds for gender-affirming surgery.

on the topic.[217] Criticism arose later, prompted by issues such as encountering problems in accessing fertility treatment:

> In 2002 came the progressive Trans Act, but then one did not think about the fact that the infertility requirement was a question of human rights, because we thought that now is the first time that it is legislated... and that was the most important thing, obviously, and there were compromises... and then, when we found out that gametes were not stored, and when there was talk about [trans] people not being suitable parents [...] then of course we started wondering what [the requirement] was based on [...] and we started looking [...] and it was based on [the idea] that men cannot give birth... it did not have any other substantiation.[218]

The infertility precondition has negatively affected trans people's access to fertility treatment, since a broad interpretation led to health care personnel refusing to assist trans applicants by referring to the Trans Act.[219] In 2009, this issue was taken up in a case before the Finnish Parliamentary Ombudsman.[220] The Ombudsman recognised that the *travaux préparatoires* of the 2002 Trans Act expressed a wish to limit the reproductive freedom of people amending their legally registered gender.[221] Yet, she considered the constitutional equality clause to be applicable,[222] which was also highlighted in the 2006 Act on Fertility Treatment.[223] Accordingly, fertility treatment was to be given to people without discrimination on the basis of gender identity or sexual orientation.[224] Furthermore, the Ombudsman crucially recognised that sterilisation was a side effect of the only existing medical treatment of people diagnosed with transsexualism in Finland, and that this form of sterilisation could not be considered voluntary.[225] The conclusion was that the applicant should have access to fertility treatment and that this interpretation should apply uniformly in the whole country.[226] While the decision was only recommendatory, it reflected a critical growing consciousness concerning trans people's reproductive rights, particularly concerning the infertility precondition, in human rights circles. Even if explicit references to international documents were absent, the emerging national criticism occurred at the same time as the growing supranational problematisation of similar requirements targeting trans people.[227]

During the 2010s, the Finnish preconditions for legal gender recognition were widely denounced by supranational and national human rights actors. Interestingly, the Finnish infertility requirement, while not requiring surgery

[217] Karanki, 6 September 2017. [218] Ibid. Translated from Finnish.
[219] This was highlighted in my interview with Lundell-Kiuru & Valleala, 6 September 2017.
[220] Eduskunnan oikeusasiamies [The Finnish Parliamentary Ombudsman], No. 2882/4/07 (2009).
[221] Ibid: 5. [222] Suomen perustuslaki [The Constitution of Finland], 731/1999, Section 6.
[223] See Eduskunnan oikeusasiamies [The Finnish Parliamentary Ombudsman], No. 2882/4/07 (2009): 8; Laki hedelmöityshoidoista [Act on Fertility Treatment] 1237/2006. Her decision was supported by the expert opinion Lahti 2008.
[224] Eduskunnan oikeusasiamies [The Finnish Parliamentary Ombudsman], No. 2882/4/07 (2009): 8.
[225] Ibid: 11. [226] Ibid. [227] See the second chapter of this work.

in practice, has been at the core of the rights debate as it was in Norway and Sweden – suggesting both transnational and supranational influence. In 2011, the infertility precondition was criticised by many civil society organisations in the light of a government initiative to establish a national Human Rights Action Programme.[228] In 2012, the Finnish Ombudsman for Equality stated that the Finnish precondition was unique, medically unfounded and legally questionable, referring to CoE recommendations,[229] constitutional regulation on equality and protection of human rights,[230] and comparative legal insights.[231] In the same year, the CoE Commissioner for Human Rights moreover severely criticised the Finnish Trans Act, and the infertility precondition in particular.[232] Similar complaints were levied against Finland, for example, in the Universal Periodic Review,[233] by the CEDAW Committee,[234] and by the European Commission.[235] Recommendations to abolish the infertility precondition were also made by domestic bodies such as the Finnish Advisory Board on Social Welfare and Health Care Ethics,[236] and the Finnish Ministry of Justice.[237] In the 2010s, civil society organisations – chief among them Seta, Trasek, the Finnish League for Human Rights and the national department of Amnesty International – ran various human rights campaigns to amend the Trans Act, involving measures such as online petitions and shadow reports to supranational institutions.[238]

During the 2010s, there were also various political initiatives to amend the law. A 2015 state report recommended a less restrictive regulation of the amendment of legal gender.[239] By then, the discrimination legislation had also been revised to include trans people.[240] The report supported the removal of the infertility precondition as:[241]

> not conforming to the European Convention on Human Rights and other international human rights obligations for our country. Transgender people's rights

[228] Salo, 4 September 2017; Karanki, 6 September 2017.

[229] CommDH/IssuePaper(2009)2; CM/Rec(2010)5 (2010).

[230] Primarily Suomen perustuslaki [The Constitution of Finland], 731/1999, Sections 6 and 22.

[231] The abolition or lack of infertility requirements in Sweden, Germany, Portugal, the UK and the Netherlands were mentioned in the report. Tasa-arvovaltuutettu [The Finnish Ombudsman for Equality] 2012: 14, 18–19.

[232] Another point of criticism was the requirement that the applicant should not be married. CommDH(2012)27: Paras 89, 91, 108.

[233] A/HRC/21/8 (2012): Para 90.8. A/HRC/36/8 (2017), Paras 48; 50; 93.46; 93.47; 93.48; 93.50; 93.51; 93.52; 93.53.

[234] CEDAW/C/FIN/CO/7 (2014): Paras 28–29.

[235] The European Commission responded to a question by MEP Miapetra Kumpula-Natri, as reported by Roivainen 2017.

[236] See Sosiaali- ja terveysministeriö [The Finnish Ministry of Social Affairs and Health] 2015: 53.

[237] Oikeusministeriö [The Finnish Ministry of Justice] 2014: 37.

[238] Salo, 4 September 2017; Karanki, 6 September 2017; Eriksson, 11 September 2017. See Trasek & Seta 2016.

[239] Sosiaali- ja terveysministeriö [The Finnish Ministry of Social Affairs and Health] 2015: 66.

[240] See Finnish Government Bill HE 19/2014.

[241] Salo, 4 September 2017; Karanki, 6 September 2017; Lundell-Kiuru & Valleala, 6 September 2017.

> to bodily integrity and protection of private life, protected as constitutional and human rights, demand that the infertility requirement is abolished from the Trans Act.[242]

National mass media reporting on the infertility precondition changed in the light of trans rights developments during the 2010s. In 2012, mass media framed the planned revision of the Trans Act as the Government preparing a law 'allowing men to give birth'.[243] Since then, mass media reporting nevertheless increasingly framed the question as one of rights, pointing out that Finland was the only Nordic country that had not abolished such requirements, that they were considered a violation of human rights at the European level and that Sweden was already paying compensation for such practices.[244]

Yet, all attempts to amend the Trans Act failed during the 2010s. A 2016 Parliamentary Bill to abolish the infertility precondition was unsuccessful.[245] The Government led by Juha Sipilä, which had a conservative voter base, did not advance any initiatives to abolish the precondition during its years in power (2015–2019),[246] strong criticism notwithstanding.[247] The amendment of the Trans Act had become a deeply politicised question, seen as having the potential of 'overthrowing the Government'.[248]

After the 2019 elections, the Government changed to a centre-left orientation. The Government led by Antti Rinne, and later Sanna Marin, included

242 Sosiaali- ja terveysministeriö [The Finnish Ministry of Social Affairs and Health] 2015: 65. Translated from Finnish.

243 See Raevaara 2012. The negative publicity made the Government withdraw any revision plans. Salo, 4 September 2017.

244 See, for example, Grünn 2017; Kervinen 2017.

245 Finnish Parliamentary Bill LA 43/2016; Yle Uutiset 2017. The precondition on marriage was subject to extensive criticism and, however unsuccessfully, even taken through a judicial process up to the ECtHR. It was amended in connection to the introduction of marriage equality, which was approved by the Finnish Parliament in 2014 and introduced in 2017. The majority of the judges of the Finnish Supreme Administrative Court and the ECtHR did not find a violation of human or constitutional rights. See Korkein hallinto-oikeus [The Finnish Supreme Administrative Court], KHO:2009:15; ECtHR, *Hämäläinen v. Finland* (2014). See also Lavapuro et al 2011: 526–527; Hellum 2016: 201.

246 The lack of political advancement is striking since a draft law had already been prepared and the individual ministers in charge supported a renewal. Salo, 4 September 2017; Karanki, 6 September 2017; Oksanen, 7 September 2017.

247 See, for example, Ihmisoikeusvaltuuskunta [The Finnish Human Rights Delegation] 2017 and Eduskunnan apulaisoikeusasiamies [Finnish Deputy Parliamentary Ombudsman] EOAK/2842/2017 (2018).

248 Oksanen, 7 September 2017. The resistance by the Finns Party and the later Blue Reform Party was particularly pivotal. See Tiusanen 2018. An organised pushback against rights pertaining to sexual orientation and gender identity in Finland is nevertheless present. This resistance manifested in, among others, a 2016 citizens' initiative to repeal equal marriage, for which no equivalent in the neighbouring countries exists. The formal initiative was rejected by Parliament in 2017, but the movement continues as a civil society organisation called 'Real Marriage' *(Aito avioliitto)*.

a revision of the legal regulations on gender recognition in its Government Programme. More specifically, the Programme stated:

> An act on the legal recognition of gender that respects people's right to self-determination will be enacted. The requirement of infertility will be removed from the act, and medical treatments will be separated from the change of legal gender.[249]

A project to revise the Trans Act was initiated by the Ministry for Social Affairs and Health in 2019.[250] In response to the slow advancement of the authorities, together with a fear that the revision project would only aim to abolish the most evident rights violations – such as the infertility precondition – trans civil society, led by the newly established organisation *Trans*, began a citizens' initiative. The initiative aspired to establish a law on legal gender recognition which would build on self-declaration and was presented before Parliament in 2021.[251] In line with the initiative, a Government Bill to introduce legal gender recognition based on self-declaration was presented before the Parliament in 2022.[252] The Act on Gender Recognition was ultimately approved by Parliament in 2023, which also meant a final elimination of the infertility precondition.[253]

5.3 A Restrained Remedial Culture

As mentioned at the beginning of this chapter, Finland is a remedially austere country in comparison to Norway and Sweden. The topic of historical sterilisation and castration laws in Finland has received minimal attention by politicians and mass media. Relevant developments in Norway and Sweden have not significantly broken through the Finnish silence. Any Finnish remedial claims differed from those of the other two countries: having appeared earlier, coming from mainly unorganised, individual victims, and centring on access to sterilisation reversal surgery, rather than compensation.

5.3.1 Sterilisation Reversal

Unlike earlier sterilisation legislation, the 1970 Sterilisation Act emphasised voluntary interventions. After it was established, some people turned to administrative courts to access reversal surgery. In the sparsely worded court

249 Prime Minister Antti Rinne's Government 2019: 93; Prime Minister Sanna Marin's Government 2019: 95.

250 A report declaring that a more restrictive or a broader revision model were both possible was published in 2020. Sosiaali- ja terveysministeriö [The Finnish Ministry of Social Affairs and Health] 2020.

251 Citizens' Initiative KAA 6/2021.

252 Government Bill HE 189/2022.

253 According to the 2023 law, the preconditions for gender legal recognition are: (i) that the applicant declares that they permanently identify with the gender in question; (ii) that they are legal adults; (iii) that they are Finnish citizens or residents. See Laki sukupuolen vahvistamisesta [Gender Recognition Act] 295/2023, Section 1.

records, there is a general lack of information about the plaintiffs and the contexts in which they were sterilised. In 1971, an early case of extraordinary appeal for nullification of a sterilisation decision in order to access reversal surgery appeared before the Finnish Supreme Administrative Court as the appeal instance for administrative decisions on sterilisation.[254] In the case, a woman had been sterilised in connection to an abortion, based on the decision of the Finnish Board of Health. The judgment did not engage in whether the intervention had been voluntary or not,[255] or whether the decision to sterilise her had been in violation of any legal norms. It referred to her presenting 'new information' before the Court, without specifying, however, what this was or how it changed the evaluation of her case.[256] The Court approved her application for nullification of the earlier decision and left the concrete decision about the access to sterilisation reversal surgery to the Board of Health.[257]

After this first decision, a dozen similar cases reached the Supreme Administrative Court, with the last one handed down in 1984. In six cases, the Court approved the application to repeal the earlier sterilisation decision based on 'new information', again never clarifying the nature of this information.[258] In five cases, it dismissed the application on the grounds that the earlier sterilisation decision had been a permission to get sterilised, not an order. This implied that there was no need to apply for a reversal of the earlier decision as it did not constitute an obstacle for sterilisation reversal surgery as an order would have been.[259] The Court also rejected one application on the basis that the plaintiff had not presented new information, yet again without mention of what such new information should have been.[260] This last rejection can be described as somewhat exceptional, since the Court in general approached these cases with a permissive attitude.

Finland seems to be the only state in the comparison where sterilisation victims have turned to the courts to access sterilisation reversal surgery. This difference is likely caused by the heavier emphasis on the state as the ultimate decision-maker in the country. The extensive interpretation of sterilisation orders in the Finnish 1935 and 1950 Sterilisation Acts, according to which former decisions formed an administrative obstacle for reversal surgery, was an exclusively Finnish interpretation of the sterilisation legislation. Indeed, access to reversal surgery has not been subject to similar authority control in Norway and Sweden.[261]

254 Korkein hallinto-oikeus [The Finnish Supreme Administrative Court], 4111/65/70 (1971).

255 Nevertheless, the fact that the sterilisation had been carried out in connection to an abortion, and that she applied for a reversal surgery, could suggest that it had been involuntary.

256 Korkein hallinto-oikeus [The Finnish Supreme Administrative Court], 4111/65/70 (1971).

257 Ibid.

258 Korkein hallinto-oikeus [The Finnish Supreme Administrative Court], 2769/65/71 (1972); 5/65/76 (1977); 1307/65/78 (1979); 2299/65/78 (1980); 3962/65/78 (1980); 5689/65/83 (1984).

259 Korkein hallinto-oikeus [The Finnish Supreme Administrative Court], 3576/65/76 (1974); 4919/65/72 (1974); 3267/65/76 (1977); 4915/65/76 (1977); 4914/65/78 (1980).

260 Korkein hallinto-oikeus [The Finnish Supreme Administrative Court], 1111/65/78 (1979).

261 As confirmed by Socialstyrelsens upplysningstjänst [The Information Service of the Swedish National Board of Health and Welfare], 28 March 2018; Knapskog, 3 May 2018.

While the related decisions did not state that the previous laws or policies constituted violations of legal or social norms, the approval of many an application in the 1970s and 1980s was a sign of a change of stance on sterilisation politics among Finnish authorities. Legal scholar and former justice at the Supreme Administrative Court, Pekka Hallberg, who sat on the bench in some of the reversal decisions, pointed out that the threshold for extraordinary appeal to nullify an administrative decision has generally been very high in Finland, particularly at the time in question. Accordingly, this points to the exceptionality of the cases, and a changing normative climate.[262] The appeals should also be understood against the background of the new legislation from 1970, emphasising personal autonomy and individual rights and eschewing forced physical interventions.[263]

5.3.2 Compensation, or No Compensation

Victims of involuntary sterilisation and castration have generally remained silent in Finland. There has been a lack of social engagement with the harm of involuntary sterilisation/castration, and an equal lacuna concerning remedies for such harm. While the victims' muteness, especially among the people subjected to historical sterilisation and castration laws, is not a uniquely Finnish trait, the lack of state engagement with its own history of sterilisation and castration stands out in comparison to Norway and Sweden. As previously mentioned, the remedial culture in Finland has generally focused on war-related harm. Discussions about the injustices carried out under the shadow of the emerging administrative state in the twentieth century – such as mistreatment of children in state care, lobotomy, sterilisation and castration – have been remarkably quieter in Finland than in Norway and Sweden.

In comparison with its neighbouring countries, the Finnish general public seems to be relatively unaware of past sterilisation practices. Mattila has highlighted that some international attention was directed at Finnish sterilisation politics after the Swedish scandal in 1997, but indicated a great contrast in the amount of public and media attention between the two countries.[264] Interestingly, even though the topic has not been ignored by Finnish mass media,[265] the sterilisation and castration history seems to have been framed as a marginal historical phenomenon – a topic of some historical, but not general public or democratic interest.

262 Hallberg, 8 July 2017. 263 This was also highlighted by Lahti, 8 September 2017.

264 Mattila, 1 September 2017. Marjatta Hietala, who has also historically investigated Finnish sterilisations and eugenics, further emphasised such Finnish national unawareness. Hietala, 11 October 2017.

265 For an early article concerning eugenic sterilisation laws in the Nordic countries which appeared in a leading Finnish newspaper, see Hietala 1995.

Unlike their Norwegian and Swedish counterparts, Finnish authorities have not commissioned any investigations concerning past historical sterilisation or castration practices. Asking Mattila about the Finnish lack of such public truth-finding, he pointed at Swedish exceptionalism, together with a strong non-retroactive approach to the sterilisation laws among Finnish authorities:

> [A]nd [the Swedish Government] appointed this big committee, this investigation, and in Finland, there has been nothing of the sort... and I understand it, very well, from the point of view, that the Sterilisation Acts were established in the correct order, approved by the Finnish Parliament... they were ordinary laws. And there was no secret activity, it was similar to all legal activity. And if we now, in hindsight, when it turns out that, for example, some premise, such as the medical one, is no longer valid... and that this would mean that the law needs to be nullified and that compensations have to be paid, then this would open a Pandora's box.[266]

A pervasive fear of the consequences which any problematisation of past practices could cause is reflected in authority statements of the time. Finnish mass media picked up on the issue in connection to the Swedish scandal in 1997, noting that Finland had implemented similar sterilisation policies and pointing out the impossibility for victims to access compensation according to existing laws.[267] In 1999, leading Finnish newspaper *Helsingin Sanomat* further pondered the question of compensation in Finland in connection to the extraordinary establishment of the Swedish Compensation Act. When asked about the topic at the time, the Minister of Social Affairs and Health, Terttu Huttu-Juntunen from the Left Alliance, replied that the Government was neither planning to address the issue of sterilisations nor to allow compensations for them. She highlighted:

> [If] one starts to dig into the history of medicine, a lot of things will be found that in the light of today's knowledge can be condemned. The knowledge at the time concerning, for example, the heredity of diseases and traits was particularly inadequate. One should learn from the mistakes made.[268]

On account of this floodgates argument, the question of compensation was left unanswered.[269]

There are some theoretical possibilities for victims of involuntary sterilisation and castration to access compensation through the Finnish Liability

[266] Mattila, 1 September 2017. Translated from Finnish.

[267] See, for example, Lindberg 1997a and 1997b. [268] Lindberg 1999. Translated from Finnish.

[269] The redress of the grievances caused by Finland's sterilisation history, particularly concerning deaf people, resurfaced in mass media and on the political agenda of the opposition in 2018. This was motivated by the activism of the Finnish Association of the Deaf, a civil society organisation pointing out that the Finnish sterilisation practices targeted deaf people in particular and that remedies such as a public apology were needed to redress their harm and trauma. Yet, the Government did not respond to these remedial claims. See Holmlund 2018a, 2018b.

Act.[270] Victims have, however, not claimed public liability in courts.[271] Taking into consideration the principle of non-retroactivity and the late development of supranational human rights norms on involuntary sterilisation and castration, but also more practical issues, such as evidence requirements and statutory limitations, turning to courts might turn out to be difficult in practice, particularly for the victims whose sterilisation or castration was carried out a long time ago. Such obstacles are affirmed in authoritative interpretation. In 1997, in the light of the Swedish mass media reports on the issue, the director of the Finnish Advisory Board on Social Welfare and Health Care Ethics of the time, Aila Lind, told national mass media that there were no possibilities for the involuntarily sterilised pursuant to historical sterilisation laws to access compensation without an extraordinarily established law.[272]

While no state investigation or remedial initiative has ever been launched for the victims of involuntary sterilisation or castration, the Finnish Advisory Board on Social Welfare and Health Care Ethics looked into possible compensation for the lobotomised in 2000.[273] Nonetheless, this initiative soon ended in a recommendation not to compensate the victims. This conclusion was reached because the interventions had been performed a long time ago, and only a small group of the lobotomy patients were still alive in 2000, meaning that few direct victims would benefit from compensation. Moreover, direct victims who were still alive would likely not be able to benefit from any compensation themselves; such compensation would benefit their relatives instead. Furthermore, a compensation to the lobotomised could open the door for other groups who would possess a similar right to compensation, such as the forcibly sterilised and castrated.[274] The decision ruled that lobotomy could be

[270] Vahingonkorvauslaki [Liability Act] 412/1974. As in Norway and Sweden, the legal evaluation of liability depends on whether involuntary sterilisations or castrations have been in accordance with the former legislation (the legislation allowing for involuntary interventions) or a violation of it. In the former case, the question becomes one of public liability according to constitutional or supranational rights standards at the time. The latter is primarily the liability (for damages or criminal liability) of the individual civil servant or medical doctor. However, similar to those in Norway and Sweden, Finnish transgressions have been treated with complete impunity by the state, reviving questions concerning public liability.

[271] This void renders it difficult to know how, for example, rules on statutory limitation would be implemented on involuntary sterilisation and castration, when personal damage(s) can be considered to be detected, etc., according to Laki velan vanhentumisesta [Statute of Limitations] 728/2003.

[272] Lindberg 1997a.

[273] Valtakunnallinen terveydenhuollon eettinen neuvottelukunta [The Finnish Advisory Board on Social Welfare and Health Care Ethics] 2000. The lobotomised have received compensation in Norway, but not in Sweden. See Arvidsson 2016: 18, 137.

[274] Valtakunnallinen terveydenhuollon eettinen neuvottelukunta [The Finnish Advisory Board on Social Welfare and Health Care Ethics] 2000: 1–5. References to forced sterilisations and castrations were made in an annex to the decision, as they were believed to be such serious interferences with the personal autonomy of the patient at the time that they had to be legislated, unlike lobotomy. The decision was evidently influenced by a formal statement on the matter by former Supreme Administrative Court justice and former ECtHR judge, Raimo Pekkanen, in 2000. While he did not see 'any formal obstacle to an extraordinary

Table 5.1 Remedies to castrated and sterilised people in Finland

	Group 1: Victims of eugenic sterilisation laws (1935–1970)	Group 2: Victims of castration laws (1935–1970)	Group 3: Trans victims (-2023)
Restitution	Yes, nullification of former decisions for a few applicants	N/A	N/A
Compensation	N/A	N/A	N/A
Rehabilitation	N/A	N/A	N/A
Satisfaction	N/A	N/A	N/A
Guarantees of non-repetition	N/A	N/A	N/A

considered to be in accordance with the legislation and the standards of care at the time from a liability perspective.[275] The decision stated that lobotomy was not a rights violation, without any substantiation being provided.[276] The mere fact that a person had been subjected to lobotomy could thus not trigger public liability. Finally, the decision pointed out that claims like this would be subject to statutory limitations.[277] Arguments pertaining to non-retroactivity and prescriptibility were thereby addressed, albeit sweepingly. The decision is important as it demonstrates Finnish authorities' persistent unwillingness to scrutinise medical practices, including sterilisation and castration, within legal parameters (Table 5.1).[278]

5.3.3 Cross-Group Comparison

A comparison between the remedies for various victim groups referred to in the Finnish context is necessarily brief because of the general lack of remedies, with the exception of successful application for nullification of sterilisation decision to access sterilisation reversal surgery for some victims.

The lack of remedies in Finland is striking. As in Sweden and Norway, victims of involuntary sterilisation and castration have generally not mobilised for remedies, possibly due to stigmatisation, shame, lack of rights consciousness,

compensatory law', he recommended that the state not establish such a law because it might 'form a precedent in other cases comparable to lobotomy'. His statement is included in Valtakunnallinen terveydenhuollon eettinen neuvottelukunta [The Finnish Advisory Board on Social Welfare and Health Care Ethics] 2002: 48–51.

275 Ibid: 3. 276 Ibid. 277 Ibid.

278 Given that a similar stance has been taken by Finnish authorities concerning more recent controversial medical practices, such as non-consensual surgeries on intersex persons, this unwillingness apparently has not been confined to the past. See Potilasvakuutuskeskus [Patient Insurance Centre], PO 2003–6434–83 (2003).

lack of a community and contact among victims, lack of organisation or particular interest among existing civil society organisations. That being said, there have been no state initiatives to remedy historical sterilisation and castration practices, even though the laws have been amended to favour an emphasis of individual interests and rights. Additionally, groups one and three have experienced difficulties in accessing fertility treatment, indicating a weak realisation of reproductive rights.[279] In comparison to Norway and Sweden, as well as many other European countries, Finland also maintained the infertility precondition for legal gender recognition for a remarkably long time.

5.4 Discussion

Just like in Sweden and Norway, rights have gained prominence by means of Finland's internationalising legal culture. While this has contributed to some apparent changes in the national liability culture, the remedial culture is more restrained in Finland than in the neighbouring countries. Potentially rights-violating practices in medical care have generally remained unquestioned by the authorities, which seem to pragmatically try to prevent a flood of claims affecting the allocation of state funds. Similarly to Swedish authority interpretation before the 1997 scandal, Finnish authorities have relied on non-retroactivity, claiming that past medical practice should not – legally or morally – be held to today's standards. Understanding these legal cultural factors is crucial to penetrate the Finnish silence.

The Finnish case is remarkably different from the Swedish and the Norwegian ones, as rather than one or two victim group(s) shaping the remedial debate and other(s) remaining silent, no group has been granted remedies. No state investigation has been launched to investigate past practices of involuntary sterilisations and castrations; this lack of truth-finding has prevented frame alignment and grievance formation among victims of past oppression. Yet, this statement not merely holds true in reference to historical practices. The absence of legal and sociocultural framing of involuntary sterilisation and castration as rights violations can also be felt in the fact that Finland was one of the few European states to have kept infertility requirements for legal gender recognition into the 2020s, even in the face of supranational legal developments supporting abolition.[280]

Lacking rights frames, Finnish victims of involuntary sterilisation and castration have not mobilised as a rule. The main exceptions to this are the few individual victims challenging their sterilisation decisions before the national

279 The general difference in remedial culture between the countries compared in this work can be seen in the Finnish compensation for infertility due to medical malpractice, which is significantly lower than its Swedish and Norwegian counterparts. In 2018, the compensation for infertility for a 30-year-old person who had become infertile due to loss of gonads was 17,688 Euros. Saarela, 7 August 2018.

280 See the second chapter of this work.

courts in order to access reversal surgery or to get legal gender recognition, not challenges in terms of public liability, however. Trans people are the only group which has mobilised collectively, with a focus on political and administrative institutions rather than courts. They have mobilised for the establishment of a law on legal gender recognition, and subsequently to amend the same law in line with emerging human rights standards. More specifically, this rights mobilisation has happened in the light of international and transnational normative developments calling infertility requirements for legal gender recognition into question, with the support of supranational human rights institutions as well as global and local NGOs. Said support has facilitated grievance formation in terms of rights on individual and intra-group levels, respectively.

In terms of external validation of victim status, Finnish mass media has only paid sporadic attention to sterilisation practices. The only interventions which have explicitly been framed as legal rights violations by mass media – in relation to emerging ECtHR judgments, Nordic developments and the Swedish 2018 Compensation Act – have been the infertility requirement targeting trans people. Yet, the recently emerging tendency to report on trans people's reproductive concerns as human rights violations stand in sharp contrast to mass media reports of a few years earlier, which implies a successful frame alignment for the group in terms of sociocultural rights consciousness.

Criticism framing the Finnish infertility requirement as a rights violation by international and national institutions, mass media and politicians, also had a surprising effect in Finland. Using human rights to 'name and shame' the country seems to have further politicised the question rather than adding momentum, especially in the period of 2015–2019 since the conservative Government in power did not wish to live up to international liberal standards of LGBT+ 'friendliness'. While the subsequent Government took a different approach with placing the revision of the Trans Act back on the political agenda, Finland showcases the most vocal political pushback to abolition of infertility requirements for legal gender recognition in the comparison. In a sense, framing in terms of rights created a sociocultural effect on the public image of the state in the Finnish case which differed greatly from that in the other countries compared, namely, state human rights advocacy being regarded as undesirable.

Part III

Rights Framing and Grievance Formation

6

From Harms to Remedies?

While the complexities of the three-pronged comparison of nations, histories and groups undertaken in this book do not easily lend themselves to being summarised, Table 6.1 gives an overview of important milestones in the establishment and abolition of sterilisation and castration practices in Sweden, Norway and Finland, and the applicable remedies. The interventions are categorised in three groups, with (1) referring to the historical, eugenic and socio-political sterilisations (1930s–1970s), (2) to the criminological and psychiatric castrations (1930s–1970s) and (3) to the compulsory sterilisations/castrations as a precondition for legal gender recognition.

The table renders visible the inconsistent remedial treatment of the groups compared, an inconsistency which this chapter aims to unpack. By conceptualising developing rights not as legal instruments, but rather as master frames, the comparison can illuminate their complex, inconsistent and situated legal and sociocultural impact. Furthermore, an investigation of the grievance formation process which victims have undergone to access remedies shows that victims have aligned with rights master frames and been socio-legally validated as rights-holders by themselves, mass media and/or public institutions to different extents. Such alignment and validation, or lack of it, have ultimately affected their recognition and redress.

6.1 Changing Cultures of Rights and Responsibilities

Legal cultures, evolving perceptions of involuntary sterilisation and castration and the development of a rights consciousness have all played a role in the states' reactions to practices of involuntary sterilisation and castration. While all three national legal cultures have increasingly emphasised rights, there are differences in how the states have come to link involuntary sterilisation and castration to existing master frames of rights.

6.1.1 Rights as a Master Frame and Competing Frames

As observed in the previous chapters, rights were traditionally not given a strong position in twentieth-century legal practice in Sweden, Norway and

Table 6.1 Comparative overview

	Sweden (S)	Norway (N)	Finland (F)
Establishment	S1) 1934 legislation	N1) 1934 legislation	F1) 1935 legislation
	S2) 1944 legislation	N2) 1934 legislation	F2) 1935 legislation
	S3) 1972 legislation	N3) administrative regulation, established in 1960–1970s	F3) 2002 legislation
Abolition	S1) 1975	N1) 1977*	F1) 1970*
	S2) 2013	N2) 1977*	F2) 1970*
	S3) 2012/2013	N3) 2016	F3) 2023
Remedy	S1) 1999 Compensation Act; investigation and publications; public apologies	N1) 2004 Compensation scheme; apologies; memorials; museum exhibitions; funds; investigations; reports and publications (only with regard to Romani victims)	F1) No remedies
	S2) No remedies	N2) No remedies	F2) No remedies
	S3) 2018 Compensation Act	N3) No remedies	F3) No remedies

* However, some involuntary interventions were still allowed in the legislative amendment, crucially those of the legally incapable. The legislation has later been amended to emphasise the consent of the patient.

Finland because of various reasons, such as cultures of consensus, universal welfare states, Nordic legal realism and a tradition of democratically elected governments. Nevertheless, the countries' commitment to human rights has been resolute, with national constitutions having been updated in connection to diligently ratified human rights treaties. The most striking progress can be seen in Sweden, where rights (both international and constitutional) have developed from being regarded as decorative, abstract guidelines to becoming binding legal norms with implications for public liability.[1] A similar development of growing emphasis on rights can be observed in Finnish and Norwegian legal cultures, albeit a less dramatic evolution than in Sweden. Critically, increasing recognition of rights in the national legal cultures has led to the establishment of rights as master frames to which legal claims can be linked.

Yet, developing master frames of rights have not automatically led to practices of involuntary sterilisation and castration becoming connected to them. In other words, the practices have not necessarily been regarded as violations of rights in conjunction to the countries committing to international human rights and establishing constitutional rights. The inconsistent framing also holds true on the supranational level, where the normative regulations on how to conceptualise and remedy these practices are fragmented. As seen in this

[1] This development is discernible in Supreme Court practice. Högsta Domstolen [The Swedish Supreme Court], NJA 2012, s. 400 (2012); NJA 2013, s. 350 (2013); NJA 2012, s. 211 (2012); and NJA 2013, s. 746 (2013). See Åhman 2016: 462–463.

book, the conceptualisation of involuntary sterilisation and castration as rights violations is relatively new and incoherently addressed by supranational institutions and bodies.[2] This incongruity is an important contributing factor to the slow national recognition of the practices as rights violations.

In the countries compared, as well as in the international community, relevant legal notions of rights as master frames were largely absent before the Second World War. In the Nordic countries, the scope of constitutional rights was strictly defined for large parts of the twentieth century. Accordingly, when the first national laws on sterilisation and castration were introduced in the 1930s and 1940s, physical and reproductive interventions against the will of individuals were generally not called into question as potential violations of rights. Yet, individual objections or concerns were raised in all three countries, even though they concerned protected interests in national criminal laws, or moral rather than legal notions of rights. Critically, in the absence of a strong master frame of rights, such contestations were easily ignored or rejected in parliamentary and expert debates. The lack of perceived rights obstacles to non-consensual interventions reflects a more general lack of universal rights consciousness at the time of the legislation's establishment. This is particularly true for the rights of marginalised groups, including their physical integrity and reproductive rights.[3]

Owing to a lack or weakness of rights as master frames in the national legal cultures, legal rights claims have been easily dismissed in favour of other, competing master frames. Often, such competing frames have been perceived to be more relevant than rights, side-lining the latter. The main competing master frame, prone to dominating political discussions on sterilisation and castration, has been that of medicine. Within this frame, sterilisation or castration is viewed as an intervention to treat a patient diagnosed with a medical condition. The procedure is as such considered to be in the best interest of the patient. From this perspective, the individual will of the patient is regarded as ideally in line with medical expertise and synonymous with the patient's interest. The patient's desires are hence regarded as secondary; if contrary to their medically perceived interests, they are considered unruly.

[2] See the second chapter of this book.

[3] While rights traditionally may not have been elements explicitly expressed in the national legal cultures, this statement holds particularly true for reproductive rights. Birth control, abortion or sterilisation have generally not been regulated as a matter of rights in any of the legal systems. Rather, laws and policies concerning reproductive and sexual health have usually been conceptualised as matters of social and family policy, related to the regulation and provision of welfare services. This can be seen in, for example, the establishment of current sterilisation and abortion laws in the three countries, which was not primarily motivated by rights. Norwegian Government Bill Ot.prp.nr. 38 (1974–1975); Norwegian Government Bill Ot.prp.nr. 46 (1976–1977); Swedish Government Bill Prop. 1975:18; Swedish Government Bill Prop. 1974:70; Finnish Government Bill HE 105/1969; Finnish Government Bill HE 60/1948. Compare with the contemporary US rights-dominated debates. Supreme Court of the United States, *Griswold v. Connecticut* (1965); *Roe v. Wade* (1973). See Siegel 2012; Case 2009.

An illustrative example of competing master frames pertaining to rights and medicine is the introduction of castration in the first half of the twentieth century as a way to treat, rather than punish, sexuality which was considered deviant, such as (particularly male) homosexuality. In the transition from criminalisation to medicalisation, same-sex sexual behaviour went from being regarded as a criminal act to being considered a medical pathology, particularly in Sweden.[4] Intriguingly, when understood as criminal sanctions, the interventions triggered resistance, seen as infringing on the rights of the people concerned. This is evident in for instance a Norwegian parliamentarian's opposition to involuntary castration depicting the practices as 'barbaric and medieval' if used for penal purposes.[5] A similar example can be seen in Finland, with one legal scholar describing castrations performed by physical force to be 'in line with the Law of Moses', yet permissible if enforced through 'softer' forms of coercion, such as institutionalisation.[6] In a medical master frame and a medicalised setting, the interventions and the coercion involved were thus regarded in a different, more permissible, scientific and modern light.

Medicalisation has also been a way of displacing the interventions from centralised state statistics as intrusions on individuals' bodies which the state ought to monitor, to decentralised medical records stored in local hospital archives. Particularly in Norway, the deficit of centralised numbers regarding historical sterilisations grounded in medical necessity and castrations carried out on trans people is an illustration of how a medical framing complicates the conceptualisation of public interest. As such, medicalisation as a competing master frame has affected not only sociocultural perceptions of the interventions but also the legal obligations of state administrations.

An effective strategy to hinder the interventions from becoming regarded as rights violations has been the claim of alterity. Such claims often align with a master frame pertaining to medicine. In Finland, where the 1935 and 1950 sterilisation and castration laws placed the least amount of emphasis on free will, the topic of rights was generally avoided by referring to the targeted group as marginal and clearly defined.[7] By employing such language, the legislation implied a focus on the undesirable minority 'other' juxtaposed to the majority population. Alterity frames were also present, albeit less evident, in the two other countries. This kind of argumentation can particularly be identified in reference to the legally incapable who could be sterilised or castrated without their consent. Portrayed as gravely feebleminded, retarded, moronic, imbecilic, deviant or dangerous, these people were considered not to understand the meaning of the interventions. As a consequence, they were regarded as

[4] See Justitiedepartementet [The Swedish Ministry of Justice] 1941a; 1941b; 1941c; Swedish Government Bill Prop. 1934:103; Swedish Government Bill Prop. 1941:13; Swedish Government Bill Prop. 1944:14.

[5] Stortinget [The Norwegian Parliament] 1934: 157–162; Haave 2000a: 106.

[6] Honkanen 1954: 44.

[7] This is particularly evident in Finnish Government Bill HE 112/1934: 19.

inappropriate decision-makers in the matter. Furthermore, it was deemed to be in their own, and society's, best interest to prevent them from engaging in sexual relations or reproduction.

Much like their establishment, the abolition and amendment of sterilisation and castration laws in the 1970s were not motivated by rights as legal instruments. Instead, the revision of the legislation was affected by an atmosphere of increasing individualism and a challenge to old dogmas. In the aftermath of sexual revolutions, anti-psychiatry movements, criticism of institutionalisation, women's movements and questioning of political elites and oppression, the Nordic countries were ratifying many newly established international human rights treaties.[8] These developments form the backdrop for the revision of sterilisation and castration laws, which were not explicitly pronounced as rights violations in any legal sense of the word by the revising authorities. Rather, the interventions were seen as unmodern and out-dated. Their perceived old-fashioned character stemmed from the development of new birth control techniques, and their prioritising social interests over individual ones. The sociocultural foundation was laid for a stronger rights culture through these changing notions of modernity and hegemonies of a good social order.[9]

When it comes to the establishment of sterilisation and castration practices targeting trans people in the period from the 1960s to the 2000s, it is important to highlight that these interventions were regarded progressive at the time. Furthermore, a strong rights master frame had long been absent in the countries investigated, influenced by the lack of supranational rights framing, resulting in the domination of medical master frames. Tellingly, the individual interest to reproduce was largely disregarded for trans people when possibilities to amend one's legally registered gender were established. Motivated by the public interest to keep gendered family relations 'in order', and guard the child's best interest,[10] a balance was struck in which

[8] Sweden ratified the CERD, ICCPR, and ICESCR in 1971; Norway ratified the CERD in 1970 and the ICCPR and ICESCR in 1972; Finland ratified the CERD in 1970 and the ICCPR and ICESCR in 1975.

[9] The break with the old was not equally profound in all countries. With changing authority and public views on mental disabilities and illnesses, an interesting matter was the possibility to sterilise the legally incapable without their consent. In Norway, the revision of the Sterilisation Act was the least dramatic overall. The 1977 Sterilisation Act maintained without further debate the possibility to sterilise and castrate people with serious mental disabilities without their consent. In Sweden, however, the *travaux préparatoires* of the 1975 Sterilisation Act emphasised a significant break with past legislation, with the Act only allowing for sterilisation upon the initiative of the applicant. No separate category of consent requirements was created for the legally incapable. Finland's revision also meant a break with the past, since the update meant a radical change of perspective and emphasis from coercion to free will. The 1970 legislation nevertheless allowed for interventions against the applicants' will when they were unable to understand the meaning of sterilisation. All laws have later been revised and amended, particularly in the light of international human rights, to underline informed consent of the legally incapable.

[10] See also Dunne 2017.

trans people's reproductive and sexual interests were subjugated. Supported by a medicalisation master frame often informed by medical experts in all the three countries of comparison, the legislators' image of the person who wanted to amend their legally registered gender was a transsexual person 'born in the wrong body',[11] who did not wish to reproduce through the reproductive organs of the 'opposite gender'.[12]

During the late twentieth century, practices of sterilisation and castration against a person's will came to be seen in a different sociocultural and legal light. Temporally, this goes hand in hand with supranational developments on the topic, creating a stronger (albeit fragmented) master frame of rights within which to understand the practices. The meaning of the practices has evolved concurrently. They have gone from being regarded as state prerogatives, and even public obligations, to control certain strata of the population, to becoming framed as rights to personal and physical autonomy, health, privacy and family life and/or equality and non-discrimination. These newfound conceptualisations have been motivated by the supranational rights developments in the field of reproduction and sexuality in particular.[13]

Increasingly important and inclusive rights legal master frames have been crucial for the conceptualisation of sterilisation or castration preconditions for legal gender recognition as rights violations. In these cases, supranational legal instruments and policy documents have provided tools with which to conceptualise victims' harms in terms of rights.[14] In Sweden, this can be seen in the process behind abolishing the infertility precondition for legal gender recognition, furthered through strategic litigation,[15] on the one hand, and the legal process to access compensation, on the other. With Swedish administrative courts framing involuntary sterilisation as a violation of human and constitutional rights in 2012,[16] the practices were viewed significantly differently in comparison to their establishment in the early 1970s. In Norway, a similar development can be observed. International and national civil society formulated rights criticism with reference to the administrative procedure, especially in respect of the castration requirement, with the result that authorities accepted the rights conceptualisation. While ratifying similar supranational

[11] See, for example, Repo 2019.

[12] In Sweden, this imagery played out through the rejection of transsexual people's will to procreate in the *travaux préparatoires*; in Norway, through the medicalised concept of 'real sex conversion', involving castration; in Finland, through a similar, medicalised understanding that only the applicants who were 'serious enough' could be allowed to amend their legally registered gender. See Justitiedepartementet [The Swedish Ministry of Justice] 1968: 52; Amnesty International 2014: 71–74; Finnish Government Bill HE 56/2001.

[13] See the second chapter of this book.

[14] See ECtHR, *Christine Goodwin v. the United Kingdom* (2002); *A.P., Garçon and Nicot v. France* (2017); CommDH/IssuePaper(2009)2; Res 1728 (2010).

[15] Kammarrätten i Stockholm [Stockholm Administrative Court of Appeal], 1968-12 (2012).

[16] Ibid; Förvaltningsrätten i Stockholm [Stockholm Administrative Court of First Instance], 45723-10 (2012).

rights instruments as its neighbours, Finland delayed the amendment of the law which makes legal gender recognition preconditioned on infertility until the 2020s, demonstrating a slower national acceptance of the rights framing.

In some cases, the practices have remained unquestioned and not been framed as rights violations, despite a general growing emphasis on rights in the national legal culture. One such case is castration, occurring in all three countries of the comparison. A fragmentary and weak conceptualisation of involuntary castrations as rights violations can also be observed at the supranational level. Castration has generally not been framed as a violation of supranational or national legal norms; its abandonment has been due to medical advancements and its perceived inefficiency instead. Rather than remedied, castration victims have been surrounded by silence and fallen into legal and sociocultural oblivion. Therefore, their harms have not been conceptualised as valid legal claims. This example shows that a changing and developing rights culture alone does not necessarily lead to oppressive practices becoming conceptualised as violations to be remedied.

6.1.2 Rights Violations and Remedies

On paper, the three countries have similar regulations on public liability, being a result of Nordic cooperation and harmonisation, building on pecuniary, rather than non-pecuniary, damages.[17] Public liability for damages is a topic generally approached with caution, which is inherently connected to the traditionally weak rights cultures. Particularly in respect of the possibility to base public liability on rights-violating legislation, the countries have adopted a careful approach.[18] The notion that Parliament itself, the most central state organ, could be in breach of the normative legal order had originally not occurred to them. Yet, with master frames of rights becoming stronger through increasing supranational commitments, a pluralising legal system and rights constitutionalisation, the idea that legislation may be contrary to superior legal norms has become less foreign. A break with past traditions is again most prominently seen in Sweden, where the Supreme Court has led the legal development of grounding public liability for damages in violations of rights protected in the ECHR and the Government Act.[19] A similar development through which rights have come to have implications for public liability can also be found in Norway and Finland.[20]

17 See Swedish Government Bill Prop. 1972:5; Norwegian Government Bill Ot.prp.nr. 48 (1965–1966); Finnish Government Bill HE 187/1973.

18 The most evident example here is Sweden, where this possibility is explicitly excluded in Skadeståndslag [Liability Act] (1972:207), Chapter 3 Section 7.

19 Högsta domstolen [The Swedish Supreme Court], NJA 2005, s. 462; NJA 2007, s. 584; NJA 2014, s. 323; and NJA 2014, s. 332.

20 See, for example, Høyesterett [The Norwegian Supreme Court], Rt. 2013 s. 588 (Besøksforbud); Korkein oikeus [The Finnish Supreme Court], KKO:2008:10.

In none of the countries investigated, involuntary sterilisations and castrations have been found to be a basis for public liability for damages. The practices have, however, not been tested in terms of liability by Finnish courts. In Sweden, a high-profile case of public liability was tried before the Chancellor of Justice in 2014, who did not find a violation of rights; the question did not appear before Swedish general courts.[21] By contrast, individual Norwegian victims of involuntary sterilisation and castration have presented their harms in terms of legal liability claims before courts on more than one occasion, from the 1950s up to the most recent cases in the 2020s. Yet, the Norwegian courts' rejection of public liability has been consistent on the basis of different legal arguments in the face of developing national and supranational rights instruments and the non-retroactivity principle.[22] The lack of remedies resulting from liability extends beyond state responsibility for rights-violating legislation, as remedies have not been based on the liability of individual public servants either.[23]

The notion that the legislator can 'break the law' has been a foreign concept in the Nordic context, which has had a detrimental impact on the remedies accessible to victims of involuntary sterilisation and castration. Tellingly, the available remedial legal framework is generally more favourable to involuntary interventions caused by medical malpractice than those by legislated state practice. As such, victims of medical malpractice benefit from specially established dispute resolution organs, standardised compensation schemes and particular legislation, often lowering evidentiary thresholds. Such special remedial treatment is, however, not awarded to the groups investigated in this book. The people who have been victimised by publicly enforced involuntary sterilisation or castration have only selectively benefited from extraordinarily established remedies in Sweden and Norway, and not at all in Finland. From a state responsibility angle, such incidental and inconsistent remedial treatment is legally questionable. In this context, state responsibility for the establishment and maintenance of oppressive sterilisation and castration policies has been treated as a moral question. As such, the issue has been excluded from systematic legal interrogation in the countries of comparison.

21 JK, Decision No. 4243-13-40 et al (2014).

22 See Eidsivating Lagmannsrett [Eidsivating Court of Appeal], Appeal No. 43/1954 (1956); Tana og Varanger Herredsrett [Tana and Varanger Court of First Instance], Case No. 36/1985 A (1985); Oslo Tingrett [Oslo Court of First Instance], Case No 17-132417TVI-OTIR/08 (2018). See also Oslo Tingrett [Oslo Court of First Instance], Case No 17-146470 TVI-OTIR/04 (2018); Borgarting Lagmannsrett [Borgarting Court of Appeal], Case No LB-2018-154220 (2020); Norges Høyesteretts ankeutvalg [The Appeals Committee of the Norwegian Supreme Court], HR-2020-1486-U (2020).

23 Even though the national legal traditions are more inclined to accept the idea that individual representatives of authorities can violate the law in their implementation of it, there is a lack of cases in which individuals have been tried for abuse of the legislation in legal or liability terms. Regardless of most laws emphasising interventions based on individual will, coercive application of the legislation took place in all countries and has been met with impunity.

In the light of assumed or *de facto* limited public liability, *ex gratia* remedies have been instituted on the basis of solidarity with the victims. Differing from compensations based on legal liability, the developing *ex gratia* compensation tradition has created a remedial rift. In Sweden, the 2018 Act on State Compensation for People who Have Obtained Legal Gender Recognition under Certain Circumstances is a manifestation of this evolution because it establishes an *ex gratia* compensation amount which is significantly lower than the compensation given to victims of involuntary sterilisation where legal liability can be established. The *travaux préparatoires* explicitly explain this disparity by making a distinction between compensations based on legal liability and *ex gratia,* respectively.[24] This development is remarkable as the first Swedish *ex gratia* compensation scheme, being the 1999 Act on Compensation to Sterilised People under Certain Circumstances, did not differentiate between remedies resulting from legal or moral state responsibility. Instead, the law established a compensation scheme which built on the idea that the amount of the compensation for the victims of historical sterilisation programmes ought to be higher than the quantity awarded to medical malpractice victims in order to also symbolically redress harms induced by previous state support for the practices.[25] Consequently, the remedial gap seems to have formed after the establishment of the 1999 compensation scheme, in the aftermath of increasing number of national compensation schemes based on *ex gratia.*[26] A similar remedial division between legal and moral responsibility can be seen in Norway, where the *ex gratia* compensation established for involuntarily sterilised Romani people also provides a significantly lower amount than the compensation paid to victims in situations where legal liability can be established.[27]

In respect of state responsibility and rights violations, there is a division between notions of rights violations in a legal and a sociocultural (often conceptualised as 'moral') sense. On account of the internationalisation of Nordic legal cultures and an increasing emphasis on rights, past oppressive treatment and earlier-established hegemonies concerning the forms of harm which deserve recognition and redress are challenged. Yet, the interventions are not legally considered violations of rights, mainly due to the lack of contemporary binding legal rules. Statutory limitations have often been used as an additional argument to the principle of non-retroactivity.[28] As a consequence, victims

[24] Socialdepartementet [The Swedish Ministry of Health and Social Affairs] 2017a; 2017b; Swedish Government Bill Prop. 2017/18:64. A similar line was drawn regarding *ex gratia* compensations for symphysiotomy victims in Ireland, see Gallen 2019: 273.

[25] See Alaattinoğlu 2017.

[26] Lag om ersättning på grund av övergrepp eller försummelser i samhällsvården av barn och unga i vissa fall [Act on Compensation for Abuse or Negligence in State Social Care of Children and Youth under Certain Circumstances] (2012:663); Lag om statlig ersättning till personer som insjuknat i narkolepsi efter pandemivaccinering [Act on State Compensation for People Suffering from Narcolepsy after Vaccination for Pandemic] (2016:417). See Arvidsson 2016.

[27] Such as in cases of medical malpractice. See Chapter 4 of this work.

[28] According to this reasoning, the sterilisation practices had unlikely been a violation of rights at the time; even if they had been, such claims are time barred.

have failed to access remedies through litigation. The practices are nevertheless frequently challenged in the light of changing public morals, incorporating broader, sociocultural notions of rights and state responsibility. This contradiction between legal and sociocultural notions of rights and rights violations has consequently given rise to an influx of *ex gratia* compensations to formerly oppressed groups in Norway and Sweden.

The argument for compensating the involuntarily sterilised has exclusively been state solidarity (*ex gratia*) so far. In Sweden, discussions pertaining to rights have been avoided, most recently so in the compensation scheme for trans victims: its *travaux préparatoires* continuously highlight that the compensation flows from solidarity with the victims, not from state responsibility for rights violations.[29]

In connection to both Swedish compensation schemes investigated in this work, the state has expressed a will to make amends for earlier practices through its references to victim solidarity and a public apology offered for historical sterilisations. Such symbolic expressions of responsibility are nevertheless in conflict with the legal format of the *ex gratia* compensations, which does not acknowledge the role of the state in the violations.[30] The situation in Norway is similar. The specially established compensation scheme for Romani victims of involuntary sterilisations has been legally based on *ex gratia*, while concurrent apologies have implied state responsibility. A government-appointed investigation in 2015 directly addressed this issue, concluding that past sterilisations constituted human rights violations in a moral, yet not legal, sense.[31] Such a statement strains the relationship between redress and recognition of state responsibility, raising questions about the role of recognition as a type of remedy for victims.[32] Provision of redress as a matter of 'benevolence and choice', rather than as a 'legal right' of the victims, can be considered to imply a certain state paternalism.[33] From the perspective of victims, the *ex gratia* compensation schemes have, however, also meant facilitated access to material redress in comparison to 'protracted and expensive' litigation, the latter alternative almost certainly involving revisiting their traumas in 'an adversarial setting'.[34] Moreover,

[29] Swedish Government Bill Prop. 2017/18:64.

[30] For criticism of *ex gratia* compensation schemes for historical gendered mistreatment in Ireland, see Gallen 2019: 274.

[31] Kommunal- og moderniseringsdepartementet [The Norwegian Ministry of Local Government and Modernisation] 2015a: 13, 78.

[32] Providing redress without recognition can be questioned from a remedial perspective. Recognition of responsibility is central to the concept of reparation and remedy. The refusal to acknowledge state responsibility means that many essential remedial aspects are neglected. Among these aspects number the symbolic effects of public apologies for not only directly affected individuals but also communities of victims, such as vulnerable groups or indirect victims; the victims' legal possibilities to seek redress based on public liability in the courts. See Shelton 2015: 123–124; Rubio-Marín 2012; 2009b.

[33] Gallen & Gleeson 2018: 55–56.

[34] On remedies for indigenous communities in Australia, see Durbach 2008: 24. The expressed sentiments were echoed by interviewees in connection to the Norwegian litigation processes furthered by trans plaintiffs. See Chapter 4 of this work.

receiving the *ex gratia* compensations under the investigated schemes of Sweden and Norway has not involved any obligation for victims to waive their claims to litigate in the future.[35]

In the comparison between the countries, Finland's public liability legislation and official rights commitments are similar to those of Sweden and Norway. However, the modern tendency to establish *ex gratia* compensation schemes for historical violations has not gained foothold in the country. This is largely due to a different sociocultural approach to the topic of state responsibility for past wrongs, rejecting any possibilities to legally or morally evaluate historical oppression *as such*.[36]

6.2 Grievance Formation: Victims as Rights-Holders

Some victims of involuntary sterilisation and castration have mobilised, while the majority has not. Similarly, some victims have accessed remedies, while others have not. In order to better understand these differences, the time has come to look closer at how the grievance formation process has led to some harms becoming recognised with remedies, while others have remained unacknowledged. The grievance formation process has occurred in relation to the master frame of rights, both in the legal and sociocultural sense. As such, apart from being used as legal instruments, rights have also been promoted as identitarian claims to align with the master frame of rights.[37] Pivotal actors participating in the frame alignment process have been victims, civil society, mass media and public institutions.

In much of the legal mobilisation scholarship, an explicit or implicit understanding is shared that people form grievances which they individually or as a group come to conceptualise in legal terms, turning to litigation to improve their positions.[38] Correspondingly, remedies are assumed to flow from violations of legal norms, such as rights.[39] A closer look at the grievance formation process nevertheless reveals more nuances of how victims' grievances and identities as rights-holders are validated internally and externally: at the personal, intra-group, public and institutional levels (Table 6.2). These types of

[35] Some *ex gratia* compensation schemes have involved such preconditions for recipients, e.g., in Ireland and Australia. See Gallen 2019; Winter 2009.

[36] An important official interpretation of state responsibility for lobotomy was marked by non-retroactivity and legal formalism in stating that national legislation equals legitimacy, rejecting debates on normative pluralism or legal and moral obligations. Valtakunnallinen terveydenhuollon eettinen neuvottelukunta [The Finnish Advisory Board on Social Welfare and Health Care Ethics] 2000. See Chapter 5 in this book.

[37] The identity creation process can be seen as a juridification of identity through rights. Golder 2015: 98–103.

[38] McCammon & McGrath 2015: 129. In the words of John Brigham, movements 'are constituted in legal terms when they see the world in those terms and organize themselves accordingly'. See Brigham 1988: 306.

[39] According to the Latin maxim *ubi jus, ibi remedium*.

Table 6.2 The forms of validation in the grievance formation process

Internal validation	External validation
Personal validation (personal identity)	Public validation (public identity)
Intra-group validation (collective identity)	Institutional validation (public identity)

validation do not necessarily happen in a certain order and are often but not always interdependent.

6.2.1 Personal Validation

In order for victims to form grievances, that is, understanding their harms as violations to be remedied, they need to create an identity as possessors of legally protected interests which have been violated.[40] In this sense, victims' individual harms become grievances which they consider rights violations. In other words, victims need to conceptualise themselves as rights-holders and as victims of rights violations. This can be considered a foundational stepping-stone for individual mobilisation. Many victims have, however, not shared their experiences or addressed the interventions with people close to them, let alone publicly, maintaining silence about the harm suffered. In the direct and indirect accounts of victims explored in this book, many express shame with regard to the interventions. As such, the interventions embody the victims' designation as unworthy of reproductive and sexual lives, an internalised oppression which may persist throughout their life.[41] This tenacious shame has often effectively prevented victims from conceptualising themselves as rights-holders wronged in a legal sense.

Yet, examples exist of individuals challenging the practices in legal and political terms. This can be seen, for example, in the case of victims writing letters of complaint to the Swedish Government before 1997 to address the sterilisations which they recognised as unjust.[42] Other examples are the individual Norwegian victims taking their compensation claims to the general courts,[43] and the Finnish victims applying for sterilisation reversal before administrative

[40] Individuals must conceptualise their individual grievances as a violation of a right which can be remedied by the law in order to seek legal recourse. McCammon & McGrath 2015: 129

[41] See the first chapter of this book.

[42] Socialdepartementet [The Swedish Ministry of Health and Social Affairs] 1999: 188.

[43] See Eidsivating Lagmannsrett [Eidsivating Court of Appeal], Appeal No. 43/1954 (1956); Oslo Tingrett [Oslo Court of First Instance], Case No 17-132417TVI-OTIR/08 (2018); Borgarting lagmannsrett [Borgarting Court of Appeal], Case No. 18-190131ASD-BORG/02 (2021); Høyesteretts ankeutvalg [The Appeals Committee of the Norwegian Supreme Court], Case No. HR-2021-1392-U (2021). See also Oslo Tingrett [Oslo Court of First Instance], Case No 17-146470 TVI-OTIR/04 (2018); Borgarting Lagmannsrett [Borgarting Court of Appeal], Case No LB-2018-154220 (2020); Norges Høyesteretts ankeutvalg [The Appeals Committee of the Norwegian Supreme Court], HR-2020-1486-U (2020).

courts.[44] Looking at these exceptional cases of resistance, the observer is struck by individual victims' lack of resources in terms of organisational infrastructure and the failure of their claims to align with rights master frames in spite of occasional successful access to remedies. Sporadically framed in terms of rights, individual claims therefore appear to fall flat. Such instances of individual mobilisation highlight varying levels of individual personal validation and rights consciousness among victims despite the lack of supporting collectives. In terms of rights, grievances have remained individual in these cases, in contrast to a conceptualisation of grievances as shared and mobilising.[45]

In the face of limited resources, many victims do not perceive mobilising to be a feasible option as it involves costs at organisational, legal, financial, mental and emotional levels. Considering that many victims – particularly those subjected to historical sterilisation laws – belonged to lower social classes, had lower attendance of formal education and were marginalised and poor, their lack of resources is further aggravated. Moreover, some victims held deep feelings of distrust for state authorities, a sentiment reiterated in direct and indirect accounts in this work. Such suspicion of state institutions has also resulted immobilising, preventing victims from advancing rights claims by means of established political or legal roads. In these cases, victims could have formed individual grievances and understood themselves as rights-holders, but failed to formally engage in mobilisation or resistance regardless.

6.2.2 Intra-group Validation

There is a difference between grievance formation at the individual and the group level.[46] Accordingly, the identity of rights-holder can be formed individually and collectively. Intra-group validation, consciousness-raising activities and a collective identity as rights-holders are actions particularly connected to collective mobilisation, in which some victim groups have engaged.

Some victims have organised collectively. In doing so, they have created political and legal spaces, gathered resources and utilised opportunities to pressure the state to abolish oppressive practices and provide access to remedies. Joint mobilisation has helped victims to transform their experiences into a common identity, building a collective whose legal and political consciousness is supported by rights instruments and rhetoric.[47] Two of the groups of victims analysed in this book stand out as being the only ones to have mobilised collectively: the Romani in Norway; trans people in all compared countries.

[44] See Chapter 5 of this book.

[45] Collective identity and legal consciousness provide a fertile ground for conceptualising grievances as shared and as rights violations. Barclay et al 2011: 9.

[46] The 'cultural transformation' happens at the personal and collective level respectively, see Chua 2022: 37.

[47] This function of legal mobilisation is highlighted in McCann 1991: 234–235.

6.2.2.1 The Mobilisation of the Norwegian Romani

Starting with the Romani people's mobilisation in Norway, the minority group has effectively organised around national rights commitments since the 1990s. At the supranational level, this can especially be noticed in how some members of the group have invoked notions of rights and state responsibility in their mobilisation. The collective mobilisation by the Norwegian Romani with pressure exerted on national authorities by means of supranational human rights mechanisms, particularly in the Council of Europe context,[48] suggests an informed involvement with rights.[49] In the late 1990s and early 2000s, group members were able to utilise the available, expanding master frame of rights, framing themselves as an ethnic minority and their grievances as ethnically discriminatory rights violations. In this exercise of frame alignment, the group crucially made use of their recent recognition as a national minority to create notions of rights-holder status, rights violations and state responsibility.

In the 1990s and 2000s, the Romani people began to mobilise in minority rights organisations,[50] helping to create a collective minority rights identity and consciousness among group members. The group has benefited from outspoken activists at the forefront of the movement, voicing the claims of more silent members, such as the victims of involuntary sterilisation. Finally, the group has also been aided by its alliance with the Norwegian Helsinki Committee, through which a range of state remedies were gained in the name of minority rights.[51]

Norwegian Romani groups have not only mobilised around involuntary sterilisation, and not even primarily so. The sterilisation narrative has only been one aspect of the claims regarding past mistreatment against the group. Yet, in comparison to other rights violations claims foregrounded, such as school bullying and discrimination, involuntary sterilisation stands out as an exceptionally grave violation, leading to permanent and directly causal, physical harm. Sterilisation performed in public hospitals and enforced through legislation also has a more direct and unquestionable connection to state responsibility compared to the responsibility of public authorities in terms of due diligence for interpersonal violence. With this in mind, the claims of

[48] A particularly important instrument was the CoE Framework Convention for the Protection of National Minorities, ratified by Norway in 1999. The impact of the rights mobilisation can also be observed in the 2003 recommendation by the CoE Advisory Committee on the Framework Convention for the Protection of National Minorities, emphasising the need for Norwegian authorities to assist abused minorities, including sterilised Romani people, and for the victims to access compensation. ACFC/INF/OP/I(2003)003 (2003): Para 33; Kommunal- og regionaldepartementet [The Norwegian Ministry of Local Government] 2003: 7. See also Ekeløve-Slydal, 7 December 2016.

[49] This phenomenon is sometimes referred to as the 'boomerang effect' of human rights. See Tsutsui & Smith 2019.

[50] At an earlier stage, religious organisations had been important for Romani mobilisation. Bergkvist, 27 January 2017.

[51] See Chapter 4 in this book.

involuntary sterilisation played a pivotal role in the group's identity formation, mobilisation and frame alignment process, despite the victims themselves not being vocal about their experiences.

Romani people's rights framing in terms of ethnic discrimination has been enforced by international criminal law, especially under genocide. The claim of genocide was never litigated, but its political invocation alone was key to successfully provoke a state response and to create remedies. Using the word 'ethnic cleansing' in the communication with the decision-makers proved to be particularly effective in instigating an investigation.[52] The first state-funded research project inquired into whether state policies were intentionally and systematically targeting the Romani population: a phrase referring to the subjective elements of the definition of genocide. While the question was eventually answered in the negative,[53] many of the past Norwegian assimilation policies have had objective elements reminiscent of genocide, crimes against humanity, or war crimes.[54] The fact that oppressive practices had existed, together with the Romani mobilisation highlighting the potential violation of international criminal law, called attention to the need for an investigation to evaluate whether the practices amounted to the alleged violations. However, the exploration was carried out under the label of 'historical mapping' instead of 'legal investigation'.[55] While it rejected the allegations of ethnic cleansing, the research functioned as a truth-finding exercise leading to a remedial response.[56]

The Norwegian institutional reaction to the mobilisation of the Romani by establishing a range of remedies, including *ex gratia* compensation, is particularly interesting in respect of access to remedies for sterilisation victims. It shows how successfully the minority created a collective identity and aligned with rights master frames in comparison to other sterilisation victims, considering that only a small minority of all historical sterilisations in Norway were carried out on Romani people.[57] The remedial scheme especially established for the group has moreover been minimally used.[58]

It is fascinating to see that the Romani minority has mobilised on the topic of past involuntary sterilisations in Norway alone. While similar groups were also vulnerable to the practices in Sweden and Finland, Romani communities and organisations in these countries have generally refrained from publicly

[52] This phrasing was also used by, for instance, MP Erling Folkvord in Parliament. Justiskomiteen [The Norwegian Parliamentary Committee on Justice] 1996: 3.

[53] See Haave 2000b; Hvinden (ed) 2000b.

[54] These measures involved forced transfer of children, involuntary sterilisations and castrations, etc. See Hvinden (ed) 2000b; and Kommunal- og moderniseringsdepartementet [The Norwegian Ministry of Local Government and Modernisation] 2015a: 92.

[55] See Hvinden (ed) 2000b. [56] See Chapter 4 in this book.

[57] See Fodstad 1999; Haave 2000a: 388.

[58] Since its establishment in 2004 until 2015, only fifteen victims applied for compensation, seven of which successfully. Kommunal- og moderniseringsdepartementet [The Norwegian Ministry of Local Government and Modernisation] 2015a: 92.

challenging such practices.[59] The Swedish and Finnish Romani communities do not seem to have conceptualised themselves as victims of sterilisation in a collective sense. Interestingly, as a consequence of the country-specific mobilisation, only Norway has framed the remedies in ethnic terms. An important contributing factor to the intra-group validation and the state response in Norway is that the Norwegian Romani minority uniquely brought the former oppressive sterilisation practices to public consciousness in the first place, setting the terms of the public debate. The following state-funded research projects focused on the sterilisation history with reference to the Romani minority, rather than investigating the practices in general.[60] This has not been the case in Sweden and Finland, where mass media and academic works were the first to publicly address the topic, without framing it as ethnic discrimination.

6.2.2.2 The Mobilisation of Trans People

Another group which has mobilised collectively, in particular through using the language of rights, is that of trans people. This group has actively used and also benefited to different extents from a proliferating rights framework condemning sterilisation/castration as a precondition for legal recognition of gender identity. Important milestones are for instance, the 2007 Yogyakarta Principles, the 2009 Commissioner for Human Rights report on gender identity and human rights, and the ECtHR decisions *YY v. Turkey* (2015) and *A.P, Garçon and Nicot v. France* (2017).[61] These emerging supranational norms, together with developing domestic non-discrimination legislation increasingly inclusive of trans identities, have coincided with the groups' mobilisation and remedial struggles. In all three countries, trans rights activists have actively referred to these developments to challenge oppressive practices as rights violations.

Unlike many other groups investigated in this work, trans victims have also been able to utilise the support of pre-existing, broader LGBT+ organisations, and their infrastructures and resources: in Sweden RFSL; in Norway FRI; in Finland Seta; internationally, TGEU, ILGA and All Out. These organisations and their networks have focused on supporting rights struggles related to gender identity and sexual orientation, both at the national and supranational levels. Mobilising in these organisations, the groups have often also profited from legal and institutional expertise on how to strategically navigate claims before judicial, political and administrative institutions.[62] This can be observed

[59] Socialdepartementet [The Swedish Ministry of Health and Social Affairs] 2000b: 240–241; Mattila 2006.

[60] In the most comprehensive account, Haave 2000a, the researcher also investigates sterilisations targeting non-Romani. Yet, this is not reflected in the title of the work. Haave, 5 December 2016.

[61] See the second chapter of this book.

[62] Vanhala has described the effect as follows: 'Collective actors, such as nongovernmental organizations and SMOs, are particularly important when considering questions of litigation

in the use of strategic litigation advanced with the assistance of legal experts in Sweden, or in the involvement of Amnesty International and other human rights organisations in Norway and Finland. The support of national LGBT+ and human rights organisations proved to be a crucial factor in the successful abolition of sterilisation/castration preconditions for legal gender recognition, particularly in Sweden and Norway.

In general terms, the mobilisation of trans victims has been similar in all three countries, with comparable rights claims being made, particularly centred on the rights regulated in the CoE framework. The targets have been the legislator, government, ombudsmen or similar administrative institutions, and also the judiciary to some extent. The national movements have benefited from each other's support, legal claims and victories. Especially the final judgment by the Stockholm Administrative Court of Appeal in 2012, stating that the infertility precondition violated human and constitutional rights has had a transnational influence and has been referred to in both Finland and Norway.[63]

The grievance formation process, particularly that through collective mobilisation, is more developed in Sweden as compared to its two neighbouring countries. Accordingly, the collective litigation process by involuntarily sterilised trans people before the Chancellor of Justice in Sweden has no direct equivalent in Finland or Norway. While the Swedish class action was ultimately unsuccessful, its relevance lies in the framing of the issue as rights violations to be remedied, raising awareness of trans people's remedial struggle, increasing political pressure on the government and paving a way for remedies.[64] Of additional importance for the Swedish trans victims was the *de facto* remedial precedent set by the 1999 Compensation Act to redress the historical sterilisations, actively used in highlighting the similarities between coercive situations by using similar terminology as well, such as 'forced sterilisation'. Using the – not legally, but politically and socioculturally – precedentary compensation scheme as a reference has also helped victims to collectively conceptualise their harms as wrongs to be remedied in the grievance formation process.

In Norway, individual trans people have also legally mobilised to have the castration precondition abolished and to access remedies with the support of broader LGBT+ and human rights organisations. A high-profile case brought before the Norwegian Equality and Anti-discrimination Ombud by a trans woman in 2014 was important to gain recognition and build momentum. The Ombud found that the invasive requirements for legal recognition of gender constituted unlawful discrimination and recommended its abolition, which

because of their ability to be "repeat players" who bring a series of test cases to various judicial venues over an extended period; this allows for coherent enforcement of rights and establishes precedent'. Vanhala 2010: 40.

63 Kammarrätten i Stockholm [Stockholm Administrative Court of Appeal], 1968-12 (2012).

64 Therefore, it is an example of rights mobilisation's many outcomes, not all court related. On such indirect outcomes, see among others McCann 1994.

added institutional weight to the claims of the trans group.[65] The individual case thus had a collective impact which went beyond the individual applicant, an effect strengthened by her acting as the face of the simultaneous Norwegian Amnesty International campaign. This connection brought the Ombud's findings to the public's attention, reinforcing the alignment with the rights master frame put forward by civil society.

The later Norwegian remedial struggle has encountered problems in aligning itself with legal and sociocultural rights frames. Remedial claims have been mainly advanced through two individually litigated cases; both were unsuccessful before the courts due to the perceived absence of binding contemporary legal obligations.[66] The reason behind the individual focus of the Norwegian mobilisation is that collective litigation has apparently not been an appealing option to trans rights activists in the country. While the lack of collective litigation might *a priori* indicate a weaker intra-group validation in comparison to the corresponding group in Sweden, this is not necessarily true. In Norway too, civil society organisations have supported the individual court cases and campaigned on the issue, building a collective identity of involuntarily castrated trans people as violated rights-holders whose harms ought to be remedied by the state. Being unable to align with legal rights frames, the group has also attempted at aligning with sociocultural rights frames. However, since the national *ex gratia* compensations for Romani sterilisations set a narrow remedial precedent, the group has drawn transnational inspiration from the 2018 Swedish compensation scheme instead, and even found some institutional support for such claims.[67] Beyond its effects in Norway, the 2018 Swedish Compensation Act has also provided transnational incentives for other European countries to remedy trans people harmed by previous sterilisation preconditions.[68]

In Finland, all legislative advancements regarding legal gender recognition have been preceded by trans rights mobilisation. There is a strong intra-group

[65] While this decision was only a recommendation without immediate legal effect, it authoritatively read national discrimination legislation in the light of recent supranational and transnational trans rights developments, being a strong incentive for the political apparatus to amend administrative practice and establish legislation. See Likestillings- og diskrimineringsombudet [The Norwegian Equality and Anti-discrimination Ombud], Decision No. 14/840 (2014); Lov om forbud mot diskriminering på grunn av seksuell orientering, kjønnsidentitet og kjønnsuttrykk [Act on Prohibition of Discrimination on the Grounds of Sexual Orientation, Gender Identity and Gender Expression], No. 58, 2013, Section 5.

[66] This was critically grounded in the principle of non-retroactivity. Oslo Tingrett [Oslo Court of First Instance], Case No 17-132417TVI-OTIR/08 (2018); Case No 17-146470 TVI-OTIR/04 (2018); Borgarting Lagmannsrett [Borgarting Court of Appeal], Case No LB-2018-154220 (2020); Norges Høyesteretts ankeutvalg [The Appeals Committee of the Norwegian Supreme Court], HR-2020-1486-U (2020).

[67] Likestillings- og diskrimineringsombudet [The Norwegian Equality and Anti-discrimination Ombud] 2020. In the light of supra- and transnational developments, the alignment of the group as rights-holders seems to better correspond to rights in a socio-cultural, rather than strictly legal, sense. Alaattinoğlu 2021.

[68] Such as in the Netherlands. Schaps 2020.

conceptualisation as rights-holders, with the mobilisation having involved the use of courts, ombudsmen institutions and citizens' initiatives.[69] In order to revise the 2002 Trans Act and its infertility precondition, the group framed the law as a rights violation in line with emerging supranational human rights standards. This framing has enjoyed the support of some state institutions,[70] and human rights civil society organisations. Individual victims and civil society organisations did, however, not judicially challenge the Finnish infertility precondition.[71] Notwithstanding trans rights activism and ECtHR developments,[72] the efforts to abolish the infertility precondition and align with rights master frames advanced more slowly in Finland than in the other countries compared in this work.

6.2.2.3 The Silent Victims

Many victim groups have not mobilised. In fact, such collective immobility appears to be more of a rule than an exception. A collective organisation or identity upon which to build their notions of rights-holder status is missing among many victims of involuntary sterilisation and castration.[73]

This book has explored how involuntary sterilisation and castration as violations of the legal order are regulated in a scattered, at times incoherent, fashion in supranational and national law.[74] The result is a weak normative system which also has implications for the identity creation of victims as rights-holders. While the trans victims and the Norwegian Romani victims have had access to the necessary resources to allow them to knowledgeably navigate and use the sparsely existing regulation to (be it successfully or unsuccessfully) align with recently emerging rights frames, with support from organisations and legal experts, the same cannot be said for other victims. The lack of resources and a recognisable and clear legal master frame within which to formulate their harms as rights violations appears to have impeded victims' chances of presenting their harm in a legally intelligible manner. Without a collective identity as rights-holders, such as a predefined or legally recognised minority, they have been prevented from creating common grievances around which to mobilise.[75] These obstacles have in turn raised the mobilisation threshold considerably.

[69] Mainly, Korkein hallinto-oikeus [The Finnish Supreme Administrative Court], KHO:1988-A-46; Eduskunnan apulaisoikeusasiamies [The Finnish Deputy Parliamentary Ombudsman] 1998; Tasa-arvovaltuutettu [The Finnish Ombudsman for Equality] 2011; 2012; Eduskunnan apulaisoikeusasiamies [Finnish Deputy Parliamentary Ombudsman] EOAK/2842/2017 (2018); Citizens' Initiative KAA 6/2021.

[70] Through Tasa-arvovaltuutettu [The Finnish Ombudsman for Equality] 2011; 2012; Eduskunnan apulaisoikeusasiamies [Finnish Deputy Parliamentary Ombudsman] EOAK/2842/2017 (2018). See Chapter 5 of this book.

[71] An individual Finnish trans person however challenged the precondition to be unmarried/have spousal consent in the ECtHR case *Hämäläinen v. Finland* (2014).

[72] Most importantly, ECtHR, *A.P., Garçon and Nicot v. France* (2017).

[73] On the cruciality of conceptualisation as collective rights-holders in the context of sexual and gender minorities in international law, see Lee 2022.

[74] See the second chapter of this work.

[75] On the importance of a collective identity, see Barclay et al 2011: 9.

6.2.3 Public Validation

The different victim groups have been publicly recognised as victims to varying degrees. This public validation of a victim identity, being conceptualised as such by mass media and by the public, has proved to be key, particularly when it comes to functioning as an incentive for the state to abolish the practices and establish remedies.[76] Changing laws, cultures and societies have affected notions of guilt and innocence in the public eye, making some victims more readily recognised as rights-holders than others.[77] In this respect, the various layers of the comparison reveal different perspectives on the validation of the victims' harms as grievable.[78] The cross-national comparison exposes how mass media in Sweden has actively framed historical sterilisation laws as wrongs to be remedied, more so than in Finland and Norway. The cross-group comparison demonstrates that the involuntarily castrated have been persistently unable to qualify as victims of rights violations according to the public. The cross-historical comparison ultimately reveals that public notions of rights violations and victimhood have only appeared in recent decades, since the 1990s in particular.

In Sweden, the mass media framing of historical sterilisation practices as outrageous and oppressive contributed to the public recognition of the victims' grievances. Contrasting the practices with the welfare state and the well-respected 'Swedish model', even comparing it to Nazi Germany, produced international headlines. In the mass media coverage, the fact that many victims of involuntary sterilisation were women was particularly highlighted as being so contradictory to the popular view of the country as a champion of gender equality.[79] Looking closer, Swedish moral and sociocultural ideals and values pertaining to rights-holder status changed remarkably during the twentieth century; this holds especially true in respect of the groups affected by the former sterilisation laws, such as women who were sexually active outside of marriage, or people with disabilities. Accordingly, people who were seen as undesirable, unfit parents or 'sterilisable' at the beginning of the century came to be regarded in a different light in later decades. State-controlled sterilisation of these groups no longer conceived as threats was therefore seen as more uncalled for at the end of the 1990s than it had before.

Against the backdrop of supranationally and constitutionally developing rights norms, such interventions began to be seen as violations of rights. While

[76] Mass media has an impact on how a question is framed, and if and how it is reported. Zald 1996: 270.

[77] According to Nils Christie's notion of 'ideal victims', the recognition of victimhood depends on the victim's contextual position and lack of perceived guilt in a wider social context. See Christie 1986. Sally Engle Merry described this tendency of requiring suffering bodies for verification of human rights violation and victimhood as a way for the human rights discourse to appear neutral and to 'rise above particular political struggles'. Merry 2007: 198.

[78] See Butler 2016. [79] See Chapter 3 of this book.

they were not regarded as legal infringements, these breaches were disturbing to sociocultural conceptualisations of rights in a developing normative order. In other words, the people subjected to involuntary sterilisation pursuant to the historical sterilisation laws better aligned with public understandings of rights-holder status and victimhood at the end of the twentieth century than they had previously. Similar changes in public attitudes with regard to this group can also be seen in Finland and Norway. Mass media reporting in the latter countries nevertheless kept a much lower profile in comparison to Sweden.[80]

No parallel normative development took place for sexual offenders, officially the main group targeted with criminological and psychiatric castrations. The castrated have been seldom conceptualised as victims, in line with contemporary public discussions about, and practices of, forced hormonal treatment – popularly referred to as 'chemical castration' – of sexual offenders, particularly perpetrators of child sexual abuse.[81] In fact, this group faces several challenges in aligning with legal and sociocultural rights frames, as they are rarely perceived as rights-holders or victims of rights violations. This also applies at the supranational level.[82] On account of a sexuality considered deviant and dangerous, (child) sexual offenders are often labelled as the worst possible criminals, who are so deprived of humanity that their harms are not publicly grievable. Instead of being publicly discussed, the practices of involuntary castration have been surrounded by silence, and their victims forgotten. Strikingly, not even changing social perceptions of homosexuality have had an effect on the recognition of the victim group of homosexual men involuntarily castrated.

When it comes to trans people, mass media has played a pivotal role in changing the general perceptions of the group. Trans rights activism has been indispensable in informing mass media about the existence of trans individuals and their situation. Mass media has generally abandoned their earlier framing of the topic as a sensational and quirky marginal issue[83] in favour of adopting a human rights-conscious reporting style, a development which has been essential to alter public perceptions of trans people. In respect of Norway, for example, many interviewees referred to documentaries and mass media reporting on trans people's existence and problems as crucial contributors to the establishment of a law on gender recognition which builds on self-ascription.[84] The changing mass media conceptualisation of trans people's sterilisation and castration as a topic of human rights has occurred simultaneously to the supranational and national legal rights developments pertaining to gender identity. Again, the medial and popular validation of the public identity of victims as

[80] See Chapters 4 and 5 in this work. [81] See, for example, Dagens Nyheter 2016.

[82] See the second chapter of this book.

[83] This attitude was present in for example Finnish mass media's reporting of the preparation to abolish the infertility requirement in 2012 as an amendment which would allow men to give birth. Raevaara 2012.

[84] See the fourth chapter in this work.

rights-holders who are entitled to recognition and redress for past rights violations has accompanied key legal milestones.

6.2.4 Institutional Validation

Public institutions have participated in framing the practices as rights violations as well. In this case, the framing has happened with reference to the victim groups as rights-holders, on the one hand, and to public institutions, governments or the states themselves as rights-friendly, on the other. In respect of the latter, sterilisation and castration practices are seen in the light of national political concerns about public image and reputational gains or losses.[85] Governments have framed involuntary sterilisation and castration as affecting the country's public image at certain times, yet not at others. This has effectively validated victims' public identity, legal status and access to justice and remedies. In the countries' varying degrees of concern about their reputation, the concept of 'rights' therefore takes on an instrumental dimension. The interventions becoming dominantly framed as rights violations in political discussions over the last decades has been a crucial incentive for their abolition and remedy. At least in some time periods, appearing 'good' or 'human rights-friendly' has been a matter of interest in all the compared countries.[86] However, this seems to have motivated and accelerated legal change in Norway and Sweden to a larger extent than in Finland.

Paradigms of a 'good' public image, as well as the importance thereof, have changed in the countries over the last century. The interventions were all seen as warranted and supported, and even regarded as progressive at their time of introduction. Not until more recently have authority-controlled sterilisation/castration practices become questioned, abolished and remedied in terms of rights. The cross-historical comparison demonstrates that rights framing has become a topic of governmental interest at the same time as the development of supranational rights instruments, especially since the 1990s.[87]

In Sweden, the involvement of the Social Democratic Party in former sterilisation practices and the consequential implications of guilt provoked a remedial response from its Government in the late 1990s.[88] It was crucial for the Government to counter the negative publicity by establishing remedies, not

[85] 'Public image' is here understood as the popular representations of a country on national and international levels. With reference to rights, a general assumption in the international community is that a positive public image equals a positive attitude and commitment of a state to human rights.

[86] Appearing 'human rights-friendly' is generally of particular importance to countries which are typically concerned about their international image. Risse & Sikkink 1999: 37–38. See also Simmons 2009: 5, 13.

[87] See the second chapter of this work.

[88] Among Swedish interviewees who highlighted the damaging publicity which the sterilisation news created were Andrén, 21 September 2016; Persson, 20 September 2016; Zaremba, 13 September 2016.

only to make amends for individual victims' harm but also to improve the state's public image as a social democratic welfare state.

In Norway, the rights-holder status of the Romani has been institutionally validated through public investigations and other remedies. During the late twentieth and early twenty-first century, the group went from being considered undesirable to becoming regarded as a national minority which ought to be protected from discrimination. Even though the sterilisation practices have never been referred to as violations of legal norms by state authorities, an indirect effect of developing supranational and national minority rights can be seen in the moral, sociocultural recognition of the minority's victimhood and the state's guilt. This recognition demonstrates the changing notions of the group as rights-holders and the state's role and responsibility in relation to the former's harms resulting from previous mistreatment.[89]

In Finland, engagement with historical sterilisation and castration practices which problematises past oppression from a current perspective is seen as inappropriate by public authorities. Potential engagement with past practices has been viewed as not merely anachronistic but also as having unforeseeable political and legal consequences, and moreover, being unnecessary from the presumed perspective of direct victims. Taking a pragmatic approach, Finnish authorities have placed less emphasis on the question of how the legacy of a sterilisation and castration history affects the public image of the state.

Public image as a sociocultural aspect of rights has been instrumental to the mobilisation of trans victims. Civil society organisations and activists have utilised notions of rights and rights commitments to call into question the state's public image, or to 'name and shame' the national governments.[90] In doing so, they have particularly contrasted infertility/sterilisation/castration preconditions for legal gender recognition with legislated rights and prohibitions of discrimination based on gender identity. This strategy has provoked an institutional response in Sweden and Norway, but was not immediately successful in Finland. The Finnish reaction can largely be attributed to political resistance to rights discourse, referring to the infertility precondition as a politicised, contentious matter.[91]

More specifically, trans civil society has socioculturally aligned with master frames of rights, provoking an institutional validation of trans people as rights-holders. By aligning with a master frame of rights, activists have challenged the previously dominating medical master frame prevalent in state institutions. This challenge has called into question the fact that trans people's recognition and interests are treated as a matter of medical expertise,

[89] See Chapter 4 in this book.

[90] In the international community, rights are used as instrumental means of persuasion and socialisation, involving the exertion of pressure on non-conforming countries through processes such as 'naming and shaming'. Risse & Sikkink 1999: 14.

[91] This reaction therefore differed from that of its neighbouring and many other European countries, which have amended such legislative requirements.

when it is actually a field which poses important legal and political questions regarding the rights of trans people. According to a rights master frame, the preconditions for legal gender recognition are a matter of constitutional review. In Norway and Sweden, this alignment effectively led to the rights framing being accepted by two conservative governments, in 2012/2013 (Sweden) and 2015/2016 (Norway), resulting in the abolition of sterilisation and castration preconditions.[92] In both countries, moreover, the opposition generally supported such amendments and criticised initial resistance by the government.[93] The general support across political party lines came to frame the question as one of apolitical rights rather than political preferences. The parliamentary embrace of the rights framing also happened without any considerable direct involvement of supranational supervisory rights institutions in both countries. However, the acceptance was parallel to the development of supranational soft law documents regarding trans people's rights, often used by civil society and at times picked up by national institutions, implying an institutional acceptance of a rights framing mainly put forward by grassroots movements.

The public image and the wish to appear human rights/trans/LGBT-friendly was crucial in the abolition of sterilisation/castration requirements for legal gender recognition in Sweden and Norway.[94] In both countries, high-profile public support for legislative amendments by key members of the respective governments was also significant.[95] Tellingly, both countries' governments only engaged with rights framing in positive terms. After legislative amendments, both governments also benefited from positive international media coverage as progressive and trans-friendly.[96] The governments therefore managed to turn the abolition of sterilisation/castration preconditions into positive news, presented as a human rights success. The governments or appointed state investigations moreover never explicitly referred to such preconditions as rights violations in the first place. A tension seems to be present between the concepts of rights 'successes' and 'failures', where the compared Nordic states more readily perceive themselves as rights vanguards, rather than violators.

[92] See Swedish Government Bill Prop. 2011/12:142; Norwegian Government Bill Prop. 74 L (2015–2016).

[93] Criticism of the government by opposition parties particularly occurred in the Swedish case. See Chapter 3 in this book.

[94] There was, hence, a sufficient degree of interest convergence. See Bell 1980.

[95] An important event in Sweden was when the Prime Minister in the face of criticism and public opinion pressure in a high-profile debate of 2012, promised to abolish the infertility precondition. Similarly, after awareness-raising campaigns and strategic litigation, in 2016, the Swedish Government decided to compensate the trans people who had been sterilised as a consequence of the earlier legislative requirement. The Norwegian trans civil society campaign for the abolishment of the castration requirement during the first half of the 2010s found similar high-profile political support in the Norwegian Minister of Health. See Chapters 3 and 4 in this work.

[96] See Ahlander 2017; Independent 2016.

Finland is in turn the only country in the comparison which has repeatedly been 'named and shamed' for upholding the infertility precondition until 2023. The criticism was not only national, but also voiced by supranational human rights institutions.[97] International mass media also reported the country's long reluctance to change the law, particularly in the light of many other European countries (including all the other Nordic countries) having amended similar preconditions.[98] The resistance of the conservative Finnish Government between 2015 and 2019 to the rights framing used by trans rights activists remains particularly interesting in this context. In terms of public image, the Government in question was less concerned about appearing 'friendly' to human rights, and trans or LGBT+ people in particular, than its neighbours.[99] In sharp contrast to its Norwegian and Swedish counterparts, the Finnish Government at the time argued that their support and domestic public image depended on the preservation of the infertility precondition. Here appears an unexpected aspect of rights instrumentalism in creating a public image. Accordingly, while the rights framing helped to depoliticise the trans sterilisations/castrations in Sweden and Norway at the time,[100] leading to successful amendments, the use of rights framing did not help to advance the change of the law in Finland. On the contrary, it even further politicised the resistance to such amendments.

Institutional validation of victims as rights-holders and their harms as justifiable legal or sociocultural claims has moreover happened to a lesser extent in Finland in comparison to its two Nordic neighbours. Finland generally provides an unfertile soil for remedial debates concerning historical violations; this stance is motivated by pragmatism rather than principle, a response springing from fear of opening a floodgate of remedial claims.[101] Despite the general Finnish remedial austerity, some historical injustices have, however, become acknowledged in restorative terms. Yet, this recognition has been restrictive, largely limited to war-related harm with a particular focus on veterans.[102] The institutional validation of historical 'victimhood' is therefore linked to specific contextual, ethnic, gendered and ability-shaped frames. The involuntarily sterilised and castrated do not easily fit within such precedents, and have failed to align.

[97] Such as the CEDAW Committee and the CoE Commissioner for Human Rights. See CEDAW/C/FIN/CO/7 (2014): Paras 28–29 and CommDH(2012)27.

[98] See, for example, Glass 2017.

[99] Reflected in the late Finnish introductions of civil partnership and equal marriage, and especially the recent backlash to the latter, Finnish politics and society seem to present a different moral environment than those of Norway and Sweden.

[100] This is a common assumption in human rights advocacy. See Merry 2007: 198.

[101] This can be seen in the pragmatic and almost immediate rejection of state responsibility in the investigation of past practices of lobotomy. Valtakunnallinen terveydenhuollon eettinen neuvottelukunta [The Finnish Advisory Board on Social Welfare and Health Care Ethics] 2000.

[102] See the fifth chapter of this book.

6.3 Fragile Rights

Exploring this 'skeleton in the closet' of the Nordic countries, which are often considered international champions of human rights, reveals more than a complicated story of how notions of human and constitutional rights have developed in the twentieth and twenty-first centuries. It also shows how rights as legal and sociocultural instruments are multidimensional and situated. As this chapter has demonstrated, the emancipatory, remedial promise inherent to rights is contingent on a number of contextually dependent enabling factors. For the promise of rights and remedies to be realised in the case of involuntary sterilisation and castration, a well-established rights master frame is needed, in conjunction with a national tradition of recognising the harms of victims of historical oppression as legally redressable. Moreover, victims have to conceptualise their own harms as legal grievances in terms of rights; be able to mobilise resources; have affluent national, transnational and supranational networks; be willing to engage in protracted and potentially costly and retraumatising struggles. Ideally, they should also appeal to society and mass media as victims. Furthermore, the public authorities should accept victims' claims as relevant and be eager to appear rights-friendly.

Without such multi-instance validation, harm framed as rights claims is at risk of coming to naught, being legally, socially and culturally unintelligible. Through their separation from 'interests' by becoming legally protected norms, 'rights' ideally appeal to the ostensibly universal, the apolitical and a sense of neutrality. At the same time, rights claims and their violations always already exist in a framework where such 'neutrality' depends on the legal, social and cultural conventions of time and place. Like the human condition, such claims are inherently vulnerable and precarious.

7

Law and Society in Change

In order to unpack the diverse contextual legal landscapes of involuntary sterilisation and castration practices and the varying measures of redress established for such mistreatment, this work has explored the meaning of grievance formation with reference to rights. As such, it has delved into questions such as why some groups of victims have mobilised for access to justice and others have not; why state authorities have provided remedies for victims in some instances and not in others; how developing supranational and constitutional rights have not only acted as legal instruments but also as sociocultural notions of identity and entitlement. Exploring possible answers to these queries, the book has put important individual instances of mobilisation under scrutiny, such as cases of strategic litigation, and furthermore investigated the more structural aspects of developing national legal and remedial cultures. In doing so, this work provides a contextualised, complexifying example of the Nordic 'rights revolution',[1] in which the international human rights law framework has provided a weak and, in many ways, unstable master frame for the legal and remedial conceptualisation of involuntary sterilisation and castration in the nations investigated.

In the book, the inconsistency in victims' access to remedies is connected to the developing socio-legal rights cultures of the countries. The increasing problematisation of involuntary sterilisation and castration as rights violations is partly explained by international and national developments with regard to rights and state responsibility conceptualisation. The interventions' place on the political agenda of states is, in other words, inherently connected to the processes through which individual rights are given a more central space in legal orders, and how an increasing number of aspects of people's lives (for example, gender identity or disability) are legally and culturally coded in terms of rights. The incorporation of rights into national legal orders, or the inclusion of references to rights instruments by courts, are in themselves sufficient for classical doctrinal understandings to speak of rights developments.[2]

[1] See, for instance, Langford et al 2019: 3–8.

[2] With regard to the Nordic countries, doctrinal scholarship has often indicated that supranational legal systems have changed the traditional national reluctance to judicial review and rights and that this has led to rights gaining a stronger foothold.

However, such accounts offer insufficient tools in a comparison seeking to understand the cultural underpinnings behind national, historical and intra-group differences. Instead of merely exploring doctrinal accounts, this book has followed a socio-legal tradition of unpacking how a rights culture *comes into being*, that is, how rights claims are socioculturally situated and depend on their users.[3]

The rights-based, grievance formation-centred theoretical and methodological tools used in this work have been specifically developed to answer the research questions posed at the outset and are tailored to the cases investigated. As such, they are valuable instruments allowing for nuance and refinement when analysing changing legal and social orders. This means that they can also be explored, applied and adapted outside the specific contexts analysed in this work, particularly suitable for those legal subjectivities at the margins of rights development. By not focusing on existing forms of mobilisation alone but also on passive and mute groups, a manifold, multi-levelled perception of rights can begin to shed light on why the promise of rights and remedies sparks change in some cases and not in others.[4]

This book does not only revolve around the practices of involuntary sterilisation and castration targeting long-marginalised groups, which are considered undesirable parts of the population body. It also explores, challenges and blurs traditional boundaries between legal margins and centres, for example, by questioning allocation of legal relevance or analysing extra-legal perspectives on the law. In so doing, it contextualises the law, on the one hand, and particularises its universalising claims, on the other. To that end, it transcends traditional legal disciplines of public and private and crosses jurisdictional boundaries of the national and international.

This work has combined doctrinal, contextual-, historical- and socio-legal approaches to law, and to rights in particular. The law is presented as an evolving set of legal rules and principles. As a historical artefact, the law is dependent on time and place.[5] In terms of mobilisation, the law seems to be a malleable, emancipatory tool for oppressed groups: not only by means of courts-centred litigation but also as a powerful, transformative cultural symbol, present in people's awareness of the status and entitlements which the

[3] This tradition can be observed in among others McCann 1994; Marshall 2005; Andersen 2005; Speed 2007; Chua 2012. A situated approach to the law is also traditionally present in Nordic feminist legal scholarship. Several examples are presented in the edited work of Nousiainen et al (eds) 2001. Furthermore, recent contributions to legal human rights scholarship are becoming increasingly focused on mobilisation and the use of human rights. See Desmet 2018; Tsutsui 2018; De Búrca 2021.

[4] Thereby, the primary interest of the research is not a normative one, for example whether rights are meaningful or harmful legal tools.

[5] The Nordic countries provide fruitful material for such historicised legal analysis, with their strong corporatist traditions and often thorough legislative *travaux préparatoires*, which document the development of legal thinking and changing constructions of social problems and solutions for them.

law may bring. In its dimension of governmentality, the law can conversely function as an instrument for the oppression of marginalised groups. Finally, from a comparative point of view, the law functions as an element of society, which is shaped by, and simultaneously shapes, societal development. Through the combination of these approaches, a multidimensional, layered understanding of the law emerges.

Bibliography[1]

Supranational Case Law

International Criminal Tribunal for the Former Yugoslavia

The Prosecutor v. Dragoljub Kunarac, Radomir Kovac and Zoran Vukovic. Trial Chamber II. IT-96-23-T & IT-96-23/1-T (22 February 2001).

International Criminal Tribunal of Rwanda

The Prosecutor v. Eliézer Niyitegeka. Trial Chamber. ICTR-96-14-T (16 May 2003).

The Prosecutor v. Jean-Paul Akayesu. Appeals Chamber. Case No. ICTR-96-4-A (1 June 2001).

The Prosecutor v. Jean-Paul Akayesu. Trial Chamber. ICTR-96-4-T (2 September 1998).

The Court of Justice of the European Union

Andrea Francovich and Danila Bonifaci v. Italian Republic. C-6/90 and C-9/90 (19 November 1991).

K.B. v. NHS Pensions Agency. C-117/01 (7 January 2004).

P v. S and Cornwall County Council. C-13/94 (30 April 1996).

Sarah Margaret Richards v. Secretary of State for Work and Pensions. C-423/04 (27 April 2006).

The European Commission of Human Rights

Roetzheim v. Germany. Application No. 31177/96 (23 October 1997).

The European Court of Human Rights

A.D. and Others v. Georgia. Application Nos. 57864/17, 79087/17 & 55353/19 (1 December 2022).

[1] All electronic sources were last accessed on 28 March 2022. Unpublished documents have been obtained by direct correspondence with the authors or downloaded from SSRN or Researchgate.

A.P., Garçon and Nicot v. France. Application Nos. 79885/12, 52471/13 & 52596/13 (6 April 2017).

B v. France. Application No. 13343/87 (25 March 1992).

Backlund v. Finland. Application No. 36498/05 (6 July 2010).

Červeňáková v. the Czech Republic. Application No. 26853/09 (23 October 2012).

Christine Goodwin v. the United Kingdom. Application No. 28957/95 (11 July 2002).

Cossey v. the United Kingdom. Application No. 10843/84 (27 September 1990).

Csoma v. Romania. Application No. 8759/05 (15 January 2013).

D.H. v. the Czech Republic. Application No. 57325/00 (13 November 2007).

Dudgeon v. the United Kingdom. Application No. 7525/76 (22 October 1981).

E v. Norway. Application No. 11701/85 (29 August 1990).

Eerikäinen and Others v. Finland. Application No. 3514/02 (10 February 2009).

G and E v. Norway. Application Nos. 9278/81 & 9415/81 (3 October 1983).

G.H. v. Hungary. Application No. 54041/14 (9 June 2015).

G.B. and R.B. v. the Republic of Moldova. Application No. 16761/09 (18 December 2012).

Grönmark v. Finland. Application No. 17038/04 (6 July 2010).

Hämäläinen v. Finland. Application No. 3735/09 (16 July 2014).

Hokkanen v. Finland. Application No. 19823/92 (23 September 1994).

I v. the United Kingdom. Application No. 25680/94 (11 July 2002).

I.G. and Others v. Slovakia. Application No. 15966/04 (13 November 2012).

Janowiec and Others v. Russia. Application Nos. 55508/07 & 29520/09 (21 October 2013).

Joëlle Gauer and Others v. France. Application No. 61521/08 (23 October 2012).

Johansson v. Finland. Application No. 10163/02 (6 September 2007).

Juppala v. Finland. Application No. 18620/03 (2 December 2008).

K.H. and Others v. Slovakia. Application No. 32881/04 (28 April 2009).

Kolk and Kislyiy v. Estonia. Application Nos. 23052/04 & 24018/04 (17 January 2006).

K.U. v. Finland. Application No. 2872/02 (2 December 2008).

L v. Lithuania. Application No. 27527/03 (11 September 2003).

L.H. v. Latvia. Application No. 52019/07 (29 April 2014).

Mocanu and Others v. Romania. Application Nos. 10865/09, 45886/07 & 32431/08 (17 September 2014).

M.P. v. Finland. Application No. 36487/12 (15 December 2016).

Muttilainen v. Finland. Application No. 18358/02 (22 May 2007).

N.B. v. Slovakia. Application No. 29518/10 (12 June 2012).

Norris v. Ireland. Application No. 10581/83 (26 October 1988).

Nunez v. France. Application No. 18367/06 (27 May 2008).

Oršuš and Others v. Croatia. Application No. 15766/03 (16 March 2010).

Rees v. the United Kingdom. Application No. 9532/81 (17 October 1987).

Ristamäki and Korvola v. Finland. Application No. 66456/09 (29 October 2013).

R.K. v. the Czech Republic. Application No. 7883/08 (27 November 2012).

Schlumpf v. Switzerland. Application No. 29002/06 (8 January 2009).

Sheffield and Horsham v. the United Kingdom. Application Nos. 22985/93 & 23390/94 (30 July 1998).

Šilih v. Slovenia. Application No. 71463/01 (9 April 2009).

Soares de Melo v. Portugal. Application No. 72850/14 (16 February 2016).

Sporrong and Lönnroth v. Sweden. Application Nos. 7151/75 & 7152/75 (23 September 1982).

Thiermann and Others v. Norway. Application No. 18712/03 (8 March 2007).
Van Kück v. Germany. Application No. 35968/97 (12 June 2003).
Van Osterwijk v. Belgium. Application No. 7654/76 (6 November 1980).
V.C. v. Slovakia. Application No. 18968/07 (8 November 2011).
Vilho Eskelinen and Others v. Finland. Application No. 63235/00 (19 April 2007).
X and Y v. the Netherlands. Application No. 8978/80 (26 March 1985).
X and Y v. Romania. Applications Nos. 2145/16 & 20607/16 (19 January 2021).
X, Y and Z v. the United Kingdom. Application No. 21830/93 (22 April 1997).
Y.Y. v. Turkey. Application No. 14793/08 (10 March 2015).

The Inter-American Court of Human Rights

Fernández Ortega et al v. Mexico. Preliminary Objection, Merits, Reparations, and Costs. Series C No. 215 (30 August 2010).
García Lucero et al v. Chile. Preliminary Objection, Merits and Reparations. Series C No. 267 (28 August 2013).
Gelman v. Uruguay. Merits and Reparations. Series C No. 221 (24 February 2011).
González et al ('Cotton Field') v. Mexico. Preliminary Objection, Merits, Reparations, and Costs. Series C No. 205 (16 November 2009).
I.V. v. Bolivia. Excepciones Preliminares, Fondo, Reparaciones y Costas [Preliminary Objections, Merits, Reparations and Costs]. Series C No. 329 (30 November 2016).
Velásquez Paiz and Others v. Guatemala. Excepciones Preliminares, Fondo, Reparaciones y Costas [Preliminary Objections, Merits, Reparations and Costs]. Series C No. 307 (19 November 2015).

The Permanent Court of International Justice

The Factory at Chorzów (Claim for Indemnity) Germany v. Poland (13 September 1928), PCIJ Reports Series A No. 17.

The Supreme National Tribunal of Poland

Poland v. Höss. 7 LRTWC 11 (11–29 March 1947).

US Military Tribunal Nuremberg

United States of America v. Greifelt et al. 13 LRTWC 1 (10 October 1947–10 March 1948).
United States of America v. Karl Brandt et al. 4 LRTWC 91–3 (21 November 1946–20 August 1947).

Supranational Advisory Opinions and Decisions

Committee against Torture

Gerasimov v. Kazakhstan, Communication No. 433/2010 (10 July 2012).

Committee on the Elimination of Discrimination against Women

A.S. v. Hungary, Communication No. 4/2004 (14 August 2006).
J.D. et al v. the Czech Republic. Communication No. 102/2016 (16 July 2019).

European Committee of Social Rights

Transgender Europe and ILGA-Europe, Complaint No. 117/2015 (15 May 2018).

Human Rights Committee

M.T. v. Uzbekistan. Communication No. 2234/2013 (23 July 2015).

The Inter-American Commission on Human Rights

I.V. v. Bolivia, Case 12.655 (merits). Report 72/14 (15 August 2014).
María Mamérita Mestanza Chávez v. Peru, Case 12.191 (friendly settlement). Report 71/03 (22 October 2003).

The Inter-American Court of Human Rights

Opinión Consultativa [Advisory Opinion], OC-24/17 (24 November 2017).

Supranational Official Documents

African Union

African Commission on Human and Peoples' Rights, *Resolution on Involuntary Sterilisation and the Protection of Human Rights in Access to HIV Services.* AU Doc. ACHPR/Res.260(LIV)13 (2013).
African Commission on Human and Peoples' Rights, *Resolution on the Right to Dignity and Freedom from Torture and Ill-treatment of Persons with Psychosocial Disabilities in Africa.* AU Doc.ACHPR/Res.343(LVIII)16 (2016).

Council of Europe

Commissioner for Human Rights, *Recommendation of the Commissioner for Human Rights Concerning Certain Aspects of Law and Practice Relating to Sterilization of Women in the Slovak Republic.* CoE Doc. CommDH(2003)12.
Commissioner for Human Rights, *Human Rights and Gender Identity.* CoE Doc. CommDH/IssuePaper(2009)2.
Commissioner for Human Rights, *Report.* CoE Doc. CommDH(2011)42.
Commissioner for Human Rights, *Report.* CoE Doc. CommDH(2012)27.
Committee of Ministers, *Recommendation on Measures to Combat Discrimination on Grounds of Sexual Orientation or Gender Identity.* CoE Doc. CM/Rec(2010)5.

Committee of Ministers, *Supervision of the Execution of Judgments and Decisions of the European Court of Human Rights*. Council of Europe Publications (2018).

CoE, *Explanatory Report to the Council of Europe Convention on Preventing and Combating Violence against Women and Domestic Violence*. CoE Doc. Explanatory Report CETS 210 (2011).

Council of Europe Advisory Committee on the Framework Convention for the Protection of National Minorities, *First Opinion on Norway*. CoE Doc. ACFC/INF/OP/I(2003)003 (2003).

CPT, *Report to the Czech Government*. CoE Doc. CPT/Inf (2007) 32.

CPT, *Report to the Czech Government*. CoE Doc. CPT/Inf (2009) 8.

European Commission against Racism and Intolerance, *Second Report on Norway*. CoE Doc. CRI(2000)33.

European Commission against Racism and Intolerance, *Third Report on Norway*. CoE Doc. CRI(2004)3.

PACE, *Condition of Transsexuals*. CoE Doc. Rec. 1117 (1989).

PACE, *Discrimination on the Basis of Sexual Orientation and Gender Identity*. CoE Doc. Res 1728 (2010).

PACE, *Putting an End to Coerced Sterilisations and Castrations*. CoE Doc. Res 1945 (2013).

PACE, *Report: Putting an End to Coerced Sterilisations and Castrations*. Written by Liliane Maury Pasquier. CoE Doc. PACE Report 13215 (2013).

PACE, *Discrimination against Transgender People in Europe*. CoE Doc. Res 2048 (2015).

European Union

European Union Agency for Fundamental Rights, *Being Trans in the European Union. Comparative Analysis of EU LGBT Survey Data*. FRA Publications (2014).

van den Brink, Marjolein; Dunne, Peter; Burri, Susanne & Timmer, Alexandra, *Trans and Intersex Equality Rights in Europe – A Comparative Analysis*. European Commission Directorate-General for Justice and Consumers (2018).

International Criminal Court

International Criminal Court, *Elements of Crimes*. International Criminal Court Publications (2011).

International Criminal Court, *Policy Paper on Sexual and Gender-based Crimes*. International Criminal Court Publications (2014).

Nordic Council

Andersen, Nina; Groes, Lis; Widemar, Ingrid G; Hækkerup, Grete & Nederström-Lundén, Judit, *Medlemsförslag om enhetlig nordisk abortlagstiftning [Member Proposal Regarding a Coherent Nordic Abortion Legislation]*. Doc No. A 109/j. Nordic Council Publications (1969).

Nordiska rådet [The Nordic Council], *Promemoria angående abortlagstiftningen [Promemoria on the Abortion Legislation]*. Unpublished (1969).

United Nations

CAT Committee, *Conclusions and Recommendations on the Czech Republic*. UN Doc. CAT/C/CR/32/2 (2004).

CAT Committee, *Conclusions and Recommendations on Peru*. UN Doc. CAT/C/PER/CO/4 (2006).

CAT Committee, *Concluding Observations on Slovakia*. UN Doc. CAT/C/SVK/CO/2 (2009).

CAT Committee, *Concluding Observations on the Czech Republic*. UN Doc. CAT/C/CZE/CO/4-5 (2012).

CAT Committee, *General Comment No. 3: Implementation of Article 14 by States Parties*. UN Doc. CAT/C/GC/3 (2012).

CAT Committee, *Concluding Observations on China with Respect to Hong Kong, China*. UN Doc. CAT/C/CHN-HKG/CO/5 (2016).

CAT Committee, *Concluding Observations on Czechia*. UN Doc. CAT/C/CZE/CO/6 (2018).

CEDAW Committee, *General Recommendation No. 19: Violence against Women*. UN Doc. A/47/38 at 1 (1992).

CEDAW Committee, *General Recommendation No. 24: Women and Health*. UN Doc. A/54/38 at 5 (1999).

CEDAW Committee, *Concluding Observations: Peru*. UN Doc. A/57/38, at 454 (2002).

CEDAW Committee, *Concluding Comments: China*. UN Doc. CEDAW/C/CHN/CO/6 (2006).

CEDAW Committee, *Concluding Comments: The Czech Republic*. UN Doc. CEDAW/C/CZE/CO/3 (2006).

CEDAW Committee, *Concluding Observations: Slovakia*. UN Doc. CEDAW/C/SVK/CO/4 (2008).

CEDAW Committee, *Concluding Observations: The Czech Republic*. UN Doc. CEDAW/C/CZE/CO/5 (2010).

CEDAW Committee, *Concluding Observations: The Netherlands*. UN Doc. CEDAW/C/NLD/CO/5 (2010).

CEDAW Committee, *Concluding Observations: Chile*. UN Doc. CEDAW/C/CHL/CO/5-6 (2012).

CEDAW Committee, *Concluding Observations: Jordan*. UN Doc. CEDAW/C/JOR/CO/5 (2012).

CEDAW Committee, *Concluding Observations on Colombia*. UN Doc. CEDAW/C/COL/CO/7-8 (2013).

CEDAW Committee, *Concluding Observations on Belgium*. UN Doc. CEDAW/C/BEL/CO/7 (2014).

CEDAW Committee, *Concluding Observations on Finland*. UN Doc. CEDAW/C/FIN/CO/7 (2014).

CEDAW Committee, *Concluding Observations on India*. UN Doc. CEDAW/C/IND/CO/4-5 (2014).

CEDAW Committee, *Concluding Observations on Peru*. UN Doc. CEDAW/C/PER/CO/7-8 (2014).

CEDAW Committee, *Concluding Observations on Slovakia*. UN Doc. CEDAW/C/SVK/CO/5-6 (2015).

CEDAW Committee, *General Recommendation No. 35: Gender-based Violence against Women*. UN Doc. CEDAW/C/GC/35 (2017).

CERD Committee, *Concluding Observations: Peru*. UN Doc. CERD/C/304/Add.69 (1999).

CERD Committee, *General Recommendation No. 25: Gender-related Dimensions of Racial Discrimination*. UN Doc. A/55/18, Annex V, 152 (2000).

CERD Committee, *Concluding Observations: Slovakia*. UN Doc. A/59/18 (2004).

CERD Committee, *Concluding Observations: The Czech Republic*. UN Doc. CERD/C/CZE/CO/7 (2007).

CERD Committee, *Concluding Observations: Slovakia*. UN Doc. CERD/C/SVK/CO/6-8 (2010).

CERD Committee, *Concluding Observations: The Czech Republic*. UN Doc. CERD/C/CZE/CO/8–9 (2011).

CERD Committee, *Concluding Observations on Slovakia*. UN Doc. CERD/C/SVK/CO/9–10 (2013).

CESCR Committee, *General Comment No. 5: Persons with Disabilities*. UN Doc. E/1995/22 at 19 (1995).

CESCR Committee, *Concluding Observations: Brazil*. UN Doc. E/C.12/1/Add.87 (2003).

CESCR Committee, *Concluding Observations: China*. UN Doc. E/C.12/1/Add.107 (2005).

CESCR Committee, *General Comment No. 22 on the Right to Sexual and Reproductive Health*. UN Doc. E/C.12/GC/22 (2016).

CRC Committee, *Concluding Observations: Austria*. UN Doc. CRC/C/15/Add.98 (1999).

CRC Committee, *Concluding Observations: Australia*. UN Doc. CRC/C/15/Add.268 (2005).

CRC Committee, *General Comment No. 9: The Rights of Children with Disabilities*. UN Doc. CRC/C/GC/9 (2007).

CRC Committee, *Concluding Observations: Australia*. UN Doc. CRC/C/AUS/CO/4 (2012).

CRC Committee, *Concluding Observations on China*. UN Doc. CRC/C/CHN/CO/3-4 (2013).

CRC Committee, *Concluding Observations on India*. UN Doc. CRC/C/IND/CO/3-4 (2014).

CRPD Committee, *Concluding Observations on Hungary*. UN Doc. CRPD/C/HUN/CO/1 (2012).

CRPD Committee, *Concluding Observations on Peru*. UN Doc. CRPD/C/PER/CO/1 (2012).

CRPD Committee, *Concluding Observations on Australia*. UN Doc. CRPD/C/AUS/CO/1 (2013).

CRPD Committee, *General Comment No. 1: Article 12, Equal Recognition before the Law*. UN Doc. CRPD/C/GC/1 (2014).

CRPD Committee, *Concluding Observations on the Republic of Korea*. UN Doc. CRPD/C/KOR/CO/1 (2014).

CRPD Committee, *Concluding Observations on Germany*. UN Doc. CRPD/C/DEU/CO/1 (2015).

CRPD Committee, *Concluding Observations on Lithuania.* UN Doc. CRPD/C/LTU/CO/1 (2015).

CRPD Committee, *Concluding Observations on the Czech Republic.* UN Doc. CRPD/C/CZE/CO/1 (2015).

CRPD Committee, *General Comment No. 3: Women and Girls with Disabilities.* UN Doc. CRPD/C/GC/3 (2016).

CRPD Committee, *General Comment No. 5: Living Independently and Being Included in the Community.* UN Doc. CRPD/C/GC/5 (2017).

CRPD Committee, *Concluding Observations on South Africa.* UN Doc. CRPD/C/ZAF/CO/1 (2018).

CRPD Committee, *General Comment No. 6: Equality and Non-discrimination.* UN Doc. CRPD/C/GC/6 (2018).

ECOSOC, *21st Session: Summary Records of the Commission on the Status of Women.* UN Doc. E/CN.6/SR.519 (1968).

ECOSOC, *Violence against Women (Addendum): Policies and Practices that Impact Women's Reproductive Rights and Contribute To, Cause or Constitute Violence against Women, Report of the Special Rapporteur on Violence against Women, Its Causes and Consequences, Radhika Coomaraswamy.* UN Doc. E/CN.4/1999/68/Add.4 (1999).

Human Rights Committee, *Concluding Observations: Japan.* UN Doc. CCPR/C/79/Add.102 (1998).

Human Rights Committee, *Concluding Observations: Peru.* UN Doc. CCPR/CO/70/PER (2000).

Human Rights Committee, *General Comment No. 28: Equality of Rights between Men and Women (Article 3).* UN Doc. CCPR/C/21/Rev.1/Add.10 (2000).

Human Rights Committee, *Concluding Observations: Slovakia.* UN Doc. CCPR/CO/78/SVK (2003).

Human Rights Committee, *Concluding Observations: The Czech Republic.* UN Doc. CCPR/C/CZE/CO/2 (2007).

Human Rights Committee, *Concluding Observations: Switzerland.* UN Doc. CCPR/C/CHE/CO/3 (2009).

Human Rights Committee, *Concluding Observations: Slovakia.* UN Doc. CCPR/C/SVK/CO/3 (2011).

OHCHR et al, *Eliminating Forced, Coercive and Otherwise Involuntary Sterilization: An Interagency Statement.* World Health Organization Publications (2014).

UN, *Beijing Declaration and Platform for Action, Fourth World Conference on Women.* United Nations Publications (1995).

UN, *Durban Declaration and Programme of Action.* United Nations Publications (2002).

UNGA, *Declaration on the Elimination of Violence against Women.* UN Doc. A/RES/48/104 (1993).

UNGA, *Report of the Committee on Elimination of Discrimination against Women.* UN Doc. A/49/38 (1994).

UNGA, *Report of the Committee on Elimination of Discrimination against Women.* UN Doc. A/54/38 (1999).

UNGA, *Economic, Cultural and Social Rights. The Right of Everyone to the Enjoyment of the Highest Attainable Standard of Physical and Mental Health: Report of the Special Rapporteur, Paul Hunt.* UN Doc. E/CN.4/2004/49 (2004).

UNGA, *Report submitted by the Special Rapporteur on the Right of Everyone to the Highest Attainable Standard of Physical and Mental health, Paul Hunt. Addendum.* UN Doc. E/CN.4/2005/51/Add.3 (2005).

UNGA, *Basic Principles and Guidelines on the Right to a Remedy and Reparation for Victims of Gross Violations of International Human Rights Law and Serious Violations of International Humanitarian Law.* UN Doc. A/RES/60/147 (2006).

UNGA, *Report of the Special Rapporteur on the Right of Everyone to the Enjoyment of the Highest Attainable Standard of Physical and Mental Health, Paul Hunt. Addendum.* UN Doc. A/HRC/4/28/Add.1 (2008).

UNGA, *Report of the Special Rapporteur on Torture and Other Cruel, Inhuman or Degrading Treatment or Punishment, Manfred Nowak.* UN Doc. A/HRC/7/3 (2008).

UNGA, *Promotion and Protection of All Human Rights, Civil, Political, Economic, Social and Cultural Rights, Including the Right to Development. Report of the Special Rapporteur on Violence against Women, its Causes and Consequences, Rashida Manjoo.* UN Doc. A/HRC/14/22 (2010).

UNGA, *Resolution Adopted by the General Assembly on the Responsibility of States for Internationally Wrongful Acts.* UN Doc. A/RES/65/19 (2010).

UNGA, *Right of Everyone to the Enjoyment of the Highest Attainable Standard of Physical and Mental Health. Report by the Special Rapporteur on the Right of Everyone to the Enjoyment of the Highest Attainable Standard of Physical and Mental Health.* UN Doc. A/66/254 (2011).

UNGA, *Report of the Special Rapporteur on Contemporary Forms of Racism, Racial Discrimination, Xenophobia and Related Intolerance, Githu Muigai.* UN Doc. A/HRC/17/49 (2011).

UNGA, *Report of the Working Group on the Universal Periodic Review: Finland.* UN Doc. A/HRC/21/8 (2012).

UNGA, *Thematic Study on the Issue of Violence against Women and Girls and Disability. Report of the Office of the United Nations High Commissioner for Human Rights.* UN Doc. A/HRC/20/5 (2012).

UNGA, *Report of the Special Rapporteur on Torture and Other Cruel, Inhuman or Degrading Treatment or Punishment, Juan E. Méndez.* UN Doc. A/HRC/22/53 (2013).

UNGA, *Report of the Special Rapporteur on Extreme Poverty and Human Rights, Magdalena Sepúlveda Carmona. Addendum.* UN Doc. A/HRC/26/28/Add.2 (2014).

UNGA, *Discrimination and Violence against Individuals based on their Sexual Orientation and Gender Identity. Report of the Office of the United Nations High Commissioner for Human Rights.* UN Doc. A/HRC/29/23 (2015).

UNGA, *Report of the Special Rapporteur on Minority Issues, Rita Izsák. Comprehensive Study of the Human Rights Situation of Roma Worldwide, with a Particular Focus on the Phenomenon of Anti-Gypsyism.* UN Doc. A/HRC/29/24 (2015).

UNGA, *Report of the Special Rapporteur on the Promotion of Truth, Justice, Reparation and Guarantees of Non-recurrence, Pablo de Greiff.* UN Doc. A/HRC/30/42 (2015).

UNGA, *Report of the Special Rapporteur on Torture and Other Cruel, Inhuman or Degrading Treatment or Punishment.* UN Doc. A/HRC/31/57 (2016).

UNGA, *Report of the Independent Expert on Protection against Violence and Discrimination based on Sexual Orientation and Gender Identity*. UN Doc. A/HRC/35/36 (2017).

UNGA, *Report of the Working Group on the Universal Periodic Review: Finland*. UN Doc. A/HRC/36/8 (2017).

UN Secretariat, *First Draft of the Genocide Convention*. UN Doc. E/447 (1947).

Judgments and Decisions by Domestic Judicial and Advisory Organs

Canada

Alberta Court of Queen's Bench, *Muir v. Alberta*. 132 D.L.R. (4th) 695 Court File No. 8903 (25 January 1996).

Finland

Eduskunnan apulaisoikeusasiamies [Finnish Deputy Parliamentary Ombudsman], *Päätös [Decision]*. Doc. No. EOAK/2842/2017 (24 October 2018).

Eduskunnan oikeusasiamies [The Finnish Parliamentary Ombudsman], *Päätös kanteluun [Decision on Complaint]*. Doc. No. 2882/4/07 (23 March 2009).

Korkein hallinto-oikeus (KHO) [The Finnish Supreme Administrative Court], Doc. No. 4111/65/70 (6 September 1971).

Korkein hallinto-oikeus (KHO) [The Finnish Supreme Administrative Court], Doc. No. 2769/65/71 (9 May 1972).

Korkein hallinto-oikeus (KHO) [The Finnish Supreme Administrative Court], Doc. No. 3576/65/76 (31 August 1974).

Korkein hallinto-oikeus (KHO) [The Finnish Supreme Administrative Court], Doc. No. 4919/65/72 (13 September 1974).

Korkein hallinto-oikeus (KHO) [The Finnish Supreme Administrative Court], Doc. No. 5/65/76 (5 April 1977).

Korkein hallinto-oikeus (KHO) [The Finnish Supreme Administrative Court], Doc. No. 3267/65/76 (5 April 1977).

Korkein hallinto-oikeus (KHO) [The Finnish Supreme Administrative Court], Doc. No. 4915/65/76 (31 August 1977).

Korkein hallinto-oikeus (KHO) [The Finnish Supreme Administrative Court], Doc. No. 1111/65/78 (29 January 1979).

Korkein hallinto-oikeus (KHO) [The Finnish Supreme Administrative Court], Doc. No. 1307/65/78 (29 January 1979).

Korkein hallinto-oikeus (KHO) [The Finnish Supreme Administrative Court], Doc. No. 2299/65/78 (8 January 1980).

Korkein hallinto-oikeus (KHO) [The Finnish Supreme Administrative Court], Doc. No. 3962/65/78 (8 January 1980).

Korkein hallinto-oikeus (KHO) [The Finnish Supreme Administrative Court], Doc. No. 4914/65/78 (8 January 1980).

Korkein hallinto-oikeus (KHO) [The Finnish Supreme Administrative Court], Doc. No. 5689/65/83 (19 April 1984).

Korkein hallinto-oikeus (KHO) [The Finnish Supreme Administrative Court], Doc. No. 1449/2/87, KHO:1988-A-46 (9 March 1988).

Korkein hallinto-oikeus (KHO) [The Finnish Supreme Administrative Court], Doc. No. 1433/1/08, KHO:2009:15 (3 February 2009).

Korkein oikeus (KO) [The Finnish Supreme Court], KKO:2008:10 (8 February 2008).

Potilasvakuutuskeskus [Patient Insurance Centre], PO 2003–6434–83 (2003).

Germany

Bundesverfassungsgericht [German Federal Constitutional Court], 1 BvR 3295/07, Rn. (1-82) (11 January 2011).

Namibia

Supreme Court of Namibia, *Government of the Republic of Namibia v. L.M. and Others* (SA 49/2012). NASC 19 (3 November 2014).

Norway

Borgarting lagmannsrett [Borgarting Court of Appeal], Case No. LB-2018-154220 (15 April 2020).

Borgarting lagmannsrett [Borgarting Court of Appeal], Case No. 18-190131ASD-BORG/02 (16 March 2021).

Eidsivating Lagmannsrett [Eidsivating Court of Appeal], Appeal No. 43/1954 (1956).

Frostating Lagmannsrett [Frostating Court of Appeal], Appeal No. 97/1949 (1950).

Høyesterett [The Norwegian Supreme Court], Rt. 1976 s. 1 (Kløfta).

Høyesterett [The Norwegian Supreme Court], Rt. 1994 s. 610 (Bølgepappkjennelsen).

Høyesterett [The Norwegian Supreme Court], Rt. 2000 s. 996 (Bøhlerdommen).

Høyesterett [The Norwegian Supreme Court], Rt. 2013 s. 588 (Besøksforbud).

Høyesteretts ankeutvalg [The Appeals Committee of the Norwegian Supreme Court], Case No. HR-2020-1486-U (16 July 2020).

Høyesteretts ankeutvalg [The Appeals Committee of the Norwegian Supreme Court], Case No. HR-2021-1392-U (29 June 2021).

Likestillings- og diskrimineringsombudet [The Norwegian Equality and Anti-discrimination Ombud], Decision No. 12/650 (28 January 2013).

Likestillings- og diskrimineringsombudet [The Norwegian Equality and Anti-discrimination Ombud], Decision No. 14/840 (23 September 2014).

Oslo tingrett [Oslo Court of First Instance], Case No. 17-146470 TVI-OTIR/04 (16 Augusti 2018).

Oslo tingrett [Oslo Court of First Instance], Case No. 17-132417TVI-OTIR/08 (18 October 2018).

Tana og Varanger herredsrett [Tana and Varanger Court of First Instance], Case No. 36/1985 A (8 October 1985).

Sweden

Förvaltningsrätten i Stockholm [Stockholm Administrative Court of First Instance], Judgment No. 45723-10 (9 March 2012).
Högsta Domstolen (HD) [The Swedish Supreme Court], NJA 1964, s. 471 (1964).
Högsta Domstolen (HD) [The Swedish Supreme Court], NJA 2003, s. 217 (6 June 2003).
Högsta Domstolen (HD) [The Swedish Supreme Court], NJA 2005, s. 462 (9 June 2005).
Högsta Domstolen (HD) [The Swedish Supreme Court], NJA 2007, s. 584 (21 September 2007).
Högsta Domstolen (HD) [The Swedish Supreme Court], NJA 2012, s. 211 (11 April 2012).
Högsta Domstolen (HD) [The Swedish Supreme Court], NJA 2012, s. 400 (15 June 2012).
Högsta Domstolen (HD) [The Swedish Supreme Court], NJA 2013, s. 350 (16 May 2013).
Högsta Domstolen (HD) [The Swedish Supreme Court], NJA 2013, s. 746 (16 July 2013).
Högsta Domstolen (HD) [The Swedish Supreme Court], NJA 2014, s. 323 (23 April 2014).
Högsta Domstolen (HD) [The Swedish Supreme Court], NJA 2014, s. 332 (23 April 2014).
JK [The Chancellor of Justice], *Skadeståndsanspråk mot staten med anledning av sterilisering enligt könstillhörighetslagen [Compensation Claim against the State Due to Sterilisation according to the Gender Recognition Act].* Decision No. 4243-13-40 et al (17 June 2014).
Kammarrätten i Stockholm [Stockholm Administrative Court of Appeal], Judgment No. 3413-04 (30 March 2005).
Kammarrätten i Stockholm [Stockholm Administrative Court of Appeal], Judgment No. 1968-12 (19 December 2012).
Regeringsrätten [The Swedish Supreme Administrative Court], Judgment no. 2751-05 (13 March 2008).

US

Supreme Court of the United States, *Marbury v. Madison.* 5 U.S. 137 (24 February 1803).
Supreme Court of the United States, *Buck v. Bell.* 274 U.S. 200 (2 May 1927).
Supreme Court of the United States, *Skinner v. Oklahoma.* 316 U.S. 535 (1 June 1942).
Supreme Court of the United States, *Griswold v. Connecticut.* 381 U.S. 479 (7 June 1965).
Supreme Court of the United States, *Roe v. Wade.* 410 U.S. 113 (22 January 1973).

Domestic Official Documents

Finland

Aborttikomitea [The Finnish Abortion Committee], *Mietintö [Report].* KM 1968:A11 (1969).
Citizens' Initiative KAA 6/2021, *Oikeus olla – kansalaisaloite oikeudenmukaisemman translain puolesta [The Right to Exist – A Citizens' Initiative for a Fairer Trans Act].*

Eduskunnan apulaisoikeusasiamies [Finnish Deputy Parliamentary Ombudsman], *Kysymys sisäasiainministeriölle [Question for the Finnish Ministry of the Interior]*. Doc. No. 2486/2/98 (4 December 1998).

Eduskunnan oikeusasiamies [The Finnish Parliamentary Ombudsman], *Letter No. 1367*. Doc. No. 683/2/91 (24 April 1991).

Finnish Government Bill HE 112/1934, *Hallituksen esitys eduskunnalle sterilisoimislaiksi [Government Bill to the Parliament regarding a Sterilisation Act]*.

Finnish Government Bill HE 58/1948, *Hallituksen esitys eduskunnalle kastroimislaiksi [Government Bill to the Parliament regarding a Castration Act]*.

Finnish Government Bill HE 59/1948, *Hallituksen esitys eduskunnalle sterilisoimislaiksi [Government Bill to the Parliament regarding aSterilisation Act]*.

Finnish Government Bill HE 60/1948, *Hallituksen esitys eduskunnalle laiksi raskaudentilan keskeyttämisestä sekä laiksi rikoslain muuttamisesta [Government Bill to the Parliament regarding an Act on Termination of Pregnancy and an Amendment of the Criminal Code]*.

Finnish Government Bill HE 104/1969, *Hallituksen esitys eduskunnalle laiksi raskaudentilan keskeyttämisestä sekä laiksi rikoslain muuttamisesta [Government Bill to the Parliament regarding an Act on Termination of Pregnancy and an Amendment of the Criminal Code]*.

Finnish Government, Bill HE 105/1969, *Hallituksen esitys eduskunnalle steriloimislaiksi [Government Bill to the Parliament regarding a Sterilisation Act]*.

Finnish Government Bill HE 106/1969, *Hallituksen esitys eduskunnalle kastroimislaiksi [Government Bill to the Parliament regarding a Castration Act]*.

Finnish Government Bill HE 187/1973, *Hallituksen esitys eduskunnalle Vahingonkorvausta koskevaksi lainsäädännöksi [Government Bill to the Parliament regarding a Liability Act]*.

Finnish Government Bill HE 309/1993, *Hallituksen esitys eduskunnalle perustuslakien perusoikeussäännösten muuttamisesta [Government Bill to the Parliament on the Revision of Constitutional Rights]*.

Finnish Government Bill HE 1/1998, *Hallituksen esitys eduskunnalle uudeksi Suomen Hallitusmuodoksi [Government Bill to the Parliament regarding a New Finnish Government Act]*.

Finnish Government Bill HE 200/2000, *Hallituksen esitys eduskunnalle laiksi virallistetusta parisuhteesta [Government Bill to the Parliament regarding an Act on Registered Partnership]*.

Finnish Government Bill HE 207/2000, *Hallituksen esitys eduskunnalle laeiksi raskauden keskeyttämisestä annetun lain ja steriloimislain muuttamisesta [Government Bill to the Parliament regarding the Amendment of the Act on Termination of Pregnancy and the Sterilisation Act]*.

Finnish Government Bill HE 56/2001, *Hallituksen esitys eduskunnalle laiksi sukupuolen vahvistamisesta eräissä tapauksissa ja eräiksi siihen liittyviksi laeiksi [Government Bill to the Parliament, Act on Legal Gender Recognition under Certain Circumstances and Connected Acts]*.

Finnish Government Bill HE 19/2014, *Hallituksen esitys eduskunnalle yhdenvertaisuuslaiksi ja eräiksi siihen liittyviksi laeiksi [Government Bill to the Parliament, Non-Discrimination Act and Related Legislation]*.

Finnish Government Bill HE 159/2014, *Hallituksen esitys eduskunnalle laiksi valtion vahingonkorvaustoiminnasta sekä eräiksi siihen liittyviksi laeiksi [Government*

Bill to the Parliament for an Act on Administration of State Liability and Some Connected Acts].

Finnish Government Bill HE 189/2022, *Hallituksen esitys eduskunnalle laiksi sukupuolen vahvistamisesta ja siihen liittyviksi laeiksi [Government Bill regarding an Act on Gender Recognition and Connected Legislation].*

Finnish Parliamentary Bill LA 43/2016, *Lakialoite laiksi transseksuaalin sukupuolen vahvistamisesta annetun lain 1 §:n muuttamisesta [Bill to Amend Section 1 of the Act on Gender Recognition of Transsexuals].*

Ihmisoikeusvaltuuskunta [The Finnish Human Rights Delegation], *Suomi rikkoo Euroopan ihmisoikeussopimusta – Ihmisoikeusvaltuuskunta vaatii translain kiirellistä uudistamista [Finland Violates the European Convention on Human Rights – The Finnish Human Rights Delegation Demands an Immediate Change of the Trans Act]* (2017).

Komitea, joka on asetettu harkitsemaan tylsämielisten y.m. sterilisoimista koskevaa kysymystä [The Finnish Committee appointed to Consider the Question of Sterilisation of the Feebleminded etc.], *Mietintö [Report].* KM 1929:5 (1929).

Lääkintöhallitus [The Finnish Board of Health], *Päätös [Decision].* Doc. No. 11083/38/71 (1971).

Lääkintöhallitus [The Finnish Board of Health], *Ohjekirje [Guidelines].* Doc. No. 3905/02/79 (1979).

Lainvalmistelukunta [The Finnish Preparatory Legislative Committee], *Ehdotus hallituksen esitykseksi eduskunnalle sterilisoimislaiksi [Proposal for Government Bill to Parliament, Sterilisation Act].* LVM 1947:3 (1947).

Lakivaliokunta [The Finnish Parliamentary Legal Affairs Committee], *Lausunto [Statement].* LaVL 4/1948 (1948)

Oikeusministeriö [The Finnish Ministry of Justice], *Seksuaali- ja sukupuolivähemmistöön kuuluvien perus- ja ihmisoikeudet Suomessa [Constitutional and Human Rights for Sexual and Gender Minorities in Finland].* OM 34/2014 (2014).

Perustuslakivaliokunta [The Finnish Parliamentary Constitutional Law Committee], *Mietintö [Report].* PeVM 25/94 (1994).

Perustuslakivaliokunta [The Finnish Parliamentary Constitutional Law Committee], *Mietintö [Report].* PeVM 3/95 (1995).

Perustuslakivaliokunta [The Finnish Parliamentary Constitutional Law Committee], *Mietintö [Report].* PeVM 10/1998 (1998).

Perustuslakivaliokunta [The Finnish Parliamentary Constitutional Law Committee], *Mietintö [Report].* PeVM 1/1999 (1999).

Prime Minister Antti Rinne's Government, *Inclusive and Competent Finland – A Socially, Economically and Ecologically Sustainable Society* (6 June 2019).

Prime Minister Sanna Marin's Government, *Inclusive and Competent Finland – A Socially, Economically and Ecologically Sustainable Society* (10 December 2019).

Sisäasiainministerö [The Finnish Ministry of the Interior], *Lausunto [Statement].* Doc. No. 37/032/98 (1 March 1999).

Suuri valiokunta [The Finnish Parliamentary Grand Committee], *Mietintö [Report].* SuVM 95/1949 (1949).

Suuri valiokunta [The Finnish Parliamentary Grand Committee], *Mietintö [Report].* SuVM 96/1949 (1949).

Suuri valiokunta [The Finnish Parliamentary Grand Committee], *Mietintö [Report].* SuVM 97/1949 (1949).

Sosiaali- ja terveysministeriö [The Finnish Ministry of Social Affairs and Health], *Työryhmän asettaminen [Appointment of Working Group]*. Doc. No. 6984/04/87 (1987).

Sosiaali- ja terveysministeriö [The Finnish Ministry of Social Affairs and Health], *Lakiesitys sukupuoleen kuulumisen vahvistamisesta eräissä tapauksissa [Legislation Draft on Gender Recognition under Certain Circumstances]*. Doc. No. STM/268/011/1991 (1991).

Sosiaali- ja terveysministeriö [The Finnish Ministry of Social Affairs and Health], *Transseksuaalien aseman kehittämistyöryhmän muistio [Memorandum of the Working Group on the Position of Transsexuals]*. STM 2000:2 (2000).

Sosiaali- ja terveysministeriö [The Finnish Ministry of Social Affairs and Health], *Sukupuolen oikeudellisen vahvistamisen edellytykset [The Preconditions for Legal Gender Recognition]*. STM 2015:23 (2015).

Sosiaali- ja terveysministeriö [The Finnish Ministry of Social Affairs and Health], *Lastensuojelun sijaishuollon epäkohdat ja lasten kaltoinkohtelu 1937–1983 [Shortcomings in Substitute Care of the Child Protection Services and Maltreatment of Children 1937–1983]*. STM 2016:22 (2016a).

Sosiaali- ja terveysministeriö [The Finnish Ministry of Social Affairs and Health], *Official Apology to Everyone Who Suffered Maltreatment in Foster Care in the Past Decades,* stm.fi/sv/-/lastensuojelun-sijaishuollossa-kaltoin-kohdelluilta-pyydettiin-anteeksi?languageId=en_US (20 November 2016b).

Sosiaali- ja terveysministeriö [The Finnish Ministry of Social Affairs and Health], *Vaihtoehtoiset sääntelymallit sukupuolivähemmistöjen oikeudellisen aseman järjestämiseksi: Translainsäädännön uudistamisen valmistelutyöryhmä [Alternative Regulatory Models to Organise the Legal Position of Gender Minorities: The Working Group to Revise the Trans Act]* (2020).

Sosiaali- ja terveysvaliokunta [The Finnish Parliamentary Social Affairs and Health Committee], Protocol No. 4/2002 (2002a).

Sosiaali- ja terveysvaliokunta [The Finnish Parliamentary Social Affairs and Health Committee], Protocol No. 6/2002 (2002b).

Sosiaali- ja terveysvaliokunta [The Finnish Parliamentary Social Affairs and Health Committee], Protocol No. 10/2002 (2002c).

Sosiaali- ja terveysvaliokunta [The Finnish Parliamentary Social Affairs and Health Committee], *Mietintö [Report]*. StVM 7/2002 (2002).

Stakes [The Finnish Centre for Research and Development on Health and Welfare], *Transseksuaalien hoito- ja tukipalvelujen kehittämistyöryhmän muistio [Report of the Working Group on the Development of Health Care and Support Services for Transsexuals]*. Stakes Report No. 18/1994 (1994).

Talousvaliokunta [The Finnish Parliamentary Commerce Committee], *Mietintö [Report]*. TaVM 3/1949 (1949).

Talousvaliokunta [The Finnish Parliamentary Commerce Committee], *Mietintö [Report]*. TaVM 4/1949 (1949).

Talousvaliokunta [The Finnish Parliamentary Commerce Committee], *Mietintö [Report]*. TaVM 5/1949 (1949).

Talousvaliokunta [The Finnish Parliamentary Commerce Committee], *Mietintö [Report]*. TaVM 16/1970 (1970).

Talousvaliokunta [The Finnish Parliamentary Commerce Committee], *Mietintö [Report]*. TaVM 17/1970 (1970).

Tasa-arvovaltuutettu [The Finnish Ombudsman for Equality], *Lisääntymiskyvyttömyysvaatimus rikkoo transsukupuolisten ihmisoikeuksia [The Infertility Requirement Violates Transgender People's Human Rights]*, www.tasa-arvo.fi/-/tasa-arvovaltuutettu-lisaantymiskyvyttomyysvaatimus-rikkoo-transsukupuolisten-ihmisoikeuksia (21 November 2011).

Tasa-arvovaltuutettu [The Finnish Ombudsman for Equality], *Selvitys sukupuolivähemmistöjen asemasta [Investigation of the Position of Gender Minorities]*. Tasa-arvojulkaisuja 2012:1 (2012).

Väestörekisterikeskus [The Finnish Population Register Centre], *Lausunto: Lääkintöhallituksen aloite väestökirja-asetuksen muuttamiseksi [Statement: The Initiative of the Finnish Board of Health to Amend the Population Registry Decree]*. Doc. No. 26/350/87 (1987).

Valtakunnallinen terveydenhuollon eettinen neuvottelukunta [The Finnish Advisory Board on Social Welfare and Health Care Ethics], *Lausuntopyyntö lobotomian aiheuttamien haittojen rahallisista korvauksista [Request for Comment on Financial Compensation for Harm caused by Lobotomy]*. Doc. No. 44/59/97 (2000).

Valtakunnallinen terveydenhuollon eettinen neuvottelukunta [The Finnish Advisory Board on Social Welfare and Health Care Ethics], *Eettisyyttä terveydenhuoltoon [Ethics in Medical Care]*. ETENE Publication 5 (2002).

Valtioneuvoston kanslia [The Finnish Prime Minister's Office], *Saamelaisten totuus- ja sovintokomission asettamispäätös [The Decision to Establish a Truth and Reconciliation Commission for the Sámi]*. Doc. No. VN/11265/2020 (2021).

Valtion Väestöpoliittinen komitea [The Finnish Population Policy Committee], *Mietintö [Report]*. KM 1941:17 (1941).

Germany

German Government Bill RegE 18/12038, *Entwurf eines Gesetzes zur strafrechtlichen Rehabilitierung der nach dem 8. Mai 1945 wegen einvernehmlicher homosexueller Handlungen verurteilten Personen und zur Änderung des Einkommensteuergesetzes [Draft Act on Criminal Law Rehabilitation of People Convicted of Consensual Homosexual Acts after 8 May 1945 and an Amendment of the Income Tax Act]* (2017).

Norway

Helsedirektoratet [The Norwegian Directorate of Health], *Veiledning i behandling av steriliseringssaker [Guidelines for Processing Sterilisation Files]*. Written by Karl Evang (1950).

Helsedirektoratet [The Norwegian Directorate of Health], *Behandlingstilbudet til transseksuelle og transpersoner i Norge: Helsedirektoratets gjennomgang og vurderinger 2011 [The Treatment Offered to Transsexual and Trans People in Norway: A 2011 Review and Evaluations by the Norwegian Directorate of Health]* (2011).

Helsedirektoratet [The Norwegian Directorate of Health], *Gjennomgang av behandlingstilbudet til transseksuelle og transpersoner [Review of the Treatments Offered to Transsexual and Trans People]* (2012).

Helsedirektoratet [The Norwegian Directorate of Health], *Rett till rett kjønn – helse till alle kjønn [Right to the Right Gender – Health for All Genders]* (2015).

Justis- og politidepartementet [The Norwegian Ministry of Justice and Public Security], *Instilling fra straffelovkomiteen, tredje del [Report from the Criminal Law Committee, Part Three]* (1932).

Justis- og politidepartementet [The Norwegian Ministry of Justice and Public Security], *Lovgivning om menneskerettigheter [Legislation on Human Rights]*. NOU 1993:18 (1993).

Justis- og politidepartementet [The Norwegian Ministry of Justice and Public Security], St.meld.nr. 44 (2003–2004), *Erstatningsordning for krigsbarn og erstatningsordninger for romanifolk/tatere og eldre utdanningsskadelidende samer og kvener [Compensation Schemes for War Children and Romani People/Tatere and Sámi and Kven Peoples Harmed by Education Policies]* (2004).

Justiskomiteen [The Norwegian Parliamentary Committee on Justice], Innst.O.nr.46, *Instilling til lov om adgang til sterilisering m.v. [Report on Act on the Access to Sterilisation etc.]* (1934).

Justiskomiteen [The Norwegian Parliamentary Committee on Justice], Innst.S.nr.39 (1996–1997), *Innstilling om forslag fra stortingsrepresentant Erling Folkvord [Report on Bill by MP Erling Folkvord*] (1996).

Justiskomiteen [The Norwegian Parliamentary Committee on Justice], Innst.O.nr.51 (1998–1999), *Innstilling om lov om styrking av menneskerettane si stilling i norsk rett [Report on Act on Reinforcing Human Rights in Norwegian Law]* (1999).

Justiskomiteen [The Norwegian Parliamentary Committee on Justice], Innst.O.nr.92 (2002–2003), *Innstilling om lov om endring i menneskerettsloven mv. [Report on Act on the Amendment of the Human Rights Act]* (2003).

Justiskomiteen [The Norwegian Parliamentary Committee on Justice], Innst.S.nr. 152 (2004–2005), *Innstilling om erstatningsordning for krigsbarn og erstatningsordninger for romanifolk/tatere og eldre utdanningsskadelidende samer og kvener [Report on Compensation Scheme for War Children and Compensation Schemes for Romani People/Tatere and Sámi and Kven Peoples Suffering from Education Policies]* (2004).

Justiskomiteen [The Norwegian Parliamentary Committee on Justice], *Innst.O.nr.115 (2008–2009), Innstilling om lov om endringar i menneskerettsloven mv. [Report on Act on Changes in the Human Rights Act etc.]* (2009).

Kommunal- og moderniseringsdepartementet [The Norwegian Ministry of Local Government and Modernisation], *Assimilering og motstand: Norsk politikk overfor tatere/romanifolket fra 1850 til i dag [Assimilation and Resistance: Norwegian Politics concerning Tatere/the Romani people from 1850 to Today]*, NOU 2015:7 (2015a).

Kommunal- og moderniseringsdepartementet [The Norwegian Ministry of Local Government and Modernisation], *Vedlegg til NOU 2015:7 [Annex to NOU 2015:7]* (2015b).

Kommunal- og regionaldepartementet [The Norwegian Ministry of Local Government], St.meld.nr. 15 (2000–2001) *Nasjonale minoritetar i Noreg – Om statleg politikk overfor jødar, kvener, rom, romanifolket og skogfinnar [National Minorities in Norway – On State Politics regarding Jews, Kven People, Roma, Romani People and Forest Finns]* (2000).

Kommunal- og regionaldepartementet [The Norwegian Ministry of Local Government], *Erstatning til tvangssteriliserte romanifolk/tatere [Compensation to Forcibly Sterilised Romani People/Tatere]* (2003).

Kommunalkomiteen [The Norwegian Parliamentary Committee on Local Government and Public Administration], Innst.S.nr. 145 (2000–2001) *Instilling fra kommunalkomiteen om Nasjonale minoritetar i Noreg – Om statleg politikk overfor jødar, kvener, rom, romanifolket og skogfinnar [Report from the Local Government Committee on National Minorities in Norway – About State Politics on Jews, Kven People, Roma, Romani People and Forest Finns]* (2001).

Kontroll- og konstitusjonskomiteen [The Norwegian Parliamentary Committee on Scrutiny and Constitutional Affairs], Innst.S.nr.172 (1993–1994) *Innstilling om ny bestemmelse av menneskerettigheter eller folkerett i Grunnloven [Report concerning the Incorporation of Human Rights Conventions in Norwegian Law on a New Regulation of Human Rights or International Law in the Constitution]* (1994).

Likestillings- og diskrimineringsombudet [The Norwegian Equality and Anti-discrimination Ombud], *Særskilt økonomisk kompensasjonsordning for personer som ble sterilisert for å endre juridisk kjønn [A Specially Established Financial Compensation Scheme for People who were Sterilised to Amend their Legally Registered Gender]*. Doc. No. 20/1049-3-HJFA (16 June 2020).

Medisinaldirektoratet [The Norwegian Directorate of Medicine], *Veiledning i behandling av steriliseringssaker [Guidelines for Processing Sterilisation Files]* (1938).

Norwegian Government Bill Ot.prp.nr. 17 (1934), *Lov om adgang til sterilisering m.v. [Act on the Access to Sterilisation Etc.]*.

Norwegian Government Bill St.prp.nr. 83 (1951), *Om innhentelse av Stortingets samtykke til at Norge tiltrer Europarådets konvensjon om beskyttelse av menneskerettighetene og de grunnleggende friheter [On Obtaining the Norwegian Parliament's Approval of Norway's Accession to the European Convention on Human Rights and Fundamental Freedoms]*.

Norwegian Government Bill Ot.prp.nr. 48 (1965–1966), *Om lov om skadeerstatning i visse forhold [On Act on Compensation under Certain Circumstances]*.

Norwegian Government Bill Ot.prp.nr. 38 (1974–1975), *Om lov om svangerskapsavbrudd [On Act on the Termination of Pregnancy]*.

Norwegian Government Bill Ot.prp.nr. 46 (1976–1977), *Om lov on sterilisering m.v. [On Act on Sterilisation etc]*.

Norwegian Government Bill Ot.prp.nr. 3 (1998–1999), *Om lov om styrking av menneskerettighetenes stilling i norsk rett [Government Bill on the Act on Reinforcing Human Rights in Norwegian Law]*.

Norwegian Government Bill St.prp.nr. 3 (1998–1999), *Om erstatning ved stråleskader etter brystkreftbehandling ved Radiumhospitalet 1975–86 [On Compensation for Radiation Damages after Breast Cancer Treatment at Radiumhospitalet 1975–86]*.

Norwegian Government Bill St.prp.nr. 67 (2000–2001), *Erstatning til norske statsborgere som satt i japansk fangenskap under 2. verdenskrig [Compensation to Norwegian Citizens who Were Prisoners of War in Japan During the Second World War]*.

Norwegian Government Bill Ot.prp.nr. 45 (2002–2003), *Om lov om endring i menneskerettsloven mv. [Government Bill on Amendment of the Human Rights Act etc]*.

Norwegian Government Bill Ot.prp.nr. 63 (2005–2006), *Om lov om endringer i lov om svangerskapsavbrudd og lov om sterilisering [On Act on Amendment in Act on Termination of Pregnancy and Act on Sterilisation]*.

Norwegian Government Bill Ot.prp.nr. 93 (2008–2009), *Om lov om endringar i menneskerettsloven mv. [Government Bill on Changes in the Human Rights Act]*.

Norwegian Government Bill Prop. 88 L (2012–2013), *Diskrimineringslovgivning [Discrimination Legislation]*.

Norwegian Government Bill Prop. 74 L (2015–2016), *Lov om endring av juridisk kjønn [Act on Amendment of Legal Gender]*.

Regjeringsadvokaten [The Office of the Attorney General of Norway], *Tilsvar til Oslo Tingrett [Plea before the Oslo Court of First Instance]*. Doc. No. 17-132417TVI-OTIR/08 (2017).

Sosialdepartementet [The Norwegian Ministry of Social Affairs], *Omstreiferne. Deres situasjon og samfunnets hjelpetiltak for dem [The Vagrants. Their Situation and Societal Aid Measures]*. NOU 1980:42 (1980).

Sosialdepartementet [The Norwegian Ministry of Social Affairs], *Utredning om lobotomi [Investigation on Lobotomy]*. NOU 1992:25 (1992).

Sosialkomiteen [The Norwegian Parliamentary Committee on Social Affairs], Innst.O.nr.62 (1976–77) *Instilling om lov om sterilisering m.v. [Report on Act on Sterilisation Etc.]* (1977).

Statens sivilrettsforvaltning [The Norwegian Civil Affairs Authority] *Søknadsskjema [Application Forms]*, www.sivilrett.no/soeknadsskjema.304224.no.html.

Stortinget [The Norwegian Parliament], *Stortingsforhandlinger [Norwegian Parliamentary Debates]* (1934).

Stortinget [The Norwegian Parliament], *Stortingsforhandlinger [Norwegian Parliamentary Debates]* (2000).

Stortinget [The Norwegian Parliament], *Stortingsforhandlinger [Norwegian Parliamentary Debates]* (2002).

Stortinget [The Norwegian Parliament], *Representantforslag 25 S (2020–2021) fra stortingsrepresentantene Nicholas Wilkinson, Solfrid Lerbrekk og Freddy André Øvstegård [Parliamentary Initiative 25 S (2020–2021) from the MPs Nicholas Wilkinson, Solfrid Lerbrekk and Freddy André Øvstegård]* (2020).

Utenriksdepartementet [The Norwegian Ministry of Foreign Affairs], St.meld.nr.21 (1999–2000) *Menneskeverd i sentrum: Handlingsplan for menneskerettigheter [Focus on Human Dignity: Action Plan for Human Rights]* (1999).

Sweden

Arbetsmarknadsdepartementet [The Swedish Ministry of Employment], *Jämställdhet i arbetslivet. Lag om jämställdhet [Equality in Working Life. Act on Equality]*. SOU 1978:38 (1978).

Delegationen för mänskliga rättigheter i Sverige [The Delegation for Human Rights in Sweden], *Ny struktur för skydd av de mänskliga rättigheterna [New Structure for the Protection of Human Rights]*. SOU 2010:70 (2010).

Justitiedepartementet [The Swedish Ministry of Justice], *Förslag till lag om sterilisering av vissa sinnessjuka, sinnesslöa eller av annan rubbning av själsverksamheten lidande personer [Proposal of Act concerning Sterilisation of Certain People who are Insane, Feebleminded or Suffering from Other Mental Disorders]*. SOU 1933:22 (1933).

Justitiedepartementet [The Swedish Ministry of Justice], *Betänkande med förslag till lagstiftning om avbrytande av havandeskap [Report with Proposal of Legislation concerning Termination of Pregnancy]*. SOU 1935:15 (1935).

Justitiedepartementet [The Swedish Ministry of Justice], *Åtgärder för bekämpande av homosexualitetens samhällsfarliga yttringar [Actions to Combat the Social Dangers of Homosexuality]*. SOU 1941:3 (1941a).

Justitiedepartementet [The Swedish Ministry of Justice], *Strafflagsberedningens promemoria med förslag till lag om kastrering m.m. [The Memorandum of the Penal Law Advisory Committee with Proposal of Castration Act etc.]*. SOU 1941:24 (1941b).

Justitiedepartementet [The Swedish Ministry of Justice], *Strafflagberedningens utlåtande med förslag till lagstiftning angående åtgärder mot homosexualitetens samhällsfarliga yttringar [The Report of the Penal Law Advisory Committee concerning Actions to Combat the Social Dangers of Homosexuality]*. SOU 1941:32 (1941c).

Justitiedepartementet [The Swedish Ministry of Justice], *Intersexuellas könstillhörighet [The Gender Recognition of Intersexuals]*. SOU 1968:28 (1968).

Justitiedepartementet [The Swedish Ministry of Justice], *Fri sterilisering [Free Sterilisation]*. SOU 1974:25 (1974).

Justitiedepartementet [The Swedish Ministry of Justice], *Medborgerliga fri- och rättigheter [Civil Freedoms and Rights]*. SOU 1975:75 (1975).

Justitiedepartementet [The Swedish Ministry of Justice], *Förstärkt skydd för fri- och rättigheter [Reinforced Protection for Freedoms and Rights]*. SOU 1978:34 (1978).

Justitiedepartementet [The Swedish Ministry of Justice], *Skadestånd och Europakonventionen [Compensation and the European Convention]*. SOU 2010:87 (2010).

Konstitutionsutkottet [The Swedish Parliamentary Committee on the Constitution], *Betänkande med anledning av propositionen 1973:90 med förslag till ny regeringsform och ny riksdagsordning m.m. jämte motioner [Report concerning Government Bill 1973:90 with Proposal of a New Government Act and a New Parliament Act etc.]*. KU 1973:26 (1973).

Konstitutionsutkottet [The Swedish Parliamentary Committee on the Constitution], *Betänkande med anledning av motioner om avslag på vilande förslag till ny regeringsform och ny riksdagsordning m.m. [Report based on Motions concerning Rejection of Proposals about a New Government Act and a New Parliament Act, etc.]*. KU 1974:7 (1974).

Konstitutionsutkottet [The Swedish Parliamentary Committee on the Constitution], *Betänkande med anledning av propositionen 1978/79:195 om förstärkt skydd för fri- och rättigheter m.m. jämte motioner [Report concerning the Government Bill 1978/79:195 on Strengthened Protection of Freedoms and Rights etc. with Bills]*. KU 1978/79:39 (1979).

Konstitutionsutkottet [The Swedish Parliamentary Committee on the Constitution], *Betänkande: Skadestånd och Europakonventionen [Report: Damages and the European Convention]*, KU 2017/18:12 (2018).

Kungliga medicinalstyrelsen [The Swedish Royal Board of Medicine], *Råd och anvisningar rörande tillämpning av steriliserings- och abortlagarna [Advice and Instructions for the Implementation of the Sterilisation and Abortion Acts]*. Meddelanden från Kungliga Medicinalstyrelsen [Messages from the Swedish Royal Board of Medicine] 84/1939 (1939).

Kungliga medicinalstyrelsen [The Swedish Royal Board of Medicine], *Råd och anvisningar rörande tillämpning av 1941 års steriliseringslag och abortlagen [Advice and Instructions for the Implementation of the 1941 Sterilisation Act and the Abortion Act]*. Meddelanden från Kungliga Medicinalstyrelsen [Messages from the Swedish Royal Board of Medicine] 88/1943 (1943).

Kungliga medicinalstyrelsen [The Swedish Royal Board of Medicine], *Råd och anvisningar rörande tillämpning av 1941 års steriliseringslag och abortlagen. Till läkare och övriga medverkande [Advice and Instructions for the Implementation of the 1941 Sterilisation Act and the Abortion Act. To Medical Doctors and Other Participants]*.

Meddelanden från Kungliga Medicinalstyrelsen [Messages from the Swedish Royal Board of Medicine] 93/1947 (1947).

Kungliga medicinalstyrelsen [The Swedish Royal Board of Medicine], *Allmän hälso- och sjukvård 1967 [Public Healthcare 1967]* (1967).

Kungliga medicinalstyrelsen [The Swedish Royal Board of Medicine], *Allmän hälso- och sjukvård 1969 [Public Healthcare 1969]* (1969).

Regeringskansliet [The Government Offices of Sweden], *Den mörka och okända historien. Vitbok om övergrepp och kränkningar av romer under 1900-talet [The Dark and Unknown History. Report on Abuse and Violations against Romani People during the 20th Century]*. Ds 2014:8.

Riksdagen [The Swedish Parliament], *Första kammaren: Motion nr. 38 [First Chamber Bill No. 38]* (1922).

Riksdagens ombudsmän [The Swedish Parliamentary Ombudsmen], *Ämbetsberättelse [Annual Report]* (1947).

Socialdepartementet [The Swedish Ministry of Health and Social Affairs], *Betänkande med förslag till steriliseringslag [Report Proposing Sterilisation Act]*. SOU 1929:14 (1929).

Socialdepartementet [The Swedish Ministry of Health and Social Affairs], *Betänkande angående sterilisering [Report Concerning Sterilisation]*. SOU 1936:22 (1936).

Socialdepartementet [The Swedish Ministry of Health and Social Affairs], *Steriliseringsfrågor i Sverige 1935–1975 – Ekonomisk ersättning [Sterilisation Issues in Sweden 1935–1975 – Financial Compensation]*. SOU 1999:2 (1999).

Socialdepartementet [The Swedish Ministry of Health and Social Affairs], *Från politik till praktik – De svenska steriliseringslagarna 1935–1975 [From Policy to Practice – The Swedish Sterilisation Laws 1935–1975]*. SOU 2000:22 (2000a).

Socialdepartementet [The Swedish Ministry of Health and Social Affairs], *Steriliseringsfrågan i Sverige [The Sterilisation Issue in Sweden]*. SOU 2000:20 (2000b).

Socialdepartementet [The Swedish Ministry of Health and Social Affairs], *Rapport över Steriliseringsersättningssnämndens verksamhet [Report concerning the Activities of the Sterilisation Compensation Committee]* (2004).

Socialdepartementet [The Swedish Ministry of Health and Social Affairs], *Ändrad könstillhörighet – förslag till ny lag [Gender Recognition – Proposal regarding New Legislation]*. SOU 2007:16 (2007).

Socialdepartementet [The Swedish Ministry of Health and Social Affairs], *Barnen som samhället svek – åtgärder med anledning av övergrepp och allvarliga försummelser i samhällsvården [The Children Let Down by Society – Actions due to Abuse and Serious Negligence in State Social Care]*. SOU 2011:9 (2011).

Socialdepartementet [The Swedish Ministry of Health and Social Affairs], *Förslag till lag om ersättning till personer som har fått ändrad könstillhörighet fastställd i vissa fall [Proposition for Act on Compensation to People who Have Obtained Legal Gender Recognition under Certain Circumstances]*. Ds 2017:6 (2017a).

Socialdepartementet [The Swedish Ministry of Health and Social Affairs], *Lagrådsremiss: Statlig ersättning till personer som fått ändrad könstillhörighet i vissa fall [Law Council Referral: State Compensation to People Have Obtained Legal Gender Recognition under Certain Circumstances]* (2017b).

Socialstyrelsen [The Swedish National Board of Health and Welfare], *Transsexuella och övriga personer med könsidentitetsstörningar. Rättsliga villkor för fastställande av könstillhörighet samt vård och stöd. [Transsexuals and Other People with Gender Identity Incongruence. Legal Conditions for Gender Recognition, Care and Support]* Socialstyrelsen 2010-6-31 (2010).

Socialutskottet [The Swedish Parliamentary Committee on Health and Welfare], *Nya regler för ändrad könstillhörighet [Changed Rules regarding Legal Gender Recognition].* Socialutskottets betänkande2011/13:SoU23 (2012).

Socialutskottet [The Swedish Parliamentary Committee on Health and Welfare], *Ersättning av staten till personer som utsatts för övergrepp eller försummelser i samhällsvården [State Compensation to People who Have Experienced Abuse or Negligence in State Social Care].* Socialutskottets betänkande 2012/13: SoU3 (2012).

Socialutskottet [The Swedish Parliamentary Committee on Health and Welfare], *Upphävande av kravet på sterilisering för ändrad könstillhörighet [The Abolition of the Sterilisation Precondition for Legal Gender Recognition].* Socialutskottets betänkande 2012/13:SoU24 (2013).

Swedish Government Bill Prop. 1934:103, *Kunglig Majestäts proposition med förslag till lag om sterilisering av vissa sinnessjuka, sinnesslöa eller andra som lida av rubbad själsverksamhet [Royal Bill with Proposal of Act on Sterilisation of Certain People who are Insane, Feebleminded or Suffering from Other Mental Disorders].*

Swedish Government Bill Prop. 1941:13, *Kunglig Majestäts proposition med förslag till lag om sterilisering m.m. [Royal Bill with Proposal of Sterilisation Act etc.]*

Swedish Government Bill Prop. 1944:14, *Kunglig Majestäts proposition med förslag till lag om kastrering, m.m. [Royal Bill with Proposal of Castration Act, etc.].*

Swedish Government Bill Prop. 1951:165, *Kunglig Majestäts proposition angående godkännande av Sveriges anslutning till Europarådets konvention angående skydd för de mänskliga rättigheterna och de grundläggande friheterna [Royal Bill concerning the Approval of Sweden Joining the Council of Europe Convention for the Protection of Human Rights and Fundamental Freedoms].*

Swedish Government Bill Prop. 1966:33, *Kunglig Majestäts proposition om förklaring enligt artikel 46 i Europarådets konvention angående skydd för de mänskliga rättigheterna och de grundläggande friheterna [Royal Bill on Declaration According to Article 46 in the Council of Europe Convention for the Protection of Human Rights and Fundamental Freedoms].*

Swedish Government Bill Prop. 1971:30, *Kunglig Majestäts proposition med förslag till lag om allmänna förvaltningsdomstolar, m.m. [Royal Bill with Proposal of Act on Administrative Courts, etc.].*

Swedish Government Bill Prop. 1972:5, *Kunglig Majestäts proposition med förslag till skadeståndslag m.m. [Royal Bill with Proposal of Liability Act etc].*

Swedish Government Bill Prop. 1972:6, *Kunglig Majestäts proposition med förslag till lag om fastställande av könstillhörighet i vissa fall [Royal Bill with Proposal of Act on Legal Gender Recognition under Certain Circumstances].*

Swedish Government Bill Prop. 1973:90, *Kunglig Majestäts propsition med förslag till ny regeringsform och ny riksdagsordning m.m. [Royal Bill with Proposal of a New Government Act and a New Parliament Act etc].*

Swedish Government Bill Prop. 1974:70, *Kunglig Majestäts proposition med förslag till abortlag, m.m. [Royal Bill with Proposal of Abortion Act etc].*

Swedish Government Bill Prop. 1975:18, *Förslag till steriliseringslag, m.m. [Proposal of Sterilisation Law, etc.].*

Swedish Government Bill Prop. 1978/79:175, *Förslag till lag om jämställdhet mellan män och kvinnor i arbetslivet, m.m. [Proposal of Act on Equality between Men and Women in Working Life, etc].*

Swedish Government Bill Prop. 1978/79:195, *Förstärkt skydd för fri- och rättigheter m.m. [Reinforced Protection for Freedoms and Rights etc].*

Swedish Government Bill Prop. 1992/93:197, *Ändring i lagen om fastställande av könstillhörighet i vissa fall, m.m. [Amendment of the Act on Legal Gender Recognition under Certain Circumstances etc].*

Swedish Government Bill Prop. 1998/99:71, *Ersättning av staten till steriliserade i vissa fall [Compensation by the State to Sterilised People under Certain Circumstances].*

Swedish Government Bill Prop. 2009/10:80, *En reformerad grundlag [A Reformed Constitution].*

Swedish Government Bill Prop. 2011/12:142, *Ändrad könstillhörighet [Legal Gender Recognition].*

Swedish Government Bill Prop. 2011/12:160, *Ersättning av staten till personer som utsatts för övergrepp eller försummelser i samhällsvården [State Compensation to People who Have Experienced Abuse and Negligence in State Social Care].*

Swedish Government Bill Prop. 2012/13:107, *Upphörande av kravet på sterilisering för ändrad könstillhörighet [Abolition of the Requirement of Sterilisation for Gender Recognition].*

Swedish Government Bill Prop. 2017/18:7, *Skadestånd och Europakonventionen [Damages and the European Convention].*

Swedish Government Bill Prop. 2017/18:64, *Statlig ersättning till personer som har fått ändrad könstillhörighet fastställd i vissa fall [State Compensation to People who Have Obtained Legal Gender Recognition under Certain Circumstances].*

Swedish Government Letter, *Redogörelse för steriliseringsfrågan i Sverige åren 1935–1975 och regeringens åtgärder [Report on the Sterilisation Issue in Sweden 1935–1975 and the Measures Taken by the Government].* Skr. 2000/01:73.

Literature

Aas, Ingeborg, *Hvordan kan samfundet beskytte sig mot åndssvake og sedelighetsforbrytere [How Society Can Protect Itself against Feebleminded People and Morality Offenders].* Olaf Norlis forlag (1932).

Aasen, Henriette S, *Rasehygiene og menneskeverd: Nasjonalsosialismens steriliseringslov av 23. juli 1942 [Racial Hygiene and Human Dignity: The National Socialist Sterilisation Act of 23 July 1942].* Kvinnerettslige studier, Institutt for offentlig rett [Studies in Women's Law, Institute for Public Law] (1989).

Ahlander, Johan, 'Sweden to Offer Compensation for Transgender Sterilizations'. *Reuters,* www.reuters.com/article/us-sweden-transgender-sterilisation-idUSKBN16Y1XA (27 March 2017).

Åhman, Karin, *Grundläggande rättigheter och juridisk metod [Fundamental Rights and Legal Method].* Norstedts juridik (2015).

Åhman, Karin, '2 kap. RF, Europakonventionen och EU:s stadga om grundläggande rättigheter – en jämförelse [The Second Chapter of the Swedish Government Act, the European Convention and the EU Charter on Fundamental Rights – A Comparison]'. In Stefan Strömberg, Charlotte Kugelberg, Petter Asp, Anders Eka, Boel Flodgren &

Mikael Mellqvist (eds), *Svensk Juristtidning 100 år [Svensk Juristtidning 100 Years Anniversary]*. Iustus (2016), 460–478.

Akre, Stein, 'Transpersoner tvunget til sterilisering [Trans People Forced into Sterilisation]'. *TV2*, www.tv2.no/a/3972687 (24 January 2013).

Alaattinoğlu, Daniela, *Svar på förslag till lag om ersättning till personer som har fått ändrad könstillhörighet fastställd i vissa fall [Answer to Proposal for Act on Compensation to People Who Have Obtained Legal Gender Recognition under Certain Circumstances]*. Doc. No. S2017/01918/FS, Statement to the Swedish Government (2017).

Alaattinoğlu, Daniela, 'Forced Sterilisation in the Istanbul Convention: Remedies, Intersectional Discrimination and Cis-Exclusiveness'. In Johanna Niemi, Lourdes Peroni & Vladislava Stoyanova (eds), *International Law and Violence against Women: Europe and the Istanbul Convention*. Routledge (2020), 173–188.

Alaattinoğlu, Daniela, 'Ersättning och gottgörelse för kastrering och sterilisering av transpersoner i Sverige och Norge [Compensation and Remedies for Castration and Sterilisation of Trans People in Sweden and Norway]'. In Anne Hellum & Anniken Sørlie (eds), *Frihet, likhet og mangfold [Freedom, Equality and Diversity]*. Gyldendal (2021), 146–178.

Alaattinoğlu, Daniela & Rubio-Marín, Ruth, 'Redress for Involuntarily Sterilised Trans People in Sweden against Evolving Human Rights Standards: A Critical Appraisal'. *Human Rights Law Review* vol. 19 no. 4 (2019), 705–732.

Alaattinoğlu, Daniela & Sørlie, Anniken, 'Sverige gir steriliserte transpersoner erstatning. Det bør Norge også gjøre [Sweden Pays Compensation to Sterilised Trans People. Norway Should Do the Same]'. *Aftenposten*, www.aftenposten.no/meninger/kronikk/i/naMMWx/sverige-gir-steriliserte-transpersoner-erstatning-det-boer-norge-ogsaa (6 June 2019).

Alanko, Antti & Achté, Kalle, 'Transsexualism'. Psychiatrica Fennica (1971), 343–358.

Alm, Erika, *"Ett emballage för inälvor och emotioner": föreställningar om kroppen i statliga utredningar från 1960- och 1970-talen ["A Wrapping for Innards and Emotions": Ideas about the Body in State Investigations from the 1960s and 1970s]*. University of Gothenburg, PhD thesis (2006).

Alvheim & Hansen Advokatfirma, *Stevning til Oslo Tingrett [Lawsuit before Oslo Court of First Instance]* (2017).

Ambos, Kai, *Treatise on International Criminal Law. Volume II: The Crimes and Sentencing*. Oxford University Press (2014).

Amnesty International, *The State Decides Who I Am*. Amnesty International Publications (2014).

Amnesty International, *A Breakthrough for Transgender People's Rights in Norway: John Jeanette's Journey*, www.amnesty.org/en/latest/campaigns/2015/04/a-breakthrough-for-transgender-peoples-rights-in-norway-john-jeanettes-journey/ (13 April 2015).

Amnesty International, *Czech Republic: Hard Won Justice for Women Survivors of Unlawful Sterilization*, www.amnesty.org/en/latest/press-release/2021/07/czech-republic-hard-won-justice-for-women-survivors-of-unlawful-sterilization/ (22 July 2021).

Amnesty International Norway, *Tvinges til sterilisering [Forced to Get Sterilised]*, www.amnesty.no/aktuelt/flere-nyheter/tvinges-til-sterilisering (25 May 2012).

Amnesty International Norway, *Støtteskriv fra Amnesty International til Oslo tingrett i sak 17-132417TVI-OTIR/08 [Amicus Curiae from Amnesty International to Oslo Court of First Instance in the Matter 17-132417TVI-OTIR/08]*. Letter to the court (2018).

Andenæs, Mads & Bjørge, Eirik, *Menneskerettene og oss [Human Rights and Us]*. Universitetsforlaget (2012).

Andersen, Ellen A, *Out of the Closets and into the Courts: Legal Opportunity Structure and Gay Rights Litigation*. The University of Michigan Press (2005).

Anderson, David, *Histories of the Hanged: The Dirty War in Kenya and the End of Empire*. Weidenfeld & Nicholson (2005).

Andersson, Olov, *En sammanställning av debatten i Dagens Nyheter augusti–oktober 1997 om steriliseringspolitiken i Sverige 1935–1976 [A Compilation of the Debate in Dagens Nyheter August–October 1997 about the Sterilisation Policies in Sweden 1935–1976]*. FUB Publications (1997).

Andersson, Olov, *Några trådar i FUB-väven. Om Riksförbundet för utvecklingsstörda barn, ungdomar och vuxna, FUB, från tidigt 1950-tal till 1980-tal [Some Threads in the FUB Fabric. On the Swedish National Association for Persons with Intellectual Disability, FUB, From the Early 1950s to the 1980s]*. FUB Publications (2002).

Andresen, Astri & Elvbakken, Kari T, 'Fødselskontroll, barnehelse og kvinners rettigheter og plikter [Birth Control, Children's Health and Women's Rights and Duties]'. *Tidsskrift for kjønnsforskning* vol. 42 no. 1–2 (2018), 67–84.

Anttila, Inkeri, *Loukatun suostumus oikeudenvastaisuuden poistavana perusteena [The Consent of the Injured Party as a Legally Justifying Ground]*. Suomalainen Lakimiesyhdistys A No. 26 (1946).

Arvidsson, Malin, *Att ersätta det oersättliga: statlig gottgörelse för ofrivillig sterilisering och vanvård av omhändertagna barn [Compensation of Irretrievable Matters: State Redress for Involuntary Sterilisation and Abuse in Out-of-Home Care for Children]*. Örebro Studies in History 18, Bokpro (2016).

Aultman, B, 'Cisgender'. *Transgender Studies Quarterly* vol. 1 no. 1–2 (2014), 61–62.

Axelsson, Majgull, *Den sterila debatten: handikapp, steriliseringar, välfärd [The Sterile Debate: Handicap, Sterilisations, Welfare]*. Thélème (1997).

Barclay, Scott, Jones, Lynn C & Marshall, Anna-Maria, 'Two Spinning Wheels: Studying Law and Social Movements'. *Studies in Law, Politics, and Society* no. 54 (2011), 1–16.

Barkan, Steven E, 'Legal Control of the Southern Civil Rights Movement'. *American Sociological Review* vol. 49 no. 4 (1984), 552–565.

Barow, Thomas, *Kein Platz im Volksheim? Die 'Schwachsinnigenfürsorge' in Schweden 1916–1945 [No Place in the People's Home? The 'Care of the Feebleminded' in Sweden 1916–1945]*. Verlag Julius Klinkhardt (2009).

Bastrup, Olav RE & Sivertsen, Aage G, *En landevei mot undergangen: utryddelsen av taterkulturen i Norge [A Road towards Destruction: The Extermination of Tatere Culture in Norway]*. Universitetsforlaget (1996).

Bell, Derrick A, '*Brown v. Board of Education* and the Interest-Convergence Dilemma'. *Harvard Law Review* vol. 93 no. 3 (1980), 518–533.

Bender, Leslie, 'Changing the Values in Tort Law'. *Tulsa Law Review* vol. 25 no. 4 (1990), 759–773.

Bengtsson, Bertil, *Det allmännas ansvar enligt skadeståndslagen [Public Liability According to the Liability Act]*. Nordstedts Juridik (1996).

Bengtsson, Bertil, 'Om *ex gratia*-ersättning [On Compensation *Ex Gratia*]'. *Svensk juristtidning* no. 3 (2009), 325–339.

Bengtsson, Bertil, 'Barnkonventionen och rättighetstänkandet [The Child Convention and Rights Thinking]'. *Advokaten* vol. 82 no. 8 (2016), 44–46.

Benjamin, Harry, *The Transsexual Phenomenon*. The Julian Press (1966).

Benjamin, Harry, 'Transvestism and Transsexualism in the Male and Female'. *The Journal of Sex Research* vol. 3 no. 2 (1967), 107–127.

Bindreiter, Uta, *Lagprövningsdebatten 1955–1966: i skärningsfältet mellan juridik och politik [The Debate on Judicial Review 1955–1966: In the Intersection of Law and Politics]*. Juristförlaget i Lund (2009).

Björkman, Maria, *Den anfrätta stammen: Nils von Hofsten, eugeniken och steriliseringarna 1909–63 [The Corroded Breed: Nils von Hofsten, Eugenics and the Sterilisations 1909–63]*. Arkiv (2011).

Black, Edwin, *War against the Weak: Eugenics and America's Campaign to Create a Master Race*. Dialog Press (2012).

Bock, Gisela, 'Racism and Sexism in Nazi Germany: Motherhood, Compulsory Sterilization, and the State'. *Signs* vol. 8 no. 3 (1983), 400–421.

Bock, Gisela, 'Antinatalism, Maternity and Paternity in National Socialist Racism'. In Gisela Bock & Pat Thane (eds) *Maternity and Gender Policies: Women and the Rise of the European Welfare States, 1880s–1950s*. Routledge (1991), 233–255.

Borgström, CA, *Tillämpningen av lagen om sterilisering i Finland [Implementation of the Sterilisation Act in Finland]*. Bidrag till kännedom av Finlands natur och folk (1958).

Bosi, Lorenzo, 'Incorporation and Democratization: The Long-term Process of Institutionalization of the Northern Ireland Civil Rights Movement'. In Lorenzo Bosi, Marco Giugni & Katrin Uba (eds), *The Consequences of Social Movements*. Cambridge University Press (2016), 338–360.

Bourke, Joanna, *Rape: A History from 1860 to the Present*. Virago (2007).

Braun, Kathrin; Herrmann, Svea L & Brekke, Ole A, 'Sterilization Policies, Moral Rehabilitation and the Politics of Amends'. *Critical Policy Studies*, vol. 8 no. 2 (2014), 203–226.

Bremer, Johan, *Asexualization: A Follow-up Study of 244 Cases*. Oslo University Press (1958).

Bremer, Signe, *Kroppslinjer: kön, transsexualism och kropp i berättelser om könskorrigering [Body Lines: Sex, Transsexualism and Body in Stories about Gender Reassignment]*. Makadam (2011).

Bremer, Pirkkoliisa, *Mikä on Trasek, mikä on transseksuaali [What is Trasek, What is Transsexual]*. Seta Publications (1991).

Brigham, John, 'Right, Rage, and Remedy: Forms of Law in Political Discourse'. *Studies in American Political Development* vol. 2 (1988), 303–316.

Broch, Lars O, '"Strict" or "Liberal" Interpretation? Comments on Norway'. In Eivind Smith (ed), *The Constitution as an Instrument of Change*. SNS Forlag (2003), 242–249.

Broberg, Gunnar & Roll-Hansen, Nils (eds), *Eugenics and the Welfare State: Norway, Sweden, Denmark, and Finland*. Michigan State University Press (2005).

Broberg, Gunnar & Tydén, Mattias, *Oönskade i folkhemmet [Unwanted in the People's Home*]. Gidlunds (1991).

Broberg, Gunnar & Tydén, Mattias, 'När svensk historia blev en världsnyhet: steriliseringspolitiken och medierna [When Swedish History Became World News: The Sterilisation Politics and the Media]'. *Tvärsnitt* vol. 20 no. 3 (1998), 2–15.

Broberg, Gunnar & Tydén, Mattias, 'Eugenics in Sweden: Efficient Care'. In Gunnar Broberg & Nils Roll-Hansen (eds), *Eugenics and the Welfare State: Norway, Sweden, Denmark, and Finland*. Michigan State University Press (2005), 77–149.

Bruzelius, Karin M, 'Hvor stor betydning har Strasbourg for norsk rett? [How Important Is Strasbourg for Norwegian Law?]'. *Rett På Sak: Aktualitetsmagasin for Domstolene* no. 4 (2008), 30–32.

Bukowska-Jakobsson, Monica; Edbom, Tobias; Fried, Ingegärd; Rydelius, Per-Anders & Henriksson, Christer, 'En kartläggning [A Mapping Exercise]'. In Socialdepartementet [The Swedish Ministry of Health and Social Affairs], *Steriliseringsfrågan i Sverige [The Sterilisation Issue in Sweden]*. SOU 2000:20 (2000), 147–278.

Burman, Kerstin & RFSL, *Ansökan om skadestånd för tvångssterilisering [Application for Compensation for Forced Sterilisation]*, www.rfsl.se/wp-content/uploads/2015/11/JK_ansokan.pdf (2013).

Butler, Judith, *Frames of War: When Is Life Grievable?* Verso Books (2016).

Cáceres, Carlos, Cueto, Marcos & Palomino, Nancy, 'Sexual and Reproductive Rights Policies in Peru: Unveiling False Paradoxes'. In Richard Parker, Rosalind Petchesky & Robert Sember (eds), *SexPolitics: Reports from the Front Lines*. Sexuality Policy Watch (2007), 127–166.

Cahn, Claude, *Human Rights, State Sovereignty and Medical Ethics. Examining Struggles Around Coercive Sterilisation of Romani Women*. Brill (2014).

Cameron, Iain, 'Normkonflikter och EKMR [Norm Conflicts and the ECHR]'. *Svensk juristtidning* no. 9 (2007), 851–861.

Case, Mary Anne, 'Perfectionism and Fundamentalism in the Application of German Abortion Laws'. In Susan H Williams (ed), *Constituting Equality: Gender Equality and Comparative Constitutional Law*. Cambridge University Press (2009), 93–106.

Center for Reproductive Rights, *Reproductive Rights in the Inter-American System for the Promotion and Protection of Human Rights*. Center for Reproductive Rights Publications (2002).

Center for Reproductive Rights; Poradna pre obcianske a l'udské práva [Centre for Civil and Human Rights] & Zoon, Ina, *Body and Soul: Forced Sterilization and Other Assaults on Roma Reproductive Freedom in Slovakia*. Center for Reproductive Rights Publications (2003).

Chabanet, Didier & Royall, Frédéric, 'From Social Movement Analysis to Contentious Politics'. In Didier Chabanet & Frédéric Royall (eds), *From Silence to Protest: International Perspectives on Weakly Resourced Groups*. Ashgate (2014), 1–18.

Charlesworth, Hilary, 'Human Rights as Men's Rights'. In Julie Peters & Andrea Wolper (eds), *Women's Rights, Human Rights: International Feminist Perspectives*. Routledge (1995), 103–113.

Charlesworth, Hilary, 'Feminist Methods in International Law'. *Studies in Transnational Legal Policy* vol. 36 (2004), 159–184.

Christie, Nils, 'The Ideal Victim'. In Ezzat A Fattah (ed), *From Crime Policy to Victim Policy*. Palgrave Macmillan (1986), 17–30.

Chua, Lynette J, 'Pragmatic Resistance, Law, and Social Movements in Authoritarian States: The Case of Gay Collective Action in Singapore'. *Law & Society Review* vol. 46 no. 4 (2012), 713–748.

Chua, Lynette J, *The Politics of Rights and Southeast Asia*. Cambridge University Press (2022).

Chua, Lynette J & Engel, David M, 'Legal Consciousness'. In Mariana Valverde, Kamari Clarke, Eve Darian-Smith & Prabha Kotiswaran (eds), *The Routledge Handbook of Law and Society*. Routledge (2021), 187–191.

Cohen, Adam, *Imbeciles: The Supreme Court, American Eugenics, and the Sterilization of Carrie Buck*. Penguin Press (2016).

Crawford, James, *State Responsibility: The General Part*. Cambridge University Press (2013).

Curran, Siobhan, 'Intersectionality and Human Rights Law: An Examination of the Coercive Sterilisations of Romani Women'. *The Equal Rights Review* vol. 16 (2016), 132–159.

Curry, Lynne, *The Human Body on Trial: A Sourcebook with Cases, Laws, and Documents*. Hackett Publishing (2002).

Dagens Nyheter, *P-pillret firar 50 år [The Pill Celebrates 50 Years]*, www.dn.se/nyheter/sverige/p-pillret-firar-50-ar/ (9 May 2010).

Dagens Nyheter, *Kastrering testas på pedofiler [Castration Is Tested on Pedophiles]*, www.dn.se/nyheter/sverige/kastrering-testas-pa-pedofiler/ (3 August 2016).

Dahlgren, Peter, 'Steril [Infertile]'. *Tidningarnas Telegrambyrå* (22 August 1986).

Dambrofsky, Gwen, 'Alberta Woman who Successfully Sued Province for Wrongful Sterilization Dies'. *Global News*, globalnews.ca/news/2580660/alberta-woman-who-successfully-sued-province-for-wrongful-sterilization-dies/ (16 March 2016).

De Búrca, Gráinne, *Reframing Human Rights in a Turbulent Era*. Oxford University Press (2021).

De Fazio, Gianluca, 'Legal Opportunity Structure and Social Movement Strategy in Northern Ireland and Southern United States'. *International Journal of Comparative Sociology* vol. 53 no. 1 (2012), 3–22.

De Los Reyes, Paulina, *Ett olösligt problem. Rapport om steriliseringslagarnas konsekvenser för romer och resande [An Unsolvable Problem. Report concerning the Consequences of the Sterilisation Laws for Romani and Travelling People]*. A2012/1901/DISK (2012).

De Los Reyes, Paulina, *Romsk och resandetillhörighet i ansökningar om sterilisering i mitten av 1940-talet [Romani and Travelling Association in Applications about Sterilisation in the Middle of the 1940s]*. A2013/1174/DISK (2013).

Della Porta, Donatella, 'In-depth Interviews'. In Donatella della Porta (ed), *Methodological Practices in Social Movement Research*. Oxford University Press (2014), 228–261.

Della Porta, Donatella, 'Democracy in Social Movements'. In Donatella Della Porta & Mario Diani (eds), *The Oxford Handbook of Social Movements*. Oxford University Press (2015), 767–780.

Demus, *Justicia de Género. Esterilización Forzada en el Perú: Delito de lesa Humanidad. [Gender Justice. Forced Sterilisation in Peru: Crime against Humanity]*. Demus (2008).

Demus, *Caso Esterilizaciones Forcadas [The Case of Forced Sterilisations]*, www.demus.org.pe/casos-emblematicos/caso-esterilizaciones-forzadas/ (8 May 2015).

Den Norske Helsingforskomite [The Norwegian Helsinki Committee], *Norsk romani-/taterpolitikk: fortid, nåtid, fremtid [Norwegian Romani/Tater Policy: Past, Present, Future]*. NHC Publications (2009).

Derlén, Mattias & Lindholm, Johan, 'Judiciell aktivism eller prejudikatbildning? En empirisk granskning av Högsta domstolen [Judicial Activism or Setting Precedents? An Empirical Examination of the Supreme Court]'. *Svensk juristtidning* no. 2 (2016), 143–159.

Desmet, Ellen, 'Methodologies to Study Human Rights Law as an Integrated Whole from a Users' Perspective: Lessons Learnt'. In Eva Brems & Saïla Ouald-Chaib (eds),

Fragmentation and Integration in Human Rights Law: Users' Perspectives. Edward Elgar Publishing (2018), 12–38.

Dittrich, Boris O, 'Sweden: Letter to the Prime Minister Regarding Transgender Law'. *Human Rights Watch*, www.hrw.org/news/2012/01/14/sweden-letter-prime-minister-regarding-transgender-law (14 January 2012).

Drake, MJ; Mills, IW & Cranston D, 'On the Chequered History of Vasectomy'. *BJU International* vol. 84 no. 4 (1999), 475–481.

D'Souza, Radha, *What's Wrong with Rights? Social Movements, Law and Liberal Imaginations*. Pluto Books (2018).

Dunne, Peter, 'Transgender Sterilisation Requirements in Europe'. *Medical Law Review* vol. 25 no. 4 (2017), 554–581.

Durbach, Andrea, '"The Cost of a Wounded Society": Reparations and the Illusion of Reconciliation'. *Australian Indigenous Law Review* vol. 12 no. 1 (2008), 22–40.

Edenheim, Sara, *Begärets lagar: moderna statliga utredningar och heteronormativitetens genealogi [The Laws of Desire: Modern State Investigations and the Genealogy of Heteronormativity]*. Brutus Östlings förlag (2005).

Edwards, Alice, 'The "Feminizing" of Torture under International Human Rights Law'. *Leiden Journal of International Law* vol. 19 no. 2 (2006), 349–391.

Edwards, Tim, *Cultures of Masculinity*. Routledge (2006).

Ehrenfreund, Norbert, *The Nuremberg Legacy: How the Nazi War Crimes Changed the Course of History*. Palgrave Macmillan (2007).

Eivergård, Mikael & Jönsson, Lars-Eric, 'Mellan tvång och frivillighet i 1,074 steriliseringsakter 1935–1975 [Between Coercion and Free Will in 1,074 Sterilisation Files 1935–1975]'. In Socialdepartementet [The Swedish Ministry of Health and Social Affairs], *Steriliseringsfrågan i Sverige [The Sterilisation Issue in Sweden]*. SOU 2000:20 (2000), 59–130.

Elkins, Caroline, *Imperial Reckoning: The Untold Story of Britain's Gulag in Kenya*. Jonathan Cape (2005).

Elmgren, Ainur, 'The Nazi's Cloven Hoof: Finnish Critiques of Legal Sterilisation'. In Johannes Kananen, Sophy Bergenheim & Merle Wessel (eds), *Conceptualising Public Health: Historical and Contemporary Struggles over Key Concepts*. Routledge (2018), 46–60.

Engesbak, Reidar, 'Gikk til sak mot staten og vant pris under Norges første Trans Pride [Went to Court Against the State and won an Award during Norway's first Trans Pride]'. *Blikk*, blikk.no/aleksander-sorlie-esben-esther-pirelli-benestad-luca-dalen-espseth/gikk-til-sak-mot-staten-og-vant-pris-under-norges-forste-trans-pride/206107 (5 September 2021).

Engs, Ruth Clifford, *The Eugenics Movement: An Encyclopedia*. Greenwood Press (2005).

Engwall, Kristina, *"Asociala och imbecilla": Kvinnorna på Västra Mark 1931–1967 ["Asocial and Imbecile": The Women at Västra Mark 1931–1967]*. Örebro University, PhD thesis (2000).

Ericsson, Kjersti, *Drift og dyd: Kontrollen av jenter på femtitallet [Drive and Virtue: The Control of Girls in the 1950s]*. Pax (1997).

Eriksson, Lars D (ed), *Pakkoauttajat [Helpers by Force]*. Tammi (1967).

Eriksson, Panda, *TransFinland: The Birth of Trans Studies as a Scholarly Field and the Parallel Development of Trans Activism in a Finnish Context*. Unpublished research paper (2017).

Erkkilä, Sven, 'Miksi steriloimislain täytäntöönpano kastraatiota koskevalta osalta on meillä epäonnistunut? [Why Has Our Implementation of the Sterilisation Act concerning Castration Failed?]'. *Vankeinhoito* no. 4–5 (1948), 74–79.

Erman, Anna, 'Skadestånd och Europakonventionen – betänkande av Utredningen om det allmännas ansvar enligt Europakonventionen [Damages and the European Convention – Report of the Investigation on Public Liability according to the European Convention]'. *Svensk juristtidning* no. 2 (2011), 189–201.

Ewig, Christina, 'Hijacking Global Feminism: Feminists, the Catholic Church, and the Family Planning Debacle in Peru'. *Feminist Studies* vol. 32 no. 3 (2006), 632–659.

Ewig, Christina, *Second-Wave Neoliberalism: Gender, Race and Health Sector Reform in Peru*. Pennsylvania State University Press (2010).

Fodstad, Hjørdis, *Møter mellom tatere og det norska samfunnet: Erfaringer fra tvangssterilisering [Meetings between Tatere and Norwegian Society: Experiences of Forced Sterilisation]*. Oslo University, Institute for Criminology, K-series No. 2-99 (1999).

Fodstad, Hjørdis, 'Erfaringen fra tvanssterilisering og andre tap [Experiences of Forced Sterilisation and Other Harm]'. In Bjørn Hvinden (ed), *Romanifolket og det norske samfunnet [The Romani People and Norwegian Society]*. Fagbokforlaget (2000), 130–159.

Foucault, Michel, *The History of Sexuality. Volume One: An Introduction*. Vintage Books (1990).

FPES, *Remissyttrande över Förslag till lag om ersättning till personer som har fått ändrad könstillhörighet fastställd i vissa fall [Comment on Proposal for Act on Compensation to People Who Have Obtained Legal Gender Recognition under Certain Circumstances]*. Report no. S2017/01918/FS (2017).

Frankenberg, Günter, 'Critical Comparisons: Re-thinking Comparative Law'. *Harvard International Law Journal* vol. 26 no. 2 (1985), 411–455.

Freyhofer, Horst H, *The Nuremberg Medical Trial*. Peter Lang Publishing (2005).

FRI, *Rettferdighet og oppreisning til transpersoner! [Justice and Redress for Trans People!]*, www.foreningenfri.no/rettferdighet-og-oppreisning-til-transpersoner/ (23 June 2020).

FTPN, *Kommentarer fra Foreningen for Transpersoner i Norge (FTP-N) til rapporten 'Behandlingstilbudet til transseksuelle og transpersoner i Norge' [Comments from the Norwegian Association of Trans People (FTP-N) to the Report 'Treatments Offered to Transsexuals and Trans People in Norway']*. Letter to the Norwegian Directorate of Health (2011).

Gallen, James, 'Redressing Gendered Mistreatment: Madgalene Laundries, Symphysiotomy and Mother and Baby Homes'. In Lyndsey Black & Peter Dunne (eds), *Law and Gender in Modern Ireland: Critique and Reform*. Hart (2019), 263–280.

Gallen, James & Gleeson, Kate, 'Unpaid Wages: The Experiences of Irish Magdalene Laundries and Indigenous Australians'. *International Journal of Law in Context* vol. 14 no. 1 (2018), 43–60.

Galton, Francis, *Inquiries into Human Faculty and Its Development*. Macmillian (1883).

Ghooi, Ravindra B, 'The Nuremberg Code – A Critique'. *Perspectives in Clinical Research* vol. 2 no. 2 (2011), 72–76.

Giles, Geoffrey J, '"The Most Unkindest Cut of All": Castration, Homosexuality and Nazi Justice'. *Journal of Contemporary History* vol. 27 no. 1 (1992), 41–61.

Glass, Jess, 'Finnish Government Opts to Keep Law that Requires Trans People to Be Sterilised'. *Pink News*, www.pinknews.co.uk/2017/08/25/finnish-government-opts-to-keep-law-that-requires-trans-people-to-be-sterilised/ (25 August 2017).

Golder, Ben, *Foucault and the Politics of Rights*. Stanford University Press (2015).

Gould, Stephen J, *The Mismeasure of Man*. Norton (1996).

Grau, Günter, *Hidden Holocaust? Gay and Lesbian Persecution in Germany, 1933–45*. Taylor & Francis (1995).

Greer, Steven & Wildhaber, Luzius, 'Revising the Debate about "Constitutionalising" the European Court of Human Rights'. *Human Rights Law Review* vol. 12 no. 4 (2012), 655–87.

Grey, Rosemary, 'The ICC's First "Forced Pregnancy" Case in Historical Perspective'. *Journal of International Criminal Justice* vol. 15 no. 5 (2017), 905–930.

Gribble, James N, Sharma, Suneeta & Menotti, Elaine, 'Family Planning Policies and their Impact on the Poor: Peru's Experience'. *International Family Planning Perspectives* vol. 33 no. 4 (2007), 176–181.

Grunewald, Karl, 'Graviditet och sterilisering hos svenska särskoleflickor under åren 1937–1956 [Pregnancy and Sterilisation among Swedish Girls in Special Schools during the Years 1937–1956]'. *Psykisk utvecklingshämning* vol. 64 no. 1–2 (1962), 3–13.

Grunewald, Karl, 'Indikationerna för sterilisering av psykiskt utvecklingsstörda måste omvärderas [The Indications for Sterilisation of Mentally Retarded Must Be Re-evaluated]'. *Svenska läkartidningen* vol. 67 no. 44 (1970a), 5096–5102.

Grunewald, Karl, 'Kritisk granskning av ansökningar om sterilisering av mentalt defekta [Critical Examination of Applications for Sterilisation by the Mentally Defective]'. *Svenska läkartidningen* vol. 67 no. 44 (1970b), 5091–5095.

Grünn, Emma, 'Sukupuolensa korjannut translain pakkosterilisaatiosta: "Se on nyt viety minulta" [A Person Who Has Undergone Gender Reassignment Comments on the Forced Sterilisation in the Trans Act: "It Has Now Been Taken Away from Me"]'. *YLE*, yle.fi/uutiset/3-9698573 (30 June 2017).

Haave, Per, *Sterilisering av tatere 1934–1977: en historisk undersøkelse av lov og praksis [Sterilisation of Tatere 1934–1977: A Historical Investigation of Legislation and Practice]*. The Research Council of Norway (2000a).

Haave, Per, 'Sterilisering av tatere – kirurgi på "rasemessig" grunnlag? [Sterilisation of Tatere – Surgery on "Racial" Grounds?]'. In Bjørn Hvinden (ed), *Romanifolket og det norske samfunnet [The Romani People and Norwegian Society]*. Fagbokforlaget (2000b), 32–73.

Haave, Per, 'Sterilisering under tvang og frivillighet [Sterilisation through Coercion and Free Will]'. *Dagbladet* (10 March 2003).

Haave, Per, 'Sterilisering av kvinner vid Svanviken arbeidskoloni (1949–1970) [Sterilisation of Women at the Svanviken Work Colony]'. In Kommunal- og moderniseringsdepartementet [The Norwegian Ministry of Local Government and Modernisation], *Vedlegg til NOU 2015:7 [Annexes to NOU 2015:7]* (2015a), 545–554.

Haave, Per, 'En paragraf til besvær: Misjonens "aksjon" for å lette adgangen til tvangssterilisering av mindreårige [A Troublesome Section: The "Action" of the Mission to Facilitate the Access to Forced Sterilisation of Minors]'. In Kommunal- og moderniseringsdepartementet [The Norwegian Ministry of Local Government and Modernisation], *Vedlegg til NOU 2015:7 [Annexes to NOU 2015:7]* (2015b), 578–590.

Haave, Per & Giæver, Øyvind, *Sterilisering på medisinsk grunnlag og sammenhengen mellom eugenikk of humangenetikk [Sterilisation on Medical Indication and the Connection between Eugenics and Human Genetics]*. The Research Council of Norway (2000).

Haavie, Siri, 'Sterilization in Norway – A Dark Chapter?'. *Eurozine* (2003), 1–20.

Hagerman, Maja, *Käraste Herman: Rasbiologen Herman Lundborgs gåta [Dearest Herman: The Riddle of the Race Biologist Herman Lundborg]*. Norstedts (2015).

Hakalehto-Wainio, Suvianna, *Valta ja vahinko: julkisen vallan käyttäjän vahingonkorvausvastuu vahingonkorvauslaissa [Power and Damage: The Legal Liability of the Administrator of Public Power]*. Talentum (2008).

Hakalehto-Wainio, Suvianna, 'Skadestånd som medel för ersättning vid kränkningar av mänskliga rättigheter [Compensation as Reparation for Human Rights Violations]'. In Karin B Mirchadani & Kristina Ståhl (eds), *Förhandlingarna vid det 39:e nordiska juristmötet i Stockholm 18–19 augusti 2011 [Negotiations at the 39th Nordic Law Meeting in Stockholm 18–19 August 2011]. De nordiske juristmøder* (2011), 237–243.

Halberstam, Jack, *Trans*: A Quick and Quirky Account of Gender Variability*. University of California Press (2018).

Halsos, Martin S, 'Norway 1842–1972: When Public Interest Demands'. In Jens Rydström & Kati Mustola (eds), *Criminally Queer: Homosexuality and Criminal Law in Scandinavia 1842–1999*. Aksant Academic Publishers (2007), 91–116.

Halvorsen, Rune, 'Etnisk mobilisering i en brytningstid [Ethnic Mobilisation in a Period of Transition]'. In Bjørn Hvinden (ed), *Romanifolket og det norske samfunnet [The Romani People and Norwegian Society]*. Fagbokforlaget (2000), 195–226.

Hancock, Ange-Marie, *Intersectionality: An Intellectual History*. Oxford University Press (2016).

Hansen, Bent S, 'Something Rotten in the State of Denmark: Eugenics and the Ascent of the Welfare State'. In Gunnar Broberg & Nils Roll-Hansen (eds), *Eugenics and the Welfare State: Norway, Sweden, Denmark and Finland*. Michigan State University Press (2005), 9–76.

Hanson, Clare, 'Biopolitics, Biological Racism and Eugenics'. In Stephen Morton & Stephen Bygrave (eds), *Foucault in an Age of Terror: Essays on Biopolitics and the Defence of Society*. Palgrave Macmillan (2008), 106–117.

Hartmann, Betsy, *Reproductive Rights and Wrongs: The Global Politics of Population Control*. Haymarket Books (2016).

Hassenstab, Christine M, *Body Law and the Body of Law: A Comparative Study of Social Norm Inclusion in Norwegian and American Laws*. De Gruyter Open (2014).

Hägglund, Göran, 'Dags att avskaffa kravet på sterilisering vid könsbyte [Time to Abolish the Requirement of Sterilisation Connected to Sex Change]'. *Dagens Nyheter* (18 February 2012).

HBRS, *Vedrørende rapport om behandlingstilbudet til pasienter med diagnosen transseksualisme [Concerning the Report on Treatments Offered to Patients Diagnosed with Transsexualism]*. Letter to the Norwegian Directorate of Health (2011).

Hedrén, Gunnar, 'Några reflektioner med anledning av den vid innevarande riksdag väckta motionen om utredning rörande sterilisering av sinnesslöa m.fl. [Some Reflections on the Parliamentary Motion on Investigation concerning Sterilisation of Feebleminded etc.]'. *Svenska läkartidningen* vol. 19 no. 14 (1922), 273–278.

Heim, Nikolaus, *Die Kastration und ihre Folgen bei Sexualstraftätern [Castration and Its Consequences on Sexual Criminals]*. Otto Schwartz & Co (1980).

Hellum, Anne, 'Making Space and Giving Voice: The CEDAW in Norwegian Law'. In Anne Hellum & Henriette Sinding Aasen (eds), *Women's Human Rights: The CEDAW in International, Regional and National Law*. Cambridge University Press (2013), 588–624.

Hellum, Anne, 'Vern mot diskriminering på grunnlag av seksuell orientering, kjønnsidentitet og kjønnsuttrykk: Noen utviklingslinjer i internasjonal og norsk rett [Protection against Discrimination Based on Sexual Orientation, Gender Identity and Gender Expression: Some Developments in International and Norwegian Law]'. In Anne Hellum, Reidun Førde, Morten Kjelland & Ulf Stridbeck (eds), *Cand. mag., cand.med., cand.jur., cand.alt: Festskrift til Aslak Syse 70 år [Cand.mag., cand. med., cand.jur., cand.alt: Commemoration of Aslak Syse 70 years]*. Gyldendal (2016), 191–213.

Hellum, Anne, 'Norwegian Equality and Anti-discrimination Reform in an Individualist and Market-oriented Context'. *NORA – Nordic Journal of Feminist and Gender Research* vol. 25 no. 3 (2017), 211–216.

Hellum, Anne, 'Individets vern mot diskriminering på grunnlag av seksuell orientering, kjønnsidentitet og kjønnsuttrykk: Et vern på majoritetens premisser? [Individual Protection against Discrimination Based on Sexual Orientation, Gender Identity and Gender Expression: Protection on the Premises of the Majority?]'. In Anne Hellum & Anniken Sørlie (eds), *Frihet, likhet og mangfold [Freedom, Equality and Diversity]*. Gyldendal (2021), 306–343.

Herzog, Dagmar, *Sexuality in Europe: A Twentieth-century History*. Cambridge University Press (2011).

Hietala, Marjatta, 'Suomalaisen naistyypin etsiminen [Looking for the Finnish Female Type]'. In Aira Kemiläinen, Marjatta Hietala & Pekka Suvanto (eds), *Mongoleja vai germaaneja? – rotuteorioiden suomalaiset [Mongols or Germanic People? – The Finns of Eugenics]*. Societas Historica Finlandiae (1985), 421–446.

Hietala, Marjatta, 'Pohjoismaihinkin säädettiin sterilisaatiolait vuoteen 1938 mennessä – Huoli ihmiskunnan laadusta synnytti rotuhygienian [Also the Nordic Countries Established Sterilisation Laws Until 1938 – Worry about the Quality of Humankind Gave Birth to Eugenics]'. *Helsingin Sanomat* (11 January 1995).

Hietala, Marjatta, 'From Race Hygiene to Sterilization: The Eugenics Movement in Finland'. In Gunnar Broberg & Nils Roll-Hansen (eds), *Eugenics and the Welfare State: Norway, Sweden, Denmark, and Finland*. Michigan State University Press (2005), 195–258.

Higuchi, A, Takita, M, Ozaki, A, Kimura, H & Watanabe, H, 'Forced Sterilization during Post-war Era in Japan'. *QJM: An International Journal of Medicine* vol. 112 no. 10 (2019), 829.

Hilson, Chris, 'New Social Movements: The Role of Legal Opportunity'. *Journal of European Public Policy* vol. 9 no. 2 (2002), 238–255.

Hilson, Chris, 'Climate Change Litigation in the UK: An Explanatory Approach (or Bringing Grievance Back In)'. In Fabrizio Fracchia & Massimo Occhiena (eds), *Climate Change: La riposta del diritto*. Editoriale Scientifica (2010), 421–436.

Hirdman, Yvonne, *Att lägga livet tillrätta: Studier i svensk folkhemspolitik [To Put Life in Order: Studies of Swedish Policies concerning the People's Home]*. Carlssons (2000).

Hirschl, Ran, 'The Nordic Counternarrative: Democracy, Human Development, and Judicial Review'. *International Journal of Constitutional Law*, vol. 9 no. 2 (2011), 449–469.

Hirschl, Ran, *Comparative Matters: The Renaissance of Comparative Constitutional Law*. Oxford University Press (2014).

Hjelmeng, Erling, 'Folkerettslig påvirkning av norsk erstatningsrett – to høyesterettsdommer [International Legal Influence on Norwegian Compensation Law – Two

Supreme Court Judgments]'. *Tidsskrift for erstatningsrett, forsikringsrett og trygderett* vol. 1 no. 3 (2016), 211–229.

Holmlund, Sofia, 'Finländska döva steriliserades – nu önskas en ursäkt av staten [Finnish Deaf People were Sterilised – Now They Ask for a State Apology]'. *Hufvudstadsbladet*, www.hbl.fi/artikel/finlandska-dova-steriliserades-nu-onskas-en-ursakt-av-staten/ (21 October 2018a).

Holmlund, Sofia, 'Politiker börjar jobba för att steriliseringar mot döva ska erkännas [Politicians Start Working for the Recognition of the Sterilisation of Deaf People]'. *Hufvudstadsbladet*, www.hbl.fi/artikel/politiker-borjar-jobba-for-att-steriliseringar-mot-dova-ska-erkannas-2/ (28 October 2018b).

hooks, bell, *Feminist Theory from Margin to Center*. South End Press (1984).

Honkanen, Toini, 'Kastroimiskysymys lainkäytön valossa [The Castration Question in the Light of Legal Implementation]'. *Lakimies* (1954), 41–55.

Honkasalo, Brynolf, 'Finlands nya lagförslag angående sterilisering [Finland's New Legislative Proposal on Sterilisation]'. *Nordisk Tidsskrift for Strafferet* vol. 23 (1935), 114–123.

Honkasalo, Julian, 'When Boys Will Not Be Boys: American Eugenics and the Formation of Gender Nonconformity as Psychopathology'. *NORMA: International Journal for Masculinity Studies* vol. 11 no. 4 (2016), 270–286.

Honkasalo, Julian, 'In the Shadow of Eugenics: Transgender Sterilisation Legislation and the Struggle for Self-determination'. In Ruth Pearce, Igi Moon, Kat Gupta & Deborah L Steinberg (eds), *The Emergence of Trans: Cultures, Politics and Everyday Lives*. Routledge (2019), 17–33.

Howe, Adrian, 'The Problem of Privatized Injuries: Feminist Strategies for Litigation'. In Martha A Fineman & Nancy S Thomadsen (eds), *At the Boundaries of Law: Feminism and Legal Theory*. Routledge (1991), 148–167.

Hoyle, Lindsay, '*V.C. v. Slovakia*: A Reproductive Rights Victory Misses the Point'. *Boston College International and Comparative Law Review* vol. 36 no. 3 (2014), 17–31.

Huffington Post, *Sweden's Transgender Sterilization Law Slammed by International Activists, Politicians*, www.huffpost.com/entry/sweden-transgender-sterilization-law-activists_n_1219878 (20 January 2012).

Hunt, Alan, 'Rights and Social Movements: Counter-hegemonic Strategies'. *Journal of Law and Society* vol. 17 no. 3 (1990), 309–328.

Husa, Jaakko, 'Nordic Constitutionalism and European Human Rights – Mixing Oil and Water?'. *Scandinavian Studies in Law* vol. 55 (2010), 101–124.

Husa, Jaakko, *The Constitution of Finland: A Contextual Analysis*. Hart Publishing (2011).

Hvinden, Bjørn, 'Innledning: Fra fordømmelse til respekt og verdighet [Introduction: From Condemnation to Respect and Dignity]'. In Bjørn Hvinden (ed), *Romanifolket og det norske samfunnet [The Romani People and Norwegian Society]*. Fagbokforlaget (2000a), 11–31.

Hvinden, Bjørn (ed), *Romanifolket og det norske samfunnet [The Romani People and Norwegian Society]*. Fagbokforlaget (2000b).

Hyde, Alan, *Bodies of Law*. Princeton University Press (2003).

ICJ-Norge, *Prosesskriv til Borgarting lagmannsrett i sak 18-190131ASD-BORG/02 [Amicus Curiae to Borgarting Court of Appeal in Case 18-190131ASD-BORG/02]*. Letter to the court (2020).

Independent, *Following in Malta's Footsteps, Norway Extends Gender Identity Laws to Children*, www.independent.com.mt/articles/2016-09-28/world-news/Following-in-Malta-s-footsteps-Norway-extends-gender-identity-laws-to-children-6736164367 (28 September 2016).

International Commission of Jurists, *Yogyakarta Principles – Principles on the Application of International Human Rights Law in Relation to Sexual Orientation and Gender Identity*. International Commission of Jurists Publications (2007).

Jacobsen, Maria H, *Prosesskrift til Oslo tingrett [Written Pleadings before the Oslo Court of First Instance]*. Case No. 17-132417TVI-OTIR/08. Unpublished (2018).

Johnston, Hank, Laraña, Enrique & Gusfield, Joseph R, 'Identities, Grievances, and New Social Movements'. In Hank Johnston, Enrique Laraña & Joseph R Gusfield (eds), *New Social Movements: From Ideology to Identity*. Temple University Press (2009), 3–35.

Karlsson Schaffer, Johan, 'Mellan ambivalens och aktivism: Norden och internationella mänskliga rättigheter [Between Ambivalence and Activism: The Nordic Countries and International Human Rights]'. *Retfærd – The Nordic Journal of Law and Justice* vol. 40 no. 1 (2017), 55–72.

Karlsson Schaffer, Johan & Langford, Malcolm, 'The Reluctant Activists: The Nordic States and International Human Rights'. Unpublished research paper (2018).

Kastari, Paavo, *Kansalaisvapauksien perustuslainturva [The Constitutional Protection of Civil Rights]*. Suomalainen Lakimiesyhdistys (1972).

Kelly, Liz, *Surviving Sexual Violence*. Polity Press (1988).

Kervinen, Elina, 'Oslolainen Noah, 20, tunsi olevansa väärässä kehossa jo viisivuotiaana – Norja vapautti translakiaan, ja Suomesta tuli ainoa sterilointia vaativa Pohjoismaa [Noah, 20 Years, from Oslo, Felt that He Was in the Wrong Body Already When He Was Five – Norway Liberalised Its Trans Act and Finland Became the Only Nordic Country Requiring Sterilisation]'. *Helsingin Sanomat*, www.hs.fi/ulkomaat/art-2000005222128.html (23 May 2017).

Kevles, Daniel, 'Eugenics and Human Rights'. *The BMJ*, vol. 319 no. 7207 (1999), 435–438.

Kierulf, Anine, 'Grunnloven som irrelevant rettskilde [The Constitution as an Irrelevant Legal Source]'. *Lov og Rett*, vol. 55 no. 3 (2016), 185–189.

Kimmel, Michael S, Hearn, Jeff & Connell, Robert W (eds), *Handbook of Studies on Men and Masculinities*. SAGE Publications (2004).

Kirves, Jenni, '"Sota ei ollut elämisen eikä muistamisen arvoista aikaa" – kirjailijat ja traumaattinen sota ["The War Was Neither a Time to Live, Nor a Time to Remember" – The Authors and the Traumatic War]'. In Sari Näre & Jenni Kirves (eds), *Ruma sota: Talvi- ja jatkosodan vaiettu historia [Ugly War: The Silenced History of the Winter and Continuation War]*. Johnny Kniga (2008), 381–425.

Klabbers, Jan, Peters, Anne & Ulfstein, Geir, *The Constitutionalization of International Law*. Oxford University Press (2009).

Knight, Kyle, 'Dispatches: Norway's Transgender Rights Transformation'. *Human Rights Watch*, www.hrw.org/news/2016/06/07/dispatches-norways-transgender-rights-transformation (7 June 2016).

Koch, Lene, 'The Meaning of Eugenics: Reflections on the Government of Genetic Knowledge in the Past and the Present'. *Science in Context* vol. 17 no. 3 (2004), 315–331.

Kolata, Jens, 'Exkurs: Kastration homosexueller Männer in der Nachkriegszeit [Excursion: Castration of Homosexual Men in the Post-War Period]'. *Der Liebe Wegen*, www.der-liebe-wegen.org/nachkriegszeit_baden-wuerttemberg_spitzenreiter_der_verfolgung/ (24 January 2017).

Koslerova, Anna, 'Illegally Sterilised Czech Women to Be Offered Compensation'. *The Guardian*, www.theguardian.com/global-development/2021/aug/04/illegally-sterilised-czech-women-to-be-offered-compensation (4 August 2021).

Kouvo, Sari, *Making Just Rights? Mainstreaming Women's Human Rights and a Gender Perspective*. Iustus (2004).

Kuechenhoff, Bernhard, 'The Psychiatrist Auguste Forel and His Attitude to Eugenics'. *History of Psychiatry* vol. 19 no. 2 (2008), 215–223.

Kühl, Stefan, *The Nazi Connection: Eugenics, American Racism, and German National Socialism*. Oxford University Press (2002).

Langford, Malcolm, Madsen, Mikael R & Karlsson Schaffer, Johan, *The Scandinavian Rights Revolution: Courts, Rights and Legal Mobilization since the 1970s*. Unpublished research paper (2019).

Lahti, Raimo, 'Vuoden 1970 abortti-, sterilisaatio- ja kastraatiolainsäädäntö [The Abortion, Sterilisation and Castration Legislation of 1970]'. In Johan Borgström, Erik Hellén, Leif Sevón & Berndt von Veh (eds), *Festskrift utgiven i anledning av Juristklubben Codex 30-års jubileum [Commemoration for the 30th Anniversary of the Lawyers' Club Codex]*. Juridiska föreningen i Finland, publikationsserie 40 (1970), 67–105.

Lahti, Raimo, 'Perhesuunnittelupolitiikka ja syntyvyyden säännöstelyä koskeva lainsäädäntömme [Our Legislation on Family Planning Policies and Birth Control]'. *Oikeus* vol. 1 no. 1 (1972), 15–40.

Lahti, Raimo, 'Uusien abortti- ja steriloimislakien vaikutus maassamme [The Effect of the New Abortion and Sterilisation Acts in Our Country]'. *Suomen Lääkärilehti* no. 28 (1973), 303–314.

Lahti, Raimo, 'Rikosseuraamukset ja niihin verrattavat pakkotoimenpiteet: Eräiden kontrollipolitiikan kysymysten tarkastelua [Criminal Sanctions and Comparable Forced Interventions: Investigation of Some Control Policy Questions]'. In Martti Majanen (ed), *Rikosoikeudellisia kirjoitelmia IV: Reino Kalervo Ellilälle omistettu [Criminal Legal Essays IV: Dedicated to Reino Kalervo Ellilä]*. Suomalainen Lakimiesyhdistys (1980), 104–122.

Lahti, Raimo, 'Voluntary or Compulsory Treatment – Some Trends in Finnish Law'. In Raphaël Dierkens (ed), *Jus Medicum*. Centrum voor Medisch Recht Rijksuniversiteit Gent (1982), 23–27

Lahti, Raimo, 'Vuoden 1970 abortti-, steriloimis-, ja kastroimislait, niiden soveltaminen sekä abortti- ja steriloimislakien muutokset vuosina 1978 ja 1985 [The 1970 Abortion, Sterilisation and Castration Acts, Their Implementation and Amendments of the Abortion and Sterilisation Acts in 1978 and 1985]'. *Suomen Lääkärilehti* vol. 18 (1985), 1809–1814.

Lahti, Raimo, 'Pakkohoito terveydenhuollossa [Forced Treatment in Health Care]'. *Sosiaalinen aikakausikirja* no. 2 (1986), 37–39.

Lahti, Raimo (ed), *Kohti rationaalista ja humaania kriminaalipolitiikkaa [Towards a Rational and Humane Criminal Policy]*. Yliopistopaino (1996).

Lahti, Raimo, 'Lääkäri ja henkilökohtaiseen koskemattomuuteen puuttuminen. Lääkintäoikeuden kehityksestä eräiden sääntelyesimerkkien valossa [The Medical

Doctor and Interventions into Personal Integrity. On the Development of Medical Law in the Light of Regulatory Examples]'. In Mirja Lohiniva-Kerkelä (ed), *Väkivalta. Seuraamukset ja haavoittuvuus. Terttu Utriaisen juhlakirja. [Violence. Consequences and Vulnerability. Commemoration of Terttu Utriainen]*. Talentum (2006), 183–206.

Lahti, Raimo, 'Ärztliche Eingriffe und das Selbstbestimmungsrecht des Individuums [Medical Interventions and Individual Autonomy]'. In Guido Britz et al (eds), *Festschrift für Heike Jung [Commemoration of Heike Jung]*. Nomos (2007), 511–528.

Lahti, Raimo, *Asiantuntijalausunto (hedelmöityshoidon kysymyksiä) [Expert Statement (Questions Regarding Fertility Treatment)]*. Report to the Finnish Parliamentary Ombudsman (2008).

Lahti, Raimo (ed), *Inkeri Anttila (1916–2013): Rikosoikeudes uudistajan ammatillinen ura ja vaikutus [Inkeri Anttila (1916–2013): The Professional Career and Impact of the Reformer of Criminal Law]*. Forum Iuris (2016).

Lambertz, Göran, 'Tankar om justitiekanslern [Thoughts on the Swedish Chancellor of Justice]'. In Sten Heckscher & Anders Eka (eds), *Festskrift till Johan Hirschfeldt [Commemoration of Johan Hirschfeldt]*. Iustus (2008), 203–223.

Laughlin, Harry H, *Eugenical Sterilization in the United States*. Psychopathic Laboratory of the Municipal Court of Chicago (1922).

Lavapuro, Juha, Scheinin, Martin & Ojanen, Tuomas, 'Rights-based Constitutionalism in Finland and the Development of Pluralist Constitutional Review'. *International Journal of Constitutional Law* vol. 9 no. 2 (2011), 505–531.

Lee, Rebecca, 'Forced Sterilization and Mandatory Divorce: How a Majority of Council of Europe Member States' Laws Regarding Gender Identity Violate the Internationally and Regionally Established Human Rights of Trans* People'. *Berkley Journal of International Law* vol. 33 no. 1 (2015), 114–152.

Lee, Po-Han, 'Struggle for Recognition: Theorising Sexual/Gender Minorities as Rights-holders in International Law'. *Feminist Legal Studies* vol. 30 no. 1 (2022), 73–95.

Le Maire, Louis, 'Danish Experiences Regarding the Castration of Sexual Offenders'. *Journal of Criminal Law and Criminology* vol. 47 no. 3 (1956), 294–310.

Lennerhed, Lena, 'Sterilisation on Eugenic Grounds in Europe in the 1930s: News in 1997 but Why?'. *Reproductive Health Matters* vol. 5 no. 10 (1997), 156–161.

Lennerhed, Lena, 'Steriliseringar och sexuell reform: Om Elise Ottesen-Jensen och Riksförbundet för sexuell upplysning [Sterilisations and Sexual Reform: On Elise Ottesen-Jensen and the Swedish Association for Sexual Education]'. In Gunnar Broberg (ed), *Fem uppsatser om steriliseringen i Sverige [Five Essays on Sterilisation in Sweden]*. Ugglan 12, Lund Studies in the History of Science and Ideas (2000), 22–46.

Lennerhed, Lena, *Sex i folkhemmet: RFSUs tidiga historia [Sex in the People's Home: The Early History of RFSU]*. Gidlunds förlag (2002).

Leppälä, Heli, *Vammaisuus hyvinvointivaltiossa [Disability in the Welfare State]*. University of Turku, PhD thesis (2014).

Lied, Vilde G, 'Vart steriliserte for å få riktig kjønn på papiret: Krev unnskyldning frå staten [Were Sterilised in Order to Get Their Real Gender on Paper: Demand Apology from the State]'. *NRK*, www.nrk.no/norge/vart-steriliserte-for-a-fa-riktig-kjonn-pa-papiret_-krev-unnskyldning-fra-staten-1.15068993 (1 July 2020).

Liljeborg, Ove, *En genomgång av 1997 års tvångssteriliseringsdebatt i svensk dagspress [A Review of the 1997 Sterilisation Debate in Swedish Daily Press]*. Levande historia (2009).

Lindberg, Marjut, 'Outo käytös ja höllö moraali riitti sterilointiin [Unusual Behaviour and Questionable Morals Was Enough for Sterilisation]'. *Helsingin Sanomat*, www.hs.fi/sunnuntai/art-2000003653509.html (31 August 1997a).

Lindberg, Marjut, 'Tutkijat: Pakkosterilointeja tehtiin vielä 1960-luvulla. Tilastoista löytyy noin 11000 viranomaisten päätöstä vuosilta 1935–70 [Researchers: Forced Sterilisations Were Still Carried Out in the 1960s. Statistics Demonstrate around 11,000 Authority Decisions during 1935–70]'. *Helsingin Sanomat*, www.hs.fi/kotimaa/art-2000003653206.html (30 August 1997b).

Lindberg, Marjut, 'Suomessa pakkosteriloitiin 11000 [In Finland 11,000 Were Forcibly Sterilised]'. *Helsingin Sanomat*, www.hs.fi/ulkomaat/art-2000003783311.html (5 March 1999).

Lindekilde, Lasse, 'Discourse and Frame Analysis'. In Donatella Della Porta (ed), *Methodological Practices in Social Movement Research*. Oxford University Press (2014), 195–227.

Lindquist, Bosse, *Förädlade svenskar [Breeded Swedes]*. Alfabeta (1991).

Liukkonen, Marjo, *Hennalan naismurhat [The Hennala Femicides]*. Vastapaino (2017).

LLH, *Angående rapportutkast "Behandlingstilbudet til transseksuelle og transpersoner i Norge" [Referring to the Draft Report 'Treatments Offered to Transsexuals and Trans People in Norway']*. Letter to the Norwegian Directorate of Health (2011).

Lohne, Jenny-Linn, 'Nye eksperter får vurdere transpersoner [New Experts Get to Evaluate Trans People]'. *VG*, www.vg.no/nyheter/innenriks/sykehus-norge/nye-eksperter-faar-vurdere-transpersoner/a/10118504/ (1 August 2013).

Lohne, Jenny-Linn, Falch-Olsen, Ida & Fagerheim, Ragnhild H, 'Ingentransland [Notransland]'. *VG*, www.vg.no/spesial/2013/transer/ (2 July 2013).

Lomfors, Ingrid, 'Berättelser från livet. Intervjuer med tvångssteriliserade i Sverige [Stories from Life. Interviews with Involuntarily Sterilised in Sweden]'. In Socialdepartementet [The Swedish Ministry of Health and Social Affairs], *Steriliseringsfrågan i Sverige [The Sterilisation Issue in Sweden]*. SOU 2000:20 (2000), 279–355.

Lundberg, Aleksa, 'Be om ursäkt för steriliseringarna [Apologise for the Sterilisations]'. *Aftonbladet*, www.aftonbladet.se/debatt/article16903339.ab (5 June 2013).

MacKinnon, Catherine, 'Rape, Genocide, and Women's Human Rights'. *Harvard Women's Law Journal* vol. 17 (1994), 5–16.

Marhoefer, Laurie, *Among Abnormals: The Queer Sexual Politics of Germany's Weimar Republic, 1918–1933*. Rutgers, The State University of New Jersey, PhD thesis (2008).

Markowitz, Lawrence P, 'How Master Frames Mislead: The Division and Eclipse of Nationalist Movements in Uzbekistan and Tajikistan'. *Ethnic & Racial Studies* vol. 32 no. 4 (2009), 716–738.

Marshall, Anna-Maria, 'Idle Rights: Employees' Rights Consciousness and the Construction of Sexual Harassment Policies'. *Law & Society Review* vol. 39 no. 1 (2005).

Mattila, Markku, 'Suomalainen rotuhygienia [Finnish Racial Hygiene]'. *Tieteessä tapahtuu* no. 8 (1997a), 20–26.

Mattila, Markku, *The Main Points of the Early Finnish Eugenic Movements*. Unpublished research paper (1997b).

Mattila, Markku, 'Suomen ruotsinkieliset ja laadukkaamman väestön vaatimus [Finland's Swedish-speakers and the Requirement for a Higher Quality Population]'. In Marja

Härmänmaa & Markku Mattila (eds), *Uusi uljas ihminen, eli modernin pimeä puoli [The Brave New Person, Or the Dark Side of Modernity]*. Atena (1998), 117–141.

Mattila, Markku, *Kansamme parhaaksi: Rotuhygienia Suomessa vuoden 1935 sterilointilakiin asti [For the Best of Our Nation: Race Hygiene in Finland until the 1935 Sterilisation Act]*. Suomen Historiallinen Seura (1999).

Mattila, Markku, *On the History of Alegal and Coercive Sterilization: Some Legal and Ethical Perspectives*. Unpublished research paper (2002).

Mattila, Markku, *Negatiivisen eugeenisen politiikan yleiskuva [The General Picture of Negative Eugenics]*. Unpublished research paper (2003).

Mattila, Markku, 'Sterilointipolitiikka ja romanit Suomessa vuosina 1950–1970 [Sterilisation Politics and the Romani in Finland during 1950–1970]'. In Antti Häkkinen, Panu Pulma & Miika Tervonen (eds), *Vieraat kulkijat - tutut talot. Näkökulmia etnisyyden ja köyhyyden historiaan Suomessa [Unfamiliar Travellers - Familiar Houses. Perspectives on the History of Ethnicity and Poverty in Finland]*. Suomalaisen Kirjallisuuden Seura (2006), 402–452.

Mattila, Markku, '"Det får ej finnas dåliga svenskar i detta land!" Rasbiologi och rashygien som vetenskapliga vapen i språkstridens Finland ["There Cannot Be Bad Swedes in this Country!" Race Biology and Racial Hygiene as Scientific Weapons in the Finland of Linguistic Battle]'. In Mats Wickström & Charlotta Wolff (eds), *Mångkulturalitet, migration och minoriteter i Finland under tre sekel [Multiculturality, Migration and Minorities in Finland During Three Centuries]*. Svenska Litteratursällskapet i Finland (2016), 271–318.

McCammon, Holly J & McGrath, Allison R, 'Litigating Change? Social Movements and the Court System'. *Sociology Compass* vol. 9 no. 2 (2015), 128–139.

McCann, Michael, 'Legal Mobilization and Social Reform Movements: Notes on Theory and Its Application'. *Studies in Law, Politics, and Society* vol. 11 (1991), 225–254.

McCann, Michael, *Rights at Work: Pay Equity Reform and the Politics of Legal Mobilization*. The University of Chicago Press (1994).

Merry, Sally E, 'Introduction: Conditions of Vulnerability'. In Mark Goodale & Sally E Merry (eds), *The Practice of Human Rights: Tracking Law between the Global and the Local*. Cambridge University Press (2007), 195–203.

Mibenge, Chiseche S, *Sex and International Tribunals: The Erasure of Gender from the War Narrative*. University of Pennsylvania Press (2013).

Modéer, Kjell Å, 'From "Rechtsstaat" to "Welfare State": Swedish Judicial Culture in Transition 1870–1970'. In W Wesley Pue & David Sugarman (eds), *Lawyers and Vampires: Cultural Histories of Legal Professions*. Hart Publishing (2003), 151–167.

Moreno, Jonathan D, 'Reassessing the Influence of the Nuremberg Code on American Medical Ethics'. *Journal of Contemporary Health Law and Policy* vol. 13 no. 2 (1997), 347–360.

Mörk, Martin & Hermansson, Magnus, 'Enskildas rättsskydd vid lagstiftarens försummelse - om estoppelargumentet i svensk rätt [The Protection of Individuals When the Legislator Is Negligent - About the Estoppel Argument in Swedish Law]'. *Svensk juristtidning* no. 3 (2008), 229–261.

Mustola, Kati, 'Finland 1889–1999: A Turbulent Past'. In Jens Rydström & Kati Mustola (eds), *Criminally Queer: Homosexuality and Criminal Law in Scandinavia, 1842–1999*. Aksant Academic Publishers (2007), 215–250.

Myhre, Eivind & Thomassen, Øyvind, 'The Construction of an Accepted Masculinity: Castration in High Security Psychiatric Institutions in Norway 1923–1945'. In Ingrid Lander, Signe Ravin & Nina Jon (eds), *Masculinities in the Criminological Field: Control, Vulnerability and Risk-taking*. Routledge (2014), 89–109.

Myrdal, Alva & Myrdal, Gunnar, *Kris i befolkningsfrågan [Crisis in the Population Matter]*. Folkutgivning (1934).

Nader, Laura, 'Introduction: Registers of Power'. In Mark Goodale & Sally E Merry (eds), *The Practice of Human Rights: Tracking Law between the Global and the Local*. Cambridge University Press (2007), 117–129.

Naffine, Ngaire, *Law and the Sexes: Explorations in Feminist Jurisprudence*. Allen & Unwin (1990).

Nair, Pooja, 'Litigating against the Forced Sterilization of HIV-positive Women: Recent Developments in Chile and Namibia'. *Harvard Human Rights Journal* vol. 23 (2010), 223–231.

Näre, Sari, '"Kuin viimeistä päivää" – sota-ajan sukupuolikulttuuri ja seksuaalinen väkivalta ["As The Last Day" – Gender Culture and Sexual Violence during War Times]'. In Sari Näre & Jenni Kirves (eds), *Ruma sota: Talvi- ja jatkosodan vaiettu historia [Ugly War: The Silenced History of the Winter and Continuation Wars]*. Johnny Kniga (2008), 335–380.

Nergelius, Joakim, *Konstitutionellt rättighetsskydd. Svensk rätt i ett komparativt perspektiv [Constitutional Protection of Rights. Swedish Law in a Comparative Perspective]*. Fritzes (1996).

Nesheim, Britt-Ingjerd, 'Prevensjon [Prevention]'. *Store Medisinske Leksikon*, sml.snl.no/prevensjon (20 February 2018).

Neuman, Scott, 'North Carolina Set to Compensate Forced Sterilization Victims'. *Kera News*, www.keranews.org/2013-07-25/north-carolina-set-to-compensate-forced-sterilization-victims (25 July 2013).

Ní Aoláin, Fionnuala, 'Sex-based Violence and the Holocaust – A Reevaluation of Harms and Rights in International Law'. *Yale Journal of Law and Feminism* vol. 12 (2000), 43–84.

Ní Aoláin, Fionnuala, Haynes, Dina F & Cahn, Naomi, 'Criminal Justice for Gendered Violence and Beyond'. *International Criminal Law Review* vol. 11 (2011), 425–443.

Niemi-Kiesiläinen, Johanna, Honkatukia, Päivi & Ruuskanen, Minna, 'Legal Texts as Discourses'. In Åsa Gunnarsson, Eva-Maria Svensson & Margaret Davies (eds), *Exploiting the Limits of Law: Swedish Feminism and the Challenge to Pessimism*. Routledge (2007), 69–88.

Nilsson, Arne, *Såna – riktiga karlar. Om manlig homosexualitet i Göteborg decennierna kring andra världskriget [Those – Real Men. On Male Homosexuality in Gothenburg in the Decades Around the Second World War]*. Kartonnage (2001).

Nordvik, Ragnhild, 'Erstatnings- og oppreisningsordninger for tatere/romanifolk [Compensation and Redress Schemes for Tatere/Romani People]'. In Kommunal- og moderniseringsdepartementet [The Norwegian Ministry of Local Government and Modernisation], *Vedlegg til NOU 2015:7 [Annexes to NOU 2015:7]* (2015), 687–697.

Nourse, Victoria, *In Reckless Hands: Skinner v. Oklahoma and the Near Triumph of American Eugenics*. W W Norton and Company (2008).

Nousiainen, Kevät, Gunnarsson, Åsa, Lundström, Karin & Niemi-Kiesiläinen, Johanna (eds), *Responsible Selves: Women in the Nordic Legal Culture.* Ashgate (2001).

Nownes, Anthony J, *Organizing for Transgender Rights: Collective Action, Group Development, and the Rise of a New Social Movement.* State University of New York Press (2019).

O'Flaherty, Michael & Fisher, John, 'Sexual Orientation, Gender Identity and International Human Rights Law: Contextualising the Yogyakarta Principles'. *Human Rights Law Review* vol. 8 no. 2 (2008), 207–248.

Ordover, Nancy, *American Eugenics: Race, Queer Anatomy, and the Science of Nationalism.* University of Minnesota Press (2003).

Oslo University Hospital, *Høringsnotat vedr utkast til rapport om "Behandlingstilbudet til transseksuelle og transpersoner i Norge" [Consultation Document referring to Draft Report "Treatments Offered to Transsexuals and Trans People in Norway"].* Letter to the Norwegian Directorate of Health (2011).

Patel, Priti, 'Forced Sterilization of Women as Discrimination'. *Public Health Reviews* vol. 38 no. 15 (2017), 1–12.

Petrén, Gustaf, 'Domstols lagprövningsrätt [Judicial Review]'. *Svensk juristtidning* no. 1 (1956), 500–509.

Pimenoff, Veronica, 'Transseksuaalisuus [Transsexualism]'. *Duodecim* vol. 109 no. 4 (1993), 368–375.

Pimenoff, Veronica, 'On the Care of Transsexuals in Finland'. *International Journal of Transgenderism* vol. 9 no. 2 (2006), 23–33.

Pimenoff, Veronica, *Geschlechtsumwandlung in Finnland 1970–2002: Eine historische und empirische Studie zu Geschlechtsumwandlungen unter den Regelungen des Kastrationsgesetzes bis zur Einführung des finnischen Transsexuellengesetzes [Gender Reassignment in Finland 1970–2002: A Historical and Empirical Study of Gender Reassignment under the Regulation of the Castration Act to the Introduction of the Finnish Transsexual Act].* University of Ulm, MD Dissertation (2008).

Polletta, Francesca, *It Was Like a Fever: Storytelling in Protest and Politics.* The University of Chicago Press (2006).

Raevaara, Tiina, 'Miehet synnyttävät, hah hah haa! [Men Give Birth, Ha Ha Ha!]'. *Suomen Kuvalehti,* suomenkuvalehti.fi/tarinoitatieteesta/miehet-synnyttavat-hah-hah-haa/ (4 February 2012).

Rastas, Merja, *Oikeus oman identiteetin mukaiseen elämään – tutkimus transseksuaalien elämästä ja asemasta Suomessa [Right to Live as Oneself: Investigation of the Life and Position of Transsexuals in Finland].* The Finnish Board of Social and Health Affairs Report No. 55 (1992).

Reinsberg, Lisa & Juaristi, Francisco R, 'IACtHR Holds Bolivia Responsible for Forced Sterilization in Landmark Judgment'. *International Justice Resource Center,* www.ijrcenter.org/2017/01/03/iacthr-holds-bolivia-responsible-for-forced-sterilization-in-landmark-judgment/ (3 January 2017).

Remes, Mikaela, Tabermann, Johannes & Mallén, Ingrid, 'Nu ska samerna få berätta sin historia som innehåller tvångsförfinskning och våld – regeringen ger 1,5 miljoner till sanningskommission [Now the Sámi People Will Tell their History Containing Forced Fennofication and Violence – The Government Gives 1,5 Million to Truth Commission]'. *YLE,* svenska.yle.fi/artikel/2018/09/04/nu-ska-samerna-fa-beratta-sin-historia-som-innehaller-tvangsforfinskning-och-vald (4 September 2018).

Renz, Flora, 'Stopping Forced Sterilisation Is Not Enough – The Limitations of the Recent ECHR Judgement on Trans Rights'. *Verfassungsblog*, verfassungsblog.de/stopping-forced-sterilisation-is-not-enough-the-limitations-of-the-recent-echr-judgement-on-trans-rights/ (13 April 2017).

Repo, Jemima, *The Biopolitics of Gender*. Oxford University Press (2015).

Repo, Jemima, 'Governing Juridical Sex: Gender Recognition and the Biopolitics of Trans Sterilization in Finland'. *Politics & Gender* vol. 38 no. 1 (2019), 83–106.

RFSL, 'RFSL om skadestånd till tvångssteriliserade transpersoner [RFSL on Compensation to Forcibly Sterilised Trans People]'. *YouTube*, www.youtube.com/watch?v=7bnSlWajw5g (30 June 2015).

RFSL, *Remissyttrande över Förslag till lag om ersättning till personer som har fått ändrad könstillhörighet fastställd i vissa fall (Ds 2017:6) [Comment on Proposal for Act on Compensation to People Who Have Obtained Legal Gender Recognition under Certain Circumstances]*. Report no. S2017/01918/FS. Statement to the Swedish Government (2017).

Risse, Thomas & Sikkink, Kathryn, 'The Socialization of International Human Rights Norms into Domestic Practices: Introduction'. In Thomas Risse, Stephen C Ropp & Kathryn Sikkink (eds), *The Power of Human Rights: International Norms and Domestic Change*. Cambridge University Press (1999), 1–38.

Robertson, Gary, 'Virginia Lawmakers OK Payout to Forced Sterilization Survivors'. *Reuters*, www.reuters.com/article/us-usa-virginia-sterilization-idUSKBN0LU2D420150226 (26 February 2015).

Roivainen, Ida, 'EU-komissio kehottaa Suomea muuttamaan translakiaan – "Rikkoo ihmisen perusoikeuksia" [The European Commission Urges Finland to Amend its Trans Act – "Violates Constitutional Rights"]'. *Aamulehti*, www.aamulehti.fi/a/200240903 (2 July 2017).

Rosef, Thea, 'Krever kompensasjon for steriliserte transpersoner: – En umenneskelig praksis [Compensation Required for Sterilised Trans People: – An Inhuman Practice]'. *VG*, www.vg.no/nyheter/innenriks/i/awmz8O/krever-kompensasjon-for-steriliserte-transpersoner-en-umenneskelig-praksis (27 June 2020).

Roll-Hansen, Nils, 'Eugenics in Scandinavia after 1945: Change of Values and Growth in Knowledge'. *Scandinavian Journal of History* vol. 24 no. 2 (1999), 199–213.

Roll-Hansen, Nils, 'Norwegian Eugenics: Sterilization as Social Reform'. In Gunnar Broberg & Nils Roll-Hansen (eds), *Eugenics and the Welfare State: Norway, Sweden, Denmark, and Finland*. Michigan State University Press (2005), 151–194.

Roll-Hansen, Nils, 'Some Thoughts on Genetics and Politics. The Historical Misrepresentation of Scandinavian Eugenics and Sterilization'. In Heike I Petermann, Peter S Harper & Susanne Doetz (eds), *History of Human Genetics: Aspects of Its Development and Global Perspectives*. Springer (2017), 167–187.

Romanifolkets landsforening [The Romani People's Association of Norway], *Satisfaction of a People: Tatere Before and Now*. Romanifolkets landsforening (2000).

Rubio-Marín, Ruth, 'Introduction: A Gender and Reparations Taxonomy'. In Rubio-Marín, Ruth (ed), *The Gender of Reparations: Unsettling Sexual Hierarchies while Redressing Human Rights Violations*. Cambridge University Press (2009a), 1–17.

Rubio-Marín, Ruth, 'Gender and Collective Reparations in the Aftermath of Conflict and Political Repression'. In Rubio-Marín, Ruth (ed), *The Gender of Reparations:*

Unsettling Sexual Hierarchies while Redressing Human Rights Violations. Cambridge University Press (2009b), 381–402.

Rubio-Marín, Ruth, 'Reparations for Conflict-related Sexual and Reproductive Violence: A Decalogue'. *William & Mary Journal of Women and the Law* vol. 19 no. 1 (2012), 69–104.

Rubio-Marín, Ruth & De Greiff, Pablo, 'Women and Reparations'. *International Journal of Transitional Justice* vol. 1 no. 3 (2007), 318–337.

Rubio-Marín, Ruth & Möschel, Mathias, 'Anti-Discrimination Exceptionalism: Racist Violence before the ECtHR and the Holocaust Prism'. *European Journal of International Law* vol. 24 no. 4 (2015), 881–899.

Rubio-Marín, Ruth & Sandoval, Clara, 'Engendering the Reparations Jurisprudence of the Inter-American Court of Human Rights: The Promise of the *Cotton Field* Judgment'. *Human Rights Quarterly* vol. 33 no. 4 (2011), 1062–1091.

Runcis, Maija, *Steriliseringar i folkhemmet [Sterilisations in the People's Home]*. Ordfront (1998).

Runcis, Maija, *Makten över barnen: tvångsomhändertagande av barn i Sverige 1928–1969 [The Power over the Children: Forced Custody of Children in Sweden 1928–1969]*. Atlas (2007).

Runcis, Maija, 'Historikern, experterna och steriliseringarna av resanderomer [The Historian, the Experts and the Sterilisations of Travelling Romani]'. In Elisabeth Elgán & Annika Sandén (eds), *Kunskapens tider: Historiska perspektiv på kunskapssamhället [Times of Knowledge: Historical Perspectives on the Society of Knowledge]*. Stockholm University Press (2016), 110–127.

Rydström, Jens, '"Sodomitical Sins Are Threefold": Typologies of Bestiality, Masturbation, and Homosexuality in Sweden, 1880–1950'. *Journal of the History of Sexuality* vol. 9 no. 3 (2000), 240–276.

Rydström, Jens, *Sinners and Citizens: Bestiality and Homosexuality in Sweden, 1880–1950*. The University of Chicago Press (2003).

Rydström, Jens, 'Piska och morot. HBT mellan stat och folkrörelse 1944–2007 [Stick and Carrot. HBT between State and Social Movement 1944–2007]'. In Marika Hedin, Urban Lundberg, Jens Rydström & Mattias Tydén (eds), *Staten som vän eller fiende? Individ och samhälle i svenskt 1900-tal [The State as Friend or Foe? Individual and Society in 20th Century Sweden]*. Institutet för framtidsstudier (2007a), 157–192.

Rydström, Jens, 'Sweden 1864–1978: Beasts and Beauties'. In Jens Rydström & Kati Mustola (eds), *Criminally Queer: Homosexuality and Criminal Law in Scandinavia 1842–1999*. Aksant Academic Publishers (2007b), 183–213.

Salmiala, Bruno, 'Onko pakkokastratio oikeus- ja kulttuurivaltiossa hyväksyttävä reaktiomuoto rikoksen seurauksena? [Is Forced Castration an Acceptable Consequence of a Crime in a Rule of Law Culture?]'. *Defensor Legis* (1951) 130–167.

Salminen, Janne, 'Den konstitutionella identiteten, förändringen och Finland [Constitutional Identity, Change and Finland]'. *Retfærd – The Nordic Journal of Law and Justice* vol. 37 no. 4 (2014), 41–65.

Sandal, Sigrid, 'Kirurgi og byråkrati: Eit historisk blikk på etablering av praksis kring kjønnsbekreftande behandling i Noreg 1952–1979 [Surgery and Bureaucracy: A Historical Glance at the Establishment of Practice surrounding Gender-affirming Treatment in Norway 1952–1979]'. In Anne Hellum & Anniken Sørlie (eds), *Frihet, likhet og mangfold [Freedom, Equality and Diversity]*. Gyldendal (2021), 42–62.

Schabas, William A, *The International Criminal Court: A Commentary on the Rome Statute*. Oxford University Press (2016).

Schaps, Karolin, 'Netherlands to Compensate Trans Victims of Forced Sterilisation'. *Reuters*, www.reuters.com/article/us-netherlands-lgbt-sterilisation-idUSKBN28B5UX (1 December 2020).

Scheingold, Stuart A, *The Politics of Rights: Lawyers, Public Policy, and Political Change*. University of Michigan Press (2004).

Scheinin, Martin, *Lausunto [Statement]*. Letter to the Finnish Ministry of Social Affairs and Health (1992).

Scheinin, Martin, 'Incorporation and Implementation of Human Rights in Finland'. In Scheinin, Martin (ed), *International Human Rights Norms in the Nordic and Baltic Countries*. Martinus Nijhoff (1996), 257–294.

Scheppele, Kim Lane, 'Constitutional Ethnography: An Introduction'. *Law & Society Review* vol. 38 no. 3 (2004), 389–406.

Schlüter, Ragnhild, *De reisende: En norsk minoritets historie og kultur [The Travellers: The History and Culture of a Norwegian Minority]*. Ad Notam Gyldendal (1993).

Schultz, Mårten, 'Rights Through Torts: The Rise of a Rights Discourse in Swedish Tort Law'. *European Review of Private Law* vol. 17 no. 3 (2009), 305–333.

Schultz, Mårten, 'Skadestånd som medel för ersättning vid kränkningar av mänskliga rättigheter [Compensation as Reparations for Human Rights Violations]'. In Karin B Mirchadani & Kristina Ståhl (eds), *Förhandlingarna vid det 39:e nordiska juristmötet i Stockholm 18–19 augusti 2011 [Negotiations at the 39th Nordic Law Meeting in Stockholm 18–19 August 2011]*. De nordiske juristmøder (2011), 217–236.

Sejersted, Fredrik, *Kontroll og konstitusjon [Control and Constitution]*. Cappelen Akademisk Forlag (2002).

Seta, 'Erilaiset häät [A Different Kind of Wedding]'. *Seta-lehti* no. 2 (1987).

Shaw, Laura, 'Iceland'. *Eugenics Archive*, eugenicsarchive.ca/discover/connections/530b9af676f0db569b00000f (24 February 2014).

Shelton, Dinah, *Remedies in International Human Rights Law*. Oxford University Press (2015).

Shriver, Thomas E, Bray, Laura A & Adams, Alison E, 'Legal Repression of Protesters: The Case of Worker Revolt in Czechoslovakia'. *Mobilization: An International Quarterly* vol. 23 no. 3 (2018), 307–328.

Siegel, Reva, 'The Constitutionalization of Abortion'. In Michel Rosenfeld & András Sajó (eds), *The Oxford Handbook of Comparative Law*. Oxford University Press (2012), 1057–1078.

Sifris, Ronli, *Reproductive Freedom, Torture and International Human Rights*. Routledge (2014).

Silver, Michael G, 'Eugenics and Compulsory Sterilization Laws: Providing Redress for the Victims of a Shameful Area in United States History', *George Washington Law Review* vol. 72 no. 4 (2004) 862–892.

Siverskog, Anna, *Queera livslopp: Att leva och åldras som lhbtq-person i en heteronormativ värld [Queer Life Courses: To Live and Age as an LGBTQ Person in a Heteronormative World]*. Linköping Studies in Art and Science No.702, PhD thesis (2016).

Simmons, Beth A, *Mobilizing for Human Rights: International Law in Domestic Politics*. Cambridge University Press (2009).

Sisula-Tulokas, Lena, *Sveda, värk och annat lidande [Pain and Other Suffering]*. Juristförbundets förlag (1995).

Smith, Andrea, *Conquest: Sexual Violence and American Indian Genocide*. Duke University Press (2005).

Smith, Carsten, 'Om Høyesteretts forhold til den Europeiske menneskerettskonvensjon [About the Norwegian Supreme Court's Relationship to the ECHR]'. *Nordisk Tidsskrift for Menneskerettigheter*, vol. 23 no. 4 (2005), 433–440.

Smith, Eivind, 'The Constitution between Politics and Law'. In Eivind Smith (ed), *The Constitution as an Instrument of Change*. SNS Forlag (2003a), 21–52.

Smith, Eivind, 'Courts and Parliament: The Norwegian System of Judicial Review of Legislation'. In Eivind Smith (ed), *The Constitution as an Instrument of Change*. SNS Forlag (2003b), 171–187.

Smith, Eivind, *Konstitusjonelt demokrati: Statsforfatningsretten i prinsipielt og komparativt lys [Constitutional Democracy: Constitutional Law in the Light of Principle and Comparison]*. Fagbokforlaget (2015).

Snow, David A & Benford, Robert D, 'Ideology, Frame Resonance, and Participant Mobilization'. *International Social Movement Research* vol. 1 (1988), 197–217.

Snow, David A & Benford, Robert D, 'Master Frames and Cycles of Protest'. In Aldon D Morris & Carol M Mueller (eds), *Frontiers in Social Movement Theory*. Yale University Press (1992), 133–155.

Snow, David A, Rochford, E Burke, Worden, Steven K & Benford, Robert D, 'Frame Alignment Processes, Micromobilization, and Movement Participation'. *American Sociological Review* vol. 51 no. 4 (1986), 464–481.

Snow, David A & Soule, Sarah A, *A Primer on Social Movements*. W W Norton & Company (2010).

Sorainen, Antu, *Rikollisia sattumalta? Naisten keskinäistä haureutta koskevat oikeudenkäynnit 1950-luvun Itä-Suomessa [Criminals by Chance? Trials on Unchastity between Women in 1950s Eastern Finland]*. University of Helsinki, PhD thesis (2005).

Sørlie, Anniken, *Retten til kjønnsidentitet som menneskerettighet: Kan norsk forvaltningspraksis' krav om irreversibel sterilisering ved endring av fødselsnummer forsvares? [The Right to Gender Identity as a Human Right: Can the Requirement in Norwegian Administrative Practice of Irreversible Sterilisation when Changing Personal Identity Number be Defended?]*. University of Oslo, Kvinnerettslig skriftserie no. 90 (2013).

Sørlie, Anniken, 'Tvungen identitet – en vurdering av norsk forvaltningspraksis' krav om irreversibel sterilisering ved endring av juridisk kjønn [Forced Identity – An Evaluation of the Requirement of Irreversible Sterilisation when Amending Legal Gender in Norwegian Administrative Practice]'. *Tidsskrift for familierett, arverett og barnevernrettslige spørsmål* vol. 12 no. 4 (2014), 272–295.

Sørlie, Anniken, 'Legal Gender Meets Reality: A Socio-Legal Children's Perspective'. *Nordic Journal of Human Rights* vol. 33 no. 4 (2015), 353–279.

Sørlie, Anniken, 'Rettighetssubjekter i endring: den fødende mannen [Legal Subjects in Change: The Man Giving Birth]'. In Ingunn Ikdahl & Vibeke Blaker Strand (eds), *Rettigheter i velferdsstaten: Begreper, trender, teorier [Rights in the Welfare State: Terms, Trends, Theories]*. Gyldendal (2016), 227–248.

Sørlie, Anniken, 'The Right to Trans-specific Healthcare in Norway: Understanding the Health Needs of Transgender People'. *Medical Law Review* (2018), 1–23.

Speed, Shannon, 'Exercising Rights and Reconfiguring Resistance in the Zapatista Juntas de Buen Gobierno'. In Mark Goodale & Sally E Merry (eds), *The Practice of Human Rights: Tracking Law between the Global and the Local*. Cambridge University Press (2007), 163–192.

Spektorowski, Alberto & Ireni-Saban, Liza, *Politics of Eugenics: Productionism, Population, and National Welfare*. Routledge (2014).

Sperfeldt, Christoph, 'Rome's Legacy: Negotiating the Reparations Mandate of the International Criminal Court'. *International Criminal Law Review* vol. 17 no. 2 (2017), 351–377.

Sprengel, Vivianne, 'Skadestånd krävs för tvångssterilisering [Compensation Is Requested for Forced Sterilisation]'. *Tidningarnas Telegrambyrå* (9 October 1987).

Sprengel, Vivianne & Dahlgren, Peter, 'Steril [Barren]'. *Tidningarnas Telegrambyrå* (12 August 1986).

Stote, Karen, *An Act of Genocide: Colonialism and the Sterilization of Aboriginal Women*. Fernwood Publishing (2015).

Sutton, Christopher JG, 'The History of Hysterectomy'. In Ibrahim Alkatout & Liselotte Mettler (eds), *Hysterectomy: A Comprehensive Surgical Approach*. Springer (2018), 1–28.

Sveriges Radio, *Kräver skadestånd för tvångssterilisering [Demand Compensation for Forced Sterilisation]*, sverigesradio.se/sida/artikel.aspx?programid=1646&artikel=5573519 (24 June 2013).

Sweet, Alec S, 'On the Constitutionalisation of the Convention: The European Court of Human Rights as a Constitutional Court'. *Yale Law School Faculty Scholarship Series*, paper 71 (2009).

Syse, Aslak, 'Om åndssvakhet og tvangssterilisering på eugenisk grunnlag [About Feeblemindedness and Forced Sterilisation on Eugenic Grounds]'. *Kritisk Juss* vol. 27 no. 1–2 (2001), 35–62.

Tamayo, Giulia, *Nada personal: Reporte de derechos humanos sobra la aplicación de la anticoncepción quirúrgica en el Perú 1996–1998 [Nothing Personal: Human Rights Report on the Application of Surgical Contraception in Peru 1996–1998]*. CLADEM (1999).

Tams, Christian J; Berster, Lars & Schiffbauer, Björn, *Convention on the Prevention and Punishment of the Crime of Genocide: A Commentary*. Hart Publishing (2014).

The Japan Times, *Records of Sterilizations under Japan's Scrapped Eugenics Law Could Help Victims Seek State Compensation*, www.japantimes.co.jp/news/2018/01/25/national/social-issues/survey-finds-records-remain-past-sterilizations-2700-japan-scrapped-eugenics-law/#.WurF39PRDBI (25 January 2018).

Theilen, Jens T, 'Depathologisation of Transgenderism and International Human Rights Law'. *Human Rights Law Review* vol. 14 no. 2 (2014), 327–342.

Thune, Jens Kristian & Stiftelsen romanifolket/taterne, *Vedr. Romanifolket/taterne – oppreisning/fonds/tilskudd [About the Romani People/Tatere – Redress/Funds/Subsidy]*. Letter to the Norwegian Ministry of Regional Government (2003).

Tidningarnas telegrambyrå, *Steril [Barren]* (21 August 1986a).

Tidningarnas telegrambyrå, *Steril, bakgrund [Barren, Background]* (12 November 1986b).

Tidningarnas telegrambyrå, *Steril [Barren]* (30 March 1987a).

Tidningarnas telegrambyrå, *En steriliserad får skadestånd [A Sterilised Gets Compensation]* (12 November 1987b).

Tiusanen, Liina, 'Helsinki pride-tapahtumaan osallistunut ministeri Tiilikainen: Translain kokonaisuudistus ei saa olla pelinappula seuraavissa hallitusneuvotteluissa [Minister Tiilikainen, who Participated in Helsinki Pride: The Complete Revision of the Trans Act Cannot Be a Pawn at the Next Negotiations for Government]'. *Suomenmaa*, www.suomenmaa.fi/uutiset/helsinki-pride-tapahtumaan-osallistunut-ministeri-tiilikainen-translain-kokonaisuudistus-ei-saa-olla-pelinappula-seuraavissa-hallitusneuvotteluissa-6.3.390662.98aa093fa1 (30 June 2018).

Tømmerås, Ane S, *Billighetserstatning – og andre offentlige erstatningsordninger [Compensation Ex Gratia – and Other Public Compensation Schemes]*. Universitetsforlaget (2002).

Tonon, Matias, 'La reparación del daño al proyecto de vida en la Corte Interamericana de Derechos Humanos [Reparation of Harm to Life Project in the Inter-American Court of Human Rights]'. *AEQUITAS Virtual* vol. 5 no. 16 (2011), 1–11.

Tranøy, Joar, '"Mindreverdig anlegg" – om sterilisering av taterjenter på skolehjem ["Inferior Features" – On Sterilisation of *Tatere* Girls at Residential Schools]'. *Materialisten* vol. 23 no. 2/3 (1995), 55–73.

Trasek & Seta, *The Cruel, Inhuman and Degrading Treatment of Trans and Intersex People in Finland*. Submission to the UN Committee against Torture (2016).

Tsuchiya, Takashi, 'Eugenic Sterilizations in Japan and Recent Demands for Apology: A Report'. *Newsletter of the Network on Ethics and Intellectual Disability* vol. 3 no. 1 (1997), 1–4.

Tsutsui, Kiyoteru, *Rights Make Might: Global Human Rights and Minority Social Movements in Japan*. Oxford University Press (2018).

Tsutsui, Kiyoteru & Smith, Jackie, 'Human Rights and Social Movements: From the Boomerang Pattern to a Sandwich Effect'. In David A Snow, Sarah A Soule, Hanspeter Kriesi & Holly J McCammon (eds), *The Wiley Blackwell Companion to Social Movements*. Wiley Blackwell (2019), 586–601.

Tydén, Mattias, *Från politik till praktik: De svenska steriliseringslagarna 1935–1975 [From Politics to Practise: The Swedish sterilisation Laws 1935–1975]*. Stockholm Studies in History (2002).

Undén, Östen, 'Några ord om domstolskontroll över lagars grundlagsenlighet [A Few Words about Judicial Constitutional Review]'. *Svensk juristtidning* no. 1 (1956), 260–263.

Van Der Ros, Janneke, *Alskens folk: Levekår, livssituasjon og livskvalitet for personer med kjønnsidentitetstematikk [All Kinds of People: Living Conditions, and Quality of Life of Individuals with Gender Identity Thematic]*. Likestillingssenteret [The Norwegian Centre for Equality] (2013).

Vanhala, Lisa, *Making Rights a Reality? Disability Rights Activists and Legal Mobilization*. Cambridge University Press (2010).

Vik, Hanne H & Skage, Alexander Ø, 'Deploying the Engagement Policy: The Significance of Legal Dualism in Norway's Support for Human Rights Treaties from the late 1970s'. *Nordic Journal of Human Rights* vol. 36 no. 3 (2018), 304–321.

Vollebæk, Knut & Plesner, Ingvill T, 'Constitutional Protection of National Minorities' Rights in Norway: Does It Matter?'. *Nordic Journal of Human Rights* vol. 32 no. 2 (2014), 176–187.

Walker, Margaret U, 'Gender and Violence in Focus: A Background for Gender Justice in Reparations'. In Rubio-Marín, Ruth (ed), *The Gender of Reparations: Unsettling*

Sexual Hierarchies while Redressing Human Rights Violations. Cambridge University Press (2009), 18–62.

Weedon, Chris, *Feminist Practice and Poststructuralist Theory*. Blackwell (1987).

Weindling, Paul, *Health, Race and German Politics between National Unification and Nazism, 1879–1945*. Cambridge University Press (1989).

Weindling, Paul, 'International Eugenics: Swedish Sterilization in Context'. *Scandinavian Journal of History*, vol. 24 no. 2 (1999), 179–197.

Weindling, Paul, 'Sterilization Compensation'. *Eugenics Archive*, eugenicsarchive.ca/discover/connections/535eeaff7095aa0000000217 (28 April 2014).

Wersäll, Fredrik, 'En offensiv Högsta domstol. Några reflektioner kring HD:s rättsbildning [An Offensive Supreme Court. Some Reflections on the Lawmaking of the Supreme Court]'. *Svensk juristtidning* no. 1 (2014), 1–8.

Wessel, Merle, 'Castration of Male Sex Offenders in the Nordic Welfare State in the Context of Homosexuality and Heteronormativity, 1930–1955'. *Scandinavian Journal of History* vol. 40 no. 5 (2015), 591–609.

Westerlund, Ulrika, 'RFSL: Ge skadestånd till tvångssteriliserade transpersoner [RFSL: Provide Compensation for Forcibly Sterilised Trans People]'. *Dagens Arena*, www.dagensarena.se/opinion/rfsl-ge-skadestand-till-tvangssteriliserade-transpersoner/ (30 June 2015).

Wickman, Jan, *Transgender Politics: The Construction and Deconstruction of Binary Gender in the Finnish Transgender Community*. Åbo Akademi University Press (2001).

Wiklund, Ola, 'The Reception Process in Sweden and Norway'. In Helen Keller & Alec S Sweet (eds), *A Europe of Rights: The Impact of the ECHR on National Legal Systems*. Oxford University Press (2008), 165–227.

Wilhelmsson, Thomas, *Senmodern ansvarsrätt. Privaträtt som redskap för mikropolitik [Late Modern Liability Law. Private Law as Tool for Micropolitics]*. Kauppakaari (2001).

Wilson, Robert A, 'Eugenics Never Went Away'. *Aeon*, aeon.co/essays/eugenics-today-where-eugenic-sterilisation-continues-now (5 June 2018a).

Wilson, Robert A, *The Eugenic Mind Project*. MIT Press (2018b).

Wind, Marlene & Follesdal, Andreas, 'Nordic Reluctance Towards Judicial Review Under Siege'. *Nordic Journal of Human Rights* vol. 27 no. 2 (2009), 131–141.

Winfield, Ann G, 'Resuscitating Bad Science: Eugenics Past and Present'. In William H Watkins (ed), *The Assault on Public Education: Confronting the Politics of Corporate School Reform*. Teachers College Press (2012), 143–159.

Winter, Stephen, 'Australia's *Ex Gratia* Redress'. *Australian Indigenous Law Review* vol. 13 no. 1 (2009), 49–61.

WPATH, Statement for Immediate Release (16 June 2010).

WPATH, *Standards of Care for the Health of Transsexual, Transgender and Gender Nonconforming People*. WPATH Publications (2012).

Yle Uutiset, *Lakialoite translain muuttamisesta odottaa sosiaali- ja terveysvaliokunnan enemmistön kantaa [Legislative Initiative Awaits the Support of the Majority in the Parliamentary Social Affairs and Health Committee]*, yle.fi/uutiset/3-9871309 (7 October 2017).

Zald, Mayer N, 'Culture, Ideology, and Strategic Framing'. In Doug McAdam, John D McCarthy & Mayer N Zald (eds), *Comparative Perspectives on Social Movements:*

Political Opportunities, Mobilising Structures, and Cultural Framings. Cambridge University Press (1996), 261–274.

Zampas, Christina, '*I.V. v. Bolivia* Decision: Forced Sterilization is Based on Harmful Stereotypes'. *Reprohealthlaw Blog*, reprohealthlaw.wordpress.com/2017/03/29/i-v-v-bolivia-decision-forced-sterilization-is-based-on-harmful-gender-stereotypes/ (29 March 2017).

Zaremba, Maciej, 'Rasren i välfärden [Racially Pure in the Welfare]'. *Dagens Nyheter* (20 August 1997a).

Zaremba, Maciej, 'De olönsamma skars bort [The Unprofitable Were Cut Off]'. *Dagens Nyheter* (21 August 1997b).

Zaremba, Maciej, *De rena och de andra: om tvångssteriliseringar, rashygien och arvssynd [The Clean Ones and the Others: On Forced Sterilisations, Racial Hygiene and Original Sin]*. WSOY (1999).

Zondag, Martin H W, 'Statens politikk mot tatere har vært feilslått og nedbrytende [The State's Policy against the *Tatere* Has Been Wrong and Oppressive]'. *NRK*, www.nrk.no/norge/_-statens-politikk-mot-tatere-har-vaert-feilslatt-og-nedbrytende-1.12387816 (1 June 2015).

Interviews and Inquiries[2]

Aasen, Cesilie, Senior Counsellor at the Norwegian Directorate of Health, e-mail correspondence on 23 November 2016.

Abelson, Lars Göran, Former Court of Appeal Chief Judge, Main Investigator in 2007 State Report on the Health Care Needs of Intersex and Transsexuals (SOU 2007:16), personal interview on 20 September 2016.

Ågren, Lisa, Archivist at the Swedish Board of Health and Welfare, e-mail correspondence on 26 November 2015.

Andrén, Carl-Gustaf, Former University Chancellor at Lund University, Main Investigator in the Swedish Sterilisation Investigation (1997–2000), personal interview on 21 September 2016.

Bengtsson, Bertil, Former Professor of Law at Uppsala University, Member of the Swedish Sterilisation Investigation (1997–2000), written interviews on 31 August 2016, 1 October 2016 and 23 November 2018.

Broberg, Gunnar, Emeritus Professor at Lund University, Department for the History of Ideas, Member of the Swedish Sterilisation Investigation (1997–2000), personal interview 20 September 2016.

Bergkvist, Johanne, Romani Representative Member of the Norwegian Investigation into Oppression of the Romani Minority (NOU 2015:7), telephone interview on 27 January 2017.

Burman, Kerstin, Legal Representative of the Sterilisation Victims of the 1972 Gender Recognition Act, telephone interview 4 February 2015, personal interview on 8 September 2016.

Drefvelin, Petter, Former Head of Public Administration, Leader of the 2003 Interdepartmental Investigation on Compensation to *Tatere*/Romani people &

[2] The titles and affiliations appearing here do not necessarily correspond to later titles and affiliations.

Skotvedt, Tove, Former Senior Counsellor and Secretary of the 2003 Interdepartmental Investigation on Compensation to *Tatere*/Romani people, personal interview on 9 December 2016.

Durbáková, Vanda, Human rights lawyer representing the applicants in *K.H. and Others v. Slovakia, V.C. v. Slovakia, N.B. v. Slovakia* and *I.G. and Others v. Slovakia*, telephone interview on 29 April 2015 and e-mail correspondence on 13 December 2017.

Duurhuus, Edel, Civil Servant at the Personal Registry at the Norwegian Tax Administration, e-mail correspondence on 29 November 2016.

Ekberg, Hedvig, Legal Counsellor at the Norwegian Association for Persons with Intellectual Disabilities (NFU), e-mail correspondence on 27 October 2016.

Ekeløve-Slydal, Gunnar, Deputy Secretary General of the Norwegian Helsinki Committee, personal interview on 7 December 2016.

Ericsson, Kjersti, Professor Emerita in Criminology at the University of Oslo & Papendorf, Knut, Professor Emeritus in Criminology and Sociology of Law, personal interview on 8 December 2016.

Eriksson, Panda, Former President of Trasek, personal interview on 11 September 2017.

Espseth, Luca Dalen, Former Advisor on Gender Diversity at FRI, Deputy Chairperson at PKI, teleconference interview on 4 January 2022.

Fodstad, Hjørdis, Associate Professor at Oslo and Akershus University College of Applied Sciences, personal interview on 14 December 2016.

Frydenlund, Stein Wolff, Former Head of the FRI Trans Political Committee and LGBT Activist in Amnesty International, former Steering Committee Member of TGEU (2014–2018), personal interview on 10 December 2016.

González-Dominguez, Marta, Legal Advisor for Latin America and the Caribbean at the Center for Reproductive Rights, teleconference interview on 5 January 2018.

Grammeltvedt, Gorm, Former Department Director at NPE, Deputy Chairman at the Norwegian National Insurance Court, personal interview on 8 December 2016; e-mail correspondence on 12 December 2016.

Haave, Per, Researcher at the Department of Community Medicine and Global Health, University of Oslo, Author of the Report *Sterilisering av tatere 1934–1977: En historisk undersøkelse av lov og praksis* (2000) and Member of the State Investigation for NOU 2015:7, personal interview on 5 December 2016.

Hallberg, Pekka, Former President of the Supreme Administrative Court of Finland; Docent at the University of Helsinki and the University of Joensuu, e-mail correspondence on 8 July 2017.

Hansen, Harald M Kvame, Association Chairman of the National Association of People with Developmental Disabilities and their Relatives (LUPE), e-mail correspondence on 7 November 2016.

Hansen, Tone Maria, Managing Director at the Norwegian Harry Benjamin Resource Centre, e-mail correspondence on 12 December 2016.

Heino, Anna, Senior Planning Officer at the Finnish Institute for Health and Welfare, e-mail correspondence on 10 August, 18 August and 23 October 2017.

Hemgård, Lisbeth, Executive Manager at Inclusion Finland FDUV & Lindholm, Mikael, Former Executive Manager at Inclusion Finland FDUV, personal interview on 7 September 2017.

Hietala, Marjatta, Professor Emerita, Department of History, Tampere University, written interview on 11 October 2017.

Ilola, Santeri, Former President of Trasek, telephone interview on 30 October 2017.

Jacobsen, Maria H, Partner at Elden Law Firm, teleconference interview on 16 December 2021.

Jacobsson, Anders, Quality Manager at the Swedish National Board of Health and Welfare, e-mail correspondence on 18 April 2017.

Jentoft, Christine M, Advisor on Gender Diversity at the Norwegian Organization for Sexual and Gender Diversity FRI, teleconference interview on 20 December 2021.

Kaatee, Patricia, Policy Advisor at the Norwegian Department of Amnesty International, personal interview on 6 December 2016.

Karanki, Antti, Former President of Trasek, personal interview on 6 September 2017; e-mail correspondence on 13 September 2017.

Karlbom, Agneta, Insurance Lawyer at the Swedish Patient Claims Panel, e-mail correspondence 30 November 2015 and personal interview on 19 September 2016.

Kempf, Françoise, Lam, Claudia & Mattioli-Zeltner, Géraldine, Advisors at the Council of Europe Commissioner for Human Rights, personal interview on 12 October 2017.

Knapskog, Arne-Birger, Senior Counsellor at the Norwegian Directorate of Health, e-mail correspondence on 3 May 2018.

Lahti, Raimo, Professor Emeritus of Law at the University of Helsinki; Secretary of the Revision Committee for the Abortion, Sterilisation, and Castration Legislation; Former Permanent Expert at the Finnish Board of Health/the National Supervisory Authority for Social Welfare and Health, personal interview on 8 September 2017.

Langseth, Helle Holst, Legal Counsellor at the Norwegian Equality and Anti-discrimination Ombud & Falch, Helene, Lawyer at the Norwegian Equality and Anti-discrimination Ombud, personal interview on 6 December 2016.

Lindvik, Jan Elisabeth, Leading Activist at the Norwegian Association of Trans People FTPN, personal interview on 7 December 2016.

Lindquist, Bosse, Author and TV Producer at *SVT Dokumentär*, personal interview on 13 September 2016.

Lindell, Karin, Former Auditor General of Sweden and External Investigator in 2010 State Report on the Health Care Needs of Transsexual People, personal interview on 15 September 2016.

Lomfors, Ingrid, Director at the Swedish Living History Forum, External Investigator in the Swedish Sterilisation Investigation (1997–2000), personal interview on 8 September 2016.

Lundell-Kiuru, Minna, Senior Officer, Specialist on Questions concerning Gender Diversity at the Finnish Ombudsman for Equality & Valleala, Aija, Senior Officer at the Finnish Ombudsman for Equality, personal interview 6 September 2017.

Mattila, Markku, Senior Researcher, Migration Institute of Finland and Docent, Tampere University, personal interview on 1 September 2017.

Moreno, Diana Carolina, Legal Fellow, Latin American & Caribbean Program, The Center for Reproductive Rights, teleconference interview on 8 January 2018.

Myrberg, Arild Johan, Senior Counsellor at the Norwegian Directorate of Health, telephone interview on 3 and 13 February 2017.

Oksanen, Pia Puu, Expert on Discrimination Based on Gender and Sexuality at Amnesty International Finland, personal interview on 7 September 2017.

Pasquier, Liliane Maury, Member of the Council of States (Switzerland), Rapporteur for PACE Report on 'Putting an End to Coerced Sterilisations and Castrations'; Tanja Kleinsorge, Head of the Secretariat, PACE Committee on Social Affairs, Health and Sustainable Development, Council of Europe & Ayşegül Elveriş, Secretary, PACE Committee on Social Affairs, Health and Sustainable Development, Council of Europe, personal interview on 12 October 2017.

Paulsrud, Kari, Leader of State Expert Investigation on Gender Identity and Gender Registration, personal interview on 9 December 2016.

Persson, Leif, Judge, Secretary in the Swedish Sterilisation Investigation (1997–2000); Deputy Chairperson in the Swedish Sterilisation Compensation Committee, personal interview on 20 September 2016.

Petersson, Stig-Åke, Archivist at the Swedish LGBTQ federation RFSL, e-mail correspondence on 17 September 2016.

Pimenoff, Veronica, Psychiatrist (MD), PhD, Author, Member of the Working Groups for the Report STM 2000:2 and for the Government Bill regarding the Finnish 2002 Trans Act, personal interview on 5 September 2017.

Plesner, Ingvill Thorson, Researcher at the Norwegian Centre for Human Rights, President of the Secretariat for Norwegian Investigation into Oppression of the Romani Minority (NOU 2015:7, 2013–2015), personal interview on 14 December 2016.

Rapo, Markus, Statistician at Statistics Finland, e-mail correspondence on 8 and 9 November 2017.

Roll-Hansen, Nils, Emeritus Professor at the University of Oslo, Department of Philosophy, Classics, History of Arts and Ideas, personal interview on 13 December 2016.

Rogalska-Hedlund, Anna, Lawyer and Former Contributor at *Centrum för rättvisa* [Centre for Justice], personal interview on 19 September 2016.

Runcis, Maija, Associate Professor of History at Stockholm University, personal interview on 7 May 2015.

Rydström, Jens, Professor at Lund University, Department of Gender Studies, telephone interview on 14 September 2016.

Saarela, Riina, Administrative Officer at the Finnish Patient Injury Board, e-mail correspondence on 7 August 2018.

Salo, Aija, Former Secretary General of Finnish LGBTI federation Seta, Senior Officer at the Office of the Non-Discrimination Ombudsman, personal interview on 4 September 2017.

Sandegård, Frida, Former Secretary General of the Swedish LGBTQI federation RFSL, personal interview on 16 September 2016.

Scheinin, Martin, British Academy Global Professor, Bonavero Institute of Human Rights, University of Oxford and Professor at the Department of Law, European University Institute, personal interview on 23 October 2017.

Sisula-Tulokas, Lena, Professor Emerita of Law, University of Helsinki, personal interview on 8 September 2017.

Skarhed, Anna, Former Swedish Chancellor of Justice, personal interview on 14 September 2016.

Socialstyrelsens upplysningstjänst [The Information Service of the Swedish National Board of Health and Welfare], e-mail correspondence on 28 March 2018.

Söderlund, Désirée, Member of the Working Group for the state report STM 2000:2, personal interview on 4 September 2017.

Sørlie, Anniken, Associate Professor, Faculty of Social Sciences, OsloMet University, personal interview on 7 December 2016.

Sørlie-Rogne, Heidi, Professional Leader of the Rights Centre of the Norwegian Federation of Organisations of Disabled People (FFO), e-mail correspondence on 26 October 2016.

Sundkvist, Elida, Specialist at the Swedish Ministry of Health and Social Affairs, written interview on 3 October and 5 December 2016.

Syse, Aslak, Emeritus Professor in Welfare and Health Law at Oslo University, Former Member of the Sterilisation Council, e-mail correspondence on 25 October 2016.

Tonning, Lena Røst, Senior Executive Officer at the Norwegian Civil Affairs Authority, e-mail correspondence on 13 March 2018.

Tystad, Arnstein, Counsellor at the Norwegian Civil Affairs Authority, e-mail correspondence on 19 October 2016.

Törngren, Erland, Unit Manager at the Swedish Legal, Financial and Administrative Services Agency, e-mail correspondence on 9 October 2020.

Van der Ros, Janneke, Associate Professor in Political Science, Lillehammer University College, teleconference interview on 2 January 2017.

Vigardt, Kai-Samuel, Romani Rights Activist, telephone interview on 1 February 2017.

Vilenius, Miika, Registrar at the Chancellor of Justice, e-mail correspondence on 26 November 2015.

Westerlund, Ulrika, Former President of the Swedish LGBTQI federation RFSL and Former Board Member of TGEU, personal interview on 16 September 2016 and telephone interview on 16 February 2015.

Wilhelmsson, Thomas, Professor Emeritus of Law at the University of Helsinki and Former Chancellor of the University of Helsinki, personal interview on 5 September 2017.

Zaremba, Maciej, Author, Journalist at Swedish newspaper *Dagens Nyheter*, personal interview on 13 September 2016.

Index

For EU product safety concerns, contact us at Calle de José Abascal, 56–1°,
28003 Madrid, Spain or eugpsr@cambridge.org.

www.ingramcontent.com/pod-product-compliance
Lightning Source LLC
LaVergne TN
LVHW062208200926
848484LV00006B/1349